THE OFFICIAL®
PRICE GUIDE TO
SCOUTING COLLECTIBLES

Y0-DNK-846

**FROM THE EDITORS OF
THE HOUSE OF COLLECTIBLES**

FOURTH EDITION

THE HOUSE OF COLLECTIBLES
NEW YORK, NEW YORK 10022

TABLE OF CONTENTS

ACKNOWLEDGMENTS

As publishers, we reach out to experts in the field to assure our readers that the price information reported reflects the most accurate accounting of the current marketplace, taking into consideration, of course, the price fluctuations between different regions of the country. To the following historians, collectors, dealers and organizations who have assisted us with the update of this book, we extend our sincere thanks:

James Clough, South Glen Falls, New York, for his editorial review of Badges; Senior and Explorer Scout Programs.

Alburtus Hoogeveen, Downey, California, for his editorial review of Jamboree and Order of the Arrow Collectibles: photographs.

Bea and Jim Stevenson, Euless, Texas, for their editorial review of Historical Items; Books; Miscellaneous Items.

Harry Thorsen, Sarasota, Florida, noted Scout historian who organized and operates the first Museum of Scouting Memorabilia in this country, for furnishing us with a rich and detailed history of the Scouting movement, including his interesting story of a personal meeting with Sir Robert Baden-Powell in the early-dawn hours of the morning at the World Jamboree in England, 1920.

Boy Scouts of America National Office, Irving, Texas.

Camp Fire, Inc. Headquarters, Kansas City, Missouri.

Girl Scouts of the United States of America Headquarters, New York, New York.

Shenandoah Area Council, Inc. BSA, Winchester, Virginia.

Finally, to the countless other contributors with whom we talked—Doug Bearce and Richard Shields, to mention two—who gave us their valuable time and wonderful background information; to the devoted Girl Scout leaders who preferred to remain anonymous, we give our wholehearted thanks.

NOTE TO READERS

MARKET REVIEW

Scouting collectibles represents a vast field. Ever since 1950, when boy scouts attending the national Jamboree at Valley Forge began to trade everything from rattlesnakes to false teeth, it has become a popular hobby for past and present scouts, as well as those who have experienced it through other people. One dealer tells the story of a customer who bought $100 worth of Order of the Arrow Flaps for his son at Christmas only to return three months later to begin buying for himself; another of his customers spent $7,000 on a computer to be able to record his collection. Beginners frequently start to collect Order of the Arrow Strips, which have become the number one most collectible area, followed close behind by the individual Council Shoulder Patches (CSP), which enjoy the number two position. In 1985, Cloisinee Hat Pins enjoyed popularity. An important dealer in Texas reports a current spark of interest in the Birch Bark Rolls. Prices fluctuate according to demand. The most volatile items are badges, Jamboree collectibles and the Order of the Arrow items. New York, California, and Illinois represent the biggest markets for collectors.

It is unfortunate—but important to report—that fakes that can be quite expensive have surfaced in the Order of the Arrow and World Jamboree patches. Take care to ensure authenticity before making any major purchase. This is best done by dealing with reputable dealers such as those found in the back of this book.

Hobbyists searching for reasonably priced Scouting memorabilia might look for Scouting games, toys and fiction books. These are colorful, affordable items. Good places to find Scouting books include The Salvation Army Thrift Stores, Goodwill, flea markets and garage sales.

Modern limited editions of collector plates, medallions, etc. have also been issued. The most famous of these is probably Rockwell's Spirit of Scouting silver medallion series designed by Norman Rockwell for the Franklin Mint. Originally issued for $117 for the series of twelve medallions, this set is now valued from $200 to $250 on the secondary market. Each sterling medallion illustrates one of the twelve Boy Scout rules of conduct.

The 75th Anniversaries of the Boy Scouts of America, Camp Fire, Inc., and Girl Scouts of America produced a flood of commemoratives that are available to collectors everywhere.

INTRODUCTION

As American as apple pie? Scouting actually began in England in 1907 when its founder, Sir Robert Baden-Powell, took a group of twenty boys off to a campsite to test his training principles. From a campsite in 1907 to a collection of sixteen million scouts and leaders in more than 150 countries and territories, scouting has become the largest volunteer youth movement in the world.

The history of boy scouting in America dates back to 1910, when a Chicago businessman named William Boyce became lost in a fog in England. He was rescued by a young scout performing his "good deed" for the day. Refusing a tip, the young scout led him back to the Boy Scout headquarters where he met and talked with Sir Robert Baden-Powell. He was so impressed by what he learned about the program that he brought the concept back to the United States when he returned home. Scouting in America has been a flourishing program ever since.

When William Boyce started the Boy Scouts of America, with the help of Ernest Seton and Daniel Beard, an adventure was launched that has since provided millions of boys and girls with character-building and maturation through a combination of self-discipline and fun. The Camp Fire program for girls followed close behind, as well as the Girl Scouts of America program. Embracing the practices of good deeds, clean living and help to the disadvantaged, the Cub Scouts, Boy Scouts, Explorer Scouts (Air Scouts, Sea Scouts), Camp Fire participants, and Girl Scouts provide a valuable benefit to America and the world.

Following the second Jamboree, which was held in 1950 at Valley Forge, Pennsylvania, individual boy scouts began trading and exchanging everything from rattlesnake skins to false teeth with other kids across the country. Trading, swapping, collecting items of all kinds pertaining to the Boy Scout movement began to be a popular diversion. The thousands of tangible items belonging to past and present members of different boy scout councils provide a record of the development of the scouting movement. Many of these collectible items are listed in this book to give you some idea of the breadth of the scouting collectibles market, as well as the value each item holds in the current market.

As you might expect, hobbyists and collectors include individuals who are or were involved in Scouting and who treasure the mementos produced by it. Also included are those who, although they were never Scouts themselves, have experienced the benefits of the program through other people, often their children. Clubs exist for collectors that offer information and valuable tips to their members. Check your area for a club; if there isn't one, you may wish to start one yourself. The bond that began years ago with Scouts themselves, has also become contagious to its collectors. It has helped build a hobby that continues to grow rapidly and will be one of the major collector fields of tomorrow.

It doesn't require a lot of money to build a collection, depending upon the items you select. Collectible items range from hat pins selling for as little as $1.50 to early Order of the Arrow collectibles that range between $400 and $2,000. It is important, however, to know the value of your chosen items so that you can get the best buy. Aside from dealers who specialize in Scouting collectibles, you may find collectible items in general antiques shops. This book has been written as a working guide to average market prices.

HOW TO BUILD A COLLECTION

There are many ways to build your collection by acquiring items from different sources. You may buy from or swap with other collectors or with former Scouts who have lost interest in the hobby. However, most of your items will probably be bought from dealers. Many of these dealers who specialize in Scouting items do business by mail-order. They will either publish lists of their stock in collector publications or print their names and addresses for you to write to them for their lists. Most lists are quite general. They may either organize them according to the type of item—i.e., books, badges, knives—or they may list only the specific items in their stock or just a sampling. This type of list is usually not in any kind of order and must be read thoroughly.

You may find that the prices for some items are different than the ones stated in this book. This is because we have listed the average selling price, using information taken from many different sources. The price you find could be higher or lower than the average. The condition of the item could be one very important reason for the difference in price. Another reason could be that the dealer is at the time overstocked on some items and understocked on others. As you read the dealers' lists, be aware that there are many reasons for differences in prices. Find the best buys for the items you want by comparing the lists of many dealers.

When you have received all your lists and compared the prices for your desired items, carefully read all information that is given with those items. Be sure to find out from the dealer:

- **Exactly what item you wish to purchase**

- *What condition it is in*

- *Whether the dealer permits returns of unsatisfactory purchases*

- *How much time is allowed for returns*

HOW TO GRADE THE CONDITION

Condition is important in all fields of collecting, including Scouting. We have set up some general guidelines for you to follow, but they must be interpreted when necessary depending on the item being purchased. The prices we include are for specimens in good to average condition. These are specimens that are in less than mint condition, but better than very worn or damaged condition. Generally, the older items from before 1920 are more difficult to find in really good condition. The age and nature of the object must be considered when evaluating price. Some of the older items may only be found in a worn state, so they may rate a higher value just because they are older. However, damaged specimens, even if they have been repaired, are never worth the value of undamaged items. Here are some more specific guidelines to follow, but again the age and nature of the item may mean a change in value:

- *Books, if they have a hardbound cover, should have no cracks in the bindings; if softbound, should have all the pages with no stains or tears.*

- *Badges or ribbons made of fabric should not be torn or badly soiled.*

- *Metals should not be badly soiled or corroded. These are very difficult, if not impossible, to clean.*

- *Uniforms should be complete with all pieces. They will probably have some fading but you should not try to correct this by redying.*

DEALERS

Doug Bearce
P. O. Box 7081
Salem, OR 97303
(503) 363-1715

The Carolina Trader
Richard E. Shields, Jr.
2429 Galloway Road
Charlotte, NC 28213

Scout Collectors Shop
James Clough
7763 Elmwood
So. Glen Falls, NY 12801
(518) 793-4037

Alburtus Hoogeveen
P. O. Box 222
Downey, CA 90241
(213) 862-6666

The Scouting Market Place
3108 15th Avenue South
Apartment 2
Minneapolis, MN 55407

Scout Stamps of the World
John Raith
P. O. Box 144
Flushing, NY 11365

Bea and Jim Stevenson
316 Sage Lane
Euless, TX 76039
(817) 354-8903

CLUBS AND PUBLICATIONS

The Illinois Traders Association, 1639 N. Hudson Avenue, Chicago, IL 60614. Dues are minimal; newsletter, mail auction on patches, and a Council Shoulder Patch Handbook with an annual supplement.

The Western Traders Association, 18036 Blue Bell East, Sonora, CA 95370. Patch collectors with quarterly newsletter. Entrance fee is $2.00 plus the $3.00 yearly dues.

The Northwest Scout Heritage Society. Dues are $5.00 per year. Publication and Trade-O-Rees. For further information write: Columbia Pacific Council, B.S.A., 2145 S.W. Front Avenue, Portland, OR 97201.

Scout Memorabilia. Scouting history, collectibles and nostalgia. Published five times a year; $5.00 annual subscription ($7.00 for foreign subscribers). Send checks to Harry D. Thorsen, Jr., Editor and Publisher, 7305 Bounty Drive, Sarasota, FL 33581. (No airmail.)

Scouts on Stamps Society International (SOSSI). This is a must for serious stamp collectors. Membership dues are $7.50 per year in U.S.A., $10.00 for surface mail or $20.00 for airmail. Write for application to Kenneth Shuker, 20 Cedar Lane, Cornwall, NY 12518.

SCOUT MUSEUMS
Courtesy of the First Federation of Scout Museums International

All Scout museums are welcome to apply for membership in the Federation of Scout Museums International. Each museum must be open to the public and provide details as requested on the application. No dues are required, but each museum is asked to send five self-addressed 39¢ stamped envelopes to the Editor of Scout Memorabilia, or those outside the U.S.A. send ten International Postage Coupons. Museums that have brochures may send 35 copies for distribution to other Scout museums. Mail to Harry Thorsen, 7305 Bounty Drive, Sarasota, FL 33581.

UNITED STATES

ARIZONA
Scout Museum of Southern Arizona
1937 E. Blacklidge Dr.
Tucson, AZ 85719 (to be opened)

CALIFORNIA
Bailey's World Scout Uniform Exhibit
2169 Highgate Rd.
Westgate Village, CA 91361

Troop 1 Scout Museum
P.O. Box 612
Huntington Beach, CA 92648

Western Museum of Scouting
13115 Washington Blvd.
Los Angeles, CA 90066

COLORADO
Koshare Indian Museum, Inc.
Otero Junior College Campus
LaJunta, CO 81050

DELAWARE
John C. Lewis Scout Museum
RD 4, Box 404
Dover, DE 19901

FLORIDA
Boy Scout Historical Exhibit
505 Riverside Dr.
Ormand Beach, FL 32074

Thorsen's Scout Memorabilia Museum
7305 Bounty Dr.
Sarasota, FL 33581

ILLINOIS
W.D. Boyce Scouting Hall of Fame
Rt. 4, 1718 N. 2525th Rd.
Ottawa, IL 61350

Gierhart's Scout Museum
803 West 10th St.
Sterling, IL 61081

Zitelman Scout Museum
708 Seminary St.
Rockford, IL 61108

INDIANA
Stone's Scout Museum
2290 West Bloomfield Rd.
Bloomington, IN 47401

KENTUCKY
National Scout Museum
Boy Scouts of America
Murray State University
Murray, KY 42071

MAINE
Brass Pounders and Scout
   Museum
3 State St.
Brewer, ME 04412

MARYLAND
Baden-Powell Historical
   Museum
9517 Kilimanjaro Rd.
Columbia, MD 21045

MASSACHUSETTS
Bussiere Scout Museum
154 Belmont Rd.
West Harwich, MA 02671

Cedar Hill Museum (Girl Scouts)
265 Beaver St.
Waltham, MA 02154

Museum of Girl Scouting
Plymouth Bay Girl Scout Council
140 Winthrop St.
Taunton, MA 02780

MICHIGAN
France Scout Museum
12417 State Rd.
Nunica, MI 49448

Washington Historical Scouting
   Museum
4772 Woodmire Dr.
Utica, MI 48087

MINNESOTA
Boy Scout History
   Interpretation Center
130 N. 3rd Ave. South
St. Paul, MN 55075

MISSISSIPPI
L.O. Crosby Jr. Visitor's Center
Scout Reservation Camp Tiak
Wiggins, MS 39577

NEW HAMPSHIRE
Lawrence Lee Scouting
   Museum & Max Silber
   Scouting Library
Camp Carpenter, BSA, RFD #6
P.O. Box 1121
Manchester, NH 03105

NEW MEXICO
Philmont Museum/
   Seton Memorial Library
Philmont Scout Ranch BSA
Cimarron, NM 87714

NEW YORK
Soundview Scouting Museum
P.O. Box 280
East Northport, NY 11731

Trailside Museum
   (Dan Beard Exhibit)
Bear Mt. State Park, NY 10911

NORTH CAROLINA
Lone Scout Memory Lodge
Camp Barnhart BSA
Rt. 2
New London, NC 28127

OHIO
Nathan L. Dauby Scout Museum
Greater Cleveland Council BSA
   Scout Center
E. 22nd St. at Woodlawn
Cleveland, OH 44115

OREGON
**Nor'west Scout Heritage
 Society**
Scouters Mt. Lodge
11300 S.E. 147th St.
Portland, OR 97236

TEXAS
**Scout Museum of Natural
 History**
Clements Scout Reservation BSA
Athens, TX 75751

UTAH
Gaudio's Boy Scout Museum
131 N. University Ave.
Provo, UT 84601

WASHINGTON
Scouting Trail Museum
10021 26th Ave., S.W.
Seattle, WA 98146

WISCONSIN
Heritage Museum of Milwaukee
County B.S.A.
3716 W. Wisconsin Ave.
Milwaukee, WI 53208

FOREIGN COUNTRIES

AUSTRALIA
**Alan Jones Museum of Scout
 Memorabilia**
Baden-Powell House
581 Murray St.
P.O. Box 467
West Perth, 6005 Australia

BELGIUM
Scout Museum of Belgium
Volmolenlaan 17
B 3000 Leuven, Belgium

CANADA
Museum of Canadian Scouting
Boy Scouts of Canada National
 Office
P.O. Box 5151, Sta. F
Ottawa, KRC-3G7 Canada

DENMARK
Scout Museum
Niels Finsens Alle 59
2860 Söborg, Denmark

ENGLAND
**Baden-Powell and Scouting
 Museum**
61 Bryning Ave.
Bispham, Blackpool, FY2 9LZ
 England

**Baden-Powell House (B-P Story
 and Exhibition)**
Queens Gate, London, SW7 5JS
 England

Gilwell Park
Chingford, London, E4 7QW
 England

FINLAND
Scout Museum
Kuikkula, SF 20510
Turku/ABO, 51 Finland

FRANCE
**Centre Charles Granvigne
 Arcenant**
21700 Nuits
St. Georges, France

GREECE
**International Scout Museum
 Exhibitions**
14 Eginis St.
Thessaloniki, 54638 Greece

ITALY
National Scout Archivio
Centro Studi Mario Mazza
via Galata 39A
16126 Genova, Italy

LUXEMBURG
Permanent Scout Exhibition
32 Grand'Rue
Wiltz, Luxemburg

MEXICO
Bibliotheque and International
Museum of Scouting in
Mexico
"Teocalli Aztec" (Gods' House)
Mexico 3 D.F.

SWEDEN
Scout Museum of Sweden
Kjesäters Folkhögskola
64300 Vingäker/0151/12000
Sweden

SWITZERLAND
Bibliotheque et Archives
Scoutes (Scout Library
and Museum)
Flamant, VY Saulnier
CH-2115 Buttes, Switzerland

Central Archives/Museum of the
Swiss Girls and Boys Scouts
Scout Center
Speichergasse 31
CH-3011 Berne, Switzerland

Marchal Scout Museum
Fschal al igne
CH 1451 Bullet, Switzerland

Note: See back of book for application for membership in the Federation of Scout Museums International.

HOW TO USE THIS BOOK

The Official Price Guide to Scouting Collectibles has been designed for maximum convenience and minimum time in using the listings. All items have been grouped into sections by type. There are main sections on *Books, Badges,* and other items, as well as special sections for *Camp Fire Girls* and *Girl Scouts material.* Within each major section are a number of divisions, for example, in *Books,* listings on song books, works of fiction and works of nonfiction. So the first step is to refer to the section that lists the type of item you want to identify or price. Next, you will find that the individual items are arranged either alphabetically or chronologically. Beside each item is a set of prices, such as: $6.00 to $8.00. These represent the current retail value for that particular item.

BOY SCOUTS

A BRIEF HISTORY

Following is a year-by-year synopsis of some of the highlights of the history of the Boy Scouts of America.

1910. Boy Scouts of America was incorporated February 8th by W.D. Boyce. James E. West appointed executive officer. Lord Robert Baden-Powell and Ernest Thompson Seton coauthor first Handbook.

1911. The National Council office was established at 200th Avenue, New York, N.Y. First American Handbook is great success. Membership—61,495.

1912. Sea Scouting for older Scouts began. *Boys Life* magazine purchased and became official. Membership—126,860.

1913. United States divided into eight districts (later to be twelve regions and then six regions). *Scouting* magazine began. Membership—115,364.

1914. First William T. Hornaday Wildlife Conservation Gold Medal presented. Membership—127,685.

1915. Fifty-seven Merit Badge pamphlets and Handbooks for Scoutmasters issued. Membership—182,303.

1916. Congress granted Federal Charter protecting name and insignia. Pioneer Scout program for rural Scouts developed. Membership—245,183.

1917. "Help Win The War" program gained country-wide recognition for the outstanding service achievements of the Boy Scouts. Membership—363,837.

1918. "The War Is Over, But Our Work is Not" slogan led Scouts into nationwide service during influenza epidemic. Scouts sold over 147 million Liberty Loan Bonds and fifty-three million Savings Stamps. Boy Scouts distributed 300 million Government leaflets and had outstanding war-garden program. Membership—418,984.

1919. First Gold Honor Medals awarded for Lifesaving, replacing Bronze and Silver Awards. Membership—462,060.

1920. First World Jamboree in London and First National Training Conference for Scout executives. Membership—478,528.

1921. Scouts rendered outstanding service in Forest Conservation, disaster areas and flood areas in Colorado and Texas. Membership—513,015.

1922. Scouts International Bureau established in London. Membership—534,415.

1923. International left-handshake adopted. Membership—587,578.

1924. "Every Scout a Swimmer" program began. Lone Scouts of America merged with Boy Scouts of America. Membership—696,620. Second World Jamboree held in Copenhagen, Denmark.

1925. Victims of Illinois tornado, California earthquake, and Louisiana fire received outstanding Boy Scout services. Membership—756,857.

1926. The first Silver Buffalo awards presented. Development of program for younger boys was begun. Membership—783,574.

1927. Eagle Palms begin. Twelve new rural merit badges added. Total merit badges now eighty-nine. "National Office" moved to Two Park Avenue, New York. Membership—785,633.

1928. Sea Scout, Paul A. Siple, accompanies Byrd's Antarctic Expedition. Membership—819,791.

1929. Third World Jamboree held at Birkenhead, England. Cub Scout program began as experiment. Membership—833,097.

1930. Cub Scout program officially began. 5,103 Cub Scouts registered. Membership—847,051.

1931. B.S.A. President, Mortimer L. Schiff, died within a month of his election. First Silver Beaver awards presented. Membership—878,358.

1932. Mortimer L. Schiff Scout Reservation, Mendham, N.J., presented by his mother in his memory. Membership—878,461.

1933. Fourth World Jamboree held at Godollo, Hungary. Membership—904,240.

1934. Radio address by President Roosevelt inspired Scouts to collect nearly two million items of clothing, furniture, food, and supplies for the needy. Membership—973,589.

1935. Proposed First National Jamboree, scheduled for Washington, D.C., cancelled due to infantile paralysis epidemic. Membership goes over one million—1,027,833.

1936. President Roosevelt broadcast invitation to National Jamboree rescheduled for July, 1937. New Handbook for Scoutmasters published. Membership—1,069,837.

1937. First National Jamboree, Washington, D.C. Fifth World Jamboree held at Vogelenzang, Holland. Membership—1,129,841.

1938. Waite Phillips donated Philturn, Rocky Mountain Scout Camp (name changed to Philmont in 1941) consisting of 35,857 acres near Cimarron, N.M. Membership—1,242,009.

1939. Scouts participated and assisted at New York World's Fair and Golden Gate Exposition. Membership—1,357,993.

1940. A program for service in national emergency and defense was adopted. Membership—1,449,412.

1941. War declared. Boy Scouts mobilized for distribution of defense bond posters, collection of aluminum and paper, Victory gardens, distribution of air raid posters, etc. Plan developed for Scouts to act as messengers, fire watchers and medical assistants. Waite Phillips contributed more acreage and also the Phil Tower building in Tulsa, Oklahoma, the income from which is to be used to support the renamed Philmont Scout Ranch. Membership—1,522,302.

1942. Scouts continued in war service collecting thirty million pounds of rubber in a two-week period. Air Scouting program developed. Membership—1,533,080.

1943. Scouts increased war service in many areas. First Silver Antelope Awards presented. Long trousers and the Scout cap were made a part of the official uniform. Membership—1,613,782.

1944. World Friendship Fund established to help restore Scouting in devastated countries. Membership—1,866,356.

1945. The General Eisenhower Gold Medal presented for outstanding achievement in waste paper collection. 20,000 Scouts also earned the General Douglas MacArthur Medal for Victory gardens. Membership—1,977,463.

1946. Camp activities became more troop centered. Grant Foundation contribution began a five-year expanded training program. Membership—2,063,397.

1947. Sixth World Jamboree in Moisson, France, hosted 32,000 Scouts from thirty-eight countries, including 1,151 from U.S.A. Membership—2,141,984.

1948. The Order of the Arrow was integrated into the National camping program. Conservation program and unit leader training emphasized. Membership—2,210,766.

1949. Age levels lowered to eight years for Cubs, eleven years old for Boy Scouts, and fourteen years old for Explorers. The crusade to "Strengthen the Arm of Liberty" inaugurated. Membership—2,579,515.

1950. The Fortieth Anniversary observed. The Second National Jamboree at Valley Forge, hosted 47,163. Training programs began at Philmont Scout Ranch. U.S. Post Office issued first Boy Scout stamp. Membership—2,795,222.

1951. "Strengthen the Arm of Liberty" concluded three-year program with 33 percent membership gain. Seventh World Jamboree at Bad Iocle, Austria hosted 13,000 Scouts. Two million pounds of clothing collected by Scouts for domestic and foreign relief. Membership—2,942,779.

1952. "Forward on Liberty's Team" launched. Scouts distributed over a million posters and thirty million Liberty Bell leaflets in a "Get-Out-the-Vote" campaign. The twenty millionth Scout was registered. Membership—3,183,266.

1953. The Third National Jamboree at Irvine Ranch, California, hosted

45,401. Scouts assisted at the Inauguration of President Eisenhower. Membership—3,395,884.

1954. National Council moved to New Brunswick, N.J. The Webelos den created to maintain interest of older Cub Scouts. Membership—3,774,015.

1955. Eighth World Jamboree conducted in Ontario, Canada, with 15,000 Scouts present. A College Scouts Reserve authorized. Membership—4,175,134.

1956. "Onward for God and My Country" program launched. Scouts distributed over a million posters and 36,000,000 Liberty Bell pamphlets in a "Get-Out-the-Vote" campaign. Membership—4,526,302.

1957. The Fourth National Jamboree held at Valley Forge, Pennsylvania, hosted 50,000 Scouts. Also Birmingham, England, hosted the World Jamboree attracting 35,000 Scouts. The Handbook for Boys passed the fifteen million mark. Membership—4,751,495.

1958. New Exploring program launched. Johnston Historical Museum begun. Membership—4,950,885.

1959. Tenth World Jamboree held in the Phillipines and new edition of the Boy Scout Handbook published. Membership—5,043,195.

1960. Scouting's Golden Jubilee Year. The Fiftieth Anniversary achievement award was offered. The Fifth National Jamboree held at Colorado Springs hosting 56,378 Scouts. U.S. Post Office issued Boy Scout Commemorative Stamp. John F. Kennedy was first U.S. President elected who had Scouting background as a youth.

1961. Plans adopted for a statue in Washington, D.C. to commemorate all who have served Scouting. Membership—5,160,958.

1962. The "Fit for Tomorrow" program launched. Membership—5,322,167.

1963. Three-year program "Scouting Can Make the Difference" launched. Philmont Scout Ranch received anonymous gift of over ten thousand acres known as the Baldy Area. The Eleventh World Jamboree was held at Marathon, Greece. Membership—5,446,910.

1964. Philmont Scout Ranch donor, Waite Phillips, died. "Strengthen America's Heritage" program launched. The Sixth National Jamboree held at Valley Forge with 52,000 attending. The Boy Scout Commemorative Tribute statue unveiled in Washington, D.C. Membership—5,585,700.

1965. "The Program of Emphasis Breakthrough for Youth" was begun for a three-year period. Golden Anniversary National Conference of the Order of the Arrow held at Indiana University. Seventh edition of Boy Scout Handbook published. The Inner-City/Rural Program launched. Membership—5,732,708.

1966. A revised Charter and By-Laws of the Boy Scouts of America was adopted. A new wing was opened at the Johnston Historical Museum. An Ernest Thompson Seton Memorial Museum and Library begun at Philmont. Membership—5,831,541.

1967. Advancement program changed to meet the challenge of reaching boys in slum ghettoes and rural poverty-stricken areas. The Twelfth World Jamboree held at Farragut State Park, Idaho, with over 12,000 attending. Membership—6,058,508.

1968. "Farm-City Week" demonstrated how Scouting serves boys both in the city and in rural areas. Young college men without previous Scouting background were invited to join the College Scouts Reserve. America's Apollo 8 spacecraft, with astronauts aboard who were former Boy Scouts, soared around the moon. Membership—6,247,160.

1969. Astronaut Neil Armstrong, a former Eagle Scout, became the first man to set foot on the moon.

Membership—6,183,086—marked the first year of membership decline since 1913.

Seventh National Jamboree held at Farragut State Park in Idaho. Over 35,000 Scouts attended.

1970. Severe unrest among the youth and the minority groups stirred high crime rate, riots, antiwar demonstrations and college campus deaths.

The Boy Scouts of America, celebrating its first sixty years, was recognized as a continuing movement for understanding of our duty to God and Country, others and self. The actions of Scouts were in direct contrast to the Hippies and Yippies of the period. Membership—6,284,284.

1971. Thirteenth World Jamboree held in the foothills of Mt. Fuji in Shizuoka Prefecture, Japan.

Project Soar focused attention on Conservation projects. Membership—6,427,026.

1972. In order to reduce travel costs and allow a greater number of National Jamboree Scout participants, two Jamborees were announced for 1973. "Jamboree West" was to take place in Idaho and "Jamboree East" in Pennsylvania.

The National Eagle Scout Association provided a way to keep Eagle Scouts affiliated with the B.S.A., even if inactive.

New Uniform options available by troop decision. "The Improved Scout Program" was announced. Membership—6,512,597 (historic high membership).

1973. The Eighth National Jamboree was attempted on a dual basis for the first time. Jamboree West was held at Farragut State Park, Idaho, hosting 28,000 Scouts and Jamboree East was held at Moraine State Park, Pennsylvania, with 44,000 Scouts in attendance. Membership—6,405,225.

1974. "Be Prepared for Life—Be Safe, Be Fit" was the theme for the year's Bicentennial program. B.S.A. recommended the Presidential Physical Fitness Program for youth and the Presidential Sports Award program for adults.

Announcement made that *Boys Life* magazine would take on a new look and a new size.

Gerald R. Ford, a former Eagle Scout, became President of the United States of America. Membership—5,803,885.

1975. Fourteenth World Jamboree, called "Nordjamb," was held in Norway. Fifteen thousand Scouts from ninety-one countries were in attendance. Membership—5,018,070.

1976. America's Bicentennial celebrated by 56,712 Cub Packs, 61,283 Scout Troops and 22,610 Explorer Posts. Membership—4,884,082.

1977. Brownsea Island was re-created at the 1977 rainsoaked National Jamboree held at Moraine Park, Pennsylvania. Membership—4,718,138.

1978. Plans made to move the National office to Dallas-Fort Worth area. Total membership figures continued to decline. Membership—4,493,491.

1979. Fifteenth World Jamboree was called Dalajamb and was to be held in Iran, but joined Dalajamb in Sweden.

James L. Tarr became Chief Scout Executive.

Important new Handbook for Boys written by Green Bar Bill Hillcourt was an immediate success. Membership—4,266,413.

1980. New Scout uniforms introduced and became popular. Downward trend in membership reversed, marking the first membership increase since 1972.

New Patrol Leaders Handbook, giving strong emphasis to the patrol method, was released with initial printing of 100,000 copies. Membership—4,296,696.

1981. The tenth National Jamboree held at Fort A. P. Hill, Virginia, in a 5,000-acre "tent city," assembled 31,000 Scouts and Scouters. The theme "Scouting's Reunion with History" and participants followed in the footsteps of America's Heritage.

Membership increases were anticipated for the second straight year.

1983. Sixteenth World Jamboree held at Calgary, Canada.

1985. At the eleventh National Jamboree, at Fort A. P. Hill, Virginia, the Boy Scouts of America celebrated its Seventy-fifth Anniversary. More than 32,000 Scouts and leaders from around the world attended. Ben H. Love became the eighth Chief Scout Executive. Members totaled 73,639,425.

FOUNDERS

ROBERT STEPHENSON SMYTH BADEN-POWELL

Robert Stephenson Smyth Baden-Powell was born in England February 22, 1857. His father, a noted clergyman and scientist, died when Robert was three years old, and his mother raised him and his four brothers and sisters. At the age of thirteen, Baden-Powell earned a scholarship to Charterhouse School in London, where he delighted classmates with his talent as an artist-caricaturist and a musical humorist. He often entertained his classmates by improvising a skit, song, or dance.

Following school, Baden-Powell began a life of travel and adventure by entering the cavalry as a Sub-Lieutenant and sailing for India in 1876.

Baden-Powell advanced rapidly in rank and supplemented his meager army pay through his published writings, which included *Reconnaissance and Scouting.* He also won honors in the dangerous sport of wild boar hunting and later wrote and illustrated another book on the sport, which he called *Pigsticking Or Hoghunting.*

His regiment, the Thirteenth Hussars, was moved to South Africa to be in position in case of war between the British and Dutch settlers. The Dutch settlers were called "Boer" from their word meaning farmer. As the war clouds formed, Baden-Powell posed as a newspaper correspondent while he scouted the mountainous area drawing maps and gaining information about the terrain and people. The conflict between the British and the Boers quieted down, but Baden-Powell's reputation as a capable scout had been established.

When the Zulu tribe of warriors, led by their Chieftain Dinizulu, began causing disturbances, Baden-Powell was dispatched to track him down. Dinizulu eventually surrendered and Baden-Powell was awarded the Chieftain's wooden beaded necklace. Years later, when Baden-Powell established the first comprehensive training course for Scoutmasters, he tied these wooden beads to leather thongs as a symbol for trained Scoutmasters to wear, naming the course "Wood Badge."

Baden-Powell became a noted intelligence agent and chief scout for the British Army, and utilized his acting and sketching abilities while playing the role of a spy. He later told of this in his book *My Adventures as a Spy.*

Baden-Powell was given command of the Fifth Dragoon Guards, where he developed a course in scouting and reconnaissance and then designed a special badge to award to men who successfully completed the course. The badge utilized the fleur-de-lys because it resembled the north point of the compass, and his trained scout "is the man who can show the way like a compass needle."

Troubles between the British and the Boers started again and Baden-Powell was dispatched to take command of the city of Mafeking, a strategically important city in South Africa. He had just sent a new book, *Aids to Scouting,* to his publisher, when the Boers attacked and surrounded Mafeking on October 13, 1899. *Aids to Scouting* was written for soldiers, not boys, but was later to play a profound role in developing the Scout movement.

Baden-Powell was determined to hold Mafeking by tricking the Boers into believing that Mafeking was well armed and strongly fortified. The siege lasted 217 days, while all of England waited anxiously for continuing reports of Baden-Powell's brilliant tactics, which continued to confuse the Boers. Finally, British forces reached Mafeking, and the Boer forces were repulsed. The public enthusiasm in England for Baden-Powell was overwhelming. He was promptly promoted to Major-General at the young age of forty-three and given the job of raising and training a ten-thousand-man force to be called the South African Constabulary. He designed their uniforms in a fashion that later was to become the first Boy Scout uniform, and their motto was, "Be Prepared."

Perhaps the most significant occurrence was the sudden and unexpected use of his book *Aids to Scouting* by the youth of the day. Thousands of children began enjoying the scouting games. One of the popular children's magazines, *Boys of the Empire,* reprinted portions of it using the title "The Boy Scouts."

While Inspector General of the Cavalry, Baden-Powell was invited to review the Boys Brigade, a youth organization that combined religion and military customs. He began to write articles for the *Boys Brigade Gazette* which appeared under the title "Scouting for Boys." The games and contests he suggested immediately proved appealing to boys. In 1907 he wrote two pamphlets titled *Boy Scouts: A Suggestion,* and then *Boy Scouts: Summary of a Scheme.* In order that his theory on a Boy Scout program be tested, Baden-Powell selected twenty-one boys from every economic level to camp for a week on Brownsea Island off the southern coast of England in July, 1907.

In this first scouting experiment, Baden-Powell instigated the use of Patrols, Patrol flags, the Troop, the honor system, uniforms, the fleur-de-lys badge, the meaningful campfire, the Koodoo horn, knot-tying, stalking, nature study, life saving, first aid, and many other scouting "methods."

The Boy Scouts had been born.

BADEN-POWELL COLLECTIBLES

BOOKS AND PAMPHLETS	Current Price Range		P/Y Avg.
☐ Adventures and Accidents, Methuen, 1934	12.00	20.00	15.00
☐ Same as above, but later printings	9.00	12.00	10.00
☐ Adventuring to Manhood, Pearson, 1936	10.00	15.00	12.00
☐ African Adventures, Pearson, 1937	10.00	15.00	11.00
☐ Aids to Scouting for N.C.O.s and Men, Gale and Polden, 1899	200.00	250.00	210.00
☐ Aids to Scoutmastership, Putnam, 1919	23.00	30.00	22.50
☐ Same as above, but later printings	11.00	15.00	11.50
☐ Alms, Methods and Needs, 1923	6.00	9.00	6.50
☐ Birds and Beast in Africa, Macmillan, 1938	13.00	17.00	13.50
☐ Canadian Boy Scout, The, Morang, 1911	75.00	110.00	76.50
☐ Downfall of Prempeh, The, Methuen, 1896	30.00	50.00	32.00
☐ Girl Guiding, Pearson, 1918	10.00	12.00	11.00
☐ Handbook for Brownies or Bluebirds, Pearson, 1920	20.00	25.00	22.50
☐ Same as above, but later printings	15.00	23.00	15.75
☐ Indian Memories, Jenkins, 1915	20.00	35.00	30.00
☐ Lessons From The Varsity of Life, Pearson, 1933	25.00	30.00	26.00
☐ Same as above, but later printings	12.00	15.00	12.50
☐ Lessons of a Lifetime, Holt, 1933	25.00	35.00	26.00
☐ Life's Snags and How to Meet Them, Pearson, 1927	12.00	18.00	13.00

	Current Price Range		P/Y Avg.
☐ **Matabele Campaign, The,** Methuen, 1897	60.00	90.00	62.00
☐ **More Sketches Of Kenya,** Macmillan, 1940	10.00	15.00	12.00
☐ **My Adventures As a Spy,** Pearson, 1915	25.00	33.00	27.00
☐ **Same as above,** but later printings	10.00	14.00	11.00
☐ **An Old Wolf's Favourites,** Lippincott, 1921	14.00	17.00	14.50
☐ **Paddle Your Own Canoe,** Macmillan, 1939	12.00	18.00	13.00
☐ **Pigsticking or Hoghunting,** Jenkins, 1889	40.00	50.00	42.00
☐ **Same as above,** but revised edition, 1924	12.00	18.00	13.00
☐ **Quick Training for War,** Jenkins, 1914	12.00	18.00	13.00
☐ **Rovering to Success,** Jenkins, 1922	15.00	20.00	15.00
☐ **Same as above,** but later printings	10.00	15.00	12.00
☐ **Scouting and Youth Movements,** McBride, 1929	10.00	12.00	10.50
☐ **Scouting for Boys,** Pearson, 1908, originally six pamphlets, per copy	60.00	75.00	63.00
☐ **Complete six**	325.00	450.00	350.00
☐ **1910 edition, complete**	70.00	100.00	75.00
☐ **1912 edition, complete**	50.00	75.00	55.00
☐ **1957 centenary edition,** reprint	10.00	20.00	12.00
☐ **Other editions**	10.00	12.00	10.50
☐ **Scouting Round the World,** Jenkins, 1935	10.00	15.00	12.00
☐ **Sea Scouting for Boys,** Brown, 1911	50.00	70.00	53.00

	Current Price Range		P/Y Avg.

☐ **Same as above,** but later editions	12.00	25.00	14.00
☐ **Sketches In Mafeking and East Africa,** Smith and Elder, 1907	150.00	200.00	160.00
☐ **Sport in War,** Heinemann........	30.00	40.00	32.00
☐ **What Scouts Can Do,** Lippincott, 1921	25.00	30.00	27.00
☐ **Same as above,** but later reprints	10.00	15.00	12.00
☐ **Wolf Cub's Handbook, The,** Macmillan, 1916.	10.00	15.00	12.00

MATERIAL

☐ **Adventuring with Baden-Powell,** 1956	4.00	6.00	4.25
☐ **Baden-Powell's Outlook,** from the Scouter, Pearson, 1941	8.00	10.00	8.50
☐ **Blazing the Trail,** Holt, 1927.....	5.00	7.00	5.25
☐ **Book of Cub Games, The,** Barclay, 1919.	5.00	7.00	5.25
☐ **Boy Scouts Imperial Jamboree, The,** Boy Scouts of America, 1924	6.00	8.00	6.25
☐ **Boy Scout Roll of Honor, The,** Eric Wood, 1914	9.00	11.00	9.50
☐ **Boy Scouts and What They Do,** 1913	9.00	11.00	9.50
☐ **Boys of the Otter Patrol, The,** LaBreton-Martin, 1910	7.00	9.00	7.25
☐ **Camping Out for Boy Scouts and Others,** Bridges, 1909	8.00	10.00	8.25
☐ **Cruise of the Calgaric, The,** Rose Kerr, 1933	7.00	10.00	7.25
☐ **Cruise of the Orduna, The,** Rose Kerr, 1938	7.00	10.00	7.25
☐ **Guiding Book, The,** Kindersley, 1925	5.00	7.00	5.10

BADEN POWELL

Robert Stephenson Smyth Baden-Powell, *Boy Scout Founder*

	Current Price Range		P/Y Avg.
☐ **He-Who-Sees-in-the-Dark,** West, 1915	8.00	10.00	8.25
☐ **How To Run a Troop,** Ernest, 1916	8.00	10.00	8.25
☐ **Laugh Boy, Laugh,** Mathiews, 1930	5.00	7.00	6.00
☐ **Letters to My Son,** James, 1912	10.00	14.00	11.00
☐ **Letters to a Patrol Leader: The Scout Law,** Phillips, 1916	5.00	7.00	5.50
☐ **Letters to a Patrol Leader: The Tenderfoot and Second Class Tests,** 1916	5.00	7.00	5.50
☐ **Look Straight Ahead,** Shepheard, 1912	4.00	6.00	4.25
☐ **Nature Stalking for Boys,** Westell	4.00	6.00	4.25
☐ **Patrol System, The,** Phillips, 1914	4.00	6.00	4.25
☐ **Peter and Veronica,** Beech, 1928	4.00	6.00	4.25
☐ **Pioneering and Map Making,** Enock, 1910	8.00	12.00	9.00
☐ **School Scout Troops,** Reynolds, 1929	4.00	6.00	4.25
☐ **Scout Book of Heroes, The,** Stokes, 1920	5.00	7.00	5.50
☐ **Scouting Sketches,** Lord Hampton, 1925	5.00	7.00	5.50
☐ **Spare Time Activities,** Gilcraft, 1929	5.00	9.00	6.00
☐ **Story of the Girl Guides, The,** Rose Kerr, 1932	4.00	6.00	4.25
☐ **Talks on Ambulance Work,** Gilcraft, 1926	4.00	6.00	4.25
☐ **Today and Tomorrow**	4.00	6.00	4.25
☐ **Training of Scout Officers, The,** 1922	5.00	7.00	5.25

	Current Price Range		P/Y Avg.
☐ **Training in Tracking,** Gilcraft, 1927	4.00	6.00	4.25
☐ **A Twenty-four-Year Hike,** Emlyn	5.00	7.00	5.25
☐ **With a Baden-Powell Scout in Gallipoli,** Priestman, 1916	8.00	10.00	8.50
☐ **With Hunter, Trapper and Scout in Camp and Field,** Miles, 1913	5.00	7.00	5.50
☐ **World Jamboree, The,** Fisher, 1929	8.00	12.00	8.50
☐ **World Rover,** Moot, 1939	4.00	6.00	4.25
☐ **Woodcraft for Boy Scouts,** Donohue, 1911	10.00	14.00	11.00

MISCELLANEOUS (Items that surface infrequently, one every two–three years.)

	Current Price Range		P/Y Avg.
☐ **Graphic, The,** articles of Baden-Powell and Mafeking, 1900	100.00	150.00	110.00
☐ **Autograph,** Baden-Powell	25.00	40.00	27.00
☐ **Original Manuscripts,** of his books with handwritten corrections	150.00	200.00	160.00
☐ **Two Lives of a Hero,** by William Hillcourt, 1964, great biography—reprint	10.00	12.00	11.00
☐ **Cardboard Coaster,** with Baden-Powell picture from Baden-Powell House	1.00	2.00	1.10
☐ **Porcelain Cup and Saucer,** with names of British Officers, including Baden-Powell	30.00	40.00	32.00
☐ **Typewritten Letters,** signed by Baden-Powell	30.00	50.00	35.00
☐ **Baden-Powell's** *Boy's Magazine,* recent lot sales:			
☐ 29 issues, 1912	40.00	—	—
☐ 49 issues, 1916	60.00	—	—
☐ 44 issues, 1914	60.00	—	—
☐ 34 issues, 1917	40.00	—	—
☐ 44 issues, 1915	60.00	—	—

	Current Price Range		P/Y Avg.
☐ **Baden-Powell Medal with Ring,** Centernario de Baden-Powell, 1957	10.00	12.00	10.50
☐ **Twelve Copies of London Times,** covering the siege of Mafeking under Baden-Powell, 1900	60.00	80.00	65.00
☐ **Eight Copies of London Times,** covering the same, criticism of Scouting and Baden-Powell's replies.	40.00	50.00	42.00
☐ **Baden-Powell House Patch**	2.00	3.00	2.10
☐ **Baden-Powell Portrait Patch,** no words	3.00	4.00	3.10
☐ **Baden-Powell Portrait Patch,** National Official Boy Scouts of America.	3.00	4.00	3.10
☐ **Photos,** of Baden-Powell.	4.00	7.00	4.25
☐ **Baden-Powell Plate,** gold edge	95.00	120.00	97.00
☐ **Baden-Powell Plate,** white with open latticework edge	110.00	140.00	112.00
☐ **Col. R.S.S. Baden-Powell Plate,** with flowers	90.00	110.00	92.00
☐ **Col. R.S.S. Baden-Powell Plate,** for seven months defender of Mafeking relieved May 17, 1900, blue floral border on plate	140.00	180.00	145.00
☐ **Lieut-Col. R.S.S. Baden-Powell Plate,** brown border	110.00	125.00	112.00
☐ **Lieut-Col. R.S.S. Baden-Powell Plate,** with flags and gold edge . . .	125.00	150.00	130.00
☐ **Lieut-Col. R.S.S. Baden-Powell Plate,** gold edge.	140.00	160.00	145.00
☐ **Major General R.S.S. Baden-Powell Plate,** brown border . . , ...	100.00	120.00	105.00
☐ **Major General R.S.S. Baden-Powell Plate,** with flags and gold edge	140.00	175.00	145.00

	Current Price Range		P/Y Avg.
☐ **Major General R.S.S. Baden-Powell Plate,** gold edge	140.00	160.00	142.00
☐ **Major General R.S.S. Baden-Powell Plate,** green and gold border..................................	120.00	140.00	125.00
☐ **Pressed Glass Plate,** Baden-Powell, Mafeking, besieged seven months, 17 May, 1900 relieved, two flags	95.00	120.00	100.00
☐ **Pottery Drinking Glass,** portrait of Lieut. Col. Robert S.S. Baden-Powell.................................	55.00	75.00	57.00
☐ **Tin Plate,** Lieut-General Baden-Powell, portrait, 10″	65.00	75.00	67.00
☐ **Porcelain Plaque,** portrait of "Col. R.S.S. Baden-Powell," 7″ x 5″....	70.00	110.00	75.00
☐ **Baden-Powell Portrait Plaque,** 7″ x 9″	70.00	110.00	75.00
☐ **Wood and Metal Plaque,** from Baden-Powell House, 3″	3.00	4.00	3.10
☐ **Baden-Powell and Lady Baden-Powell,** Thank-you postcard	3.00	5.00	3.10
☐ **Postcard,** Baden-Powell War Memorial, Australia	3.00	5.00	3.10
☐ **Color Portrait,** poster of Baden-Powell, 17″ x 12″..................	15.00	20.00	15.50
☐ **Color Portrait Poster,** Baden-Powell, l7″ x 20″	15.00	20.00	15.50
☐ **Poster #56,** "The Scout Jamboree," Baden-Powell being cheered by scouts, in color, 12″ x 14″	6.00	8.00	6.25
☐ **Black-and-White Portrait,** Baden-Powell, 22″ x 29″..................	7.00	10.00	7.50
☐ **Ceramic Tile Portrait,** Baden-Powell, 6″ square	70.00	90.00	72.00
☐ **Portrait Cigarette Cards,** Baden-Powell, fourteen different..........	125.00	150.00	130.00

	Current Price Range		P/Y Avg.
☐ **Color Portrait,** Baden-Powell, 8″ x 10″, framed in cherry wood under glass, from Boy Scout World Headquarters, London, 1930s...........	65.00	90.00	70.00
☐ **Portrait,** Baden-Powell with an English Scout......................	3.00	5.00	3.75
☐ **Handkerchief,** portrait of Baden-Powell in center with one Lord and three Generals, "Our Heroes"	25.00	35.00	27.00
☐ **Original Pen Sketches,** by Baden-Powell..............................	60.00	100.00	63.00
☐ **Original Vanity Fair Lithograph,** Baden-Powell with certificate of authenticity, titled "Boy Scouts," also "Mafeking," each, 8″ x 14″, 1911	40.00	60.00	45.00
☐ **Color Print,** of Baden-Powell's water color "My House in the Woods," 1911	5.00	10.00	5.50
☐ **Phonograph Records,** set of two, Columbia Gramaphone Co., a lecture on Boy Scout Training by Baden-Powell, 12″, 1927	125.00	200.00	130.00
☐ **Cassette Recording,** of above....	10.00	12.00	10.50
☐ **Baden-Powell's Recorded Voice,** farewell speech, 10″ phonograph record, Nixa Co., England.........	12.00	20.00	13.00
☐ **Baden-Powell's Scouts,** an official history, 1961	5.00	15.00	6.00
☐ **Sheet Music,** Baden-Powell march................................	10.00	15.00	11.00
☐ **Metallic Stickers,** Baden-Powell's Bust, brass-colored, from Baden-Powell's House, 2½″ oval	2.00	3.00	2.10

ERNEST THOMPSON SETON

Canadian-born Ernest Thompson Seton was an organizer, artist, illustrator, naturalist, and fiction writer. A man of great and varied talents, he had, in July, 1902, organized a boys' youth movement based on American-Indian lore which he called "Woodcraft Indians." The group used the tribal form of government with a chief, medicine man, braves and utilized American Indian symbols and legends.

Seton met with Baden-Powell in England in 1906 to discuss common principles and goals. The following year, Baden-Powell helped revise Seton's "Birch Bark Roll," a type of manual for the Woodcraft Indians. In the early organizational meetings to develop the Boy Scouts of America, Seton indicated he would bring his Woodcraft Indians into the suggested Boy Scouts of America. He was appointed Chairman of the Organizational Committee with Executive Powers in June, 1910, and the Boy Scouts of America opened its doors in a small office in New York. Subsequently he utilized his great genius in developing the *Official Handbook*, uniforms, ranks, and many of the great things in Scouting.

A clash of personalities developed between Seton, Chief Scout from 1910 to 1915, and James E. West, another powerful figure. The disagreements between the two increased until 1915, when Seton resigned as Chief Scout. The post of Chief Scout was not used again for thirty years.

In 1916, when the Boy Scouts of America received a charter from Congress, it specified that Scout Leaders were required to be citizens of the United States. Since Seton was still a Canadian, he left the movement and attempted to reinstate the Woodcraft Indians, but it never became a vital organization again.

SETON COLLECTIBLES (Few collectors in the field. More interest in Canada, his birthplace.)

BOOKS AND PAMPHLETS	Current Price Range		P/Y Avg.
☐ **Animals,** Selections from Life Histories, The Nature Library, Doubleday, 1926, color plates	12.00	17.00	12.50
☐ **Animal Heroes,** Scribner, 1905	11.00	13.00	11.50

	Current Price Range		P/Y Avg.
☐ **Same as above,** but later editions	5.00	7.00	5.50
☐ **Same as above,** printed by Grosset & Dunlap	4.00	6.00	4.25
☐ **Animals Worth Knowing,** The Little Nature Library, Doubleday, 1928	8.00	10.00	8.50
☐ **Arctic Prairies,** Scribners, 1911 ...	25.00	40.00	30.00
☐ **Same as above,** but later printings	10.00	15.00	12.00
☐ **Same as above,** but printed by Universal Press and Seton Press	10.00	15.00	12.00
☐ **Bannertail: The Story of a Gray Squirrel,** Scribner, 1922	13.00	17.00	13.50
☐ **Biography of an Arctic Fox,** Century, 1909	14.00	18.00	14.50
☐ **Biography of a Grizzly, The,** Century, 1900	12.00	15.00	10.50
☐ **Same as above,** but later printings	6.00	8.00	6.25
☐ **Same as above,** but printed by Grosset & Dunlap	3.00	5.00	3.25
☐ **Blazes on the Trail,** Little Peegno Press, 1928, three pamphlets: I Life Craft or Woodcraft;	4.00	5.00	4.10
☐ **II Rise of the Three Woodcraft**	4.00	5.00	4.10
☐ **III Spartans of the Three Pamphlets: West**	4.00	5.00	4.10
☐ **Same as above,** but set of all three	14.00	18.00	14.50
☐ **Famous Animal Stories,** Tudor, 1934	10.00	14.00	10.50
☐ **Forester's Manual, The,** Doubleday, 1912	20.00	30.00	25.00
☐ **Four Books in Braille,** Lobo, Redruff, Raggylug, Vixen, Pennsyl-			

	Current Price Range		P/Y Avg.

vania Institution for the Blind, 1900 .... **5.00** / **10.00** — **5.50**

☐ **Gospel of the Redman**, with Julia Seton, Doubleday, 1936 .... **20.00** / **35.00** — **22.00**

☐ **Great Historic Animals**, Scribner, 1937 .... **10.00** / **15.00** — **12.00**

☐ **Johny Bear, Lobo and Other Stories**, Modern Standard Authors, Scribner, 1935 .... **8.00** / **11.00** — **8.25**

☐ **Krag and Johny Bear, Scribner, 1901** .... **9.00** / **12.00** — **9.25**

☐ **Same as above**, but later printings .... **3.00** / **5.00** — **3.25**

☐ **Krag: The Kootenay Ram and Other Stories**, University of London Press, 1929 .... **6.00** / **9.00** — **6.50**

☐ **Legend of the White Reindeer**, Constable, 1915 .... **7.00** / **9.00** — **7.50**

☐ **Library of Pioneering and Woodcraft**, Doubleday, 1925, Reissue of six previously published books in a matching set: I Rolf in the Woods; II Wild Animal Ways; III Two Little Savages; IV Book of Woodcraft and Indian Lore; V Woodland Tales; VI Wild Animals at Home, per set .... **30.00** / **50.00** — **40.00**

☐ **Life Histories of Northern Animals**, Scribner, two volumes, 1909 .... **150.00** / **225.00** — **157.00**

☐ **Lives of Game Animals**, Doubleday, four volumes, 1925–1928, sometimes issued as four volumes in eight parts........................ **140.00** / **200.00** — **145.00**

☐ **Lives of the Hunted**, Scribner, 1901 .... **10.00** / **12.00** — **10.50**

☐ **Same as above**, but later printings................................... **6.00** / **8.00** — **6.50**

☐ **Little Warhorse**, Constable, 1915 **8.00** / **12.00** — **8.50**

	Current Price Range		P/Y Avg.
☐ **Lobo and Other Stories,** Hodder, c. 1927	6.00	9.00	6.50
☐ **Lobo; Bingo; The Pacing Mustang,** State, 1930	6.00	9.00	6.50
☐ **Lobo, Rag, and Vixen,** Scribner, 1899	10.00	14.00	11.00
☐ **Same as above,** but later printings	6.00	8.00	6.50
☐ **Mainly About Wolves,** Methuen London, 1937	8.00	12.00	8.50
☐ **Monarch: The Big Bear of Tallac,** Scribner, 1904	14.00	18.00	15.00
☐ **Same as above,** but printed by Constable	6.00	8.00	6.50
☐ **Natural History of the Ten Commandments, The,** Scribner, 1907, (later Doubleday printed this as *The Ten Commandments in the Animal World*)	15.00	25.00	17.00
☐ **Preacher of Cadar Mountain,** Doubleday, 1917	10.00	14.00	11.00
☐ **Other printings,** Doubleday	6.00	9.00	6.50
☐ **Other printings,** Grosset & Dunlap	4.00	6.00	4.50
☐ **Raggylug and Other Stories,** Hodder, 1927	7.00	9.00	7.50
☐ **Rolf in the Woods,** Doubleday, 1911	9.00	12.00	9.50
☐ **Santana, the Hero Dog of France,** Phoenix Press, 1945, only 500 numbered copies, 300 autographed	100.00	150.00	105.00
☐ **Sign Talk,** Doubleday, 1918	30.00	40.00	32.00
☐ **Slum Cat, The,** Constable, London, 1915	8.00	12.00	8.50
☐ **Trail of the Sandhill Stag,** Scribner, 1899	15.00	30.00	17.00

	Current Price Range		P/Y Avg.
☐ **Same as above,** but later printings..........................	6.00	8.00	6.50
☐ **Same as above,** but limited edition of 250, leather-bound.......	50.00	60.00	52.00
☐ **Twelve Pictures of Wild Animals,** Scribner, no text, 1901.............	75.00	100.00	85.00
☐ **Two Little Savages,** Doubleday, 1900................................	12.00	16.00	12.50
☐ **Same as above,** but later printingo................	7.00	9.00	7.50
☐ **Wild Animals at Home,** Doubleday, 1913.............................	10.00	12.00	10.50
☐ **Same as above,** Grosset & Dunlap..........................	5.00	7.00	5.25
☐ **Wild Animals I Have Known,** American Printing House for the Blind, 1900, N.Y., point system ...	7.00	11.00	7.50
☐ **Wild Animals I Have Known,** Scribner, 1898, first printing with omission page 25..................	60.00	80.00	65.00
☐ **Same as above,** but second printing, without omission.......	30.00	40.00	32.00
☐ **Same as above,** but later printings................................	8.00	10.00	8.50
☐ **Same as above,** but printing by Grosset & Dunlap..............	4.00	5.00	4.10
☐ **Wild Animal Play for Children, The,** Doubleday and Curtis, 1900, musical...........................	15.00	20.00	16.00
☐ **Wild Animal Ways,** Doubleday, 1916..............................	14.00	16.00	14.50
☐ **Same as above,** but other printings................................	5.00	7.00	5.50
☐ **Same as above,** but printed by Houghton Mifflin.................	4.00	5.00	4.10
☐ **Woodland Tales,** Doubleday, 1921................................	7.00	10.00	7.50

	Current Price Range		P/Y Avg.
☐ **Woodmyth and Fable,** Century, 1905	14.00	16.00	14.50

BIRCH BARK ROLLS, THE (There is a current spark of interest in these collectibles.)

☐ **American Woodcraft,** Ladies Home Journal, seven articles, first edition, 1902 May–November, each	25.00	40.00	30.00
☐ **Birch Bark Roll,** Brieger, twentieth edition, 1925	25.00	40.00	30.00
☐ **Birch Bark Roll,** twenty-first edition, 1927	20.00	30.00	25.00
☐ **Birch Bark Roll of the Woodcraft Indians,** Doubleday, Page, sixth edition, 1906	50.00	60.00	50.00
☐ **Birch Bark Roll of the Woodcraft Indians,** Doubleday, Page, seventh edition, 1907 December, 1906	50.00	60.00	52.00
☐ **Birch Bark Roll of the Woodcraft Indians,** Doubleday, Page, eighth edition, 1907	50.00	60.00	52.00
☐ **How to Play Indian,** Curtis Pub. Co., second edition, 1903	40.00	50.00	45.00
☐ **Laws of the Seton Indians,** Camp Cong. Secy's Report, Boston, fourth edition, 1905 April 26	40.00	50.00	45.00
☐ **Laws of the Seton Indians,** Association Boys, New York Y.M.C.A., fifth edition, 1905 June	40.00	50.00	45.00
☐ **Manual of the Woodcraft Indians,** Doubleday, fourteenth edition, 1915	30.00	35.00	32.50
☐ **Book of Woodcraft and Indian Lore, The,** Doubleday, eleventh edition, 1912	20.00	25.00	21.00

	Current Price Range		P/Y Avg.
☐ **Book of Woodcraft and Indian Lore, The,** Doubleday, twelfth edition, 1915	20.00	25.00	21.00
☐ **Boy Scouts of America, The,** Doubleday, Page, tenth edition, 1910	200.00	300.00	225.00
☐ **Red Book, The; Or, How to Play Indian,** Seton, third edition, 1904	40.00	50.00	42.50
☐ **Woodcraft Boys, Woodcraft Girls, How to Begin,** Woodcraft HQ, thirteenth edition, 1915 Dec.	20.00	30.00	22.50
☐ **Woodcraft Manual for Boys,** Doubleday, sixteenth edition, 1917	20.00	30.00	25.00
☐ **Woodcraft Manual for Boys,** Woodcraft League, Doubleday, seventeenth edition, 1918	20.00	30.00	25.00
☐ **Woodcraft Manual for Girls,** Doubleday, fifteenth edition, 1916	20.00	30.00	25.00
☐ **Woodcraft Manual for Girls,** Woodcraft League, Doubleday, eighteenth edition, 1918	20.00	30.00	25.00

ILLUSTRATIONS AND MATERIAL (Little collector interest. Few items available.)

☐ **Animals of a Sagebrush Ranch,** Rand McNally, 1931	5.00	7.00	5.50
☐ **Animal Story Book, The,** volume VI of Young Folks Library, Hall and Locke, 1902	5.00	7.00	5.50
☐ **Animal Tracks and Hunter Signs,** Julia Seton, Doubleday, 1958	6.00	9.00	6.50
☐ **By a Thousand Fires,** Julia Seton, Doubleday	12.00	14.00	12.50
☐ **Bird Portraits,** Ralph Hoffman, Ginn, 1901	22.00	30.00	24.00

	Current Price Range		P/Y Avg.
☐ **Bird World,** J.H. Stickney, Ginn, 1898	9.00	11.00	9.50
☐ **Bird Life,** Frank Chapman, Appleton, 1897	9.00	11.00	9.50
☐ **Boy Training,** John L. Alexander, Association Press, 1911	7.00	10.00	7.50
☐ **Camp Craft,** Warren H. Miller, Scribner, 1915	6.00	9.00	6.50
☐ **Century Dictionary,** 24 volumes, 1000 Seton illustrations, 1889	30.00	50.00	32.00
☐ **First Across the Continent,** Noah Brooks, Scribner, 1901	7.00	9.00	7.50
☐ **Four-Footed Americans and Their Kin,** Mabel Osgood Wright, Macmillan, 1898	10.00	14.00	10.50
☐ **Gorm, The Giant of the Club,** Julia Seton, Philosophers, 1944	3.00	5.00	3.50
☐ **Handbook of Birds of Eastern North America,** Frank Chapman, Appleton, 1895	6.00	8.00	6.50
☐ **Nimrod's Wife,** Grace Gallatin Seton, Doubleday, 1907	8.00	11.00	8.50
☐ **Our Winter Birds,** Chapman, Appleton, 1918	8.00	12.00	8.50
☐ **Outdoorman's Handbook, The,** Warren H. Miller, Angler's Guide Co., 1916	6.00	8.00	6.50
☐ **Queens Gift Book, The,** Hodder...	6.00	9.00	6.50
☐ **Rhythm of the Redman, The,** Julia M. Buttree, Barnes, 1930.......	9.00	12.00	9.50
☐ **Same as above,** but reprint, 1968..............................	4.00	6.00	4.50
☐ **Scribner Treasury, The,** Scribner, 1953	3.00	5.00	3.50

	Current Price Range		P/Y Avg.
☐ **Social Activities for Men and Boys,** Chesley, Association Press, 1910	7.00	10.00	7.50
☐ **Trail and Campfire Stories,** Julia Seton, Appleton, 1940..............	10.00	12.00	10.50
☐ **They Were Open Range Days,** Thompson, World Press, 1946	18.00	24.00	19.00
☐ **Wild Animals of North America,** National Geographic Society, 1918	12.00	14.00	12.50
☐ Same as above, but later printings................................	5.00	8.00	5.25
☐ **A Woman Tenderfoot,** Grace Gallatin Seton-Thompson, Doubleday, 1900	8.00	14.00	9.00
☐ **World of Ernest Thompson Seton, The,** Samson, Knopf, 1976	20.00	25.00	21.00

MISCELLANEOUS

☐ **Journal of the Century, The,** Article by Ernest Thompson Seton, Viking Press	5.00	8.00	5.50
☐ **Seton's Autograph,** in an autograph book	50.00	75.00	52.00
☐ **Ernest Thompson Seton: A Biographical and Bibliographical Sketch,** Doubleday, Page, 1925....	25.00	35.00	27.00
☐ **Menton Magazine,** full-page biographical sketch of Seton and sepia photo, 6/15/19	6.00	8.00	6.50
☐ **Trail and Campfire Stories,** Seton Press, 1968.........................	4.00	6.00	4.50
☐ **Wiley,** Ernest Thompson Seton's America, Devin, 1954.............	7.00	10.00	7.50
☐ **Seton Comic Book,** "Wild Animals I Have Known"	8.00	10.00	8.50
☐ Same as above, but "Lives of the Hunted"	8.00	10.00	8.50

	Current Price Range		P/Y Avg.

☐ **Beaver,** pencil and wash, initialed E.T.S., 5″ x 6¼″, 1886 .... 140.00 175.00 145.00

☐ **Carberry,** Manitoba, pencil, signed, 5″ x 7″, 1882 .... 160.00 200.00 165.00

☐ **Coati,** pencil and wash, initialed E.T.S., bear sketch on reverse, 4″ x 8″ 120.00 150.00 125.00

☐ **Deer Studies,** pencil and watercolor, initialed E.T.S., 3″ x 6¼″, 1894 .... 140.00 175.00 145.00

☐ **Follow Deer,** pencil, initialed E.T.S., illustrated on both sides, 7″ x 9½″, 1886 .... 140.00 175.00 145.00

☐ **Gophers,** ink and watercolor, initiated E.T.S., 4½″ x 7½″, 1883 ..... 160.00 200.00 165.00

☐ **Original Prints,** from Scribner, "Pictures of Wild Animals," 12 different prints, unsigned, 1901 ...... 30.00 35.00 30.50

☐ **Tito and Her Brood,** Scribner, print on heavy paper, 10″ x 13″, 1900 .... 30.00 35.00 30.50

☐ **Youth's Companion Bird Portfolio,** 12 prints by Ernest Thompson Seton, 9¼″ x 13½″, c. 1901 .... 60.00 75.00 61.00

☐ **Original Watercolor "French Wolf,"** used in *Lives of Game Animals,* signed by Ernest Thompson Seton, 3¾″ square 250.00 300.00 255.00

VOICE RECORDINGS

☐ **Victor Blue Label #55136** 50.00 60.00 55.00
   Three Sioux Scouts (The Voices of the Night) written and recorded by Ernest Thompson Seton Chief of the Woodcraft League An Indian Story with bird and animal calls

	Current Price Range		P/Y Avg.
☐ **Columbia #A3131**................	50.00	60.00	55.00
Wild Animal Calls—			
The Death of the Old Lion			
The Hunting Wolves			
Ernest Thompson Seton			
(Chief Scout)			
☐ **Columbia #A3132**................	50.00	60.00	55.00
Wild Animal Calls—			
My First Meeting with a Lynx			
The Elks' Battle			
Ernest Thompson Seton			
(Chief Scout)			
☐ **Columbia #A1331**................	50.00	60.00	55.00
Scout Patrol Calls			
Ernest Thompson Seton			
Chief Scout, Boy Scouts of America			
☐ **Cassette Recording of the 4**.....	10.00	—	—

DANIEL CARTER BEARD

Daniel Carter Beard was another giant personality responsible for the development of the Boy Scouts of America. Artist, writer, naturalist, and conservationist, he founded a group known as "The Sons of Daniel Boone," which promoted camping and the outdoor life.

He became a legend in his own time as Mark Twain's illustrator and the leading advocate of conservation. President Theodore Roosevelt once named Dan Beard as the one who "inspired" him.

Uncle Dan was an important figure at the early organizational meeting of the Boy Scouts of America and he quickly pledged to merge his "Sons of Daniel Boone" into the new movement. He was as good as his word and continued to actively support Scouting as National Scout Commissioner until his death at age ninety-one. He was undoubtedly the most colorful and best remembered of all Scouters.

BEARD COLLECTIBLES (Books seldom in circulation.)

BOOKS AND PAMPHLETS

☐ **American Boy's Book of Birds and Brownies of the Woods**, Lippincott, 1923.......................	17.00	23.00	17.50

The American Boy's Handy Book, Dan Beard, Scribners, 1882, $12.50–$17.50

	Current Price Range		P/Y Avg.
☐ **Same as above,** but later reprints	7.00	10.00	7.50
☐ **American Boy's Book of Bugs, Butterflies and Beetles,** Lippincott, 1915	17.00	25.00	18.00
☐ **Same as above,** but later printings	8.00	12.00	8.50
☐ **American Boy's Book of Signs, Signals and Symbols,** Lippincott, 1918	14.00	18.00	14.50
☐ **Same as above,** but later printings	5.00	7.00	5.25
☐ **American Boy's Book of Sport,** Scribner, 1896	20.00	28.00	21.00
☐ **American Boy's Handybook of Camplore and Woodcraft,** Lippincott, 1920	12.00	18.00	12.50

	Current Price Range		P/Y Avg.
☐ **Same as above,** but later printings..................	6.00	8.00	6.50
☐ **American Boy's Handybook, What to Do and How to Do it,** Scribner, 1882.....................	17.00	25.00	17.50
☐ **Same as above,** but later printings..................	5.00	7.00	5.50
☐ **American Boy's Book of Wild Animals,** same as 1907 *Animal Book,* Lippincott, 1921.............	10.00	14.00	10.50
☐ **Animal Book and Campfire Stories,** Moffat, 1907	25.00	30.00	25.50
☐ **Black Wolf Pack,** Scribner, 1922...	12.50	16.00	13.00
☐ **Boat Building and Boating,** Scribner, 1911	15.00	20.00	15.50
☐ **Boy Heroes of Today,** Brewer, Warren, and Putnam, 1932........	9.00	12.00	9.50
☐ **Boy Pioneers of the Buckskin Men,** Pamphlet, 1911.............	3.00	5.00	3.50
☐ **Boy Pioneers, Sons of Daniel Boone,** Scribner, 1909	22.00	30.00	22.50
☐ **Buckskin Book and Buckskin Calendar, The,** 1911	22.00	30.00	22.50
☐ **Buckskin Book for Buckskin Men and Boys,** Lippincott, 1929	15.00	20.00	15.50
☐ **Dan Beard Talks to Scouts,** talkingbook with phonograph record, Garden City, 1940	30.00	40.00	32.00
☐ **Do It Yourself,** Lippincott, 1925	10.00	14.00	11.00
☐ **Field and Forest Handybook, New Ideas for Out of Doors,** Scribner, 1906	16.00	20.00	16.50
☐ **Same as above,** but later printings..................	4.00	7.00	4.50
☐ **Hardly a Man is Now Alive,** Autobiography, Doubleday, 1939.....	20.00	30.00	25.00
☐ **Jack of All Trades, New Ideas for American Boys,** Scribner, 1900....	14.00	18.00	14.50

		Current Price Range		P/Y Avg.

	Current Price Range		P/Y Avg.
☐ **Same as above,** but reprint of later as *Fair Weather Ideas*	6.00	8.00	6.50
☐ **Moonlight and Six Feet of Romance,** Webster, 1892	14.00	18.00	14.50
☐ **Same as above,** but later reprints	6.00	8.00	6.50
☐ **Shelters, Shacks and Shanties,** Scribner, 1914	25.00	33.00	25.50
☐ **Wisdom of the Woods,** Lippincott, 1926	12.00	17.00	12.50

ILLUSTRATIONS AND MATERIAL

	Current Price Range		P/Y Avg.
☐ **Boys Book of Sports,** Maurice Thompson Century, 1886	10.00	15.00	10.50
☐ **Campers Own Book,** 1913	8.00	12.00	8.50
☐ **Captain Jinks,** Edward Crosby Hero, Funk and Wagnalls, 1902	4.00	6.00	4.50
☐ **Dan Beard, Boy Scout,** Mason	7.00	9.00	7.50
☐ **Dan Beard, Scoutmaster of America,** Blassingame 1972	6.00	8.00	6.50
☐ **First Aid for the Injured,** J. C. Zwetsch Whitman, 1937	3.00	5.00	3.50
☐ **Guns and Gunning,** J. Stevens Arms, Bellmore H. Brown, 1908	9.00	11.00	9.50
☐ **Hat and the Man, The,** Henry Irving Dodge, Dillingham, 1897	7.00	10.00	7.50
☐ **Laugh Boy, Laugh,** Franklin Mathiews, Appleton, 1930	5.00	7.00	6.00
☐ **Little People and Their Homes in the Meadows, Woods, and Waters,** S. T. Hook, Scribner, 1888	6.00	8.00	6.50
☐ **Sportsman's Paradise, The,** B. A. Watson, Lippincott, 1888	6.00	8.00	6.50
☐ **Story of Dan Beard, The,** Webb 1958	6.00	8.00	6.50

MISCELLANEOUS	Current Price Range		P/Y Avg.
☐ **Bum Elee's Chance,** limited edition reprint of 500 original illustrations	7.00	10.00	7.50
☐ **Capital and Labor Sharing the Burden of Life,** pen and ink drawing, 11″ x 27″, 1892..............	130.00	150.00	135.00
☐ **In the Sweat of Thy Face Shalt Thee Eat Bread,** 17″ x 20″, signed	140.00	175.00	145.00

The following 5 pictures are illustrations for Kipling's *Jungle Book* as used in *St. Nicholas* magazines:

☐ **"Shere Khan,"** original pen and ink sketch, a roaring lion in tall grass, signed, 10½″ x 14¼″, 1894 ..	120.00	150.00	125.00
☐ **"Men Always Play with Their Mouths,"** original pen and ink sketch, signed, 10½″ x 14″, 1894 ..	120.00	150.00	125.00
☐ **Group of Indians Stoning a Woman,** original pen and ink sketch, signed, similiar sketches both sides, 10½″ x 13¼″, 1894 ...	120.00	150.00	125.00
☐ **Elephants Uprooting Bamboo Platform and the People on Them,** original pen and ink sketch, signed, 12½″ x 15½″	120.00	150.00	125.00
☐ **"Letting the Jungle In"**, original pen and ink sketch, signed, 14″ x 22½″	120.00	150.00	125.00
☐ **Typewritten Letter,** by Dan Beard on Boy Scout of America letterhead. Signed by Beard	20.00	30.00	21.00
☐ **Autographed Photo,** of Beard....	20.00	25.00	20.50
☐ **Dan Beard Medallion,** sterling silver, limited edition of 10,000, issued by Rockland County Council, 1974, in numbered boxes	30.00	40.00	31.00

	Current Price Range		P/Y Avg.
☐ **Same as above,** but gold, limited edition of 5,000	60.00	75.00	62.00
☐ **Same as above,** solid brass	15.00	20.00	15.50
☐ **Picture Promotional Book,** for The Dan Beard Outdoor School, 32 pages, 1931	15.00	25.00	17.00
☐ **Picture Postcard,** Dan Beard's home in Redding, Connecticut	7.00	8.00	7.25
☐ **Photos,** of Dan Beard.............	4.00	10.00	4.50
☐ **Photo Postcard,** from Dan Beard Camp	10.00	12.00	10.50
☐ **Photo Postcard,** signed by Beard	20.00	30.00	21.00
☐ **Photo Postcard,** Dan Beard in white buckskins....................	5.00	7.00	5.75
☐ **Portrait,** of Dan Beard	7.00	10.00	7.50
☐ **Postcard,** "A Healthy Group of Boy Scouts," including Dan Beard, official Boy Scout of America......	5.00	7.00	5.25

WILLIAM D. BOYCE

Every Scout is familiar with the story of the American businessman William D. Boyce, who was helped by a young boy in 1909 while lost in a London fog. When Boyce attempted to pay him for his assistance, the boy said, "No thank you, sir. I am a Scout. I can't take anything for helping."

We would prefer to end the story by relating how Boyce talked to Baden-Powell and then returned to the United States of America where he began the Boy Scouts of America, which was an immediate success.

Actually, the story of Boyce and Scouting is more complex and interesting. He incorporated the Boy Scouts of America in Washington, D.C., on February 8, 1910, but he was unable to get any organizational momentum. In May, through Y.M.C.A. Director Edgar Robinson, he met with Ernest Thompson Seton and Daniel Beard and it was through the combined talents of all these men that the scouting movement got off to a successful start in the United States.

Interestingly, Boyce pledged $1,000.00 per month to pay expenses, but stipulated that Scouting must be open to all boys regardless of race, color, or creed.

Lone Scout, July 1918,
Collectibles of W. Boyce,
$3.00–$5.00 each

Almost immediately thereafter, Boyces' strong will clashed with that of James E. West, and Boyce disappeared from the scouting scene until, in January, 1915, he incorporated the Lone Scouts of America. This was basically a rival group that centered to the needs of rural boys living in remote areas, where there were not enough boys to form a troop.

The boys were encouraged to submit material for the *Lone Scout* magazine, a weekly publication. The Lone Scouts remained a strong and useful boys' organization until 1924, when it was merged into the Boy Scouts of America. Over one half million boys had participated during that period. The rural Scouting program of the Boy Scouts of America thereafter fulfilled the needs of these former Lone Scouts.

BOYCE COLLECTIBLES (Few collectible items available.)

MISCELLANEOUS	Current Price Range		P/Y Avg.
☐ Black-and-White Photo...........	1.00	2.00	1.10
☐ Booster Button	5.00	6.00	5.25
☐ Contributor Cards or Credit Cards, green, gray, yellow	5.00	6.00	5.25
☐ Copy of Constitution	6.00	8.00	6.50
☐ Gold Quill Award	20.00	22.00	20.50
☐ Illustrated Africa, 1925	6.00	8.00	6.50
☐ Lone Scout Magazine, 1918–1923	4.00	5.00	4.25

	Current Price Range		P/Y Avg.
☐ Lone Scout Magazine, 1927–1930	3.00	4.00	3.10
☐ Lone Scout Magazine, 1940–1950	2.00	3.00	2.10
☐ Lone Scout Magazine, 3/22/19, shows all badges	7.00	10.00	7.50
☐ Lone Scout of America, first-degree book	10.00	12.00	10.50
☐ Lone Scout of America, second-degree book	12.00	14.00	12.50
☐ Lone Scout of America, third-degree book	14.00	16.00	14.50
☐ Lone Scout of America, fourth-degree book	14.00	16.00	14.50
☐ Lone Scout of America, fifth-degree book	16.00	18.00	16.50
☐ Lone Scout of America, sixth-degree book	16.00	18.00	16.50
☐ Lone Scout of America, seventh-degree book	18.00	20.00	18.50
☐ Lone Scout Pin, first degree	8.00	10.00	8.50
☐ Lone Scout Pin, second degree ...	12.00	15.00	12.50
☐ Lone Scout Pin, third degree	15.00	17.00	15.50
☐ Lone Scout Pin, fourth degree ...	16.00	18.00	16.50
☐ Lone Scout Pin, fifth degree	16.00	18.00	16.50
☐ Lone Scout Pin, sixth degree	16.00	18.00	16.50
☐ Lone Scout Pin, seventh degree...	18.00	20.00	18.50
☐ Lone Scout Pin, bronze membership..............................	12.00	15.00	12.50
☐ Lone Scout Pin, gold membership	23.00	27.00	23.50
☐ Lone Scout Pin, Sagamore Lodge	18.00	20.00	18.50
☐ Lone Scout Pin, silver membership	19.00	22.00	19.50
☐ Lone Scout Pin, Tepee Lodge....	18.00	20.00	18.50
☐ Lone Scout Pin, Totem Pole Lodge..............................	18.00	20.00	18.50

	Current Price Range		P/Y Avg.
☐ **Lone Scout Pin,** W. D. Boyce Chief Totem	110.00	15.00	10.50
☐ **Membership Application**	4.00	5.00	4.25
☐ **Official Handbook**	20.00	30.00	25.00
☐ **Postcard,** W. D. Boyce Monument, Ottawa, Il	2.00	4.00	2.25
☐ **Reprint Edition,** 1918 Lone Scout of America degree books, 1–7	10.00	12.00	10.50
☐ **Service Bars:**			
☐ Bronze, 6 months...............	7.00	9.00	7.50
☐ Silver, 1 year	10.00	12.00	10.50
☐ Gold, 2 years	12.00	15.00	12.50
☐ **Sullivan,** Boyce of Ottawa, 1976 ...	2.00	3.00	2.10
☐ **W. D. Boyce Memorabilia,** collector's button	.50	1.00	.60

JAMES E. WEST

James E. West was the first Chief Scout Executive who took the job on a temporary basis in 1911, and stayed on to mold and lead the Boy Scouts of America for thirty-two years, until his retirement in 1943, when he was given the title of Chief Scout of the United States.

West was orphaned at age six and crippled at age seven while in an orphanage. He proved himself in every possible manner throughout his sad and sometimes cruel childhood. He organized study and recreational programs for the other orphaned children and accomplished many needed reforms before his crusades for improvements caused his expulsion from the orphanage.

He worked his way through high school and law school and became a crusading attorney for the rights of children. Already a nationally prominent figure, West was the unanimous choice to lead the newly organized Boy Scouts of America.

West was an extremely strong personality and is described best as ''brusque and forceful.'' When he was questioned on his authority, he boomed, ''I *am* the Boy Scouts of America.''

He was a giant and millions of scouts owe a great debt to James E. West.

WEST COLLECTIBLES

	Current Price Range		P/Y Avg.
☐ **Article in the Nature Almanac,** 1927	1.00	3.00	1.50
☐ **Benjamin, Call to Adventure,** West fwd. 1934	2.00	3.00	2.25
☐ **Black-and-White Photograph,** 3" x 4", mint..........................	2.00	—	—
☐ **Boy Scout of America Letter,** signed by James E. West	7.00	10.00	7.50
☐ **Lone Scout of the Sky,** 1927.....	6.00	7.00	6.10
☐ **Lone Scout of the Sky,** 1928.....	3.00	5.00	3.50
☐ **Making the Most of Yourself,** 1942	7.00	9.00	7.50
☐ **Plastic Coin,** scout memorabilia collector...........................	1.00	2.00	1.10
☐ **Boys Book of Honor, The,** West and Lamb, 1931	6.00	8.00	6.50
☐ **Trained for Citizenship,** article from *Review of Reviews*, 1916	1.00	3.00	1.10

BADGES

MEDALLIONS

This section contains Scout Medallions, Good Luck Charms, tokens, and pocket pieces. Some are official issue and others are nonofficial, but Scout-oriented. This list does not include pins or award medals.

The Excelsior Shoe Company of Portsmouth, Ohio, issued the first advertising coin, which was given to boys who purchased the first "Boy Scout Shoe."

	Current Price Range		P/Y Avg.
☐ **Excelsior Shoe Coin,** company emblem on face, horseback rider, dated July, 1910..................	9.00	12.00	9.50

Boy Scouts of America Paperweight, *bronze, 3″,* **$5.00–$7.50**

	Current Price Range		P/Y Avg.
☐ **Excelsior Shoe Coin,** good luck symbols on back, dated July, 1910	9.00	12.00	9.50
☐ **Excelsior Shoe Coin,** good luck symbols, states, "Membership Emblem of the Boy Scouts Club," no date	12.00	14.00	12.50
☐ **Excelsior Shoe Coin,** Scout on horseback, no date	12.00	15.00	12.50
☐ **Rotary Club International,** good luck coin, 1½″, 1920	10.00	18.00	10.50

*Boy Scouts of America, yearly theme, paperweight, bronze, 2¹/₂",
1964, $5.00–$10.00*

	Current Price Range		P/Y Avg.
☐ **Second National Jamboree,** official, bronze, Washington kneeling, wording on back, Washington's head does not break wording at top on original coin but it does on the 1973 replica, 1950	10.00	15.00	18.00
☐ **Twenty-fifth Anniversary National Convention,** Alpha Phi Omega, silver, emblem, 1950	8.00	11.00	8.50
☐ **B.S.A. Vote Campaign,** "Get Out the Vote" campaign, Washington praying, 1952, silver color	3.00	5.00	4.25
☐ Same as above, Gold color	3.00	10.00	—

Fiftieth Anniversary Boy Scouts of America Paperweight,
bronze, 2¹⁄₂″ diameter, 1960, $7.50–$15.00

	Current Price Range		P/Y Avg.
☐ **Youth of the Scout World,** scouts signaling, eagle on back, bronze, 1952	4.00	6.00	4.25
☐ **Third National Jamboree,** official, bronze, covered wagon front, wording on back of original, 1953	35.00	50.00	40.00
☐ **Same as above,** Silver	75.00	100.00	80.00
☐ **Third National Jamboree,** replica, has outline of the state of California without wording, 1953	2.00	5.00	3.00
☐ **Fortieth Anniversary of Mormon Scouts,** Mormon Temple on front, wording on back, 1953	5.00	7.50	4.00

	Current Price Range		P/Y Avg.
☐ **National Jamboree Circle B Roundup**, 1953....................	5.00	7.00	5.25
☐ **Fourth National Jamboree**, official, bronze, Washington kneeling on front, wording on back, head breaks wording at top but on the replica Washington head is below wording, 1957	7.50	12.50	12.00
☐ **Scout Tower at Valley Forge**, official, bronze, Washington praying on front, wording on back, 1957	12.00	15.00	12.50
☐ **Fiftieth Anniversary of B.S.A.**, official, bronze, Fiftieth Anniversary emblem, scout oath on back, 1960.....	6.00	8.00	6.50
☐ **Fiftieth Anniversary of B.S.A.**, official, bronze, scout badge on front, scout oath on back, 1960	4.00	6.00	4.50
☐ **Fiftieth Anniversary of B.S.A.**, sterling silver, 1960................	18.00	23.00	18.50
☐ **Fifth National Jamboree**, official, bronze, "For God or Country" emblem on front, three scenic views on back, 1960	5.00	7.00	5.25
☐ **Strengthening America's Heritage**	4.00	5.00	4.25
☐ **Sixth National Jamboree**, official, bronze, George Washington kneeling with knee $\frac{1}{16}$" from numeral 19, replica has larger figure of Washington and his knee is $\frac{3}{16}$" from numeral 19, 1964	5.00	7.00	5.25
☐ **Wonderful World of Scouting**, sold at New York World's Fair, bronze, Boy Scout emblem on front..........................	3.00	4.00	3.10
☐ **AMF Explorer Coin**, bronze, "I played Dick Weber," 1964	3.00	4.00	3.10
☐ **AMF Explorer Coin**, bronze, "I played Ben Hogan," 1964.........	3.00	4.00	3.10

	Current Price Range		P/Y Avg.

- ☐ **AMF Explorer Coin**, bronze, "I qualified for Swim Tests," 1964 .... — 3.00 — 4.00 — 3.10
- ☐ **Twelfth World Jamboree**, official, bronze, world scout badge on front, scout sign on back, "For Friendship," 1967 .... — 5.00 — 8.00 — 5.50
- ☐ **Twelfth World Jamboree**, white plastic, jambo insignia, "I am Indian too" on back, 1967 .... — 2.00 — 3.00 — 2.10
- ☐ **Pocket Piece**, official, bronze, scout law and emblem on front, scout oath on back, 1968 .... — 3.00 — 4.00 — 3.10
- ☐ **Seventh National Jamboree**, official, bronze, the deer's nose on the original is almost touching the "J" in Jamboree, in the replica, the deer's nose is ⅛″ from the "J," 1969 .... — 4.00 — 6.00 — 4.25
- ☐ **Key Chain Piece**, official, bronze, Cub Scouts, wolf on front, promise on back, 1970 .... — 2.00 — 4.00 — 2.10
- ☐ **Forty-fifth Anniversary National Convention**, Alpha Phi Omega, crest on front, wording on back, 1970 .... — 4.00 — 5.00 — 4.10
- ☐ **Thirteenth World Jamboree**, official, bronze, scout badge on front, Statue of Liberty on back, USA-B.S.A., 1971 .... — 5.00 — 7.00 — 5.25
- ☐ **Boy Power–Man Power**, official, silver or bronze, boy power insignia on front, Scout oath on back, 1971 .... — 4.00 — 5.00 — 4.10
- ☐ **Project SOAR**, official, bronze, SOAR emblem front, boy power–man power emblem on back, 1971 .... — 2.00 — 4.00 — 2.25

	Current Price Range		P/Y Avg.
☐ **Thirteenth World Jamboree,** solid 24 K gold, 12 grams, in box, 1971	145.00	160.00	145.00
☐ **Spirit of Scouting,** designed by Norman Rockwell for Franklin Mint, sterling silver, set of 12 depicting scout laws, 1972	250.00	350.00	250.00
☐ **Pocket Piece,** official, bronze, Cub Scouts, square, wolf on front, promise on back, 1972	3.00	4.00	3.10
☐ **Eighth National Jamboree,** official, goldine, back has map of U.S.A., Jambo emblem on front, replica is identical	3.00	4.00	3.10
☐ **Bicentennial Coin,** official, bronze, old style flag on front, "Gift" on back with wording, 1973...........	3.00	4.00	3.10
☐ **Rockland County Scouts Fiftieth Anniversary,** bronze, gold, or silver, Dan Beard on front, scout cooking on back, encased in old style scout handbook, bronze, 1974	12.00	15.00	12.50
☐ **The Scout Oath,** official, bronze, silver or gold, Wittnauer Mint, 12 pictures of oath, motto and slogan, scout sign on back, silver, 1974	240.00	300.00	245.00
☐ **Bicentennial Coin,** official, bronze, Bunker Hill flag on front, wording on back, 1974	4.00	5.00	4.25
☐ **Bicentennial Coin,** official, bronze, old style flag on front, "Gift" on back, 1976..........................	3.00	4.00	3.25
☐ **National Jamboree Souvenir Coin Set,** in frame, 1937–73	10.00	15.00	11.00
☐ **Irish Jamboree,** B.S.A. contingent, c. 1978	4.00	6.00	4.25

	Current Price Range		P/Y Avg.
☐ **Colorado Day B.S.A.**, set of coins, bronze, silver and gold, 8/1/76, limited edition..........................	80.00	100.00	85.00
☐ **Region Seven Necklace Medallion**, 14 K gold.....................	20.00	35.00	22.00
☐ **James E. West Coin**, plastic	1.00	2.00	1.10
☐ **Lady Baden-Powell Coin**, Universal Declaration of Human Rights, 7/8", 1973..........................	1.00	2.00	1.10
☐ **Honoring Boy Scouts**, bronze, scout with staff on front, wording on back	3.00	5.00	3.20
☐ **Good Turn Pocket Piece**, official, bronze, first-class badge on front, wording on back, also found with Tenderfoot badge front	3.00	7.50	3.00
☐ **Presentation Medallion**, official, bronze, world emblem on front, engravings on back	3.00	4.00	3.10
☐ **Sea Explorers Bronze Medallion**	3.00	4.00	3.10
☐ **B.S.A. National Meeting**, 1980	2.00	4.00	2.25

MEDALS

The "Medal" in Scouting is reserved as a symbol of personal high achievement of service to God, Country and fellow man.

	Current Price Range		P/Y Avg.
☐ **Ace Medal**, for sale of $250.00 World War I Savings Stamps......	100.00	125.00	105.00

AWARD MEDALS 1917 SERIES

The 1917 Series of Award Medals were irregular-shaped and designed to be used for a variety of awards.

	Current Price Range		P/Y Avg.
☐ **Contest Award Medal**, bronze....	35.00	45.00	37.00
☐ **Contest Award Medal**, silver	40.00	50.00	42.00
☐ **Contest Award Medal**, gold-plated	60.00	80.00	62.00

OCTAGON-SHAPED AWARD MEDALS, 1929 SERIES

The octagon-shaped award medals were available beginning in 1929 and were popular throughout the 1930s. They were available in the following subjects: Track, Field, First Aid, Swimming, Signaling, Cooking, Bugling, Knife and Axe, Knot-Tying, Camping, Wall-Scaling, Firemaking, Handicraft, Tent-Pitching, Tower-Building, Archery, Canoeing and Bridge-Building.

All of these medals were issued in bronze, silver, and gold.

☐ **Bronze Medals**	20.00	25.00	21.00
☐ **Silver Oxidized Medals**	25.00	30.00	26.00
☐ **Rose Gold Plated Medals**	30.00	40.00	32.00

CURRENT CUB CONTEST MEDALS

☐ **Cub Scout Pinewood Derby**, bronze, silver, and gold medals .:................................	3.00	4.00	3.10
☐ **Same as above**, but in plastic....................................	1.00	2.00	1.10
☐ **1970 Series**, octagon-shaped, red and white ribbons, available in bronze, silver and gold finishes ...	2.00	4.00	2.50

EAGLE MEDALS

Grateful acknowledgment is made of the assistance of *Scout Memorabilia* publisher Harry D. Thorsen, Jr., to use the following descriptive information on Eagle Medals. This information was compiled by collector-scouter Bernard B. Miller of New York and published in *Scout Memorabilia*. All Eagle Medals were solid silver.

Eagle Scout Medals, with presentation case, $60.00–$80.00

	Current Price Range		P/Y Avg.
☐ **First Eagle Medal,** scrawny Eagle and a dull appearance, 1912–1925	150.00	200.00	155.00
☐ **Second Eagle Medal,** finely engraved design with feathers on both sides, 1925–1930	120.00	150.00	125.00

	Current Price Range		P/Y Avg.
☐ **Third Eagle Medal,** not as well engraved, has curved wings and no "B.S.A.," 1930s and 1940s	50.00	75.00	55.00
☐ **Fourth Eagle Medal,** no "B.S.A.," flat back, 1950s and 1960s........	35.00	60.00	40.00
☐ **Fifth Eagle Medal,** resumed the "B.S.A.," finely engraved on both sides, 1970s to present............	30.00	40.00	42.00
Note: Newer ones have been put out and are not silver, $3.00–$4.00; newer varieties range + $20.00–$40.00.			
☐ **Same as above,** but full presentation kit	70.00	80.00	72.00

MISCELLANEOUS MEDALS

	Current Price Range		P/Y Avg.
☐ **Colin H. Livingstone Award,** for Victory Bond Sales, bronze. National award but very few were issued, 1918.........................	800.00	1200.00	850.00
☐ **Cub Scout Religious Awards**	8.00	12.00	8.50
☐ **Den Mothers Training Award,** blue and gold ribbon	12.00	15.00	12.50
☐ **General Douglas MacArthur Medal,** World War II for Victory Gardens	25.00	35.00	26.00
☐ **General Eisenhower Medal,** World War II for Waste Paper Collection	15.00	25.00	20.00
☐ **Grub Scout Button,** World War I	40.00	50.00	41.00
☐ **Honor Medal,** awarded for life-saving at risk of their own life.........	350.00	400.00	355.00
☐ **Hornaday Badge,** awarded to a Scout or Explorer for outstanding service or environmental quality within a council	50.00	60.00	50.50

	Current Price Range		P/Y Avg.
☐ **Hornaday Bronze Medal**, identical in design and is awarded for exceptional conservation service	150.00	200.00	155.00
☐ **Hornaday Conservation Award Pin**....................................	40.00	60.00	42.00
☐ **Hornaday Conservation Silver Medal**, award for outstanding work in conservation	200.00	250.00	205.00
☐ **Hornaday Silver Medal**, the highest conservation award to a Scout or Explorer. There is a limit of six annual awards for unusual and distinguished service to conservation.....	300.00	350.00	310.00
☐ **Medal of Merit**, awarded for outstanding act of service not necessarily risking own life	200.00	300.00	210.00
☐ **Scout Religious Awards**	12.00	15.00	12.50
☐ **Scouters Key**, green and white ribbon...............................	5.00	7.50	6.00
☐ **Scouters Key**, all green ribbon, gold-filled	25.00	30.00	25.50
☐ **Scouters Training Award**	5.00	8.00	5.50
☐ **Scouters Training Award** gold-filled................................	15.00	20.00	16.00
☐ **Silver Antelope Award**, given to adult volunteers for distinguished service to youth in the region	175.00	225.00	180.00
☐ **Silver Beaver Award**, given to adult volunteers for outstanding service to youth on a council basis...................................	50.00	100.00	60.00
☐ **Silver Buffalo Award**, given to adults in recognition of distinguished service to youth on a national basis	300.00	500.00	400.00
☐ **Silver Faun**, the highest award made to lady scouters.............	300.00	500.00	325.00

	Current Price Range		P/Y Avg.
☐ **United States Treasury War Service Award,** for sale of ten or more Liberty Bonds in World War I. The circular medal was earned by 78,699 scouts, and in addition 39,969 bars were earned by holders of medals for achievement in drives subsequent to the one in which they won the first award. ...			
☐ Medal Alone	30.00	35.00	30.50
☐ Medal and Bar	60.00	75.00	61.00
☐ **Various Adult Scouting Awards ...**	10.00	100.00	77.00
☐ **War Garden Medal,** 1917	60.00	80.00	63.00
☐ **War Savings Stamp Achievement Award,** for sale of twenty-five books of stamps, with blue ribbon, 1918	40.00	50.00	41.00
☐ **William T. Hornaday Gold Medallion,** awarded to an adult scout or Explorer leader for unusual and distinguished service to conservation or environmental quality. Not more than one medal can be awarded annually	1000.00	1200.00	1050.00

METAL BADGES

There have been literally thousands of different metal badges signifying the rank or office in scouting. Different manufacturers, wartime material shortages, and altered designs have added to the difficulty in presenting an authoritative chronological listing. The following is a representative listing of metal badges which shows the approximate dates of their circulation.

	Current Price Range		P/Y Avg.

- ☐ **"BSA" Monogram,** was optional but popular in the early years of scouting, made in both brass and bronze, worn on the coat collar or on the sleeve 25.00 30.00 25.50
- ☐ **Heavy Metal Troop Numerals,** similar to above, both were phased out in the late 1920s.............. 10.00 15.00 10.50

COLLAR PINS

- ☐ **Assistant Field and Assistant District Executive,** gold on red..... 15.00 25.00 20.00
- ☐ **Assistant Scout Executive,** silver, red, and gold.................. 15.00 25.00 20.00
- ☐ **Assistant Scoutmaster,** green and gold 20.00 30.00 25.00
- ☐   **Same as above,** but late 1930s 15.00 25.00 20.00
- ☐ **District and Field Commissioner,** blue, silver, and gold 17.50 25.00 20.00
- ☐ **Field and District Scout Executive,** silver and gold on red........ 20.00 35.00 25.50
- ☐ **Local Council Employee,** bronze and red enamel, no background.... 15.00 25.00 20.00
- ☐ **National Field Scout Commissioner,** purple, silver, and gold ... 50.00 75.00 40.50
- ☐ **Neighborhood Commissioner,** blue and gold.................... 15.00 20.00 16.00
- ☐ **President of Local Council,** gold on blue background 17.50 30.00 20.00
- ☐ **Scout Commissioner,** blue and silver...................... 17.50 25.00 22.00
- ☐ **Scout Executive,** silver and red.... 20.00 35.00 24.00
- ☐ **Scoutmaster,** green and silver finish, without circular background, c. 1920s 30.00 40.00 35.00
- ☐   **Same as above,** but with circular background, began late 1930s............................ 25.00 35.00 30.50

	Current Price Range		P/Y Avg.

Note: The small ⅝" lapel pin was used for street clothing. The larger ⅞" size was the collar pin.

HAT PINS

	Current Price Range		P/Y Avg.
☐ **Eagle Scout,** sterling silver with enameled red, white, and blue background, safety clasp, for use on lapel or hat	55.00	75.00	56.00
☐ **First Class,** heavy brass and crude clasp, 1½", c. 1930s..............	10.00	17.50	13.00
☐ **First Class,** heavy gold gilt medal, clasp pin back, c. 1916..........	20.00	22.00	20.50
☐ **First Class,** with stars near the top of the wings, c. 1920s	17.50	22.50	20.50
☐ **Same as above,** but with stars lower on the wings, c. 1940s....	12.50	17.50	15.50
☐ **First Class,** rare 3"	75.00	95.00	77.00
☐ **First Class,** Patrol Leader, oxidized silver	50.00	75.00	40.50
☐ **Second Class,** heavy gold gilt medal, clasp pin back, c. 1916......	10.00	15.00	12.00
☐ **Senior Patrol Leader,** silver metal superimposed on background of green bars, introduced in early 1920s	25.00	45.00	35.00
☐ **Same as above,** but with dark brass and dark green enamel	25.00	40.00	30.00
☐ **Same as above,** but with gold gilt and light green enamel......	25.00	40.00	35.50
☐ **Star Scout and Life Scout,** lapel pins were sometimes worn as hat pins, and had various clasps, not as popular as the larger first-class hat pin	7.50	12.50	10.00

Note: Life Scout preceded Star Scout until 1924.

	Current Price Range		P/Y Avg.
☐ **Tenderfoot,** heavy gold gilt medal, highly polished clasp pin back, c. 1916	5.00	10.00	7.00

MINIATURE PINS

☐ **Assistant Deputy Scout Commissioner,** light blue	20.00	25.00	25.50
☐ **Assistant Scoutmaster,** background of red enamel	20.00	25.00	20.50
☐ **Deputy Scout Commissioner,** dark blue............................	20.00	25.00	20.50
☐ **First Class,** safety clasp, solid gold, early teens...................	5.00	10.00	8.50
☐ **National Councilman,** purple	30.00	35.00	30.50
☐ **Scout Commissioners,** dark blue with gold wreath	17.50	25.00	20.00
☐ **Scoutmaster,** background of green enamel.......................	15.00	25.00	20.00
☐ **Troop Committeeman,** white	20.00	25.00	20.50

MERIT BADGES

Merit Badge collecting is definitely one of the most rewarding and often most confusing areas of Boy Scout memorabilia. The confusion is caused by the many varieties of the individual badges, name changes, design changes, color and cloth changes and valuation determinations.

TYPE A, 1910 to 1934. The "Square Cut" Merit Badges were embroidered on wide rolls of material and then cut out in rectangles or squares. The edges of Type A would unravel unless hemmed and were usually sewed abutting each other on the right sleeve of the uniform and later on a false sleeve that pulled over the right uniform sleeve. Still later, the Merit Badge sash was introduced.

The Merit Badge design was embroidered within a green ring. Often this ring appears to be a yellow-green in shading. Generally speaking, Type A is the most valuable, even though they were used for almost twenty-five years, because a great number of them were cut down to the green embroidered circle to facilitate sewing them without a hem. Also, many of these Type A badges were sewn to woolen uniform sleeves and they suffered greater wear or were thrown away later when the uniform became moth damaged.

TYPE B, 1934 to 1936, wide crimped edge. This was the manufacturer's first answer to facilitating the sewing-on of Merit Badges. As part of the manufacturing process, the Badge was made in a round shape and the unhemmed edges were "bent under" or "folded under" or "crimped." This process left a space on the outside of the green (or yellow) embroidered circle of about 3/16″. This Type B is usually called the "wide crimped edge" variety because subsequent varieties had only about 1/16″ of material left outside of the green embroidered circle. Because the wide crimped edge type was used for only about three years, its value is often near that of the earlier Type A.

TYPE C, 1936 to 1947, tan or brown, colored narrow crimped Merit Badges. This was the first of two color variations in the narrow crimped edge. The colors are brown tone ranging from tan to brown. The cloth materials vary greatly from a fine to a rough twill. Apparently, wartime shortages and changes in manufacturers were responsible for the variations in Type C, but the edge was crimped to about 1/16″ from the green embroidered circle.

The Air Scout program of the 1940s had Merit Badges with blue embroidered circles which command about a 30 percent to a 50 percent premium in value.

TYPE D, 1947–1959, khaki-color narrow crimped edge. Type D is the same as Type C, except the color was a definite khaki rather than brown or tan. The edge was also crimped to about 1/16″ of the green embroidered circle.

TYPE E, 1959–1970, rolled edge. Type E was the first of a series without hems or crimped edges. It is a complete circle without any additional cloth material on the outside of the embroidered circle. The design was still embroidered on a khaki-colored twill material.

TYPE F, 1970 to present, fully embroidered. This current style is the most colorful because it is 100 percent embroidered in many colors and has either a silver-white or a light olive-green embroidered circle. Some of these badges were introduced prior to 1970, but in 1970 all Merit Badges were redesigned to the fully embroidered style with a cloth backing. Around 1972, a plastic material was added during the manufacturing process in order to hold the stitching more securely.

CONDITION AND VALUATION

The Merit Badge was earned with great effort and pride, so it was only natural that a scout would promptly attach it to his uniform or Merit Badge sash. Therefore, most Merit Badges are "used," not "mint." The "mint" variety usually came from the Council service spring cleaning after a new type had been introduced. The price quoted is for a badge in very good to excellent "used" condition. It will be clean, not faded; not unraveled or torn, and all the cloth material, as defined earlier, will be present.

The valuation depends on the number believed to have been earned within the time duration of each type. To the right of the badge title appears the grand total reported earned, and next to each listed type is the total number reported earned during the years that each type of badge was being used. For example, only 430 scouts earned the earliest style of the Citrus Fruit Culture badge, so it should be worth considerably more than the 141,181 Athletic badges issued during the same time period. This system has much to offer in determining the relative supply or scarcity of each badge, but admittedly it is not without flaws. Often, the design was changed within the time span reported. This is an honest attempt to report the relative values of each of some 178 badges over a seventy-year time span with six major design changes.

The totals have been gleaned from the Boy Scouts of America Annual Reports to Congress, and often many Councils would send in their tally reports too late to appear in the correct year. Often, the totals of each type will not balance with the grand total appearing in the most recent report to Congress.

	Current Price Range		P/Y Avg.
☐ **Aerodynamics**, 6,693, 1942–1952.			
☐ **Type C**, 3,878 issued	7.50	15.00	5.25
☐ **Type D**, 2,795 issued	1.00	8.00	5.00
☐ **Aeronautics**, 19,708, used same badge as Suspended Aviation Merit Badge, 1942–1952.			
☐ **Type C**, 13,691 issued	7.50	10.00	3.10
☐ **Type D**, 6,017 issued	1.00	8.00	5.00
☐ **Agriculture**, 84,535, replaced by Food Systems in 1978.			
☐ **Type A**, 18,005 issued	8.00	12.00	9.00
☐ **Type B**, 3,508 issued	4.00	15.00	8.00

	Current Price Range		P/Y Avg.
☐ **Type C,** 12,836 issued..........	3.00	4.00	3.10
☐ **Type D,** 16,792 issued..........	1.00	8.00	5.00
☐ **Type E,** 16,201 issued..........	1.00	2.00	1.10
☐ **Type F,** 17,293 issued..........	.80	1.00	.90
☐ **Airplane Design,** 5,938, 1942–1952.			
☐ **Type C,** 3,251 issued............	10.00	20.00	5.10
☐ **Type D,** 1,687 issued............	10.00	20.00	6.10
☐ **Airplane Structure,** 12,131, 1942–1952.			
☐ **Type C,** 6,763 issued............	7.50	15.00	4.10
☐ **Type D,** 5,368 issued............	6.00	12.50	4.10
☐ **American Business,** 22,015, 1967.			
☐ **Type E,** 6,832 issued	1.00	2.00	1.10
☐ **Type F,** 15,183 issued	.80	1.00	.90
☐ **American Cultures,** 738, new in 1979.			
☐ **Type F,** 738 issued	.80	1.00	.90
☐ **American Heritage,** 26,083, new in 1975.			
☐ **Type F,** 26,083 issued	.80	1.00	.90
☐ **Angling,** became Fishing in 1951 and the design remained the same. Annual earned Merit Badges increased from 4,013 in 1951 to 26,557 in 1955.			
☐ **Type A,** 7,874 issued	9.00	15.00	10.00
☐ **Type B,** 2,692 issued	4.00	9.00	7.50
☐ **Type C,** 16,347 issued..........	2.00	3.00	2.10
☐ **Animal Industry,** 375,028, replaced by Animal Science in 1975.			
☐ **Type A,** 37,951 issued..........	6.00	10.00	6.50
☐ **Type B,** 20,579 issued..........	4.00	15.00	8.00
☐ **Type C,** 80,573 issued..........	1.00	2.00	1.10
☐ **Type D,** 76,652 issued..........	1.00	2.00	1.10
☐ **Type E,** 88,292 issued..........	.80	1.00	.90

	Current Price Range		P/Y Avg.
☐ Type F, 70,981 issued	.80	1.00	.90
☐ Archery, 377,138.			
☐ Type A, 3,056 issued	10.00	16.00	10.50
☐ Type B, 796 issued	4.00	15.00	8.00
☐ Type C, 3,466 issued	5.00	6.00	5.10
☐ Type D, 25,595 issued..........	2.00	3.00	2.10
☐ Type E, 122,931 issued.........	.80	1.00	.90
☐ Type F, 221,294 issued....	.80	1.00	.90
☐ Architecture, 120, 288.			
☐ Type A, 8,529 issued	10.00	17.00	10.60
☐ Type B, 1,646 issued	4.50	15.00	8.00
☐ Type C, 7,376 issued	4.00	5.00	4.10
☐ Type D, 14,322 issued..........	3.00	4.00	3.10
☐ Type E, 30,790 issued	1.00	2.00	1.10
☐ Type F, 57,625 issued	.80	1.00	.90
☐ Art, 531,081.			
☐ Type A, 22,434 issued	7.00	11.00	7.50
☐ Type B, 6,410 issued	4.00	15.00	8.00
☐ Type C, 43,964 issued	2.00	3.00	2.10
☐ Type D, 152,960 issued.........	1.00	2.00	1.10
☐ Type E, 158,569 issued.........	.80	1.00	.90
☐ Type F, 146,744 issued.........	.80	1.00	.90
☐ Astronomy, 193,249.			
☐ Type A, 7,082 issued	8.00	13.00	8.50
☐ Type B, 1,737 issued	4.00	15.00	8.00
☐ Type C, 11,257 issued...........	3.00	4.00	3.10
☐ Type D, 32,225 issued..........	2.00	3.00	2.10
☐ Type E, 68,426 issued	1.00	2.00	1.10
☐ Type F, 72,522 issued	.80	1.00	.90
☐ Athletics, 877,331.			
☐ Type A, 141,181 issued	5.00	7.00	5.50
☐ Type B, 47,466 issued..........	4.00	15.00	8.00
☐ Type C, 190,244 issued	1.00	2.00	1.10
☐ Type D, 169,022 issued.........	1.00	2.00	1.10
☐ Type E, 173,409 issued.........	.80	1.00	.90
☐ Type F, 156,009 issued.........	.80	1.00	.90
☐ Atomic Energy, 42,876.			
☐ Type E, 18,415 issued	1.00	2.00	1.10

	Current Price Range		P/Y Avg.
☐ Type F, 24,461 issued	.80	1.00	.90
☐ Automobiling, 177,353, discontinued in 1961.			
☐ Type A, 68,355 issued..........	7.00	9.00	7.50
☐ Type B, 13,250 issued..........	4.00	15.00	8.00
☐ Type C, 39,995 issued..........	2.00	3.00	2.10
☐ Type D, 47,519 issued..........	1.00	2.00	1.10
☐ Type E, 8,234 issued	.80	1.00	.90
☐ Automotive Safety, 147,902, replaced by Traffic Safety in 1975.			
☐ Type E, 67,366 issued..........	.80	1.00	.90
☐ Type F, 79,536 issued..........	.80	1.00	.90
☐ Aviation, 124,701, was dropped in 1942 and Aeronautics replaced it, using the same design. Aviation was reactivated in 1952.			
☐ Type A, 11,955 issued..........	13.00	16.00	13.50
☐ Type B, 2,891 issued	4.00	15.00	8.00
☐ Type C, 8,006 issued	4.00	5.00	4.50
☐ Type D, 22,288 issued..........	3.00	4.00	3.50
☐ Type E, 19,727 issued..........	1.00	2.00	1.50
☐ Type F, 59,834 issued..........	.80	1.00	.90
☐ Basketry, 952,298.			
☐ Type A, 33,743 issued..........	7.00	11.00	7.50
☐ Type B, 13,279 issued..........	4.00	15.00	8.00
☐ Type C, 49,540 issued..........	2.00	3.00	2.10
☐ Type D, 125,153 issued..........	1.00	2.00	1.10
☐ Type E, 257,879 issued.........	.80	1.00	.90
☐ Type F, 472,704 issued.........	.80	1.00	.90
☐ Beekeeping, 44,616.			
☐ Type A, 6,822 issued	10.00	20.00	11.00
☐ Type B, 1,342 issued	4.00	15.00	8.00
☐ Type C, 5,596 issued	4.00	5.00	4.10
☐ Type D, 9,715 issued	3.00	4.00	3.10
☐ Type E, 9,433 issued	1.00	2.00	1.10
☐ Type F, 11,708 issued..........	.80	1.00	.90
☐ Beef Production, 75,650, replaced by Animal Science in 1975.			

	Current Price Range		P/Y Avg.
☐ **Type A**, 3,764 issued	17.00	22.00	17.50
☐ **Type B**, 2,254 issued	4.00	15.00	8.00
☐ **Type C**, 12,131 issued..........	3.00	4.00	3.50
☐ **Type D**, 19,290 issued..........	2.00	3.00	2.50
☐ **Type E**, 20,138 issued..........	.80	1.00	.90
☐ **Type F**, 18,073 issued	.80	1.00	.90
☐ **Bird Study**, 467.			
☐ **Type A**, 112,117 issued	5.00	7.00	5.50
☐ **Type B**, 35,021 issued...........	4.00	5.00	8.00
☐ **Type C**, 142,899 issued	2.00	3.00	2.10
☐ **Type D**, 100,303 issued.........	2.00	3.00	2.10
☐ **Type E**, 43,702 issued..........	.80	1.00	.90
☐ **Type F**, 29,333 issued..........	.80	1.00	.90
☐ **Blacksmithing**, 27,147.			
☐ **Type A**, 13,148 issued..........	10.00	16.00	10.50
☐ **Type B**, 2,811 issued	4.00	15.00	8.00
☐ **Type C**, 7,893 issued	4.00	5.00	4.10
☐ **Type D**, 3,295 issued	5.00	6.00	5.10
☐ **Bookbinding**, 390,697.			
☐ **Type A**, 83,850 issued..........	6.00	8.00	6.10
☐ **Type B**, 32,125 issued..........	4.00	15.00	8.00
☐ **Type C**, 104,643 issued	2.00	3.00	2.10
☐ **Type D**, 101,031 issued	1.00	2.00	1.10
☐ **Type E**, 41,508 issued..........	.80	1.00	.90
☐ **Type F**, 27,540 issued..........	.80	1.00	.90
☐ **Botany**, 71,783.			
☐ **Type A**, 12,196 issued..........	9.00	16.00	9.50
☐ **Type B**, 2,609 issued..........	4.00	15.00	8.00
☐ **Type C**, 7,632 issued	4.00	5.00	4.10
☐ **Type D**, 10,319 issued..........	3.00	4.00	3.10
☐ **Type E**, 17,658 issued..........	.80	1.00	.90
☐ **Type F**, 21,369 issued..........	.80	1.00	.90
☐ **Bugling**, 137,537.			
☐ **Type A**, 20,508 issued..........	8.00	12.00	8.50
☐ **Type B**, 5,399 issued	4.00	15.00	8.00
☐ **Type C**, 21,191 issued..........	3.00	4.00	3.10
☐ **Type D**, 25,216 issued..........	3.00	4.00	3.10
☐ **Type E**, 38,051 issued..........	.80	1.00	.90

	Current Price Range		P/Y Avg.
☐ **Type F**, 27,172 issued	.80	1.00	.90
☐ **Business**, 72,958, 1966.			
☐ **Type A**, 14,617 issued	8.00	14.00	8.50
☐ **Type B**, 3,975 issued	4.00	15.00	8.00
☐ **Type C**, 16,543 issued	3.00	4.00	3.10
☐ **Type D**, 21,914 issued	3.00	4.00	3.10
☐ **Type E**, 15,909 issued	1.00	2.00	1.10
☐ **Camping**, 2,373,138.			
☐ **Type A**, 117,797 issued	5.00	7.00	5.25
☐ **Type B**, 32,985 issued	4.00	15.00	8.00
☐ **Type C**, 149,658 issued	1.00	2.00	1.10
☐ **Type D**, 405,260 issued	.80	1.00	.90
☐ **Type E**, 920,817 issued.........	.80	1.00	.90
☐ **Type F**, 746,621 issued.........	.80	1.00	.90
☐ **Canoeing**, 1,354,702.			
☐ **Type A**, 17,550 issued..........	8.00	14.00	8.50
☐ **Type B**, 7,231 issued	4.00	15.00	8.00
☐ **Type C**, 43,425 issued..........	2.00	3.00	2.10
☐ **Type D**, 167,321 issued	.80	1.00	.90
☐ **Type E**, 525,831 issued	.80	1.00	.90
☐ **Type F**, 593,344 issued.........	.80	1.00	.90
☐ **Carpentry**, 548,539.			
☐ **Type A**, 207,097 issued	5.00	6.00	5.25
☐ **Type B**, 52,423 issued	4.00	15.00	8.00
☐ **Type C**, 199,254 issued	1.00	2.00	1.10
☐ **Type D**, 89,765 issued..........	1.00	2.00	1.10
☐ **Cement Work**, 48,142, discontinued, 1952.			
☐ **Type A**, 14,738 issued..........	9.00	14.00	9.50
☐ **Type B**, 5,333 issued	5.00	7.00	5.25
☐ **Type C**, 20,171 issued..........	3.00	4.00	3.10
☐ **Type D**, 10,007 issued..........	3.00	4.00	3.10
☐ **Chemistry**, 191,597.			
☐ **Type A**, 31,372 issued..........	9.00	15.00	9.50
☐ **Type B**, 9,171 issued	4.00	15.00	8.00
☐ **Type C**, 32,693 issued..........	2.00	3.00	2.10
☐ **Type D**, 30,906 issued..........	2.00	3.00	2.10
☐ **Type E**, 52,063 issued..........	1.00	2.00	1.10

	Current Price Range		P/Y Avg.
☐ **Type F**, 35,392 issued	1.00	2.00	1.10
☐ **Citizenship in Community,** 1,515,351.			
☐ **Type D**, 248,012 issued	1.00	2.00	1.10
☐ **Type E**, 534,318 issued.........	.80	1.00	.90
☐ **Type F**, 733,021 issued.........	.80	1.00	.90
☐ **Citizenship in Home,** 875,446.			
☐ **Type D**, 342,569 issued	.80	1.00	.90
☐ **Type C**, 532,877 issued.........	.80	1.00	.90
☐ **Citizenship in Nation,** 1,203,706.			
☐ **Type D**, 248,012 issued	1.00	2.00	1.10
☐ **Type E**, 467,800 issued.........	.80	1.00	.90
☐ **Type F**, 487,894 issued.........	.80	1.00	.90
☐ **Citizenship in World,** 309,694.			
☐ **Type F**, 309,694 issued.........	.80	1.00	.90
☐ **Citrus Fruit Culture,** 4,587, 1931–1954.			
☐ **Type A**, 430 issued	21.00	26.00	21.50
☐ **Type B**, 1,269 issued	4.00	15.00	8.00
☐ **Type C**, 1,602 issued	8.00	10.00	8.50
☐ **Type D**, 1,286 issued	6.00	8.00	6.50
☐ **Civics,** 526,551, discontinued about 1951.			
☐ **Type A**, 159,304 issued	5.00	7.00	5.25
☐ **Type B**, 49,727 issued..........	4.00	15.00	8.00
☐ **Type C**, 167,520 issued	2.00	3.00	2.10
☐ **Type D**, 150,000 approx. issued	1.00	2.00	1.10
☐ **Coin Collecting,** 335,480.			
☐ **Type C**, 3,595 issued	5.00	6.00	5.25
☐ **Type D**, 41,365 issued..........	2.00	3.00	2.10
☐ **Type E**, 150,564 issued.........	.80	1.00	.90
☐ **Type F**, 139,956 issued.........	.80	1.00	.90
☐ **Communications,** 283,530.			
☐ **Type E**, 7,537 issued	4.00	5.00	4.25
☐ **Type F**, 275,993 issued.........	.80	1.00	.90
☐ **Computers,** 46,993, 1967.			
☐ **Type E**, 5,842 issued	4.00	5.00	4.25

	Current Price Range		P/Y Avg.
☐ **Type F**, 41,151 issued	1.00	2.00	1.10
☐ **Conservation**, 117,925, discontinued, 1952.			
☐ **Type A**, 45,937 issued..........	8.00	10.00	8.50
☐ **Type B**, 9,763 issued	4.00	15.00	8.00
☐ **Type C**, 39,135 issued..........	2.00	3.00	2.10
☐ **Type D**, 23,080 issued..........	3.00	4.00	3.10
☐ **Conservation of National Resources**, 446,592, cumulative total is approximate, 1966–1974.			
☐ **Type E**, 240,220 issued........	.80	1.00	.90
☐ **Type F**, 206,372 issued........	.80	1.00	.90
☐ **Consumer Buying**, 8,686, new in 1975.			
☐ **Type F**, 8,686 issued	1.00	2.00	1.10
☐ **Cooking**, 2,965,310.			
☐ **Type A**, 188,405 issued	5.00	7.00	5.25
☐ **Type B**, 59,026 issued..........	4.00	15.00	8.00
☐ **Type C**, 248,305 issued	1.00	2.00	1.10
☐ **Type D**, 638,324 issued........	.80	1.00	.90
☐ **Type E**, 1,107,064 issued.......	.80	1.00	.90
☐ **Type F**, 724,186 issued.........	.80	1.00	.90
☐ **Corn Farming**, 70,469, replaced by Plant Science, 1975.			
☐ **Type A**, 3,794 issued	10.00	16.00	10.50
☐ **Type B**, 4,205 issued	4.00	15.00	8.00
☐ **Type C**, 6,817 issued	4.00	5.00	4.10
☐ **Type D**, 19,374 issued..........	3.00	4.00	3.10
☐ **Type E**, 19,330 issued..........	2.00	3.00	2.10
☐ **Type F**, 16,949 issued	1.00	2.00	1.10
☐ **Cotton Farming**, 13,939, replaced by Plant Science, 1975, 1931.			
☐ **Type A**, 956 issued	19.00	24.00	20.00
☐ **Type B**, 915 issued	4.00	15.00	8.00
☐ **Type C**, 2,005 issued	5.00	7.00	5.25
☐ **Type D**, 3,753 issued	4.00	5.00	4.25
☐ **Type E**, 2,717 issued	4.00	5.00	4.25
☐ **Type F**, 3,593 issued	1.00	2.00	1.10

	Current Price Range		P/Y Avg.
☐ **Craftsmanship, 95,871.**			
☐ **Type A**, 95,871 issued	7.00	15.00	7.50
☐ **Cycling, 363,040.**			
☐ **Type A**, 100,658 issued	8.00	12.00	8.50
☐ **Type B**, 9,173 issued	4.00	15.00	8.00
☐ **Type C**, 34,038 issued............	2.00	3.00	2.10
☐ **Type D**, 51,702 issued............	1.00	2.00	1.10
☐ **Type E**, 82,849 issued	.80	1.00	.90
☐ **Type F**, 84,620 issued	.80	1.00	.90
☐ **Dairying, 95,958, replaced by Animal Science in 1975.**			
☐ **Type A**, 15,311 issued..........	11.00	14.00	11.50
☐ **Type B**, 4,814 issued	4.00	15.00	8.00
☐ **Type C**, 18,057 issued............	3.00	4.00	3.10
☐ **Type D**, 25,068 issued............	2.00	3.00	2.10
☐ **Type E**, 18,995 issued............	1.00	2.00	1.10
☐ **Type F**, 13,713 issued..........	.80	1.00	.90
☐ **Dentistry, 16,189, new in 1975.**			
☐ **Type F**, 16,189 issued..........	.80	1.00	.90
☐ **Dog Care, 298,839.**			
☐ **Type D**, 89,005 issued..........	1.00	2.00	1.10
☐ **Type E**, 102,686 issued..........	1.00	2.00	1.10
☐ **Type F**, 107,148 issued..........	.80	1.00	.90
☐ **Drafting, 150,699.**			
☐ **Type E**, 59,927 issued..........	2.00	3.00	2.25
☐ **Type F**, 90,772 issued	.80	1.00	.90
☐ **Dramatics, 30,533, 1932–1966.**			
☐ **Type A**, 633 issued	21.00	26.00	21.50
☐ **Type B**, 1,991 issued	9.00	11.00	9.50
☐ **Type C**, 5,862 issued	4.00	5.00	4.10
☐ **Type D**, 11,179 issued	3.00	4.00	3.10
☐ **Type E**, 10,868 issued	2.00	3.00	2.10
☐ **Electricity, 504,829.**			
☐ **Type A**, 81,489 issued..........	8.00	12.00	8.50
☐ **Type B**, 15,380 issued..........	4.00	15.00	8.00
☐ **Type C**, 61,766 issued..........	2.00	3.00	2.10
☐ **Type D**, 86,374 issued..........	1.00	2.00	1.10
☐ **Type E**, 152,477 issued.........	.80	1.00	.90

	Current Price Range		P/Y Avg.
☐ **Type F**, 107,343 issued.........	.80	1.00	.90
☐ **Electronics**, 65,662.			
☐ **Type E**, 19,923 issued	1.00	2.00	1.10
☐ **Type F**, 45,739 issued	.80	1.00	.90
☐ **Emergency Preparedness**, 285,041.			
☐ **Type F**, 285,041 issued.........	.80	1.00	.90
☐ **Energy**, 7,358, new in 1976.			
☐ **Type F**, 7,358 issued	.80	1.00	.90
☐ **Engineering**, 20,689, 1967.			
☐ **Type E**, 2,691 issued	1.00	2.00	1.10
☐ **Type F**, 17,998 issued	.80	1.00	.90
☐ **Farm and Ranch Management**, 726, new in 1980.			
☐ **Type F**, 726 issued.............	1.00	2.00	1.10
☐ **Farm Arrangements**, 44,854, replaced by Farm and Ranch Management in 1980.			
☐ **Type E**, 22,543 issued..........	.80	1.00	.90
☐ **Type F**, 22,311 issued	.80	1.00	.90
☐ **Farm Home**, 135,295, discontinued, 1959.			
☐ **Type A**, 28,005 issued..........	9.00	14.00	9.50
☐ **Type B**, 3,966 issued	4.00	15.00	8.00
☐ **Type C**, 51,892 issued..........	2.00	3.00	2.10
☐ **Type D**, 51,432 issued..........	1.00	2.00	1.10
☐ **Farm Layout**, 89,017, discontinued, 1959.			
☐ **Type A**, 12,393 issued..........	10.00	16.00	10.50
☐ **Type B**, 9,232 issued	4.00	15.00	8.00
☐ **Type C**, 32,334 issued..........	2.00	3.00	2.10
☐ **Type D**, 35,058 issued..........	1.00	2.00	1.10
☐ **Farm Mechanics**, 148,434.			
☐ **Type A**, 28,005 issued..........	10.00	12.00	10.50
☐ **Type B**, 6,703 issued	4.00	15.00	8.00
☐ **Type C**, 14,557 issued..........	3.00	4.00	3.10

	Current Price Range		P/Y Avg.
☐ Type D, 31,657 issued..........	1.00	2.00	1.10
☐ Type E, 26,366 issued..........	1.00	2.00	1.10
☐ Type F, 41,146 issued..........	.80	1.00	.90
☐ **Farm Records,** 52,786, replaced by Farm and Ranch Management 1980.			
☐ Type A, 6,445 issued.............	10.00	19.00	10.50
☐ Type B, 3,019 issued.............	4.00	15.00	8.00
☐ Type C, 9,186 issued.............	3.00	4.00	3.10
☐ Type D, 12,125 issued..........	2.00	3.00	2.10
☐ Type E, 11,005 issued..........	1.00	2.00	1.10
☐ Type F, 10,917 issued..........	.80	1.00	.90
☐ **Fingerprinting,** 412,237.			
☐ Type C, 11,377 issued..........	3.00	4.00	3.10
☐ Type D, 64,507 issued..........	1.00	2.00	1.10
☐ Type E, 132,835 issued..........	.80	1.00	.90
☐ Type F, 203,518 issued..........	.80	1.00	.90
☐ **Firemanship,** 2,129,128.			
☐ Type A, 380,005 issued	5.00	6.00	5.25
☐ Type B, 76,277 issued..........	4.00	15.00	8.00
☐ Type C, 277,285 issued..........	1.00	2.00	1.10
☐ Type D, 520,460 issued	.80	1.00	.90
☐ Type E, 580,814 issued..........	.80	1.00	.90
☐ Type F, 294, 287 issued	.80	1.00	.90
☐ **First Aid,** 3,620,952.			
☐ Type A, 249,085 issued	5.00	6.00	5.25
☐ Type B, 82,057 issued..........	4.00	15.00	8.00
☐ Type C, 358,980 issued	1.00	2.00	1.10
☐ Type D, 652,013 issued	.80	1.00	.90
☐ Type E, 1,040,021 issued.......	.80	1.00	.90
☐ Type F, 1,238,796 issued.......	.80	1.00	.90
☐ **First Aid to Animals,** 357,235.			
☐ Type A, 173,184 issued	5.00	6.00	5.25
☐ Type B, 43,379 issued..........	3.00	4.00	3.25
☐ Type C, 81,312 issued..........	1.00	2.00	1.10
☐ Type D, 26,526 issued..........	1.00	2.00	1.10

	Current Price Range		P/Y Avg.
☐ **Type E,** 32,834 issued	.80	1.00	.90
☐ **Type F,** with white background	15.00	25.00	20.00
☐ **Fish and Wildlife Management,** 121,576.			
☐ **Type F,** 121,576 issued	.80	1.00	.90
☐ **Fishing,** 1,002,624, was ''Angling'' until 1951.			
☐ **Type D,** 215,239 issued	1.00	2.00	1.10
☐ **Type E,** 367,670 issued	.80	1.00	.90
☐ **Type F,** 419,714 issued	.80	1.00	.90
☐ **Food Systems,** 1,971.			
☐ **Type F,** 1,971 issued	.80	1.00	.90
☐ **Forage Crops,** 22,312, replaced by Plant Science in 1975.			
☐ **Type E,** 16,197 issued	.80	1.00	.90
☐ **Type F,** 6,115 issued	.80	1.00	.90
☐ **Forestry,** 669,145.			
☐ **Type A,** 24,848 issued	9.00	15.00	9.50
☐ **Type B,** 8,919 issued	4.00	15.00	8.00
☐ **Type C,** 43,918 issued	2.00	3.00	2.10
☐ **Type D,** 195,609 issued	.80	1.00	.90
☐ **Type E,** 247,376 issued	.80	1.00	.90
☐ **Type F,** 148,475 issued	.80	1.00	.90
☐ **Foundry Practice,** 13,980, discontinued, 1952.			
☐ **Type A,** 5,945 issued	12.00	19.00	12.50
☐ **Type B,** 2,131 issued	4.00	15.00	8.00
☐ **Type C,** 3,899 issued	5.00	6.00	5.10
☐ **Type D,** 2,005 issued	5.00	6.00	5.10
☐ **Fruit and Nut Growing,** 14,644, replaced by Food Systems, 1978.			
☐ **Type D,** 2,719 issued	5.00	6.00	5.10
☐ **Type E,** 6,063 issued	3.00	4.00	3.10
☐ **Type F,** 5,862 issued	.80	1.00	.90
☐ **Fruit Culture,** 11,865, discontinued about 1954.			
☐ **Type A,** 3,267 issued	17.00	22.00	17.25
☐ **Type B,** 1,499 issued	4.00	15.00	8.00

		Current Price Range		P/Y Avg.
☐	Type C, 4,180 issued	5.00	6.00	5.10
☐	Type D, 2,919 issued	5.00	6.00	5.10
☐ **Gardening, 301,805.**				
☐	Type A, 33,740 issued..........	9.00	11.00	9.50
☐	Type B, 9,271 issued	4.00	15.00	8.00
☐	Type C, 38,346 issued	2.00	3.00	2.10
☐	Type D, 59,765 issued..........	1.00	2.00	1.10
☐	Type E, 70,009 issued	.80	1.00	.90
☐	Type F, 90,074 issued	.80	1.00	.90
☐ **Genealogy, 40,592.**				
☐	Type F, 40,592 issued	.80	1.00	.90
☐ **General Service, 32,876.**				
☐	Type F, 32,876 issued	.80	1.00	.90
☐ **Geology, 165,693.**				
☐	Type D, 13,826 issued	.80	1.00	.90
☐	Type E, 64,734 issued	1.00	2.00	1.10
☐	Type F, 87,133 issued	.80	1.00	.90
☐ **Golf, 6,197, new in 1976.**				
☐	Type F, 6,197 issued	.80	1.00	.90
☐ **Grasses, Legumes, and Forage Crops, discontinued about 1960.**				
☐	Type C, 3,207 issued	5.00	6.00	5.10
☐	Type D, 5,076 issued	4.00	5.00	4.10
☐ **Handicapped Awareness, 57, new in 1980.**				
☐	Type F, 57 issued..............	1.00	2.00	1.10
☐ **Handicraft, 600,451.**				
☐	Type A, 249,506 issued	5.00	6.00	5.25
☐	Type B, 88,837 issued	4.00	15.00	8.00
☐	Type C, 262,108 issued	.80	1.00	.90
☐ **Hiking, 951,850.**				
☐	Type A, 20,904 issued..........	10.00	12.00	10.50
☐	Type B, 6,756 issued	4.00	15.00	8.00
☐	Type C, 29,601 issued	2.00	3.00	2.10
☐	Type D, 178,510 issued..........	.80	1.00	.90
☐	Type E, 394,649 issued..........	.80	1.00	.90
☐	Type F, 321,443 issued..........	.80	1.00	.90

	Current Price Range		P/Y Avg.

☐ **Hog Production,** 74,997, previously Hog and Pork Production, replaced by Animal Science, 1975.

☐ **Type A,** 4,916 issued	12.00	20.00	12.50
☐ **Type B,** 4,073 issued	4.00	15.00	8.00
☐ **Type C,** 14,627 issued..........	3.00	4.00	3.10
☐ **Type D,** 21,799 issued..........	2.00	3.00	2.10
☐ **Type F,** 12,483 issued	.80	1.00	.90

☐ **Home Repairs,** 2,089,278, 1945.

☐ **Type C,** 118,897 issued	1.00	2.00	1.10
☐ **Type D,** 749,846 issued	.80	1.00	.90
☐ **Type E,** 700,707 issued.........	.80	1.00	.90
☐ **Type F,** 519,828 issued.........	.80	1.00	.90

☐ **Horsemanship,** 270,341.

☐ **Type A,** 21,305 issued..........	10.00	12.00	10.50
☐ **Type B,** 4,248 issued	4.00	15.00	8.00
☐ **Type C,** 25,616 issued	2.00	3.00	2.10
☐ **Type D,** 61,156 issued..........	1.00	2.00	1.10
☐ **Type E,** 79, 522 issued	.80	1.00	.90
☐ **Type F,** 78,494 issued..........	.80	1.00	.90

☐ **Indian Lore,** 298,271, 1931.

☐ **Type A,** 1,389 issued	12.00	24.00	12.50
☐ **Type B,** 1,260 issued	4.00	15.00	8.00
☐ **Type C,** 6,878 issued	4.00	5.00	4.25
☐ **Type D,** 28,576 issued..........	2.00	3.00	2.10
☐ **Type E,** 99,724 issued..........	.80	1.00	.90
☐ **Type F,** 160,444 issued.........	.80	1.00	.90

☐ **Insect Life,** 96,463.

☐ **Type A,** 5,707 issued	19.00	35.00	20.00
☐ **Type A, "Spider"**	50.00	100.00	65.00
☐ **Type A, "Bug"**..................	19.00	35.00	20.00
☐ **Type B,** 573 issued	4.00	15.00	8.00
☐ **Type C,** 3,749 issued	5.00	6.00	5.10
☐ **Type D,** 15,822 issued..........	2.00	3.00	2.10
☐ **Type E,** 38,533 issued..........	1.00	2.00	1.10
☐ **Type F,** 32,078 issued	.80	1.00	.90

☐ **Interpreting,** 41,351, discontinued, 1952.

	Current Price Range		P/Y Avg.
☐ **Type A,** 19,603 issued..........	11.00	14.00	11.50
☐ **Type B,** 3,998 issued	4.00	15.00	8.00
☐ **Type C,** 13,038 issued	3.00	4.00	3.10
☐ **Type D,** 4,719 issued	3.00	4.00	3.10
☐ **Invention,** 151, one of the original Merit Badges, it was discontinued in about 1917.			
☐ **Type A,** 151 approximately issued ....,,.	40.00	50.00	42.00
☐ **Journalism,** 71,274.			
☐ **Type A,** 4,976 issued ,..	12.00	20.00	12.50
☐ **Type B,** 2,230 issued	4.00	15.00	8.00
☐ **Type C,** 6,178 issued	4.00	5.00	4.10
☐ **Type D,** 7,691 issued	3.00	4.00	3.10
☐ **Type E,** 22,997 issued	1.00	2.00	1.10
☐ **Type F,** 27,202 issued	.80	1.00	.90
☐ **Landscape Architecture,** 24,018, 1967.			
☐ **Type E,** 5,763 issued	1.00	2.00	1.10
☐ **Type F,** 18,255 issued	.80	1.00	.90
☐ **Landscape Gardening,** 28,665.			
☐ **Type A,** 2,675 issued	12.00	23.00	12.50
☐ **Type B,** 937 issued	4.00	15.00	8.00
☐ **Type C,** 4,952 issued	4.00	5.00	4.10
☐ **Type D,** 10,650 issued..........	2.00	3.00	2.10
☐ **Type E,** 9,451 issued	.80	1.00	.85
☐ **Law,** 14,358, new in 1975.			
☐ **Type F,** 14,358 issued	.80	1.00	.85
☐ **Leathercraft,** 249,361, discontinued, 1952.			
☐ **Type A,** 121,612 issued	5.00	7.00	5.25
☐ **Type B,** 23,919 issued..........	4.00	15.00	8.00
☐ **Type C,** 69,142 issued	1.00	2.00	1.10
☐ **Type D,** 34,688 issued..........	1.00	2.00	1.10
☐ **Leatherwork,** 594,693, previously Leatherworking.			
☐ **Type A,** 24,134 issued..........	10.00	12.00	10.50
☐ **Type B,** 4,480 issued	4.00	15.00	8.00

	Current Price Range		P/Y Avg.
☐ Type C, 14,777 issued..........	3.00	4.00	3.10
☐ Type D, 70,199 issued..........	1.00	2.00	1.10
☐ Type E, 168,670 issued.........	.80	1.00	.85
☐ Type F, 312,433 issued.........	.80	1.00	.85
☐ Lifesaving, 1,929,638.			
☐ Type A, 143,360 issued	5.00	7.00	5.25
☐ Type B, 43,372 issued..........	4.00	15.00	8.00
☐ Type C, 189,730 issued	1.00	2.00	1.10
☐ Type D, 355,295 issued	.80	1.00	.85
☐ Type E, 705,809 issued.........	.80	1.00	.85
☐ Type F, 492,072 issued.........	.80	1.00	.85
☐ Machinery, 161,231.			
☐ Type A, 25,671 issued..........	10.00	12.00	10.50
☐ Type B, 7,545 issued	4.00	15.00	8.00
☐ Type C, 36,268 issued..........	2.00	3.00	2.10
☐ Type D, 49,010 issued..........	1.00	2.00	1.10
☐ Type E, 20,981 issued..........	1.00	2.00	1.10
☐ Type F, 21,756 issued	.80	1.00	.90
☐ Mammals, 201,076.			
☐ Type F, 201,076 issued.........	.80	1.00	.85
☐ Marksmanship, 290,966, ended 1966.			
☐ Type A, 34,869 issued..........	9.00	11.00	9.50
☐ Type B, 7,473 issued	4.00	15.00	8.00
☐ Type C, 24,746 issued..........	3.00	4.00	3.25
☐ Type D, 88,625 issued..........	1.00	2.00	1.10
☐ Type E, 135,253 issued.........	.80	1.00	.85
☐ Masonry, 146,579.			
☐ Type A, 35,646 issued..........	9.00	11.00	9.25
☐ Type B, 6,374 issued	4.00	15.00	8.00
☐ Type C, 25,935 issued..........	2.00	3.00	2.10
☐ Type D, 32,905 issued..........	1.00	2.00	1.10
☐ Type E, 22,451 issued	.80	1.00	.85
☐ Type F, 23,268 issued	.80	1.00	.85
☐ Mechanical Drawing, 174,673, 1933–1964.			
☐ Type A, 2,491 issued	15.00	23.00	15.50
☐ Type B, 7,827 issued	4.00	15.00	8.00

		Current Price Range		P/Y Avg.
☐	Type C, 46,835 issued..........	2.00	3.00	2.10
☐	Type D, 68,554 issued..........	1.00	2.00	1.10
☐	Type E, 48,966 issued..........	.80	1.00	.85
☐	**Metals Engineering, 14,952.**			
☐	Type F, 14,952 issued..........	.80	1.00	.85
☐	**Metalwork, 601,487.**			
☐	Type A, 51,575 issued..........	8.00	10.00	8.25
☐	Type B, 28,782 issued,.. ...	4.00	15.00	8.00
☐	Type O, 121,194 issued........	1.00	2.00	1.10
☐	Type D, 118,069 issued	1.00	2.00	1.10
☐	Type E, 101,108 issued.........	.80	1.00	.85
☐	Type F, 177,679 issued..........	.80	1.00	.85
☐	**Mining, 8,036, discontinued in 1937.**			
☐	Type A, 6,677 issued	16.00	20.00	16.50
☐	Type B, 1,359 issued	4.00	15.00	8.00
☐	**Model Design and Building, 130,446.**			
☐	Type E, 21,417 issued..........	1.00	2.00	1.10
☐	Type F, 109,029 issued.........	.80	1.00	.85
☐	**Motorboating, 166,328.**			
☐	Type E, 65,123 issued..........	.80	1.00	.85
☐	Type F, 101,205 issued.........	.80	1.00	.85
☐	**Music, 865,351.**			
☐	Type A, 61,168 issued..........	7.00	9.00	7.25
☐	Type B, 15,943 issued..........	4.00	15.00	8.00
☐	Type C, 107,664 issued	1.00	2.00	1.10
☐	Type D, 165,014 issued	.80	1.00	.85
☐	Type E, 275,129 issued.........	.80	1.00	.85
☐	Type F, 240,433 issued.........	.80	1.00	.85
☐	**Nature, 1,114,807.**			
☐	Type D, 259,724 issued	.80	1.00	.85
☐	Type E, 538,724 issued.........	.80	1.00	.85
☐	Type F, 316,359 issued.........	.80	1.00	.85
☐	**Nut Culture, 3,503, discontinued, 1954.**			
☐	Type A, 948 issued	15.00	24.00	15.50
☐	Type B, 850 issued	4.00	15.00	8.00

	Current Price Range		P/Y Avg.
☐ **Type C**, 1,050 issued	12.00	15.00	12.50
☐ **Type D**, 735 issued	12.00	15.00	12.50
☐ **Oceanography**, 51,457.			
☐ **Type E**, 14,039 issued	.80	1.00	.85
☐ **Type F**, 37,418 issued	.80	1.00	.85
☐ **Orienteering**, 88,283, new in 1973.			
☐ **Type F**, 88,283 issued	.80	1.00	.85
☐ **Painting**, 413,721.			
☐ **Type A**, 42,105 issued..........	9.00	11.00	9.50
☐ **Type B**, 21,345 issued..........	4.00	15.00	8.00
☐ **Type C**, 33,586 issued..........	2.00	3.00	2.10
☐ **Type D**, 73,443 issued..........	1.00	2.00	1.10
☐ **Type E**, 31,351 issued	.80	1.00	.85
☐ **Type F**, 111, 891 issued	.80	1.00	.85
☐ **Pathfinding**, 598,085, discontinued in 1952.			
☐ **Type A**, 189,166 issued	5.00	7.00	5.25
☐ **Type B**, 63,852 issued..........	4.00	15.00	8.00
☐ **Type C**, 226,931 issued	1.00	2.00	1.10
☐ **Type D**, 118,236 issued	1.00	2.00	1.10
☐ **Personal Finances**, 65,503.			
☐ **Type E**, 65,503 issued	.80	1.00	.85
☐ **Personal Health**, 1,014,833, discontinued in 1952.			
☐ **Type A**, 332,664 issued	5.00	6.00	5.10
☐ **Type B**, 81,928 issued..........	4.00	15.00	8.00
☐ **Type C**, 419,452 issued	1.00	2.00	1.10
☐ **Type D**, 180,789 issued	.80	1.00	.85
☐ **Personal Health**, 1,256,930.			
☐ **Type E**, 50,387 issued	.80	1.00	.85
☐ **Type F**, 47,706 issued..........	.80	1.00	.85
☐ **Personal Management**, 257,941.			
☐ **Type F**, 257,941 issued.........	.80	1.00	.85
☐ **Pets**, 392,614, started August, 1958.			
☐ **Type D**, 3,924 issued	4.00	5.00	4.10
☐ **Type E**, 142,420 issued.........	1.00	2.00	1.10
☐ **Type F**, 246,270 issued.........	.80	1.00	.85

	Current Price Range		P/Y Avg.
☐ **Photography,** 225,824.			
☐ **Type A,** 25,202 issued..........	10.00	12.00	10.50
☐ **Type B,** 13,415 issued..........	4.00	15.00	8.00
☐ **Type C,** 27,648 issued..........	2.00	3.00	2.10
☐ **Type D,** 42,373 issued..........	.80	1.00	.85
☐ **Type E,** 46,159 issued..........	.80	1.00	.85
☐ **Type F,** 71,027 issued..........	.80	1.00	.85
☐ **Physical Development,** 268,299, discontinued in 1952.			
☐ **Type A,** 97,586 issued..........	7.00	9.00	7.50
☐ **Type A, "Extended Thumb"** ..	75.00	100.00	85.00
☐ **Type B,** 16,286 issued..........	4.00	15.00	8.00
☐ **Type C,** 122,399 issued........	1.00	2.00	1.10
☐ **Type D,** 62,028 issued..........	1.00	2.00	1.10
☐ **Pigeon Raising,** 48,655, started 1933.			
☐ **Type A,** 697 issued.............	21.00	26.00	21.50
☐ **Type B,** 800 issued.............	4.00	15.00	8.00
☐ **Type C,** 10,050 issued..........	3.00	4.00	3.10
☐ **Type D,** 13,488 issued..........	1.00	2.00	1.10
☐ **Type E,** 15,146 issued..........	1.00	2.00	1.10
☐ **Type F,** 9,971 issued	.80	1.00	.85
☐ **Pioneering,** 1,438,044.			
☐ **Type A,** 163,890 issued	5.00	7.00	5.25
☐ **Type B,** 32,950 issued..........	4.00	15.00	8.00
☐ **Type C,** 189,822 issued	1.00	2.00	1.10
☐ **Type D,** 268,230 issued	1.00	2.00	1.10
☐ **Type E,** 399,996 issued.........	.80	1.00	.85
☐ **Type F,** 383,156 issued.........	.80	1.00	.85
☐ **Plant Science,** 8,518, new in 1975.			
☐ **Type F,** 8,518 issued	.80	1.00	.85
☐ **Plumbing,** 239,704.			
☐ **Type A,** 39,682 issued..........	9.00	11.00	9.25
☐ **Type C,** 22,116 issued..........	3.00	4.00	3.10
☐ **Type D,** 82,101 issued..........	1.00	2.00	1.10
☐ **Type E,** 81,214 issued..........	.80	1.00	.85
☐ **Type F,** 94,544 issued..........	.80	1.00	.85
☐ **Pottery,** 98,458.			

	Current Price Range		P/Y Avg.
☐ **Type A,** 9,889 issued	12.00	19.00	12.50
☐ **Type B,** 2,940 issued	4.00	15.00	8.00
☐ **Type C,** 3,201 issued	5.00	6.00	5.25
☐ **Type D,** 11,853 issued	2.00	3.00	2.10
☐ **Type E,** 24,523 issued	1.00	2.00	1.10
☐ **Type F,** 46,052 issued	.80	1.00	.85
☐ **Poultry Keeping,** 164,039, originally Poultry Farming, replaced by Animal Science, 1975.			
☐ **Type A,** 42,500 issued	9.00	11.00	9.25
☐ **Type B,** 7,270 issued	4.00	15.00	8.00
☐ **Type C,** 41,458 issued	2.00	3.00	2.10
☐ **Type D,** 40,779 issued	2.00	3.00	2.10
☐ **Type E,** 17,680 issued	1.00	2.00	1.10
☐ **Type F,** 14,352 issued	.80	1.00	.85
☐ **Printing,** 279,975, it appears that an error was made in compiling the cumulative totals in the early 1930s. As a result, these figures are unbalanced.			
☐ **Type A,** 23,737 issued..........	10.00	12.00	10.50
☐ **Type B,** 5,000 issued	4.00	15.00	8.00
☐ **Type D,** 33,449 issued..........	1.00	2.00	1.10
☐ **Type E,** 827,917 issued.........	.80	1.00	.85
☐ **Type F,** 395,564 issued.........	.80	1.00	.85
☐ **Public Health,** 1,439,395.			
☐ **Type A,** 266,164 issued	5.00	6.00	5.10
☐ **Type B,** 54,051 issued	4.00	15.00	8.00
☐ **Type C,** 346,849 issued	1.00	2.00	1.10
☐ **Type D,** 362,637 issued	1.00	2.00	1.10
☐ **Type E,** 300,751 issued.........	.80	1.00	.85
☐ **Type F,** 108,943 issued.........	.80	1.00	.85
☐ **Public Speaking,** 511,311, started 1932.			
☐ **Type A,** 1,444 issued	12.00	23.00	12.50
☐ **Type B,** 3,620 issued	4.00	15.00	8.00
☐ **Type C,** 17,969 issued	3.00	4.00	3.25
☐ **Type D,** 162,866 issued	1.00	2.00	1.10

	Current Price Range		P/Y Avg.
☐ **Type E, 251,895 issued**.........	.80	1.00	.85
☐ **Type F, 73,517 issued**	.80	1.00	.85
☐ **Pulp and Paper, 14,435.**			
☐ **Type F, 14,435 issued**	.80	1.00	.85
☐ **Rabbit Raising, 118,721, 1943.**			
☐ **Type C, 7,975 issued**	4.00	5.00	4.10
☐ **Type D, 35,796 issued**..........	1.00	2.00	1.10
☐ **Type E, 36,472 issued**	.80	1.00	.85
☐ **Type F, 38,478 issued**	.80	1.00	.85
☐ **Radio, 61,934,** it appears that an error was made in compiling the cumulative totals in the 1930s; therefore, these figures are unbalanced.			
☐ **Type A, 6,475 issued**	12.00	20.00	12.50
☐ **Type B, 1,261 issued**	4.00	15.00	8.00
☐ **Type C, 4,000 issued**	5.00	6.00	5.10
☐ **Type D, 21,737 issued**..........	2.00	3.00	2.10
☐ **Type E, 23,496 issued**	1.00	2.00	1.10
☐ **Type F, 16,701 issued**	.80	1.00	.85
☐ **Railroading, 83,563.**			
☐ **Type D, 18,871 issued**..........	3.00	4.00	3.10
☐ **Type E, 37,695 issued**	1.00	2.00	1.10
☐ **Type F, 26,997 issued**	.80	1.00	.85
☐ **Reading, 1,259,007.**			
☐ **Type A, 50,129 issued**..........	8.00	10.00	8.50
☐ **Type B, 30,419 issued**	4.00	15.00	8.00
☐ **Type C, 174,932 issued**	1.00	2.00	1.10
☐ **Type D, 274,838 issued**	.80	1.00	.85
☐ **Type E, 448,487 issued**	.80	1.00	.85
☐ **Type F, 280,151 issued**	.80	1.00	.85
☐ **Reptile Study, 280,842.**			
☐ **Type A, 43,497 issued**..........	9.00	11.00	9.50
☐ **Type B, 8,827 issued**	4.00	15.00	8.00
☐ **Type C, 38,760 issued**	2.00	3.00	2.10
☐ **Type D, 32,318 issued**..........	2.00	3.00	2.10
☐ **Type E, 64,891 issued**	.80	1.00	.85
☐ **Type F, 92,549 issued**	.80	1.00	.85

	Current Price Range		P/Y Avg.
☐ **Rifle and Shotgun Shooting,** 306,281.			
☐ **Type E,** 77,500 issued	.80	1.00	.85
☐ **Type F,** 228,781 issued	.80	1.00	.85
☐ **Rocks and Minerals,** 21,016, 1938–1953.			
☐ **Type C,** 9,669 issued	3.00	4.00	3.10
☐ **Type D,** 11,347 issued	2.00	3.00	2.10
☐ **Rowing,** 948,699, 1933.			
☐ **Type A,** 3,994 issued	17.00	21.00	17.50
☐ **Type B,** 10,498 issued	4.00	15.00	8.00
☐ **Type C,** 60,755 issued	2.00	3.00	2.10
☐ **Type D,** 157,112 issued	.80	1.00	.85
☐ **Type E,** 364,451 issued	.80	1.00	.85
☐ **Type F,** 351,889 issued	.80	1.00	.85
☐ **Safety,** 1,956,780.			
☐ **Type A,** 118,238 issued	5.00	7.00	5.25
☐ **Type B,** 73,102 issued	4.00	15.00	8.00
☐ **Type C,** 343,5111 issued	1.00	2.00	1.10
☐ **Type D,** 413,527 issued	.80	1.00	.85
☐ **Type E,** 558,225 issued	.80	1.00	.85
☐ **Type F,** 450,177 issued	.80	1.00	.85
☐ **Salesmanship,** 149,902.			
☐ **Type A,** 9,093 issued	12.00	19.00	12.50
☐ **Type B,** 3,995 issued	4.00	15.00	8.00
☐ **Type C,** 14,510 issued	3.00	4.00	3.10
☐ **Type D,** 27,232 issued	1.00	2.00	1.10
☐ **Type E,** 36,798 issued	.80	1.00	.85
☐ **Type F,** 58,214 issued	.80	1.00	.85
☐ **Scholarship,** 1,024,145.			
☐ **Type A,** 125,983 issued	5.00	7.00	5.25
☐ **Type B,** 35,978 issued	4.00	15.00	8.00
☐ **Type C,** 113,419 issued	1.00	2.00	1.10
☐ **Type D,** 312,519 issued	.80	1.00	.85

		Current Price Range		P/Y Avg.
☐	**Type E,** 287,406 issued.........	.80	1.00	.85
☐	**Type F,** 148,840 issued.........	.80	1.00	.85
☐ **Sculpture,** 78,935.				
☐	**Type A,** 2,779 issued	17.00	22.00	17.50
☐	**Type B,** 822 issued	4.00	15.00	8.00
☐	**Type C,** 2,024 issued	5.00	7.00	5.25
☐	**Type D,** 12,234 issued..........	3.00	4.00	3.10
☐	**Type E,** 23,966 issued..........	.00	1.00	.85
☐	**Type F,** 37,110 issued	.80	1.00	95
☐ **Seamanship,** 20,659, discontinued in 1964.				
☐	**Type A,** 5,981 issued	16.00	20.00	16.50
☐	**Type A, "Black Anchor"**	100.00	150.00	90.00
☐	**Type B,** 1,170 issued	4.00	15.00	8.00
☐	**Type C,** 4,696 issued	4.00	5.00	4.10
☐	**Type D,** 5,469 issued	3.00	4.00	3.10
☐	**Type E,** 3,343 issued	2.00	3.00	2.10
☐ **Sheep Farming,** 30,607, replaced by Animal Science in 1975.				
☐	**Type A,** 2,312 issued	17.00	22.00	17.50
☐	**Type B,** 1,193 issued	4.00	15.00	8.00
☐	**Type C,** 4,715 issued	4.00	5.00	4.10
☐	**Type D,** 7,527 issued	2.00	3.00	2.10
☐	**Type E,** 7,187 issued	1.00	2.00	1.10
☐	**Type F,** 7,673 issued	.80	1.00	.85
☐ **Signaling,** 88,076.				
☐	**Type A,** 28,719 issued..........	9.00	12.00	9.50
☐	**Type B,** 4,955 issued	4.00	15.00	8.00
☐	**Type C,** 11,827 issued..........	3.00	4.00	3.10
☐	**Type D,** 10,120 issued..........	2.00	3.00	2.10
☐	**Type E,** 18,958 issued..........	1.00	2.00	1.10
☐	**Type F,** 13,497 issued	.80	1.00	.85
☐ **Skating,** 26,729, new in 1973.				
☐	**Type F,** 26,729 issued	.80	1.00	.85
☐ **Skiing,** 83,381, c. 1940.				
☐	**Type C,** 2,438 issued	5.00	7.00	5.50

		Current Price Range		P/Y Avg.
☐	**Type D**, 6,636 issued	3.00	4.00	3.10
☐	**Type E**, 25,364 issued	1.00	2.00	1.10
☐	**Type F**, 48,943 issued	.80	1.00	.85
☐ **Small Boat Sailing**, 83,400.				
☐	**Type E**, 12,745 issued	1.00	2.00	1.10
☐	**Type F**, 70,655 issued	.80	1.00	.85
☐ **Small Grains**, 14,906, replaced by Plant Science in 1975, 1943–1975.				
☐	**Type C**, 1,257 issued	6.00	8.00	6.25
☐	**Type D**, 4,898 issued	3.00	4.00	3.10
☐	**Type E**, 4,612 issued	2.00	3.00	2.10
☐	**Type F**, 4,139 issued	.80	1.00	.85
☐ **Soil and Water Conservation**, 617,651.				
☐	**Type D**, 110,063 issued	.80	1.00	.85
☐	**Type E**, 364,219 issued	.80	1.00	.85
☐	**Type F**, 143,369 issued	.80	1.00	.85
☐ **Soil Management**, 14,618, discontinued in 1952.				
☐	**Type A**, 4,722 issued	16.00	20.00	16.50
☐	**Type B**, 3,030 issued	4.00	15.00	8.00
☐	**Type C**, 4,667 issued	4.00	5.00	4.10
☐	**Type D**, 2,199 issued	4.00	5.00	4.10
☐ **Space Exploration**, 52,628.				
☐	**Type F**, 52,628 issued	.80	1.00	.85
☐ **Sports**, 399,336.				
☐	**Type F**, 399,336 issued	.80	1.00	.85
☐ **Stalking**, 9,966, discontinued in 1952.				
☐	**Type A**, 3,487 issued	18.00	22.00	12.50
☐	**Type B**, 980 issued	4.00	15.00	8.00
☐	**Type C**, 2,678 issued	5.00	7.00	5.25
☐	**Type D**, 2,821 issued	5.00	6.00	5.10
☐ **Stamp Collecting**, 337,029, 1931.				
☐	**Type A**, 10,736 issued	9.00	16.00	9.50
☐	**Type B**, 9,817 issued	4.00	15.00	8.00
☐	**Type C**, 41,046 issued	2.00	3.00	2.10
☐	**Type D**, 89,499 issued	.80	1.00	.85

		Current Price Range		P/Y Avg.
☐	**Type E,** 114,257 issued.........	.80	1.00	.85
☐	**Type F,** 71,674 issued	.80	1.00	.85
☐	**Surveying,** 104,173.			
☐	**Type A,** 14,191 issued..........	11.00	14.00	11.50
☐	**Type B,** 3,681 issued	4.00	15.00	8.00
☐	**Type C,** 9,536 issued	3.00	4.00	3.10
☐	**Type D,** 24,489 issued..........	1.00	2.00	1.10
☐	**Type E,** 25,979 issued	.80	1.00	.85
☐	**Type F,** 26,297 issued ,..	.80	1.00	.85
☐	**Swimming,** 3,420,119.			
☐	**Type A,** 258,239 issued	5.00	6.00	5.25
☐	**Type B,** 77,008 issued...........	4.00	15.00	8.00
☐	**Type C,** 309,212 issued	1.00	2.00	1.10
☐	**Type D,** 603,279 issued	.80	1.00	.85
☐	**Type E,** 1,190,185 issued.......	.80	1.00	.85
☐	**Type F,** 981,536 issued..........	.80	1.00	.85
☐	**Taxidermy,** 10,344, discontinued in 1953.			
☐	**Type A,** 4,393 issued	16.00	20.00	16.50
☐	**Type B,** 2,102 issued...........	4.00	15.00	8.00
☐	**Type C,** 2,358 issued	5.00	7.00	5.25
☐	**Type D,** 1,491 issued	5.00	6.00	5.10
☐	**Textiles,** 60,055.			
☐	**Type A,** 14,452 issued..........	11.00	14.00	11.50
☐	**Type B,** 2,597 issued..........	4.00	15.00	8.00
☐	**Type C,** 7,293 issued	4.00	5.00	4.25
☐	**Type D,** 6,838 issued	3.00	4.00	3.10
☐	**Type E,** 7,821 issued	1.00	2.00	1.10
☐	**Type F,** 21,054 issued	.80	1.00	.85
☐	**Theater,** 26,041, 1967.			
☐	**Type E,** 6,030 issued	1.00	2.00	1.10
☐	**Type F,** 20,022 issued	.80	1.00	.85
☐	**Traffic Study,** 22,662, new in 1975.			
☐	**Type F,** 22,662 issued	.80	1.00	.85
☐	**Truck Transportation,** 34,820, new in 1973.			
☐	**Type F,** 34,820 issued	.80	1.00	.85

	Current Price Range		P/Y Avg.
☐ **Veterinary Science**, 12,255, new in 1973.			
☐ **Type F**, 12,255 issued	.80	1.00	.85
☐ **Water Skiing**, 81,312, 1969.			
☐ **Type E**, 12,551 issued	.80	1.00	.85
☐ **Type F**, 68,761 issued	.80	1.00	.85
☐ **Weather**, 161,388.			
☐ **Type A**, 11,644 issued..........	13.00	16.00	13.50
☐ **Type B**, 4,342 issued	4.00	15.00	8.00
☐ **Type C**, 19,017 issued..........	3.00	4.00	3.10
☐ **Type D**, 39,447 issued..........	1.00	2.00	1.10
☐ **Type E**, 42,414 issued..........	.80	1.00	.85
☐ **Type F**, 44,524 issued	.80	1.00	.85
☐ **Wilderness Survival**, 191,320.			
☐ **Type F**, 191,320 issued..........	.80	1.00	.85
☐ **Wildlife Management**, 290,903, discontinued.			
☐ **Type D**, 91,922 issued..........	1.00	2.00	1.10
☐ **Type E**, 198,981 issued..........	.80	1.00	.85
☐ **Wood Carving**, 871,693.			
☐ **Type A**, 102,562 issued	5.00	7.00	5.25
☐ **Type B**, 34,370 issued..........	4.00	15.00	8.00
☐ **Type C**, 134,031 issued	1.00	2.00	1.10
☐ **Type D**, 192,264 issued	1.00	2.00	1.10
☐ **Type E**, 211,128 issued..........	.80	1.00	.85
☐ **Type F**, 197,338 issued..........	.80	1.00	.85
☐ **Wood Turning**, 78,102, discontinued in 1952.			
☐ **Type A**, 8,749 issued	15.00	19.00	15.50
☐ **Type B**, 9,977 issued	4.00	15.00	8.00
☐ **Type C**, 38,709 issued..........	2.00	3.00	2.10
☐ **Type D**, 20,667 issued..........	2.00	3.00	2.10
☐ **Woodwork**, 784,351.			
☐ **Type A**, 106,094 issued	5.00	7.00	5.25
☐ **Type B**, 44,659 issued..........	4.00	15.00	8.00
☐ **Type C**, 184,426 issued	1.00	2.00	1.10
☐ **Type D**, 167,813 issued	1.00	2.00	1.10
☐ **Type E**, 151,687 issued.........	.80	1.00	.85

	Current Price Range		P/Y Avg.
☐ **Type F**, 129,672 issued.........	.80	1.00	.85
☐ **World Brotherhood**, 130,785, discontinued in 1972.			
☐ **Type D**, 51,266 issued...........	2.00	3.00	2.25
☐ **Type E**, 75,508 issued............	.80	1.00	.85
☐ **Zoology**, 65,022, discontinued in 1973.			
☐ **Type A**, 6,127 issued	16.00	20.00	16.50
☐ **Type B**, 8,255 issued	4.00	15.00	8.00
☐ **Type C**, 18,005 issued...........	3.00	4.00	3.10
☐ **Type D**, 10,740 issued........ ...	2.00	3.00	2.10
☐ **Type E**, 17,562 issued	1.00	2.00	1.10
☐ **Type F**, 3,433 issued	.80	1.00	.85

BOOKS

DIARIES

"A Mint of Scout Information in Your Pocket" was the accurate description given the early Scout diaries. The pocket-size (3 inches by 4¾ inches) diary contained a broad range of topics helpful and interesting to the scout.

The pages were thin and ranged from 192 to 256. The scout usually tired of writing in the diary after two or three months, but continued to carry it for the information it contained.

These are in demand by serious collectors assembling a complete collection. There is a slight escalation in price for more recent years, because fewer have been printed.

Year	Current Price Range		P/Y Avg.
☐ **1913**	27.00	33.00	27.50
☐ **1915**	23.00	30.00	23.50
☐ **1916**	23.00	30.00	23.50
☐ **1917**	20.00	25.00	20.50
☐ **1918**	17.00	19.00	17.50
☐ **1919**	17.00	19.00	17.50

	Current Price Range		P/Y Avg.
☐ 1920	15.00	17.00	15.50
☐ 1921	15.00	17.00	15.50
☐ 1922	14.00	16.00	14.50
☐ 1923	14.00	16.00	14.50
☐ 1924	14.00	16.00	14.50
☐ 1925	14.00	16.00	14.50
☐ 1926	14.00	16.00	14.50
☐ 1927	13.00	15.00	13.50
☐ 1928	13.00	15.00	13.50
☐ 1929	12.00	14.00	12.50
☐ 1930	12.00	14.00	12.50
☐ 1931	12.00	14.00	12.50
☐ 1932	10.00	12.00	10.50
☐ 1932	10.00	12.00	10.50
☐ 1933	10.00	12.00	10.50
☐ 1934	8.00	10.00	8.50
☐ 1935	8.00	10.00	8.50
☐ 1936	8.00	10.00	8.50
☐ 1937 (Jamboree Edition)	10.00	12.00	10.50
☐ 1938	8.00	10.00	8.50
☐ 1939	8.00	10.00	8.50
☐ 1940	8.00	10.00	8.50
☐ 1941	8.00	10.00	8.50
☐ 1942	8.00	10.00	8.50
☐ 1943	6.00	8.00	6.50
☐ 1944	5.00	7.00	5.50
☐ 1945	5.00	7.00	5.50
☐ 1946	5.00	7.00	5.50
☐ 1947	5.00	7.00	5.50
☐ 1948	5.00	7.00	5.50
☐ 1949	5.00	7.00	5.50
☐ 1950 (Jamboree Edition)	8.00	10.00	8.50
☐ 1951	4.00	6.00	5.00
☐ 1952	4.00	6.00	5.00
☐ 1953	4.00	5.00	4.50
☐ 1954	4.00	6.00	5.00
☐ 1955	4.00	6.00	5.00
☐ 1956	4.00	5.00	4.50

	Current Price Range		P/Y Avg.
☐ 1957	4.00	5.00	4.50
☐ 1958	4.00	5.00	4.50
☐ 1959	4.00	5.00	4.50

FIELDBOOKS

The first printing of the Fieldbook, called the "Scout Fieldbook," was written by William "Green Bar Bill" Hillcourt in 1944. This book was quickly accepted by Boy Scouts and Scouters throughout the country and sold nearly a million copies in its first edition. At present the Fieldbook is in its second edition. Since 1944, the name of the book has been changed twice. In 1967, the new edition was changed to "Fieldbook for Boys and Men." The name was changed again in 1973 to "Fieldbook." This book is dedicated to preparedness, outdoor living, and nature lore, and is most certainly one of the most useful and interesting books in a Scout's library.

☐ **First Edition—Scout Fieldbook.**
Soft brown cover with picture of Scout cooking......................

Year	Printing	Quantity in 1000s			
☐ 1944 .... 1 ....500			12.00	15.00	10.50
☐ 1947 .... 2 .... 50			10.00	12.00	10.50
☐ 1948 .... 3 .... 50			10.00	12.00	10.50
☐ 1949 .... 4 .... 50			10.00	12.00	10.50
☐ 1950 .... 5 .... 50			8.00	10.00	9.00
☐ 1951 .... 6 .... 60			8.00	10.00	9.00
☐ 1952 .... 7 .... 60			8.00	10.00	9.00
☐ 1953 .... 8 .... 60			8.00	10.00	9.00
☐ 1954 .... 9 .... 60			8.00	10.00	9.00
☐ 1955 ....10 .... 70			6.00	8.00	7.00
☐ 1956 ....11 .... 70			6.00	8.00	7.00
☐ 1957 ....12 .... 75			6.00	8.00	7.00
☐ 1958 ....13 .... 75			6.00	8.00	7.00
☐ 1969 ....14 .... 60			6.00	8.00	7.00

	Current Price Range		P/Y Avg.

☐ **Second Edition—Fieldbook for Boys and Men.** Green cover showing two Explorers backpacking in mountains. . . . .

Year	Printing	Quantity in 1000s			
☐ 1967 .... 1 ....400			3.00	4.00	3.10
☐ 1969 .... 2 ....100			3.00	4.00	3.10
☐ 1970 .... 3 .... 85			3.00	4.00	3.10
☐ 1971 .... 4 .... 40			3.00	5.00	3.25
☐ 1972 .... 5 .... 80			3.00	4.00	3.10

☐ Name changed to **Fieldbook.** New cover shows a lakeside camping scene. . . . .

☐ 1973 .... 6 .... 80			2.00	5.00	2.25
☐ 1976 .... 7 .... 70			2.00	5.00	2.25
☐ 1976 .... 8 .... 70			2.00	4.00	2.20
☐ 1977 .... 9 .... 65			2.00	3.00	2.25

☐ Reprint of Second Edition—name changed to **Boy Scout Fieldbook.** Cover shows three Explorer Scouts hiking. This book contains sixteen pages of Norman Rockwell scouting pictures in color. Made available to the general public for the first time. . . . .

☐ 1978 ....10 .... 60			4.00	6.00	4.25
☐ 1979 ....11 .... 60			4.00	6.00	4.25
☐ 1980 ....12 .... 60			4.00	6.00	4.25

BOY SCOUT HANDBOOKS

Probably the most collectible of all Scouting memorabilia is *The Boy Scout Handbook.*

In 1910, the first attempt was entitled *Official Handbook* and the cover indicated authorship by Ernest Thompson Seton and Lt. General Sir Robert S. S. Baden-Powell. It combined many of the features of Baden-Powell's *Scouting for Boys* and Seton's Woodcraft Indian manual *The Birch Bark Roll.*

The cover of the second attempt of 1910 dropped the name of Lt. General Robert S. S. Powell from the cover and also eliminated the printing from certain pages which were particularly "British" in content, and these pages were left blank for note-taking. It was called *The Official Manual.* There are seven variations of the original edition of 1910, with a total combined printing of 68,900.

Since 1911, there have been nine editions and about 114 printings. It is sometimes difficult to distinguish early "printings" from "reprints," as the terms were sometimes used interchangeably.

In the first editions, from 1911 to 1927, there were thirty-nine printings entitled *The Official Handbook for Boys.*

The name was changed to *Revised Handbook for Boys* for another thirty-nine printings from 1927 to 1946, which covered editions three and four. The twelve printings of edition five were called *Handbook for Boys,* and the fourteen printings of editions six and seven were entitled *Boy Scout Handbook.* The eighth edition of five printings was entitled the *Scout Handbook* and the current ninth edition by "Green Bar Bill" Hillcourt is entitled *The Official Boy Scout Handbook.*

Acknowledgment is gratefully made to two Scouters who have made excellent studies of the Scout Handbook, Jeff Snowden of Fort Collins, Colorado, in his monograph *The Boy Scout Handbook 1911 to 1980,* and Harris M. Tanner of Holyoke, Massachusetts, for his scholarly work *A Bibliography of the Boy Scout Handbook.*

Price ranges are for "fair to good" condition to "very good to fine" condition.

ORIGINAL 1910 EDITION VARIATIONS	Current Price Range		P/Y Avg.
☐ **Variation I,** brown and gold hardcover Seton and Baden-Powell as authors, contains blank pages	200.00	300.00	255.00
☐ **Variation II,** same as above, but no blank pages.........................	200.00	300.00	285.00
☐ **Variation III,** same as above, except green on white soft cover, marked "Price 25¢ net"..........	200.00	300.00	245.00
☐ **Variation IV,** brown and gold hardcover, shows Seton as only author, pages 33 to 43 are blank..........	200.00	300.00	240.00

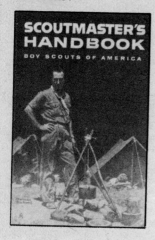

Scoutmaster's Handbook, 5th edition, 11th printing, 1970, cover by Norman Rockwell, $3.00–$5.00

	Current Price Range		P/Y Avg.
☐ **Variation V,** green and white soft cover, shows Seton as only author, ''Price 25¢ net'' on cover..........	200.00	300.00	225.00
Variation VI, red lambskin binding, gold scout seal on cover, presented at Baden-Powell dinner on September 22, 1910, 100 copies believed printed—maybe more—several autographed may run much higher.............................	250.00	1000.00	230.00
☐ **Variation VII,** green hardcover with embossed ''Campfire Edition''	200.00	400.00	195.00

Patrol Leaders Handbook, 1965 printing, copyright 1950, **$2.00–$3.00**

FIRST EDITION

In June 1911, James E. West and all available Scout personnel hand-bound 5,000 copies of the new handbook and sent them to leading educators, requesting their review and comment. These "Proof Copies" were instrumental in gaining valuable immediate support for the scouting movement.

Cover picture by artist Gordon Grant shows a Scout waving his hat. Jeff Snowden in his well-done comparison of handbooks notes that this first edition left out many things we now take for granted as important parts of scouting: mapping and map use, compass, conservation, poison plants, knife and axe, description of troop-leader position and the scout handclasp.

	Current Price Range		P/Y Avg.
☐ **Black on brown cover**, some blank pages, title page marked "Proof Copy," proof, June 1911, 320 pages	150.00	350.00	165.00
☐ **Same as above**, except no blank pages, proof, June 1911, 320 pages...............................	150.00	350.00	155.00
Same as above, but not marked "Proof," first printing, August 1911, 400 pages	160.00	200.00	165.00
☐ **Reproduction of the 1911 Handbook**, hardcover, limited edition, to celebrate the seventieth anniversary of the Handbook for Boys in 1970	10.00	15.00	10.50
☐ **Glossy Reprint**, same as above but soft cover, made in larger quantities	5.00	10.00	5.50
☐ **Reprint**, same as above, but hardcover, published for sale in commercial book stores................	12.00	14.00	12.25
☐ **Every Boy's Library Edition**, 1911 handbook	160.00	190.00	165.00

SECOND EDITION

This edition has the same cover and is available in hardcover and soft cover.

	Current Price Range		P/Y Avg.
☐ **Black on brown cover,** first printing, November 1911, 404 pages....	125.00	200.00	155.00
☐ **Black on dark red cover,** title page says "Reprint 2nd Edition," second printing, December 1911, 404 pages	100.00	200.00	150.00
☐ **Black on brown cover,** third printing, May 1912, 404 pages.........	100.00	150.00	130.00
☐ **Red leatherette cover,** same as above	125.00	175.00	145.00
☐ **Black on dark red cover,** fourth printing, July 1912, 404 pages	75.00	100.00	80.00
☐ **Red leatherette cover,** same as above	75.00	100.00	80.00
☐ **Black on dark red cover,** fifth printing, January 1913, 404 pages	75.00	100.00	80.00
☐ **Red leatherette cover,** same as above	75.00	100.00	80.00
☐ **Black on dark red cover,** sixth printing, May 1913, 416 pages	75.00	100.00	80.00
☐ **Red leatherette cover,** same as above	75.00	100.00	80.00
☐ **Black on orange cover,** seventh printing, October 1913, 416 pages	75.00	100.00	80.00
☐ **Red leatherette cover,** same as above	75.00	100.00	80.00
☐ **Black on light green cover,** eighth printing, December 1913, 416 pages	75.00	100.00	80.00
☐ **Red leatherette cover,** same as above	75.00	100.00	80.00
☐ **Black on dark red cover,** ninth printing, February 1914, 440 pages	75.00	100.00	80.00

	Current Price Range		P/Y Avg.
☐ **Red leatherette cover,** same as above	50.00	100.00	90.00
☐ **Black on dark red cover,** tenth printing, March 1914, 440 pages ...	50.00	100.00	90.00
☐ **Red leatherette cover,** same as above	50.00	100.00	70.00
☐ **Every Boy's Library Edition,** red and black seal	40.00	75.00	60.00

THIRD EDITION

The third edition cover, by artist J. C. Leyendecker, shows one scout signaling and one scout with binoculars. Three errors appear on this cover. The signaling scout is using Morse code flags to send semaphore. This error was finally corrected in 1921, after fourteen printings. The scout is sending a nonexisting semaphore letter, and this was corrected after five printings in 1916. The scout badge was missing the knot until the printing of December, 1916.

The Scout handclasp was introduced in 1914 as three fingers extended on the right hand. This was changed to a three-fingered left-hand handshake in 1923, and in 1972 it was changed to a standard left hand handshake to conform to that of other scouting countries.

	Current Price Range		P/Y Avg.
☐ **Silver cover "Revised Edition,"** marked 11th edition on title page, eleventh printing, November 1915, 472 pages	50.00	100.00	75.00
☐ **Every Boy's Library Edition,** same as above	40.00	75.00	60.00
☐ **Silver cover,** twelfth printing, January 1915, 472 pages	50.00	90.00	70.00
☐ **Black cloth binding,** same as above	50.00	90.00	65.00
☐ **Silver cover, "13th Edition"** on title page, thirteenth printing, March 1915, 464 pages...................	50.00	90.00	70.00

	Current Price Range		P/Y Avg.

☐ **Silver cover,** "13th edition 1916" on title page, reprint, thirteenth printing, April 1916, 464 pages.... 60.00 85.00 70.00

☐ **Silver-green cover,** "14th edition" on cover, fourteenth printing, June 1916, 498 pages............ 50.00 75.00 60.00

☐ **Red cover,** "15th edition," cover revised with signaling scout now on left, knot added to badge, fifteenth printing, December 1916, 498 pages............ 50.00 60.00 80.00

☐ **Red cover,** "sixteenth edition" on cover, sixteenth printing, May 1917, 498 pages............ 50.00 75.00 60.00

☐ **Light green cover,** "17th edition" on cover, seventeenth printing, December 1917, 498 pages.......... 50.00 75.00 65.00

☐ **Light green cover,** "18th edition" on cover, eighteenth printing, May 1918, 498 pages.................. 50.00 75.00 65.00

☐ **Light green cover,** title page reads "eighteenth edition reprint," nineteenth printing, December 1918, 496 pages.......................... 50.00 70.00 63.00

☐ **Light green cover** 50.00 70.00 63.00

☐ **Every Boy's Library Edition,** twentieth printing, May 1919, 496 pages........................... 40.00 60.00 47.00

☐ **Light green cover,** twenty-first printing, December 1919, 496 pages................................... 40.00 60.00 55.00

☐ **Light green cover,** twenty-second printing, June 1920, 492 pages ... 30.00 50.00 35.00

☐ **Original Gordon Grant cover,** hard copy........................... 30.00 50.00 45.00

☐ **Light green cover,** twenty-third printing, January 1921, 488 pages............................... 30.00 50.00 35.00

	Current Price Range		P/Y Avg.
☐ **Same as above,** but marked "Galahad Edition"	30.00	50.00	40.00
☐ **Oliver cover,** Semaphore flags used and uniforms and equipment updated, twenty-fourth printing, June 1921, 488 pages.............	25.00	50.00	35.00
☐ **Olive cover,** twenty-fifth printing, February 1922, 512 pages	25.00	50.00	32.00
☐ **Olive cover,** twenty-sixth printing, August 1922, 512 pages...........	25.00	50.00	32.00
☐ **Olive cover,** twenty-seventh printing, April 1923, 512 pages	25.00	50.00	32.00
☐ **Olive cover,** twenty-eighth printing, May 1923, 512 pages..........	25.00	50.00	32.00
☐ **Olive cover,** twenty-ninth printing, January 1924, 512 pages	25.00	50.00	32.00
☐ **Olive cover,** thirtieth printing, May 1924, 512 pages.....................	25.00	45.00	32.00
☐ **Olive cover,** thirty-first printing, January 1925, 512 pages	25.00	45.00	32.00
☐ **Olive cover,** thirty-second printing, May 1925, 512 pages..........	25.00	45.00	32.00
☐ **Olive cover,** thirty-third printing, August 1925, 512 pages...........	25.00	45.00	32.00
☐ **Olive cover,** thirty-fourth printing, August 1926, 512 pages...........	25.00	45.00	32.00
☐ **Olive cover,** thirty-fifth printing, July 1926, 512 pages..............	25.00	45.00	32.00
☐ **Olive cover,** thirty-sixth printing, March 1927, 512 pages	25.00	45.00	32.00
☐ **Olive cover,** thirty-seventh printing, May 1927, 512 pages.........	25.00	45.00	32.00

FOURTH EDITION

This is the first scout handbook with a Norman Rockwell cover. Title on cover is *Handbook for Boys,* and title page reads, 'Revised Handbook for Boys, First Edition."

This was the first major rewriting of the handbook, and many improvements appear. The neckerchief was optional until the early 1920s, and this edition discusses its wear and uses. For the first time, The Boy Scouts of America history appears in the Handbook.

Hardcover copies were made in all printings.

The first thirty-two printings from November 1927 through May 1940 had the profile of a Scout on a dark blue background.

	Current Price Range		P/Y Avg.
☐ **First Printing**, November 1927, 638 pages	15.00	30.00	22.00
☐ **Second Printing**, November 1927, 638 pages	17.50	30.00	22.00
☐ **Third Printing**, December 1927, 638 pages	10.00	25.00	17.00
☐ **Fourth Printing**, January 1928, 638 pages	10.00	25.00	17.00
☐ **Fifth Printing**, January 1928, 638 pages	10.00	25.00	17.00
☐ **Sixth Printing**, March 1928, 646 pages	10.00	25.00	17.00
☐ **Seventh Printing**, November 1928, 646 pages	10.00	25.00	17.00
☐ **Eighth Printing**, January 1929, 646 pages	10.00	25.00	17.00
☐ **Ninth Printing**, April 1929, 646 pages	10.00	25.00	17.00
☐ **Tenth Printing**, August 1929, 646 pages	10.00	25.00	17.00
☐ **Eleventh Printing**, January 1930, 646 pages	10.00	25.00	17.00
☐ **Twelfth Printing**, April 1930, 646 pages	10.00	25.00	17.00
☐ **Thirteenth Printing**, December 1930, 650 pages	10.00	25.00	17.00
☐ **Fourteenth Printing**, March 1931, 650 pages	10.00	25.00	17.00
☐ **Fifteenth Printing**, June 1931, 646 pages	10.00	25.00	17.00

	Current Price Range		P/Y Avg.
☐ **Sixteenth Printing,** April 1932, 650 pages	10.00	25.00	17.00
☐ **Seventeenth Printing,** November 1932, 650 pages..................	10.00	20.00	17.00
☐ **Eighteenth Printing,** July 1933, 658 pages	10.00	20.00	17.00
☐ **Nineteenth Printing,** December 1933, 658 pages..................	10.00	20.00	17.00
☐ **Twentieth Printing,** regular edition, September 1934, 658 pages...	10.00	20.00	17.00
☐ **Twenty-first Printing,** March 1935, 658 pages..................	10.00	20.00	17.00
☐ **Silver cover,** Twenty-fifth Anniversary Edition with four page insert ...	100.00	150.00	125.00
☐ **Twenty-second Printing,** September 1935, 658 pages...........	10.00	20.00	15.00
☐ **Twenty-third Printing,** March 1936, 660 pages..................	10.00	20.00	15.00
☐ **Twenty-fourth Printing,** October 1936, 660 pages..................	10.00	20.00	15.00
☐ **Twenty-fifth Printing,** December 1936, 668 pages..................	10.00	20.00	13.50
☐ **Twenty-sixth Printing,** March 1937, 668 pages..................	10.00	20.00	12.50
☐ **Twenty-seventh Printing,** September 1937, 668 pages...........	10.00	20.00	12.50
☐ **Twenty-eighth Printing,** February 1938, 668 pages..................	10.00	20.00	12.50
☐ **Twenty-ninth Printing,** April 1938, 668 pages	10.00	20.00	12.50
☐ **Thirtieth Printing,** November 1938, 676 pages..................	9.00	17.50	10.50
☐ **Thirty-first Printing,** October 1939, 676 pages..................	9.00	17.50	10.50
☐ **Thirty-second Printing,** October 1940, 676 pages..................	9.00	17.50	10.50
☐ **Thirty-third Printing,** with ads, December 1940, 680 pages	9.00	17.50	12.50

	Current Price Range		P/Y Avg.
☐ **Same as above**, without ads ...	9.00	17.50	10.00
☐ **Thirty-fourth Printing**, with ads, December 1941, 680 pages	9.00	17.50	10.25
☐ **Same as above**, without ads ...	9.00	17.50	8.50
☐ **Thirty-fifth Printing**, with ads, December 1942, 680 pages	7.50	15.00	10.50
☐ **Same as above**, without ads ...	7.00	14.00	7.50
☐ **Thirty-sixth Printing**, eight-color plates, December 1943, 608 pages	7.00	14.00	7.50
☐ **Thirty-seventh Printing**, book size to 4⅛" x 6⅝" to save paper in wartime, September 1944, 570 pages	7.00	12.00	7.50
☐ **Thirty-eighth Printing**, September 1945, 570 pages	6.00	12.00	6.50
☐ **Thirty-ninth Printing**, June 1946, 570 pages	6.00	12.00	6.50

FIFTH EDITION

Artist Don Ross's cover shows five happy hiking scouts wearing campaign hats. Cover colors are green and brown. This cover was used for only two printings. The nature material is reduced and lashing appears for the first time. This is also the first handbook to include the scout slogan, "Do a Good Turn Daily."

The third printing of the fifth edition introduced a new cover by artist Don Ross of three scouts wearing overseas caps around a campfire with the ghost-like image of an Indian Chief formed by smoke in the background. The cover was changed due to the switch from campaign hats.

	Current Price Range		P/Y Avg.
☐ **First Printing**, with advertising, June 1948, 566 pages	6.00	12.00	10.50
☐ **Same as above**, but without advertising	4.00	7.50	5.50
☐ **Second Printing**, April 1949, 566 pages	4.00	7.50	5.50
☐ **Third Printing**, April 1950, 566 pages	4.00	7.50	5.50

	Current Price Range		P/Y Avg.
☐ **Fourth Printing,** last four pages unnumbered, January 1951, 564 pages	4.00	7.50	4.50
☐ **Fifth Printing,** June 1952, 568 pages	3.00	7.50	4.50
☐ **Sixth Printing,** June 1953, 568 pages	3.00	7.50	4.50
☐ **Seventh Printing,** June 1954, 566 pages	3.00	7.50	4.50
☐ **Eighth Printing,** February 1955, 568 pages	3.00	7.50	4.50
☐ **Ninth Printing,** January 1956, 568 pages	3.00	7.50	4.50
☐ **Tenth Printing,** January 1957, 568 pages	5.00	7.50	6.50
☐ **Eleventh Printing,** same with four-page insert to commemorate fifteen-millionth handbook, October 1957, 568 pages..................	3.00	7.50	4.25
☐ **Twelfth Printing,** September 1958, 568 pages..................	3.00	7.50	4.25

SIXTH EDITION

The Norman Rockwell cover of a hiking scout shows his belt backward. This was corrected after seven printings. This was the only Rockwell cover painted specifically for a handbook cover to honor the Fiftieth Anniversary of the Boy Scouts of America in 1960.

Green Bar Bill Hillcourt was selected to author this improved handbook, which was entitled *The Boy Scout Handbook.* The size of the book increased from 4⅛″ × 6⅝″ to 5⅜″ × 8″, and multicolored pages were used for eye appeal.

☐ **First Printing,** November 1959, 480 pages	2.50	5.00	3.50
☐ **Second Printing,** August 1960, 478 pages	2.50	5.00	3.50
☐ **Third Printing,** August 1961, 478 pages	2.50	5.00	3.50

	Current Price Range		P/Y Avg.
☐ **Fourth Printing**, September 1962, 478 pages	2.50	5.00	3.50
☐ **Fifth Printing**, March 1963, 478 pages	2.50	5.00	3.50
☐ **Sixth Printing**, January 1964, 478 pages	2.50	5.00	3.50
☐ **Seventh Printing**, March 1965, 472 pages	2.50	5.00	3.50

SEVENTH EDITION

That giant of Scouting, Bill Hillcourt, was again selected to author the seventh edition on the eve of his retirement as a professional scouter. The seventh edition was required due to a change in advancement requirements.

This is the first handbook to use multiethnic scouts, including an oriental scout and a black scout on the back cover. Artist Don Lupo.

	Current Price Range		P/Y Avg.
☐ **First Printing**, September 1965, 488 pages	2.00	5.00	2.25
☐ **Second Printing**, April 1966, 448 pages	2.00	5.00	2.25
☐ **Third Printing**, January 1967, 448 pages	2.00	5.00	2.25
☐ **Fourth Printing**, February 1968, 448 pages	2.00	5.00	2.25
☐ **Fifth Printing**, January 1969, 448 pages	2.00	5.00	2.25
☐ **Sixth Printing**, February 1970, 448 pages	2.00	5.00	2.25
☐ **Seventh Printing**, January 1971, 448 pages	4.00	8.00	4.50

EIGHTH EDITION

The first three printings of the eighth edition showed four scouts in red berets and blue neckerchiefs around a telescope. Background was a two-tone green. This Scout Handbook was printed on recycled paper through the fourth printing.

The last two printings featured another cover by artist Joseph Csatari. It shows a group of active scouts and a back-packing burro in a colorful display of scouting activity. This handbook contained the revised progress award requirements that became mandatory January 1, 1978.

The period covered by this handbook spanned the move to inner-city activities rather than the traditional "great outdoors" emphasis.

Nine pages are devoted to "Harmful Habits," including smoking, alcohol, and drugs.

This edition is colorfully illustrated and contains the complete merit badge requirements.

	Current Price Range		P/Y Avg.
☐ **First Printing,** June 1972, 480 pages	2.50	5.00	3.50
☐ **Second Printing,** February 1973, 480 pages	2.50	5.00	3.50
☐ **Third Printing,** January 1975, 480 pages	2.50	5.00	3.50
☐ **Fourth Printing,** July 1976, 480 pages	2.50	5.00	3.50
☐ **Fifth Printing,** December 1977, 480 pages	2.50	5.00	4.50

NINTH EDITION

That Greatest of all American Scouts, Green Bar Bill Hillcourt, came out of retirement and devoted one more year of his life to write the completely revised and inspired *Official Boy Scout Handbook,* ninth edition. In 1977 he had told National Headquarters that the eighth edition was "dull and irrelevant, and that was the reason for the decline in membership."

Green Bar Bill had written the sixth and seventh editions, and they had sold about 680,000 copies per year, but the eighth edition was selling only about 380,000 copies annually.

"We had forgotten the first thing you have to be relevant to are the boys themselves. Scouting is based on camping and hiking, and learning things that will make it possible for you to stand on your own feet. That's where you begin, you begin by having fun with your friends," said Green Bar Bill as he restored the relevancy to the handbook.

The cover depicts a scout troop cooking and canoeing in Norman Rockwell's "Come and Get It."

Through the courtesy of Harry D. Thorsen, Jr., publisher of *Scout Memora-*

bilia, we are presenting the following listing of the ten printing variations of the new *Official Handbook.* This list was prepared by Green Bar Bill Hillcourt and published as a supplement to *Scout Memorabilia,* volume 16, number three. We do not list a price guide here because prices are being developed. As Harry Thorsen pointed out in *Scout Memorabilia,* many of these variations are still available and can be found in local scout service centers or in department stores that are distributors for the National Supply Service of the Boy Scouts of America.

FIRST PRINTING—FEBRUARY, 1979.

Variation A. Title on cover in black only, no Boy Scouts of America on the spine. Foreword (page five) by Harvey Price, Chief Scout Executive; star maps (pages 316–17, 319, and 321) with black sky, and compass on page 576 centered.

Variation B. Blank pages front and back to prevent loss of title page, otherwise as printing A above.

Variation C. Title on cover in blue and red, Boy Scouts of America on spine. Star maps (pages 316–17, 319, and 321) with blue sky; compass on page 576 off center; otherwise as printing B above.

Variation D. Stars on page 319 overprinted in red (purple), otherwise as printing C above.

SECOND PRINTING—JUNE, 1979.

Variation A. Title on cover in black only, no Boy Scouts of America on spine. No blank pages front and back; foreword (page five) by J. L. Tarr, Chief Scout Executive.

Variation B. Title on cover in blue and red, Boy Scouts of America on spine. Blank pages front and back; otherwise as printing A above.

Variation C. Some copies with Simon and Schuster on the spine.

THIRD PRINTING—MARCH, 1980.

Author's picture eliminated from title page, hiking, camping, and cooking skill awards on page 457 changed to Family Living, Communications, and Environment.

FOURTH PRINTING—FEBRUARY, 1981.

Variation A. Author's picture reinstated on title page, 53 illustrations re-done with new uniforms. Land Between the Lakes Gateway high adventure base eliminated (page 172), metric measurements on pages 198–99 rearranged, Family Living, Communications, and Environment skill awards changed back from page 457 of third printing to hiking, camping, and cooking. New merit badge, Handicapped Awareness, added (page 468), merit badges rearranged on pages 468–470, and Pigeon Raising eliminated (page 470); otherwise as second printing B.

Variation B. Limited number of commemorative copies with beige-colored sheet in front of title page, on which is printed the wording of the insert in the thirty-millionth copy presented to President Ronald Reagan on February 5th, 1981.

PATROL LEADERS HANDBOOK

William Green Bar Bill Hillcourt tells an interesting story concerning his authorship of the first *Handbook for Patrol Leaders.* Green Bar Bill, an enthusiastic scout from Denmark, planned a bicycle tour of the United States following his completion of pharmacy school in his homeland. Through American professional Scouts, whom he had met at the 1925 World Jamboree in Copenhagen, Bill obtained a temporary job at National Headquarters doing manual work.

A loading platform accident at Scout Headquarters in 1920 left Bill with a broken leg and hobbling around on crutches. It was at this time that he encountered Chief Scout Executive James E. West and convinced him that the Boy Scouts of America needed a handbook for Patrol Leaders, and soon Green Bar Bill was given the job of creating it.

The *Handbook for Patrol Leaders* has been revised and has been translated into numerous languages, selling around two million copies.

The first *Handbook for Patrol Leaders* has a cover by artist Hy Hintermeister showing a solitary scout dreaming of high adventure around his campfire. There was a green background.

In 1935, in celebration of the silver anniversary of the Boy Scouts of America, the book was published with a silver cover. This continued through 1949.

	Current Price Range		P/Y Avg.
☐ **First Printing**, 1929	14.00	20.00	14.50
☐ **Second Printing**, 1930	11.00	16.00	11.50
☐ **Third Printing**, 1931	12.00	18.00	12.50
☐ **Fourth Printing**, 1933	12.00	14.00	12.50
☐ **Fifth Printing**, 1935	10.00	12.00	10.50
☐ **Sixth Printing**, 1936	8.00	10.00	8.50

	Current Price Range		P/Y Avg.
☐ Seventh Printing, 1937	8.00	10.00	8.50
☐ Eighth Printing, 1938	8.00	10.00	8.50
☐ Ninth Printing, 1939	8.00	10.00	8.50
☐ Tenth Printing, 1941	8.00	10.00	8.50
☐ Eleventh Printing, 1942	8.00	10.00	8.50
☐ Twelfth Printing, 1943	8.00	10.00	8.50
☐ Thirteenth Printing, 1944	8.00	10.00	8.50
☐ Fourteenth Printing, 1945	7.00	9.00	7.60
☐ Sixteenth Printing, 1946	7.00	9.00	7.50
☐ Seventeenth Printing, 1948	7.00	9.00	7.50
☐ Eighteenth Printing, 1949	7.00	9.00	7.50

The World Brotherhood Edition of *Handbook for Patrol Leaders* was a revised work that received worldwide usage.

☐ First Printing, 1950	3.00	5.00	3.50
☐ Second Printing, 1952	3.00	5.00	3.50
☐ Third Printing, 1952	3.00	5.00	3.50
☐ Fourth Printing, 1953	3.00	5.00	3.50
☐ Fifth Printing, 1954	3.00	5.00	3.50
☐ Sixth Printing, 1955	3.00	5.00	3.50

Handbook for Patrol Leaders, issued in 1956, has a revised preface but no change in content.

☐ Seventh Printing, 1956	2.00	4.00	2.25
☐ Eighth Printing, 1957	2.00	4.00	2.25
☐ Ninth Printing, 1959	2.00	3.00	2.10
☐ Tenth Printing, 1959	2.00	3.00	2.10
☐ Eleventh Printing, 1961	2.00	3.00	2.10
☐ Twelfth Printing, 1961	2.00	3.00	2.10
☐ Thirteenth Printing, 1962	2.00	3.00	2.10
☐ Fourteenth Printing, 1963	2.00	3.00	2.10
☐ Fifteenth Printing, 1963	2.00	3.00	2.10
☐ Sixteenth Printing, 1964	2.00	3.00	2.10
☐ Seventeenth Printing, 1965	2.00	3.00	2.10
☐ Eighteenth Printing, 1965	2.00	3.00	2.10

Patrol Leaders Handbook has a revised text and shows a Patrol Leader and his Patrol on a Compass Hike.

	Current Price Range		P/Y Avg.
☐ **First Printing,** 1967	2.00	3.00	2.10
☐ **Second Printing,** 1968	1.00	2.00	1.10
☐ **Third Printing,** 1969	1.00	2.00	1.10
☐ **Fourth Printing,** 1970	1.00	2.00	1.10

Patrol and Troop Leadership has a new text and a green cover with a cartoon-type picture of a patrol meeting in upper right-hand corner.

☐ **First Printing,** 1972	1.00	2.00	1.10
☐ **Second Printing,** 1975	1.00	2.00	1.10
☐ **Third Printing,** 1977	1.00	2.00	1.10
☐ **Fourth Printing,** 1978	1.00	2.00	1.10

The Official Patrol Leaders Handbook, a completely revised text with contributions by Green Bar Bill and Keith Monroe, was first published in 1980.

☐ **Patrol Leaders Program Notebook,** 1959	1.00	2.00	1.10

SCOUTMASTERS HANDBOOK

First printed in a pamphlet as a proof edition. Original printings were probably in lots of about 2,000, but the exact printing numbers are not known.

FIRST EDITION 1912–1919

☐ **Proof Copy,** with a Bertillion section, 1912, 203 pages	150.00	200.00	175.00
☐ **Proof Copy,** without Bertillion section, 1912, 161 pages	150.00	200.00	175.00
☐ **Same as above,** except 1,000 copies printed without indicating "Proof," 1912	150.00	200.00	175.00

	Current Price Range		P/Y Avg.
☐ **Proof copy,** no cover, 1913, 344 pages	150.00	175.00	165.00
☐ **First Printing,** bound in tan hardcover, includes Jameson of Editorial Board, 1913–14...............	40.00	60.00	50.00
☐ **Second Printing,** Presbrey replaces Jameson, 1913–14.........	40.00	60.00	50.00
☐ **Seventh Printing,** cover page indicates 1913–14, but advertisement shows 1915, 1916	30.00	50.00	47.00
☐ **Eighth Printing,** 1918.............	30.00	50.00	47.00
☐ **Ninth Printing,** 1919	30.00	50.00	42.00

SECOND EDITION 1920–1935

☐ **First Printing,** 1920	15.00	25.00	16.00
☐ **Second Printing,** 1920............	15.00	25.00	16.00
☐ **Third Printing,** 1922	15.00	25.00	16.00
☐ **Fourth Printing,** 1923.............	15.00	25.00	15.50
☐ **Fifth Printing,** 1923	15.00	25.00	15.50
☐ **Sixth Printing,** 1924	13.00	20.00	13.50
☐ **Seventh Printing,** 1924...........	13.00	20.00	13.50
☐ **Eighth Printing,** 1925.............	10.00	17.00	10.50
☐ **Ninth Printing,** 1926	10.00	17.00	10.50
☐ **Tenth Printing,** 1926...............	15.00	17.00	15.25
☐ **Eleventh Printing,** 1927	10.00	17.00	10.50
☐ **Twelfth Printing,** 1927............	10.00	17.00	10.50
☐ **Thirteenth Printing,** 1928	10.00	15.00	10.50
☐ **Fourteenth Printing,** 1929........	10.00	15.00	10.50
☐ **Fifteenth Printing,** 1930	10.00	15.00	10.50
☐ **Sixteenth Printing,** 1932	10.00	15.00	10.50
☐ **Seventeenth Printing,** 1934	10.00	15.00	10.50
☐ **Eighteenth Printing,** 1934........	10.00	12.00	10.25
☐ **Nineteenth Printing,** 1935........	10.00	12.00	10.25

THIRD EDITION 1936–1945

The third edition was published in two separate volumes, as indicated on the title page and on the spine. The separate volumes contained different information. The two-volume system was dropped in 1947 with the appearance of the fourth edition written by Green Bar Bill Hillcourt.

VOLUME I	Current Price Range		P/Y Avg.
☐ First Printing, Fall–December 1936	8.00	10.00	8.50
☐ Second Printing, Spring–February 1937	8.00	10.00	8.50
☐ Third Printing, November 1937	8.00	10.00	8.50
☐ Fourth Printing, October 1938	8.00	10.00	8.50
☐ Fifth Printing, March 1939	8.00	10.00	8.50
☐ Sixth Printing, November 1940	8.00	9.00	7.50
☐ Seventh Printing, May 1941	7.00	9.00	7.50
☐ Eighth Printing, March 1942	7.00	9.00	7.50
☐ Ninth Printing, February 1943	7.00	9.00	7.50
☐ Tenth Printing, July 1944	7.00	9.00	7.50
☐ Eleventh Printing, December 1944	7.00	9.00	7.50
☐ Twelfth Printing, March 1945	7.00	9.00	7.50
☐ Thirteenth Printing, October 1945	7.00	9.00	7.50

VOLUME II			
☐ First Printing, Spring–March 1937	8.00	10.00	8.50
☐ Second Printing, Winter–March 1938	8.00	10.00	8.50
☐ Third Printing, December 1938	8.00	10.00	8.50
☐ Fourth Printing, November 1939	8.00	10.00	8.50
☐ Fifth Printing, April 1941	7.50	10.00	8.50
☐ Sixth Printing, February 1942	7.50	10.00	8.50
☐ Seventh Printing, July 1942	7.50	10.00	8.50
☐ Eighth Printing, October 1943	7.50	10.00	8.50
☐ Ninth Printing, October 1944	7.50	10.00	8.50
☐ Tenth Printing, April 1945	7.50	10.00	8.50

	Current Price Range		P/Y Avg.

	Current Price Range		P/Y Avg.
☐ **Eleventh Printing,** December 1945	7.50	10.00	8.50

FOURTH EDITION 1947–1957

☐ **First Printing,** September 1947	4.00	6.00	5.25
☐ **Second Printing,** February 1948 ...	4.00	6.00	5.25
☐ **Third Printing,** October 1948	4.00	6.00	5.25
☐ **Fourth Printing,** January 1950 ...	4.00	6.00	5.25
☐ **Fifth Printing,** June 1951	4.00	6.00	5.25
☐ **Sixth Printing,** September 1952....	3.00	5.00	4.25
☐ **Seventh Printing,** December 1953	3.00	5.00	4.25
☐ **Eighth Printing,** December 1954...	3.00	5.00	4.25
☐ **Ninth Printing,** December 1955	3.00	5.00	4.25
☐ **Tenth Printing,** December 1956 ...	3.00	5.00	4.25
☐ **Eleventh Printing,** December 1957	3.00	5.00	4.25

FIFTH EDITION 1959–1970

Name changed to *Scoutmaster's Handbook.*

☐ **First Printing,** July 1959	2.50	5.00	4.25
☐ **Second Printing,** July 1960.......	2.50	5.00	4.25
☐ **Third Printing,** June 1961	2.50	5.00	4.25
☐ **Fourth Printing,** June 1962.......	2.50	5.00	4.25
☐ **Fifth Printing,** June 1963	2.50	5.00	4.25
☐ **Sixth Printing,** October 1964	2.50	5.00	4.25
☐ **Seventh Printing,** November 1965	2.50	5.00	4.25
☐ **Eighth Printing,** November 1966...	2.00	4.00	3.50
☐ **Ninth Printing,** October 1967.....	2.00	4.00	3.50
☐ **Tenth Printing,** November 1968..	2.00	4.00	3.50
☐ **Eleventh Printing,** August 1970....	2.00	4.00	3.50

SIXTH EDITION 1972

☐ **First Printing,** 1972	1.50	3.00	2.25
☐ **Second Printing,** 1972............	1.50	3.00	2.25
☐ **Third Printing,** 1973	1.50	3.00	2.25

	Current Price Range		P/Y Avg.
☐ **Fourth Printing,** 1975.............	1.50	3.00	2.25
☐ **Fifth–Tenth Printings,** 1976–1980	1.50	3.00	2.25

SONG BOOKS

Most of us remember with great nostalgia the good times around camp fires. A good portion of the meaningful camp fire experience were the songs we sang. It is still fun to browse through the song books of our scouting days.

☐ **Boy Scout Song Book,** 1913.....	20.00	25.00	21.00
☐ **Boy Scout Song Book,** linen cover, 1917	14.00	17.00	15.00
☐ **Boy Scout Song Book,** 1920.....	9.00	14.00	10.00
☐ **Boy Scout Song Book,** condensed edition, 1924	8.00	11.00	8.50
☐ **Official Song Book for Scouts,** 1929	5.00	7.00	5.50
☐ **Camp Songs,** 1930	5.00	6.00	5.25
☐ **Songs Scouts Sing,** first printing, June 1930	6.00	8.00	6.25
☐ **Songs Scouts Sing,** second printing, July 1930......................	4.00	6.00	4.25
☐ **Songs Scouts Sing,** third printing, 1931	4.00	6.00	4.25
☐ **Songs Scouts Sing,** fourth printing, 1934................................	3.00	5.00	3.25
☐ **Songs Scouts Sing,** fifth printing, 1935	3.00	5.00	3.25
☐ **Songs Scouts Sing,** sixth printing, 1937	3.00	5.00	3.15
☐ **Songs Scouts Sing,** seventh printing, January 1939.............	3.00	5.00	3.00
☐ **Songs Scouts Sing,** eighth printing, November 1939...............	3.00	6.00	2.75

	Current Price Range		P/Y Avg.
☐ Songs Scouts Sing, ninth printing, 1941	2.00	4.00	2.25
☐ Songs Scouts Sing, tenth printing, 1942	2.00	4.00	2.25
☐ Songs Scouts Sing, eleventh printing, 1943	2.00	4.00	2.25
☐ Songs Scouts Sing, twelfth printing, 1944	2.00	4.00	2.25
☐ Songs Scouts Sing, thirteenth printing, 1945	2.00	4.00	2.25
☐ Songs Scouts Sing, fourteenth printing, 1946	2.00	4.00	2.25
☐ Songs Scouts Sing, fifteenth printing, 1948	2.00	4.00	2.25
☐ Boy Scout Song Book, 1954	3.00	5.00	3.50
☐ Boy Scout Song Book, 1956	2.00	3.00	2.00
☐ Boy Scout Song Book, 1958	2.00	3.00	2.00
☐ Boy Scout Song Book, revised, new cover and binding, 1963	3.00	5.00	3.00
☐ Boy Scout Song Book, 1966	1.00	2.00	.75
☐ Boy Scout Song Book, new cover, 1970	1.00	2.00	.75
☐ Boy Scout Song Book, 1972	1.00	2.00	.75
☐ Scout Song Book, 1972			
☐ Pocket Edition of Favorite Scout Songs, 1927	2.00	5.00	1.25
☐ BSA Song Sheet, "Let's Sing," 1944	1.00	2.00	1.25
☐ North Shore Area Council Boy Scout Song Book, 1920	5.00	8.00	5.25

WORKS OF FICTION

With the early overwhelming enthusiasm for scouting came a great outpouring of exciting fiction designed to capture the reading interest of young American boys. A great amount of this took the form of fifty-cent novels called "potboilers."

A successful novelist of the time, Edward Stratemeyer, would hire semi-experienced writers to produce action-filled books following his outlines. Unfortunately, the authors were not usually conversant with scouting principles and the results reflected badly on the purposes of scouting. The usual format was to picture "The Boy Scouts" in heroic and reckless stunts. Flying airplanes, jumping from racing trains, capturing armed and dangerous criminals, practicing war games and various death defying activities, were all pictured as typical scouting activities.

By 1912, James E. West, Chief Scout Executive, determined the current fictionalized version of the Boy Scouts was doing harm to the movement and to the boys who devoured the "potboilers." West hired Franklin K. Mathiews as Chief Scout Librarian and gave him broad authority to do whatever was necessary to counteract the unauthorized fiction series.

Mathiews prevailed upon important publishers of the time to realize the dangers inherent in the current philosophy of their publications and proposed that the Boy Scouts of America would support better-quality publications. Famous writers, including Zane Grey, Richard Harding Davis, Jack London, and John Masefield, rallied to the cause.

Mathiews hired Percy Keese Fitzhugh, an experienced writer and Scouter, to produce a series of more wholesome books to counteract the Tom Swift unauthorized version of The Boy Scouts. Fitzhugh created the Tom Slade series. With the Boy Scouts of America endorsement, this series was highly successful.

In 1913, the first issues of "Every Boy's Library" met with immediate success. In the foreword, James E. West attacks "cheap juvenile literature" that "exploits" the taste of youth. Fitzhugh produced the *Tom Slade, Roy Blakeley, Pee Wee Harris, Westy Martin,* and *Mark Gilmore* series, totaling over sixty volumes.

BANNER BOY SCOUTS, THE

By George A. Warren, Cupples and Leon, Publishers, World Publishing Co.

Title	Current Price Range		P/Y Avg.
☐ Banner Boy Scouts, The, 1912 ..	3.00	5.00	3.75
☐ Banner Boy Scouts Afloat, The, 1913	3.00	5.00	3.75
☐ Banner Boy Scouts in the Air, The, 1937	3.00	5.00	3.75
☐ Banner Boy Scouts Mystery, The, 1937	3.00	5.00	3.75

	Current Price Range		P/Y Avg.

☐ **Banner Boy Scouts Snowbound, The**, 1916 .... 3.00   5.00   3.75
☐ **Banner Boy Scouts on a Tour, The**, 1912 .... 3.00   5.00   3.75

BEST FROM BOY'S LIFE COMICS, THE
By various authors, Gilbertson World-Wide Publications.

☐ **Number 1**, October 1957.......... 4.00   5.00   4.50
☐ **Number 2**, June 1958.............. 4.00   5.00   4.50
☐ **Number 3**, April 1958 .... 4.00   5.00   4.50
☐ **Number 4**, July 1958.............. 4.00   5.00   4.50
☐ **Number 5**, October 1958.......... 4.00   5.00   4.50

BOB HANSON SERIES, THE
By Russell G. Carter, Penn Publishing Company.

☐ **Bob Hanson, Eagle Scout**, 1923 .. 6.00   8.00   5.00
☐ **Bob Hanson, First Class Scout**, 1922 .... 6.00   8.00   5.00
☐ **Bob Hanson, Scout**, 1921 .... 6.00   8.00   5.00
☐ **Bob Hanson, Tenderfoot**, 1921 .. 6.00   8.00   5.00

BOY PATROL SERIES, THE
By Edward Ellis, John C. Winston Company.

☐ **Around the Council Fire**, 1913 .... 6.00   8.00   6.50
☐ **Boy Patrol on Guard, The**, 1913 .. 6.00   8.00   6.50

BOY SCOUT EXPLORERS, THE
By Don Palmer, Cupples and Leon Company.

☐ **Boy Scout Explorers at Emerald Valley, The**, 1955 .... 3.00   5.00   3.25
☐ **Boy Scout Explorers at Headless Hollow, The**, 1957 .... 3.00   5.00   3.25
☐ **Boy Scout Explorers at Treasure Mountain, The**, 1955 .... 3.00   5.00   3.25

	Current Price Range		P/Y Avg.

BOY SCOUT LIFE SERIES, THE
Barse and Hopkins, Publishers.

	Current Price Range		P/Y Avg.
☐ **Boy Scout Firefighters, The,** Irwing Crump, 1917	3.00	5.00	4.15
☐ **Boy Scout Trailblazers, The,** F. H. Cheley, 1917	3.00	5.00	4.15
☐ **Boy Scout Treasure Hunters, The,** C. Lerrigo, 1917	3.00	5.00	4.25
☐ **Boy Scouts A-Float,** W. Walden, 1918	3.00	5.00	4.25
☐ **Boy Scouts in Africa, The,** Capt. A. P. Corcoran, 1923	3.00	5.00	4.25
☐ **Boy Scouts Courageous,** F. K. Mathiews, 1918	3.00	5.00	4.25
☐ **Boy Scouts of the Lighthouse, The,** F. Moulton McLane, 1917	3.00	5.00	4.15
☐ **Boy Scouts of the Robin Hood Patrol, The,** C. Lerrigo, 1927	3.00	5.00	4.15
☐ **Boy Scouts of the Round Table Patrol, The,** C. Lerrigo, 1924	3.00	5.00	4.15
☐ **Boy Scouts on the Trail,** John Garth, 1920	3.00	5.00	4.25

BOY SCOUT SERIES, THE
By Captain John Blaine, Saalfield Publishing Company.

	Current Price Range		P/Y Avg.
☐ **Boy Scouts in England, The,** 1916	3.00	5.00	3.25
☐ **Boy Scouts in Europe, The,** 1916	3.00	5.00	3.25
☐ **Boy Scouts in France, The,** 1915	3.00	5.00	3.25
☐ **Boy Scouts in Germany, The,** 1916	3.00	5.00	3.25
☐ **Boy Scouts in Italy, The,** 1916	3.00	5.00	3.25
☐ **Boy Scouts with Joffre, The,** 1919	3.00	5.00	3.25

	Current Price Range		P/Y Avg.
☐ Boy Scouts in The Netherlands, The, 1916	3.00	5.00	3.25
☐ Boy Scouts in Russia, The, 1916	4.00	5.00	4.25
☐ Boy Scouts in Servia, The, 1916	4.00	5.00	4.25
☐ Boy Scouts on a Submarine, The, 1918	4.00	5.00	4.25
☐ Boy Scouts in Turkey, The, 1916	4.00	5.00	4.25
☐ Boy Scouts on the Western Front, The, 1919	4.00	5.00	4.25

By Thronton W. Burgess, Penn Publishing Company.

☐ Boy Scouts on Lost Trail, The, 1914	4.00	7.00	4.50
☐ Boy Scouts on Swift River, The, 1913	4.00	7.00	4.50
☐ Boy Scouts in a Trapper's Camp, The, 1915	4.00	7.00	4.50
☐ Boy Scouts of Woodcraft Camp, The, 1912	4.00	7.00	4.50

By Herbert Carter, A. L. Burt Publishing Company.

☐ Boy Scouts Afoot in France, The; or, With the Red Cross Corps at the Marne, 1917	3.00	5.00	3.50
☐ Boy Scouts Along the Susquehanna, The; or, Silver Fox Patrol Caught in a Flood, The, 1915	3.00	5.00	3.50
☐ Boy Scouts at the Battle of Saratoga, The; or, Story of General Burgoyne's Defeat, The, 1915	3.00	5.00	3.50
☐ Boy Scouts Through the Big Timber, The; or, Search for the Lost Tenderfoot, The, 1913	3.00	5.00	3.50

	Current Price Range		P/Y Avg.
☐ Boy Scouts in the Blue Ridge, The; or, Marooned Among the Moonshiners, 1913	3.00	5.00	3.50
☐ Boy Scouts in Dixie, The; or, Strange Secret of Alligator Swamp, The, 1914...............	3.00	5.00	3.50
☐ Boy Scouts First Campfire, The; or, Scouting with the Silver Fox Patrol, 1913	3.00	5.00	4.25
☐ Boy Scouts in the Maine Woods, The; or, New Test for the Silver Fox Patrol, The, 1913	3.00	5.00	3.25
☐ Boy Scouts in the Rockies, The; or, Secret of the Hidden Silver Mine, The, 1913..................	3.00	5.00	3.25
☐ Boy Scouts on Sturgeon Island, The; or, Marooned Among the Game-Fish Poachers, The, 1914	3.00	5.00	3.50
☐ Boy Scouts on the Trail, The; or, Scouting Through the Big Game Country, 1913....................	3.00	5.00	3.25
☐ Boy Scouts on the War Trails in Belgium, The; or, Caught Between Hostile Enemies, 1916	3.00	5.00	3.25

By Brewar Corcoran, The Page Company.

	Current Price Range		P/Y Avg.
☐ Boy Scouts in Africa, 1924.......	4.00	5.00	3.25
☐ Boy Scouts at Camp Lowell, The, 1922	4.00	5.00	3.25
☐ Boy Scouts of Kendallville, The, 1918	4.00	5.00	3.25
☐ Boy Scouts of the Wolf Patrol, The, 1920	4.00	5.00	3.25

	Current Price Range		P/Y Avg.

By Thomas Y. Crowell Company.

☐ **Along the Mohawk Trail; or, Boy Scouts on Lake Champlain**, P.K. Fitzhugh, 1912......................	6.00	9.00	6.50
☐ **Boy Scouts in Lumber Camp**, James Otis, 1913..................	6.00	9.00	6.50
☐ **Boy Scouts in the Maine Woods**, James Otis, 1911	6.00	9.00	6.50
☐ **For Uncle Sam Boss; or, Boy Scouts at Panama**, P.K. Fitzhugh, 1913	8.00	10.00	6.50
☐ **In the Path of La Salle; or, Boy Scouts on the Mississippi**, P.K. Fitzhugh, 1914......................	6.00	9.00	6.50
☐ **Pluck on the Trail; or, Boy Scouts in the Rockies**, Edward L. Sabin, 1912	6.00	9.00	6.50

By George Durston, Saalfield Publishing Company.

☐ **Boy Scout Aviators**, large and small size, 1921	3.00	5.00	3.25
☐ **Boy Scout on Duty, A**, large size only, 1927	3.00	5.00	3.25
☐ **Boy Scout Firefighters, The**, small size only, 1921	3.00	5.00	3.25
☐ **Boy Scout Pathfinders, The**, small size only, 1921	3.00	5.00	3.25
☐ **Boy Scouts Afloat**, large and small size, 1921	3.00	5.00	3.25
☐ **Boy Scout's Bravery, A**, large size only, 1921	3.00	5.00	3.25
☐ **Boy Scouts in Camp**, large and small size, 1921	3.00	5.00	3.25
☐ **Boy Scout's Campaign, A**, large size only, 1927	3.00	5.00	3.25
☐ **Boy Scouts' Challenge, The**, small size, only, 1921	3.00	5.00	3.25

	Current Price Range		P/Y Avg.
☐ Boy Scouts' Champion Recruit, The, small size only, 1921	3.00	5.00	3.25
☐ Boy Scouts DeFrance, small size only, 1921	3.00	5.00	3.25
☐ Boy Scout's Discovery, A, large size only, 1927	3.00	5.00	3.25
☐ Boy Scout's Mission, A, large size only, 1927	3.00	5.00	3.25
☐ Boy Scouts to the Rescue, large and small size, 1921..............	3.00	5.00	3.50
☐ Boy Scout's Secret, A, large size only, 1927	3.00	5.00	3.50
☐ Boy Scouts on the Trail, large and small size, 1921	3.00	5.00	3.25
☐ Boy Scout's Victory, large and small size, 1921	3.00	5.00	3.25

By Walter P. Eaton, W.A. Wilde Publisher.

☐ Boy Scouts of Berkshire, 1912 ..	5.00	7.00	5.25
☐ Boy Scouts at Crater Lake, 1922	5.00	7.00	5.25
☐ Boy Scouts in Death Valley, 1939	5.00	7.00	5.25
☐ Boy Scouts in the Dismal Swamp, 1913.....................	5.00	7.00	5.25
☐ Boy Scouts in Glacier Park, 1918	5.00	7.00	5.25
☐ Boy Scouts at the Grand Canyon, 1932	5.00	7.00	5.25
☐ Boy Scouts on Green Mountain Trail, 1929........................	5.00	7.00	5.25
☐ Boy Scouts on Kata Hidin, 1924	5.00	7.00	5.25
☐ Boy Scouts in the White Mountains, 1914	5.00	7.00	5.25
☐ Boy Scouts of the Wild Cat Patrol, 1915.........................	5.00	7.00	5.25
☐ Peanut, Cub Reporter, 1916	5.00	7.00	5.25
☐ Young Scoutmaster, The, ...	5.00	7.00	5.25

WALTER P. EATON

Boy Scouts of the Wildcat Patrol, Walter P. Eaton, W. A. Wilde Co., 1915, $5.00–$7.50

By Maj. A. L. Fletcher, A. Donahue and Company, Publishers.

	Current Price Range		P/Y Avg.
☐ Boy Scout Pathfinders; or, Strange Hunt for the Beaver Patrol, The, 1913	3.00	5.00	3.25
☐ Boy Scout Rivals; or, A Leader of the Tenderfoot Patrol, 1913	3.00	5.00	3.25
☐ Boy Scouts in Alaska; or, Camp on the Glacier, The, 1913	5.00	7.00	5.50
☐ Boy Scouts in the Coal Caverns; or, Light in Tunnel Six, 1913	3.00	5.00	3.25
☐ Boy Scouts in the Everglades; or, Island of Lost Channel, The, 1913	3.00	5.00	3.25
☐ Boy Scouts on the Great Divide; or, Ending of the Trail, The, 1913	3.00	5.00	3.25
☐ Boy Scouts on a Long Hike; or, To the Rescue in the Black Water Swamp, 1913	3.00	5.00	3.25

	Current Price Range		P/Y Avg.

☐ **Boy Scouts in Northern Wilds; or, Signal from the Hills, The,** 1913 — 3.00 5.00 3.25

☐ **Boy Scouts on Old Superior; or Tale of the Pictured Rocks, The,** 1913 — 3.00 5.00 3.25

☐ **Boy Scout's Signal Sender; or, When Wig Wag Knowledge Paid,** 1913 .... — 3.00 5.00 3.50

☐ **Boy Scout's Test of Courage; or, Winning The Merit Badge,** 1913 ... — 3.00 5.00 3.50

☐ **Boy Scout's Woodcraft Lesson; or, Proving Their Mettle in the Field,** 1913 .... — 3.00 5.00 3.50

By Edward Griggs, Saalfield Publishing Company.

☐ **Boy Scout Hero, A,** 1921 .... — 4.00 6.00 4.50
☐ **Boy Scout Patriot, A,** 1921 .... — 4.00 6.00 4.50
☐ **Boy Scout on the Trail, A,** 1921 .. — 4.00 6.00 4.50
☐ **Boy Scout's Adventure, A,** 1921 .. — 4.00 6.00 4.50
☐ **Boy Scout's Chance, A,** 1921 .... — 4.00 6.00 4.50
☐ **Boy Scout's Courage, A,** 1921 .... — 4.00 6.00 4.50
☐ **Boy Scout's Daring, A,** 1921 ...... — 4.00 6.00 4.50
☐ **Boy Scout's Destiny, A,** 1921 .... — 4.00 6.00 4.50
☐ **Boy Scout's Holiday, A,** 1921 .... — 4.00 6.00 4.50
☐ **Boy Scout's Mystery, A,** 1921 ... — 4.00 6.00 4.50
☐ **Boy Scout's Struggle, A,** 1921 .... — 4.00 6.00 4.50
☐ **Boy Scout's Success, A,** 1921 .... — 4.00 6.00 4.50

By William Heyiger, D. Appleton and Company.

☐ **Don Strong, American,** 1920 ..... — 7.00 9.00 7.50
☐ **Don Strong, Patrol Leader,** 1918 .. — 7.00 9.00 7.50
☐ **Don Strong of the Wolf Patrol,** 1916 .... — 7.00 9.00 7.50

	Current Price Range		P/Y Avg.

By Rupert Sargent Holland, Lippincott Publishing Company.

☐ Boy Scouts of Birchbark Island, The, 1911	5.00	7.50	6.25
☐ Boy Scouts of Snowshoe Lodge, The, 1915	5.00	7.50	6.25
☐ Sea Scouts of Birchbark Island, The, 1936	5.00	7.50	6.25

By Isabel K. Hornibrood, Houghton Mifflin Company.

☐ Captain Curly's Boy	6.00	9.00	6.50
☐ Coxwain Drake of the Sea Scouts, 1920	6.00	9.00	6.50
☐ Drake and the Adventurer's Cup, 1922	6.00	9.00	6.50
☐ Drake of Troop One, 1916	6.00	9.00	6.50
☐ Lost in Maine Woods	6.00	9.00	6.50
☐ Scout Drake in War Time	6.00	9.00	6.50
☐ Scout of Today, A, 1913	6.00	9.00	6.50

By Marshall Jenkins, D. Appleton and Company.

☐ Doings of Troop 5, The, 1914	6.00	8.00	6.25
☐ Freshman Scout at College, A, 1914	6.00	8.00	6.25
☐ Jackel Patrol of Troop 5, The, 1915	6.00	8.00	6.25
☐ Norfolk Boy Scouts, The, 1916	6.00	8.00	6.25
☐ Troop 5 at Camp, 1914	6.00	8.00	6.25

By Maj. Robert Maitland and George Durston, Saalfield Publishing Company.

☐ Boy Scout Automobilists, The, 1912	3.50	5.00	3.75
☐ Boy Scout Aviators, The, 1912	3.50	5.00	3.75
☐ Boy Scout Pathfinders, The, 1912	3.50	5.00	3.75
☐ Boy Scouts Afloat, The, 1912	3.50	5.00	3.75

	Current Price Range		P/Y Avg.
☐ Boy Scouts with the Allies, The, 1915	3.50	5.00	3.75
☐ Boy Scouts Before Belgrade, The, 1915	3.50	5.00	3.75
☐ Boy Scouts in Camp, The, 1912	3.50	5.00	3.75
☐ Boy Scouts' Challenge, The, 1912	3.50	5.00	3.75
☐ Boy Scouts' Champion Recruit, The, 1912	3.50	5.00	3.75
☐ Boy Scouts with the Cossacks, The, 1915	3.50	5.00	3.75
☐ Boy Scout Fire Fighters, The, 1912	3.00	5.00	3.50
☐ Boy Scouts Under Fire in France, The	3.00	5.00	3.50
☐ Boy Scouts in Front of Warsaw, The, 1916	3.00	5.00	3.50
☐ Boy Scouts under the Kaiser, 1915	3.00	5.00	3.50
☐ Boy Scouts with King George, The, 1915	3.00	5.00	3.50
☐ Boy Scouts at Leige, 1915	3.00	5.00	3.50
☐ Boy Scouts under the Red Cross, The, 1916	3.00	5.00	3.50
☐ Boy Scouts to the Rescue, The, 1912	3.00	5.00	3.50
☐ Boy Scouts under the Stars and Stripes, The, 1918	3.00	5.00	3.50
☐ Boy Scouts' Test, The, 1916	3.00	5.00	3.50
☐ Boy Scouts on the Trail, The, 1912	3.00	5.00	3.50
☐ Boy Scouts' Victory, The, 1912	3.00	5.00	3.50
☐ Boy Scouts in the War Zone, 1919	3.00	5.00	3.50

	Current Price Range		P/Y Avg.

By Lt. Howard Payson, Hurst and Company.

☐ Boy Scouts with the Allies in France, The, 1915	3.00	5.00	3.50
☐ Boy Scouts and the Army Airship, The, 1911	3.00	5.00	3.50
☐ Boy Scouts' Badge of Courage, The, 1917	3.00	5.00	3.50
☐ Boy Scouts on Belgian Battlefields, The, 1915	3.00	5.00	3.50
☐ Boy Scouts' Campaign for Preparedness, The, 1916	3.00	5.00	3.50
☐ Boy Scouts at the Canadian Border, The, 1918	3.00	5.00	3.50
☐ Boy Scouts of the Eagle Patrol, The, 1911	3.00	5.00	3.50
☐ Boy Scouts' Mountain Camp, The, 1912	3.00	5.00	3.50
☐ Boy Scouts at the Panama Canal, The, 1913	4.00	5.00	4.25
☐ Boy Scouts at the Panama-Pacific Exposition, The, 1915	4.00	5.00	4.25
☐ Boy Scouts on the Range, The, 1911	4.00	5.00	4.25
☐ Boy Scouts for Uncle Sam, The, 1912	4.00	5.00	4.25
☐ Boy Scouts under Fire in Mexico, The, 1914	4.00	5.00	4.25
☐ Boy Scouts under Sealed Orders, The, 1916	4.00	5.00	4.25

By Leslie W. Quirk, Little, Brown and Company.

☐ Boy Scouts of the Black Eagle Patrol, The, 1915	7.00	10.00	7.50
☐ Boy Scouts on Crusade, The, 1917	7.00	10.00	7.50
☐ Boy Scouts of Lakeville High, The, 1920	7.00	10.00	7.50

	Current Price Range		P/Y Avg.

By G. Harvey Ralphson, Donahue Publishing Company.

☐ Boy Scout Electricians; or, Hidden Dynamo, The, 1913..........	4.00	5.00	4.25
☐ Boy Scouts in an Airship; or, Warning from the Sky, The, 1912	4.00	5.00	4.25
☐ Boy Scouts in Belgium; or, Imperiled in a Trap, 1912	4.00	5.00	4.25
☐ Boy Scouts Beyond the Arctic Circle; or, Lost Expedition, The, 1913	4.00	5.00	4.25
☐ Boy Scouts in California; or, Flag on the Cliff, The, 1913	4.00	5.00	4.25
☐ Boy Scouts' Camera Club; or, Confessions of a Photograph, The, 1913	4.00	5.00	4.25
☐ Boy Scouts in the Canal Zone; or, Plot Against Uncle Sam, The, 1911	3.00	5.00	4.25
☐ Boy Scouts on the Columbia River; or, Adventures in a Motor Boat, 1912........................	3.00	5.00	4.25
☐ Boy Scouts with the Cossacks; or, Poland Recaptured, 1916	3.00	5.00	4.25
☐ Boy Scouts in Death Valley; or, City in the Sky, The, 1914	3.00	5.00	4.25
☐ Boy Scouts on Hudson Bay; or, Disappearing Fleet, The, 1914	3.00	5.00	4.25
☐ Boy Scouts in Mexico; or, On Guard With Uncle Sam, 1911	3.00	5.00	4.25
☐ Boy Scouts on Motorcycles; or, With the Flying Squadron, 1912 ..	3.00	5.00	4.25
☐ Boy Scouts in the North Sea; or, Mystery Sub, The, 1915.........	3.00	5.00	4.25
☐ Boy Scouts in the Northwest; or, Fighting Forest Fires, 1912	3.00	5.00	4.25

	Current Price Range		P/Y Avg.
□ Boy Scouts on Open Plains; or, Roundup Not Ordered, The, 1914	3.00	5.00	4.25
□ Boy Scouts in the Phillipines; or, Key to the Treaty Box, The, 1911	3.00	5.00	4.25
□ Boy Scouts in Southern Waters; or, Spanish Treasure Chest, The, 1915	3.00	5.00	4.25
□ Boy Scouts in a Submarine; or, Searching an Ocean Floor, 1912	3.00	5.00	4.25
□ Boy Scouts under the Kaiser; or, Uhlan's Escape, The, 1916	3.00	5.00	4.25

Note: Title changed at World War I to "The Boy Scouts' Mysterious Signal; or, Perils of the Black Bear Patrol" and also "Boy Scouts in the Verdun Attack; or, Perils of the Black Bear Patrol."

By Capt. V. T. Sherman, Donahue Publishing Company.

□ Scouting the Balkans in a Motorboat; or, An Escape from the Dardanelles, 1913	3.00	5.00	3.50
□ Boy Scouts with Joffre; or, Trenches in Belgium, The, 1913	3.00	5.00	3.50
□ Boy Scout's Signal, The; or, Camp on the Cliff, The, 1913	3.00	5.00	3.50
□ Call of the Beaver Patrol, The; or, A Break in the Glacier, 1913	3.00	5.00	3.50
□ Capturing a Spy; or, A New Peril, 1913	3.00	5.00	3.50
□ An Interrupted Wig Wag; or, A Boy Scout Trick, 1913	3.00	5.00	3.50
□ A Lost Patrol; or, Scout Tactics to the Front, 1913	3.00	5.00	3.50
□ Perils of an Air Ship, The; or, Boy Scouts in the Sky, 1913	3.00	5.00	3.50

Boy Scouts Yearbook,
edited by Mathiews,
$10.00–$17.50

	Current Price Range		P/Y Avg.
☐ Runaway Balloon, The; or, Beseiged Scouts, The, 1913	3.00	5.00	3.50
☐ War Zone of the Kaiser, The; or, Boy Scouts of the North Sea, 1913	3.00	5.00	3.50

BOY SCOUT YEARBOOKS
By Franklin K. Mathiews, D. Appleton and Company.

☐ Boy Scouts Yearbook, The, 1915	16.00	24.00	18.00
☐ Boy Scouts Yearbook, The, 1916	16.00	22.00	17.00
☐ Boy Scouts Yearbook, The, 1917	12.00	20.00	12.50
☐ Boy Scouts Yearbook, The, 1918	12.00	20.00	12.50
☐ Boy Scouts Yearbook, The, 1919	15.00	20.00	15.50
☐ Boy Scouts Yearbook, The, 1920	10.00	14.00	10.50
☐ Boy Scouts Yearbook, The, 1921	10.00	14.00	10.50

	Current Price Range		P/Y Avg.
☐ Boy Scouts Yearbook, The, 1922	10.00	14.00	10.50
☐ Boy Scouts Yearbook, The, 1923	9.00	14.00	9.50
☐ Boy Scouts Yearbook, The, 1924	9.00	14.00	9.50
☐ Boy Scouts Yearbook, The, 1925	9.00	13.00	9.25
☐ Boy Scouts Yearbook, The, 1926	8.00	12.00	8.60
☐ Boy Scouts Yearbook, The, 1927	8.00	12.00	8.50
☐ Boy Scouts Yearbook, The, 1928	8.00	12.00	8.50
☐ Boy Scouts Yearbook, The, 1929	8.00	12.00	8.50
☐ Boy Scouts Yearbook, The, 1930	8.00	12.00	8.50
☐ Boy Scouts Yearbook, The, 1931	8.00	12.00	8.50
☐ Boy Scouts Yearbook, The, 1932	8.00	12.00	8.50
☐ Fun in Fiction, 1938	6.00	9.00	6.50
☐ Ghost and Mystery Stories, 1933	7.00	10.00	7.50
☐ Stories of Adventurous Fliers, 1943	5.00	8.00	5.50
☐ Stories of Boy Heroes, 1942	5.00	8.00	5.50
☐ Stories of Boy Scouts Courageous, 1944	5.00	8.00	5.50
☐ Stories Boys Like Best, 1945	8.00	12.00	8.50
☐ Stories of Brave Boys and Fearless Men, 1934	7.00	10.00	7.50
☐ Stories of Daring and Danger, 1939	6.00	9.00	6.25
☐ Stories of Dogs, 1935	7.00	10.00	7.50
☐ Stories of Patriots and Pioneers, 1937	7.00	10.00	7.50

	Current Price Range		P/Y Avg.
☐ **Wild Animal Stories**, 1940........	6.00	9.00	6.50
☐ **Yearbook of Patriotic Stories,** 1941	5.00	8.00	5.50
☐ **Yearbook of Sport Series**, 1936	7.00	10.00	7.50

BOY SCOUTS, THE
By Ralph Victor, A. L. Chatterton, Publishers, Platt and Rick, Publishers.

☐ **Boy Scouts' Air Craft**, 1912......	3.00	5.00	3.50
☐ **Boy Scouts in the Black Hills,** 1913	3.00	5.00	3.50
☐ **Boy Scouts in the Canadian Rockies**, 1911......................	3.00	5.00	3.50
☐ **Boy Scouts' Canoe Trip**, 1911...	3.00	5.00	3.50
☐ **Boy Scouts' Motorcycles**, 1911....	3.00	5.00	3.50
☐ **Boy Scouts in the North Woods,** 1913	3.00	5.00	3.50
☐ **Boy Scouts' Patrol**, 1911.........	3.00	5.00	3.50

BOY SCOUTS OF THE AIR BOOKS
By Gordon Stuart, Reilly and Britton, Publishers.

☐ **Boy Scouts of the Air on Baldcrest, The**, 1922	3.00	5.00	3.50
☐ **Boy Scouts of the Air in Belgium, The**, 1915	3.00	5.00	3.50
☐ **Boy Scouts of the Air at Cape Peril, The**, 1921....................	3.00	5.00	3.50
☐ **Boy Scouts of the Air in the Dismal Swamp, The**, 1920	3.00	5.00	3.50
☐ **Boy Scouts of the Air at Eagle Camp, The**, 1912	3.00	5.00	3.50
☐ **Boy Scouts of the Air on Flathead Mountain, The**, 1913	3.00	5.00	3.50
☐ **Boy Scouts of the Air on the French Front, The**, 1918	3.00	5.00	3.50

Boy Scouts of the Air at Eagle Camp, Stuart, $3.50–$6.00

	Current Price Range		P/Y Avg.
☐ Boy Scouts of the Air on the Great Lakes, The, 1914	3.00	5.00	3.50
☐ Boy Scouts of the Air at Greenwood School, The, 1912	3.00	5.00	3.50
☐ Boy Scouts of the Air in Indian Land, The, 1912	3.00	5.00	3.50
☐ Boy Scouts of the Air in the Lone Star Patrol, The, 1916	3.00	5.00	3.50
☐ Boy Scouts of the Air on Lost Island, The, 1917	3.00	5.00	3.50
☐ Boy Scouts of the Air in the Northern Wilds, The, 1912	3.00	5.00	3.50
☐ Boy Scouts of the Air with Pershing, The, 1919	3.00	5.00	3.50

Note: Gordon Stuart was a pseudonym of H. S. Sayler. After his death in 1913, the name was used by G. N. Madison and H. Bedford Jones, who completed the series.

	Current Price Range		P/Y Avg.

BOY SCOUTS OF TROOP FIVE SERIES
By T. I. Thurston, Revell Publishing Company.

☐ Billy Burns of Troop 5, The, 1916	8.00	10.00	8.50
☐ Scoutmaster of Troop 5, The, 1912	8.00	10.00	8.50

BOY'S LIFE LIBRARY BOOKS, THE
By various authors, Random House Publishers.

☐ Boy's Life Book of Baseball Stories, The, 1964	3.00	4.00	3.25
☐ Boy's Life Book of Basketball Stories, The, 1966	3.00	4.00	3.25
☐ Boy's Life Book of Flying Stories, The, 1964	3.00	4.00	3.25
☐ Boy's Life Book of Football Stories, The, 1963	3.00	4.00	3.25
☐ Boy's Life Book of Horse Stories, The, 1963	3.00	4.00	3.25
☐ Boy's Life Book of Mystery Stories, The, 1963	3.00	4.00	3.25
☐ Boy's Life Book of Outer Space Stories, The, 1964	3.00	4.00	3.25
☐ Boy's Life Book of Sport Series, The, 1965	3.00	4.00	3.25
☐ Boy's Life Book of Wild Animal Stories, The, 1965	3.00	4.00	3.25
☐ Boy's Life Book of World War II Stories, The, 1965	3.00	4.00	3.25
☐ Mutiny in the Time Machine, 1963	3.00	4.00	3.25

CLOUD PATROL SERIES, THE
By Irving Crump, Grosset & Dunlap, Publishers.

☐ Cloud Patrol, The, 1929	3.00	5.00	3.50
☐ Craig of the Cloud Patrol, 1931	3.00	5.00	3.50

Dan Carter Cub Scout, Mildred A. Wirt, Cupples & Leon Co., $2.50–$5.00

	Current Price Range		P/Y Avg.
☐ Pilot of the Cloud Patrol, The, 1929	3.00	5.00	3.50

DAN CARTER BOOKS
By Mildred A. Wirt, Cupples and Leon Company.

☐ Dan Carter and the Cub Honor, 1953	3.00	5.00	3.25
☐ Dan Carter Cub Scout, 1949	3.00	5.00	3.25
☐ Dan Carter and the Great Carved Face, 1952	3.00	5.00	3.25
☐ Dan Carter and the Haunted Castle, 1951	3.00	5.00	3.25
☐ Dan Carter and the Money Box, 1950	3.00	5.00	3.25
☐ Dan Carter and the River Camp, 1949	3.00	5.00	3.25

EAGLE SCOUT SERIES, THE
By Norton H. Jonathan, Goldsmith Publishing Company.

☐ Lost Empire, The, 1934	4.00	6.00	4.25
☐ Movie Scout, The, 1934	4.00	6.00	4.25

	Current Price Range		P/Y Avg.
☐ Mystery of the Midnight Flyer, The	4.00	6.00	4.25
☐ Speedway Cyclone, The, 1934...	4.00	6.00	4.25

HICKORY RIDGE BOY SCOUTS, THE
By Capt. Alan Douglas, New York Publishing Company.

☐ Afloat; or, Adventures on Watery Trails, 1917	3.00	5.00	3.50
☐ Campfires of the World Patrol, The, 1913	3.00	5.00	3.50
☐ Endurance Test; or, How Clear Grit Won the Day, 1913	3.00	5.00	3.50
☐ Fast Nine; or, a Challenge from Fairfield, 1913....................	3.00	5.00	3.50
☐ Great Hike; or, Pride of the Khaki Troop, The, 1913	3.00	5.00	3.50
☐ Pathfinder; or, Missing Tenderfoot, The, 1913	3.00	5.00	3.50
☐ Storm Bound; or, a Vacation Among the Snow Drifts, 1915 ...	3.00	5.00	3.50
☐ Tenderfoot Squad; or, Camping at Raccoon Bluff, 1919	3.00	5.00	3.50
☐ Under Canvas; or, Hunt for the Cartaret Ghost, The, 1915	3.00	5.00	3.50
☐ Woodcraft; or, How a Patrol Leader Made Good, 1913	3.00	5.00	3.50

Note: Victory Boy Scout Series is the reprint edition of Hickory Ridge Scouts.

JERRY HICKS SERIES, THE
By William Heyliger, Grosset & Dunlap, Publishers.

☐ Jerry Hicks, Explorer, 1930	6.00	8.00	6.50
☐ Jerry Hicks, Ghost Hunter, 1929 ..	6.00	8.00	6.50
☐ Jerry Hicks and His Gang, 1929 ..	6.00	8.00	6.50
☐ Yours Truly, Jerry Hicks, 1929 ..	6.00	8.00	6.50

LUCKY BOY SCOUTS SERIES, THE

By Elmer H. Sherwood, Whitman Publishing Company.

	Current Price Range		P/Y Avg.
☐ Lucky the Boy Scout, 1916	3.00	5.00	3.50
☐ Lucky Finds a Friend	3.00	5.00	3.50
☐ Lucky and His Friend Steve	3.00	5.00	3.50
☐ Lucky and His Travels	3.00	5.00	3.50
☐ Lucky on an Important Mission ..	3.00	5.00	3.25
☐ Lucky In the Northwest, 1917 ...	3.00	5.00	3.50
☐ Lucky the Young Navy Man, 1917	3.00	5.00	3.50
☐ Lucky the Young Soldier, 1917 ...	3.00	5.00	3.25
☐ Lucky the Young Volunteer	3.00	5.00	3.25

Note: Both *Lucky* and *Ted Marsh* series are the same except that, in *Ted Marsh*, two books are sometimes combined.

MARK GILMORE SERIES, THE

By Percy Keese Fitzhugh, official Boy Scout fiction writer, Grosset & Dunlap, Publishers.

☐ Mark Gilmore, Scout of the Air, 1930	4.00	7.00	6.50
☐ Mark Gilmore, Speed Flyer, 1931	4.00	7.00	6.50
☐ Mark Gilmore's Lucky Landing, 1931	4.00	7.00	6.50

PEE-WEE HARRIS BOOKS, THE

By Percy Keese Fitzhugh, Grosset & Dunlap, Publishers.

☐ Pee-Wee Harris, 1922	4.00	6.00	5.00
☐ Pee-Wee Harris, Adrift, 1922.....	4.00	6.00	5.00
☐ Pee-Wee Harris: As Good As His Word, 1925	4.00	6.00	5.00
☐ Pee-Wee Harris on the Briny Deep, 1928........................	4.00	6.00	5.00
☐ Pee-Wee Harris in Camp, 1922....	4.00	6.00	5.00

	Current Price Range		P/Y Avg.
☐ Pee-Wee Harris in Darkest Africa, 1929	8.00	12.00	10.00
☐ Pee-Wee Harris: Fixer, 1924	4.00	6.00	5.00
☐ Pee-Wee Harris F.O.B. Bridgeboro, 1923	4.00	6.00	5.00
☐ Pee-Wee Harris in Luck, 1922	4.00	6.00	5.00
☐ Pee-Wee Harris: Mayor for a Day, 1926	4.00	6.00	5.00
☐ Pee-Wee Harris and the Sunken Treasure, 1927	4.00	6.00	5.00
☐ Pee-Wee Harris on the Trail, 1922	3.00	5.00	3.50
☐ Pee-Wee Harris Turns Detective, 1930	8.00	16.00	9.00

ROY BLAKELEY BOOK, THE

By Percy Keese Fitzhugh, Grosset & Dunlap, Publishers.

☐ Roy Blakeley at the Haunted Camp, 1922	4.00	6.00	5.00
☐ Roy Blakeley, His Story, 1920	4.00	6.00	5.00
☐ Roy Blakeley: Lost, Strayed or Stolen, 1921	4.00	6.00	5.00
☐ Roy Blakeley on the Mohawk Trail, 1925	4.00	6.00	5.00
☐ Roy Blakeley up in the Air, 1931	4.00	6.00	5.00
☐ Roy Blakeley's Adventures in Camp, 1920	4.00	6.00	5.00
☐ Roy Blakeley's Bee-Line Hike, 1922	4.00	6.00	5.00
☐ Roy Blakeley's Camp on Wheels, 1920	4.00	6.00	5.00
☐ Roy Blakeley's Elastic Hike, 1926	4.00	6.00	5.00
☐ Roy Blakeley's Funny Bone Hike, 1922	4.00	6.00	5.00
☐ Roy Blakeley's Go-As-You-Please Hike, 1929	4.00	6.00	5.00

Left to Right: **The Boy Scouts of the Eagle Patrol,** by Lt.
Howard Payson, Hurst and Co., 1911, **$3.00–$5.00; Pee-Wee
Harris: Fixer,** by Percy Fitzhugh, Grosset and Dunlap Publishing,
1924, **$3.00–$5.00**

	Current Price Range		P/Y Avg.

☐ Roy Blakeley's Happy-Go-Lucky Hike, 1928	4.00	6.00	5.00
☐ Roy Blakeley's Motor Caravan, 1921	4.00	6.00	5.00
☐ Roy Blakeley's Path Finder, 1920	4.00	6.00	5.00
☐ Roy Blakeley's Roundabout Hike, 1926	4.00	6.00	5.00
☐ Roy Blakeley's Silver Fox Patrol, 1920	4.00	6.00	5.00
☐ Roy Blakeley's Tangled Trail, 1924	4.00	6.00	5.00
☐ Roy Blakeley's Wild Goose Chase, 1930	4.00	6.00	5.00

SCOUT PATROL BOYS SERIES, THE
By Jack Wright, World Syndicate Publishing Company.

☐ Scout Patrol Boys at Circle U Ranch, The, 1933	3.00	5.00	3.25
☐ Scout Patrol Boys Exploring in Yucatan, The, 1933	3.00	5.00	3.25
☐ Scout Patrol Boys in the Frozen South, The, 1933	3.00	5.00	3.25
☐ Scout Patrol Boys and the Hunting Lodge Mystery, The, 1933	3.00	5.00	3.25

STERLING BOY SCOUTS BOOKS
By S. M. Robert Shaler, Hurst Co., Publishers.

☐ Boy Scout Forest Fire Fighters, 1915	3.00	5.00	3.50
☐ Boy Scouts As Country Fair Guides, 1915	3.00	5.00	3.50
☐ Boy Scouts of the Field Hospital, 1915	3.00	5.00	3.50
☐ Boy Scouts for City Improvement, 1914	3.00	5.00	3.50
☐ Boy Scouts of the Flying Squadron, 1914	3.00	5.00	3.50

The Boy Scouts of the Signal Corps, Robert Shaler, Hurst & Co., 1914, $3.00–$5.00

	Current Price Range		P/Y Avg.
☐ Boy Scouts of the Geological Survey, 1914	3.00	5.00	3.50
☐ Boy Scouts in the Great Flood, 1915	3.00	5.00	3.50
☐ Boy Scouts for Home Protection, 1916	3.00	5.00	3.50
☐ Boy Scouts of the Life Saving Crew, 1914	3.00	5.00	3.50
☐ Boy Scouts in the Mobilization Camp, 1916	3.00	5.00	3.50
☐ Boy Scouts with the Motion Picture Players, 1915	3.00	5.00	3.50
☐ Boy Scouts of the Naval Reserve, 1914	3.00	5.00	3.50
☐ Boy Scouts on Picket Duty, 1914	3.00	5.00	3.50
☐ Boy Scouts and the Prize Pennant, 1914	3.00	5.00	3.50

	Current Price Range		P/Y Avg.

☐ **Boy Scouts with the Red Cross,**
1915 .... 3.00 5.00 3.50
☐ **Boy Scouts on the Roll of Honor,**
1916 .... 3.00 5.00 3.50
☐ **Boy Scouts in the Saddle, 1914...** 3.00 5.00 3.50
☐ **Boy Scouts of the Signal Corps,**
1914 .... 3.00 5.00 3.50

TAD SHELDON BOY SCOUTS SERIES

By John F. Wilson, Sturgis and Walton Co., Macmillan, Publishers.

☐ **Tad Sheldon, Boy Scout, 1913....** 3.00 5.00 3.25
☐ **Tad Sheldon's Fourth of July,**
1913 .... 3.00 5.00 3.25

TED MARSH BOY SCOUT SERIES

By Elmer H. Sherwood, Whitman Publishing Company.

☐ **Ted Marsh, the Boy Scout** 6.00 9.00 6.50
☐ **Ted Marsh and the Enemy** 6.00 9.00 6.50
☐ **Ted Marsh on an Important Mis-**
sion 6.00 9.00 6.50
☐ **Ted Marsh, the Young Volun-**
teer 6.00 9.00 6.50

TOM SLADE BOOKS, THE

By Percy Keese Fitzhugh, Grosset & Dunlap, Publishers.

☐ **Parachute Jumper, The: A Tom**
Slade Story, 1930 .... 4.00 5.00 4.25
☐ **Tom Slade at Bear Mountain,**
1925 .... 4.00 5.00 4.25
☐ **Tom Slade at Black Lake, 1920 ...** 4.00 5.00 4.25
☐ **Tom Slade, Boy Scout of the Mo-**
tion Pictures, 1915 .... 4.00 5.00 4.25
☐ **Tom Slade with the Boys Over**
There, 1918 .... 4.00 5.00 4.25
☐ **Tom Slade with the Colors,**
1918 .... 4.00 5.00 4.25

	Current Price Range		P/Y Avg.
☐ Tom Slade with the Flying Corps., 1919	4.00	5.00	4.25
☐ Tom Slade, Forest Ranger, 1926	4.00	5.00	4.25
☐ Tom Slade at Haunted Cavern, 1929	4.00	5.00	4.25
☐ Tom Slade, Motorcycle Dispatch Beaver, 1918	4.00	5.00	4.25
☐ Tom Slade on Mystery Trail, 1921	4.00	5.00	4.25
☐ Tom Slade In the North Woods, 1927	4.00	5.00	4.25
☐ Tom Slade on Overlook Mountain, 1923	4.00	5.00	4.25
☐ Tom Slade Picks a Winner, 1924	4.00	5.00	4.25
☐ Tom Slade on the River, 1917	4.00	5.00	4.25
☐ Tom Slade's Double Dare, 1922	4.00	5.00	4.25
☐ Tom Slade at Shadow Isle, 1928	4.00	5.00	4.25
☐ Tom Slade at Temple Camp, 1917	4.00	5.00	4.25
☐ Tom Slade on a Transport, 1918	3.00	5.00	4.25

WESTY MARTIN BOOKS, THE

By Percy Keese Fitzhugh, Grosset & Dunlap, Publishers.

	Current Price Range		P/Y Avg.
☐ Out West with Westy Martin, a four-in-one book containing #1–4, 1924	6.00	9.00	6.50
☐ West Martin, 1924	4.00	5.00	4.25
☐ Westy Martin in the Hand of the Purple Sage, 1929	4.00	5.00	4.25
☐ Westy Martin on the Mississippi, 1930	4.00	5.00	4.25
☐ Westy Martin on the Old Indian Trails, 1928	4.00	5.00	4.25
☐ Westy Martin in the Rockies, 1925	4.00	5.00	4.25
☐ Westy Martin on the Santa Fe Trail, 1926	4.00	5.00	4.25

	Current Price Range		P/Y Avg.
☐ **Westy Martin in the Sierras,** 1931	4.00	5.00	4.25
☐ **Westy Martin in the Yellowstone,** 1924	4.00	5.00	4.25

WORKS OF NONFICTION. (There is not a big demand for nonfiction works by collectors.)

Through the years, the Boy Scouts of America have endeavored to publish literature to provide every Scout and Leader with the fullest enjoyment and understanding of the huge Scout Program. Below is a compiled list of nonfictional books devoted to this purpose. Also included in this list are books that are not published by the Boy Scouts of America but dedicated to them or intended for their use.

☐ **Adventuring for Senior Scouts,** Boy Scouts of America, 1939	8.00	10.00	8.50
☐ **American Boy Scouts, Plays and Pastime,** 1912	15.00	20.00	15.75
☐ **Antarctic Scout,** Chappell, 1959	5.00	8.00	6.00
☐ **Arts and Crafts, A Practical Handbook,** Ickis, 1943	6.00	8.00	6.50
☐ **Be Expert with Maps and Compass,** Kjellstrom	2.00	3.00	2.25
☐ **Big Book of Scoutcraft, The,** Townsend, 1929	7.50	12.50	10.75
☐ **Big Book of Woodcraft, The,** Townsend, 1929	10.00	14.00	10.75
☐ **Book of American Indian Games,** MacFarlan, 1958	6.00	8.00	6.25
☐ **Book of Arts and Crafts,** Ickis and Esh, 1954	7.00	9.00	7.50
☐ **Book of Outdoor Winter Activities,** Peterson and Edgson, 1962	4.00	6.00	4.25

	Current Price Range		P/Y Avg.
☐ **Book of Winter Sports**, White, 1925	10.00	15.00	8.25
☐ **Boycraft Booklet, a Good Turn Habit**, 1926	4.00	5.00	3.25
☐ **Boy Rangers of America, Official Handbook**, 1926	10.00	15.00	12.00
☐ **Boys Book of Camp Life**, Jessup, 1920	7.00	9.00	7.50
☐ **Boy Scout Around The World, A**, Huld	4.00	5.00	4.25
☐ **Boy Scout With Byrd, A**, Siple, 1931	5.00	7.00	5.50
☐ **Boy Scout Book of Indoor Hobby Trails**, Mathiews, 1939	5.00	7.00	6.00
☐ **Boy Scout of True Adventure**, 1931	4.00	6.00	4.25
☐ **Boy Scout Encyclopedia**, first printing, Gant, 1952	4.00	6.00	4.25
☐ **Boy Scout Entertainments**, Lisle, 1918	8.00	12.00	8.50
☐ **Boy Scouts' and Girls' Open Air Clubs**, Russell, 1912	6.00	9.00	6.50
☐ **Boy Scouts In Grizzly Country**, Douglas	4.00	6.00	4.25
☐ **Boy Scout and His Law, The**, Chalmers	3.00	5.00	2.25
☐ **Boy Scout Movement Applied by the Church, The**, Richardson and Loomis, 1919	5.00	7.00	5.25
☐ **Boy Scout with the Sea Devil, A**, Martain, 1930	4.00	6.00	4.25
☐ **Boy Scout Camp Book, The**, Cave, 1914	15.00	20.00	15.50
☐ **Boy Scout's Camp Book**, Carrington, 1918	25.00	35.00	27.50
☐ **Boy Scout's Camp and Hike Book, The**, Cave, 1928	25.00	35.00	27.50

	Current Price Range		P/Y Avg.
☐ **Boy Scout's Hike Book, The,** Cave, 1913	15.00	20.00	15.50
☐ **Boy Scout's Life of Lincoln,** Tarbell, 1941	4.00	6.00	4.25
☐ **Boy Scouts and the Oregon Trail,** Putnam, 1930	5.00	7.00	5.50
☐ **Boy Scout Tests and How to Pass Them,** 1912	25.00	35.00	27.50
☐ **Boy Scout Story, The,** Oursler, 1955	9.00	11.00	9.50
☐ **Building a Popular Movement,** Levy, 1940	7.50	10.00	11.00
☐ **Cabin Craft and Outdoor Living,** Meinecke	6.00	8.00	6.50
☐ **Call to Adventure,** Benjamin, 1934	4.00	6.00	4.25
☐ **Camping,** Kephart, 1933	8.00	10.00	8.50
☐ **Camping for Boys,** Gibson, 1911	6.00	8.00	6.25
☐ **Camping and Scout Lore,** Townsend, 1930	9.00	12.00	9.50
☐ **Camp and Outing Activities,** Cheley and Baker, 1919	6.00	9.00	6.50
☐ **Camp Program Book, The,** Hammatt, 1951	6.00	8.00	6.25
☐ **Camp Sites and Facilities,** Boy Scouts of America, 1950	4.00	5.00	4.25
☐ **Camp and Trail,** Outing, White, 1907	11.00	13.00	11.50
☐ **Cubmaster's Packbook,** first edition, 1932	6.00	8.00	6.50
☐ **Cub Scout Magic Book,** 1965	1.00	2.00	1.25
☐ **Den Chief's Denbook,** 1949	3.00	4.00	3.25
☐ **Games and Recreational Methods,** Smith, 1925	7.00	9.00	7.50
☐ **Golden Anniversary Book of Scouting,** 1959	15.00	20.00	16.00
☐ **Harper's Camping and Scouting,** 1911	7.00	11.00	7.50

The Boy Scouts on Sturgeon Island, by Herbert Carter, copyright 1914, A. L. Burt Publishing Co., $6.00–$8.00

	Current Price Range		P/Y Avg.
☐ **Hiking,** Morgan, 1927	4.00	6.00	4.25
☐ **How-to Book of Cubbing,** first printing, 1938	8.00	10.00	8.50

	Current Price Range		P/Y Avg.
☐ How-to Book of Scouting, 1938 ...	10.00	15.00	12.00
☐ How to Run a Scout Camp, Lewis, 1918	4.00	6.00	4.25
☐ How to Run a Troop, Young, 1919	4.00	6.00	4.25
☐ How and Why for Scouts, England, 1934	3.00	5.00	3.25
☐ Indian Scout Talks, Eastman	8.00	12.00	8.50
☐ Information Book of the Cub Movement, 1929	12.00	15.00	12.50
☐ Jacknife Cookery, Wilder, 1946 ..	6.00	8.00	6.50
☐ The Knights of the Holy Grail and the Boy Scouts, Powell, 1911	9.00	12.00	9.50
☐ Lost on a Mountain in Maine, Fendler, 1939	3.00	5.00	3.50
☐ Manual of Cooking for Boy Scouts, A, Kellogg	2.00	3.00	1.25
☐ Matching Mountains with the Boy Scout Uniform, Reimer, 1929	15.00	20.00	16.00
☐ Minute Tapioca Book, one of the first on Scouting, Alexander, 1910	85.00	110.00	87.50
☐ Modern Camping Guide, First Edition, Mortin, 1940	4.00	6.00	4.25
☐ Mountain Boyhood, Mills, 1926....	4.00	6.00	4.25
☐ Naturebook for Scout Leaders, 1926	12.00	16.00	12.50
☐ Nature Stalking for Boys, England, 1909	12.00	15.00	12.50
☐ Night Scouting, Thomson, 1939 ...	4.00	6.00	4.25
☐ Old Scoutmaster's Poems, The, Matlock, 1937......................	10.00	15.00	10.50
☐ Personally Speaking, Boy Scouts of America, Lucas, 1965..........	1.00	2.00	.75
☐ Pine Tree Patrol, The, Wilder, 1918	20.00	30.00	24.00
☐ Practical Hints to Scoutmaster, Cheeseman, 1934	4.00	6.00	4.25

	Current Price Range		P/Y Avg.
☐ Real Book about Indians, The, Gorham, 1953	3.00	5.00	3.25
☐ Resourceful Scouts in Action, MacPeck...........................	3.00	5.00	3.25
☐ Saints for Scouts, Flahive, 1960...	4.00	5.00	4.00
☐ Scouting for Leadership, The Scariest Thing in the World, Cheley, 1924............................	7.00	10.00	7.50
☐ Scouting Marches On, History of the Boy Scouts of America, Murray, 1937..........................	18.00	25.00	18.50
☐ Scouting in Rhode Island, 1910–1962	10.00	15.00	12.00
☐ Scouting for Rural Boys, Manual for Leaders, 1938.................	6.00	9.00	6.50
☐ Scouting with a Neckerchief, Longfellow, 1927	4.00	6.00	4.50
☐ Scout Law in Action, MacPeck, 1966	3.00	5.00	3.25
☐ Scout Leaders in Action, MacPeck	3.00	5.00	3.25
☐ Scout Oath in Action, MacPeck ...	3.00	5.00	3.25
☐ Scout Book of Observation, McKay, 1923......................	4.00	6.00	4.25
☐ Thirteen Years of Scout Adventure, 1923	15.00	20.00	15.50
☐ Three Boy Scouts in Africa, Douglas, Martin, and Oliver	3.00	5.00	3.25
☐ Three Scout Naturalists in the National Parks, Kelley, Edgeman and Chick..........................	5.00	7.00	5.25
☐ Tracks and Tracking, Brunner, 1912	10.00	14.00	10.50
☐ Tracks and Trails, Boy Scouts of America, Rossell, 1928	4.00	7.50	1.75
☐ Uncle Sam's Outdoor Magic, Fitzhugh	10.00	13.00	10.50

Left to Right: **Matching Mountains with the Boy Scout Uniform,** *by Edward F. Reimer, E. P. Dutton and Co. Inc., 1929,* **$15.00–$20.00;** **Golden Anniversary Book of Scouting,** *Golden Press, New York, cover by Norman Rockwell, 1959,* **$15.00–$20.00**

	Current Price Range		P/Y Avg.
☐ **Wild Life Conservation,** Hornaday	3.00	5.00	3.25
☐ **Youth-Hope of the World,** Geiss, 1972	4.00	6.00	4.25

EQUIPMENT

AXES

Bow saws are emphasized to a greater degree today because they are safer in the hands of young Scouts than hand axes and felling axes. Axes and Boy Scouts attract each other like magnets, and there have been numerous official issues since 1911, when the Plumb "Anchor Brand" first appeared in the Handbook with the die-stamped Scout emblem.

	Current Price Range		P/Y Avg.
☐ **Bridgeport,** one-piece steel axe began in 1930 as Boy Scout model 1424 without sheath and 1425 with sheath. The first models had a squared off Butt (or Poll) and the steel shoulder was reinforced	30.00	40.00	32.50
☐ **Same as above,** but style changed to a rounded Butt (or Poll), and the reinforced shoulder was reduced. Color changed to green	23.00	30.00	22.50
☐ **Same as above,** but color changed to red, and rubber handle added	15.00	25.00	15.75
☐ **Collins,** Boy Scout model 1507 appeared about 1925 and apparently was discontinued about 1933. It is somewhat heavier than the other axes	19.00	22.00	19.50

Plumb "Anchor Brand" Axe, *solid steel special temper, axe pattern hickory handle, non-rusting finish,* **$30.00–$50.00**

	Current Price Range		P/Y Avg.

☐ **Plumb "Anchor Brand,"** was given quite a buildup in the 1911 Handbook—"Any local hardware dealer can suggest quite a variety of good axes which may be used by the Scout, but because of quality and price, the Boy Scout axe is suggested. Weight without handle, 12 oz. Made of one piece of solid steel special temper, axe pattern hickory handle, missionized hand-forged, non-rusting finish, axe scabbard or shield, blade is die-stamped with the Plumb Anchor Brand and the first-class emblem. A scout decal appears on the hickory handle." ....

	30.00	50.00	35.00

☐ **Plum Canoe,** has a 1¾ lb. head and a 19″ hickory handle, no nail puller, Boy Scout model 1266, began about 1972.....................

	11.00	15.00	11.50

☐ **Plumb Hand,** was later assigned Boy Scout model 1510 with sheath and model 1002 without sheath. The imprint "Anchor Brand" was dropped around 1920 and subsequent models were stamped "Plumb" or "Genuine Plumb." The Scout emblem appeared in different sizes, shapes, and locations on the head. These models, unlike the original "Anchor Brand," had nail pullers ....

	16.00	20.00	16.50

☐ **Plum Voyager,** 1132 began in 1933. It has a more tapered head and no nail puller. In about 1970, a red plastic substance was used to

	Current Price Range		P/Y Avg.

keep the head tight; "Voyager" was stamped on the handle	15.00	19.00	15.75
☐ **Same as above,** but name was changed to the Pack axe around 1970 and no stamping on handle. Boy Scout model remained 1510	8.00	12.00	8.50
☐ **True Temper Jet Rocket,** model 1270, rubber handle and chrome with longer tapered blade, 1957	10.00	15.00	11.00
☐ **Saf-T-Head,** produced briefly in the early 1940s by Vaughan and Bushnell Company, steel handle with rubber grips........................	20.00	35.00	21.50
☐ **Unknown Manufacturer,** third axe had parkerized head, cream and red painted handle, 1940–1950 ...	8.00	12.00	8.50

KNIVES AND SHEATH KNIVES

The official knives are listed by manufacturers in the approximate order of their issue.

A "mint" knife is factory-fresh as the day it was manufactured. It has not been carried or sharpened. A "good" knife will have no more than 25% blade wear and slight cracks in the handle material; but the stamping is clearly visible to the naked eye. No blades are broken, changed or repaired. All prices quoted here are for Mint to V.G.

Knife-collecting has had a rapid growth in the past decade and prices on used knives have increased rapidly. The price difference between Mint and Good is approximately 50%. So, if a knife is appraised in this work at $100.00 Mint, its value in "only good" condition would be $50.00

OFFICIAL BOY SCOUT KNIVES

NEW YORK KNIFE COMPANY (HAMMER BRAND)

New York Knife Company of Walden, New York, produced the first official Boy Scout knife in 1910 or 1911. Their first advertisement appeared in the 1911 *Handbook for Boys*. The company manufactured under the trademark

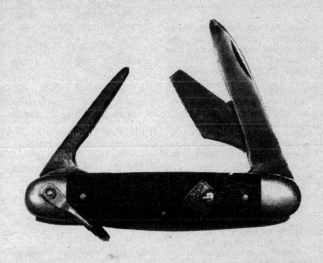

Cub Scout Knife, *blue handle, gold metal, raised cub emblem,*
$8.00–$12.50

"Hammer Brand," and went out of business in 1931. It manufactured very
high-quality knives, which are much in demand by knife collectors.

	Current Price Range	P/Y Avg.

☐ **Model 1004,** four-blade utility knife
 was actually the first standard four-
 bladed scout utility knife, mea-

	Current Price Range		P/Y Avg.

sured 3¾" with a bone stag handle with shield and etching the same as above, shield is etched "Be Prepared" 150.00 200.00 175.00

☐ **Model 1005,** two-blade easy-open with smooth ebony handle measuring 3¾", "Be Prepared" on long shield and etched on the blade, produced from 1910 until 1926.... 150.00 200.00 175.00

☐ **Model 1566,** same as above, but with oval shield, measured 3¾", shield began in 1926, oval shield has First-Class BSA emblem design 75.00 100.00 125.00

☐ **Model 1567** smaller 3⅝" version of number 1566, was stamped "B S 4 Official" on tang, made from 1926 to 1930, oval First-Class design shield 125.00 150.00 130.00

☐ **Same as above,** but clip blade replaced by spear blade, oval First-Class design shield 125.00 150.00 135.00

☐ **Model 1568,** same as above, except with heavy dagger blade and spiral boring tool, oval shield, made from 1926 until 1930, oval First-Class design shield................ 75.00 100.00 135.00

REMINGTON AND PAL

Remington Arms Company of New York produced high-quality Scout knives in many variations from about 1923 until they sold their knives division to Pal Cutlery Company in 1937. Pal used the remaining Remington parts until they ran out and then substituted lesser-quality Pal blades. Pal ceased to produce the official Scout knife in the early part of World War II, when they converted to making military knives. It is not unusual to find some of the last knives manufactured containing some Remington and some Pal blades. Many of the Pal Knives had black handles instead of brown-bone stag.

Model 1996 Imperial Knife, 3¾", four-blade black handle with gray plastic shield, $10.00–$20.00

The Remington has the greatest number of variations, and therefore offers the greatest hobby interest and challenge to the collector. The following are some of the variations that may be found by the ardent collector enthusiast. These variations will help to identify the manufacturing date.

VARIATIONS IN SHIELDS

The first shield was an acorn outline with the First-Class emblem engraved thereon. Remington used this same acorn shield on others of their nonofficial models to signify the knife contained an awl. The acorn shield was used until about 1927.

Western Sheath Knife, *saber blade, leather ring handle, $15.00–$25.00*

Their second shield was a "cut out" First-Class emblem. This is probably the rarest emblem used, and apparently was made only in 1927.

Most of their knives were made with a circular shield with the First-Class emblem engraved thereon. These started about 1928 and continued through the Pal knife.

In the early 1920s the Remington Company began to honor the Scouts who received the "Heroism Medal" by presenting them with a specially engraved "The Remington Award for Heroism" on an acorn shield. Judging by their advertisements, it is thought the knife was a standard-sized R.S. 3333. This would be the rarest collectible knife.

VARIATIONS IN SIZES

The most popular model was the standard size 3¾" four-blade model R.S. 3333. This was assigned number 1496 in the Scout Catalog and apparently became number 1495 when later made by Pal Cutlery Co.

The second most popular was their narrow 3⅝″ four blade model R. 4233. This was identical to the Girl Scout model R4373, but it had pinched bolsters. It could be more easily held in the small hand or carried in the pocket but the reduced size of the blades allowed them to be easily broken. The Scout catalog identifies this as number 1497.

The rarest, according to size, was the middle sized 3½″ three-bladed model. The awl was not included. This was model R4783 and was apparently introduced in about 1934 in only the circle shield, Boy Scouts of America number 1494. This apparently became Boy Scouts of America model 1493 when made later by Pal Cutlery Company.

VARIATIONS IN CAN-OPENERS

The first can-opener was a D-shaped, one-piece opener, which dulled quickly. On July 28, 1924, they applied for a patent on a two-piece riveted can-opener invented by Carl W. Tillmanns. The back portion was made of a softer and tougher spring steel, and the blade was made of a high-carbon steel, which would stay sharp longer. The opener could be used effectively on cans with rims or on rimless cans.

The second can-opener variation was this two-piece type with only the name "Remington" stamped thereon. This was produced from July 28, 1924, until the patent was granted on July 12, 1927.

The third can-opener variation started shortly after July 1927, and then Patent number 1,635,649 was stamped on the back portion under the name "Remington." This stamping of the patent number was used until about 1931 or 1932.

The fourth can-opener variation is the same opener but without the name Remington or the patent number, and begins about 1931 or 1932 and runs until Pal ran out of these parts in 1939 and reverted to the cheaper one-piece opener.

The remaining can-opener variation has to do with the fingernail left tab on the back part of the opener. Originally, this tab was made vertically or perpendicular to the handle. This required that a separate cut be made in the liner and handle material to receive this tab when the can-opener was closed. In 1927 this tab was changed to a parallel position, so that it came to rest on top of the handle and thus the cutout notch in the handle was eliminated. Beginning shortly after Remington stopped stamping the patent number on the blade, in about 1932, they started using a round dowel type of finger-nail tab lift.

VARIATIONS IN SCREWDRIVER-CAPLIFTER

Remington initially used a short screwdriver, caplifter blade, which measured about 1⅛″ from the end of the handle to the tip of the blade. This was found until about 1930 and then, until 1931, they utilized a long blade of approximately 1⅞″. This long blade tended to twist and bend, so it was soon changed to a medium-sized blade of about 1½″. It is difficult to date a Remington based on the size of this blade, because a broken one would often be ground down to a smaller size, but only the longest blade size had a bump on the inside edge about ¼" from the knife end when opened. Even if the tip has been ground down, this bump might help identify it.

VARIATIONS IN TANG STAMPINGS

The Remington Company stamped their identifying mark on the master blade (and sometimes other blades) using about eleven different stamps, but we are concerned only with four of them. These are not particularly reliable, but may be helpful in identifying the year of manufacture if used in connection with the other information.

All four variations involve a circle.

Variation #1. Has "Remington U M C" in block letters within the circle and nothing on the outside of the circle, used about 1921 to 1924.

Variation #2. Is the same as #1, but has "Made in U.S.A." on the outside of the circle, used about 1924 to 1933.

Variation #3. Has "Remington" in block lettering inside the circle without "U M C," "Made in U.S.A." is on the outside of the circle, used about 1933 to 1935.

Variation #4. Is the same as #3, but "Remington" is in script rather than block lettering, used from about 1935 on.

We will attempt to summarize the above factors and divide the Remington models into four phases based on their probable dates of manufacture.

	Current Price Range		P/Y Avg.
☐ **Phase I,** will likely have the one-piece can opener, the short-style screwdriver without a "bump," the variation #1 tang stamp, an acorn shield, and a vertical (or perpendicular) nail lift tab on the can-opener, earliest from about 1923 to late 1924........			
☐ Standard Size R S 3333........	100.00	125.00	110.00
☐ Small Size R 4233..............	150.00	175.00	160.00

	Current Price Range		P/Y Avg.

☐ **Time Phase 2,** the Remington will likely have the two-piece can-opener variation #2 with Remington and no patent number, the short-style screwdriver without a "bump," the variation #2 tang stamp, a vertical (or perpendicular) nail lift tab on the can-opener, and either an acorn shield or a "cut-out" First-Class shield, but a round shield is also possible, from late 1924 until late 1927..............

	Current Price Range		P/Y Avg.
☐ **Standard Size R S 3333,** with cut-out shield....................	150.00	175.00	165.00
☐ **Standard Size RS 3333,** with acorn shield	100.00	125.00	110.00
☐ **Standard Size R S 3333,** with round shield	75.00	100.00	85.00
☐ **Small Size R 4233,** with cut-out shield............................	150.00	175.00	160.00
☐ **Small Size R 4233,** with acorn shield............................	125.00	150.00	140.00
☐ **Small Size R 4233,** with round shield	100.00	125.00	110.00

☐ **Time Phase 3,** will likely have the patent number stamped under "Remington" on the two-piece can-opener variation #3, either a short or a long screwdriver, but not a medium size, the variation #2 tang stamping, a parallel lift tab on the can-opener. The type of shield is not controlling in identifying this phase, except that the later ones would have the round shield, from late 1927 until about 1932. ....

☐ **Standard Size R S 3333**........	75.00	100.00	85.00

	Current Price Range		P/Y Avg.
☐ **Small Size R 4233**..............	100.00	125.00	110.00
☐ **Time Phase 4,** will likely have the two-piece can-opener without Remington or the patent number, a medium-sized screwdriver, the variation #3 tang marking, a parallel lift tab or the round dowel lift tab and the round shield, from about late 1932 until 1935................			
☐ **Standard Size R S 3333**........	75.00	100.00	80.00
☐ **Small Size R 4233**..............	100.00	125.00	110.00
☐ **Medium Size R 4783**	100.00	125.00	110.00
☐ **Time Phase 5,** would likely have either variation #4 tang stamp or a Pal tang stamp, a round shield, a two-piece can-opener without markings or a Pal one-piece opener and possibly a rough black handle material, from 1935 through use of remaining parts after sale to Pal Cutlery Company.			
☐ **Standard Size R S 3333,** in either black or brown handle....	50.00	75.00	60.00
☐ **Medium Size R 4783,** with Pal stampings	50.00	100.00	60.00

LANDERS, FRARY AND CLARK (UNIVERSAL)

Landers, Frary and Clark of New Britain, Connecticut, was an eighty-year-old cutlery company when they started producing official Boy Scout knives in 1930. They produced under their trade name "Universal" until they discontinued Scout knives in 1940.

☐ **Model 1564,** three-blade, $3^3/8''$, three blades consisted of spear blade, combination screwdriver and bottle-opener and can-opener, introduced in 1934...................	75.00	100.00	85.00

	Current Price Range		P/Y Avg.

☐ **Model 1586,** standard four-blade 3¾" with black stag bone handle and long narrow shield imprinted with "Boy Scout," one-piece spear type can-opener, "Universal" stamped on blade, manufacturer's model number 03662 . . . . — 75.00 — 100.00 — 85.00

☐ **Same as above,** with new shield with First-Class emblem, can-opener is conventional type, manufacturer's model number 1585 . . . . — 50.00 — 75.00 — 60.00

☐ **Same as above,** but medium-size 3⅜", rare . . . . — 100.00 — 150.00 — 120.00

NOVELTY KNIFE COMPANY

Novelty Knife Company of Canton, Ohio, was a producer of cheaply made advertising knives with transparent handles covering photographic pictures.

They produced such a knife officially for the Boy Scouts in limited quantities in the 1920s. The transparent handle depicts scouts in a lake camping scene and has "Be Prepared" and the First-Class emblem as part of the picture. These knives are extremely rare because they clouded and deteriorated rapidly.

☐ **Standard Size,** four-bladed as described above . . . . — 100.00 — 150.00 — 120.00

☐ **Same as above,** with compass inserted in handle . . . . — 100.00 — 150.00 — 120.00

ULSTER KNIFE COMPANY

Ulster Knife Company of Ellenville, New York, began making high-quality official Boy Scout Knives in 1921. Their earliest tang stamping apparently was "Ulster Knife Company" and was changed to "Ulster, Dwight Devine & Sons," and later in about 1965 to "Ulster, U.S.A." There is more confusion than price differential among the earlier two markings. The later marking is currently used.

There is a curious number of variations on this shield. Initially, the eagle was erroneously looking to its own left and this was changed to an eagle with a long thin neck and head looking to its right. Then there was a long fat-necked eagle with practically no chest, and finally the standard-sized First-Class emblem eagle.

	Current Price Range		P/Y Avg.
☐ **Model 1502,** standard 3¾″, four-blade, introduced in 1922 and discontinued in 1940, manufacturer's number 47553, shield shaped "shield" in bone handle with First-Class Scout design	50.00	75.00	60.00
☐ **Same as above,** but tang stamping is "O V B," which stands for "Our Very Best." This was the trademark of the large Chicago hardware company, Hibbard, Spencer and Bartlett, which had distribution rights to hardware stores, shield-shaped "shield" in bone handle with First-Class Scout design	75.00	100.00	85.00
☐ **Model 1503,** same as above, but medium size 3⅜″, same blades, began in 1925, discontinued in 1932, manufacturer's number 47488L5	75.00	100.00	85.00
☐ **Model 1513,** standard size 3¾″, three-blade introduced in 1933, heavy spear blade, can-opener and combination screwdriver and can-opener, discontinued in 1940, shield-shaped "shield" in bone handle with First-Class Scout design	40.00	60.00	50.00
☐ **Model 1128,** Sea Scout (Mariner's model) had one large blade and one marlin spike, introduced in 1933 and the shield was added in			

	Current Price Range		P/Y Avg.

about 1935, etching on blade is "Official Sea Scouts Knife, B S A" with First-Class emblem **100.00** **150.00** **125.00**

Later model Ulsters are identified by a small, round metal crest with a Tenderfoot emblem. These were manufactured in various models from 1963 to the present. In 1980 the handle material was changed to an ivory-colored material.

☐ **Model R 1996,** standard 3¾", four-blade, brown simulated stag bone handle, "Official Knife Boy Scouts of America" and Tenderfoot emblem etched on blade. The first knife has a solid brown handle and was the earliest model followed in about 1970 by a two-tone handle that looked more like bone stag **9.00** **15.00** **10.00**

☐ **Model 1036,** same as above, but handle is solid brown with very fine grooves, "Stainless" stamped on tang and etched on blade, was introduced in about 1970 and discontinued in 1976 .... **20.00** **25.00** **22.00**

☐ **Model T 1996,** same as above, but ivory-colored handle, introduced in 1980 .... **6.00** **10.00** **7.00**

☐ **Model R 1046,** five-blade, 3¾", has standard four blades plus a Phillips head screwdriver and brown handle **6.00** **10.00** **7.50**

☐ **Same as above,** but ivory handle, introduced in 1980.......... **6.00** **10.00** **7.50**

CATTARAUGUS CUTLERY COMPANY

Cattaraugus Cutlery Company of Little Valley, New York, produced excellent-quality knives under the trade name *Whitt-L-Craft*. Their products are much in demand by knife collectors and their official Scout knives, produced only from 1933 until 1940 or 1941, are very rare.

Cattaraugus produced only two models and the only variations known to the author are in the shields and the tang markings.

	Current Price Range		P/Y Avg.
☐ **Model 1087,** four-blade medium size 3⅜", bone stag handle, Whitt-L-Craft Boy Scouts of America and the First-Class emblem etched on large blade. The four blades consist of large spear point, small blade with 45-degree offset point, hollow chisel blade, and a bottle-opener. Manufacturer's model number D2589	75.00	100.00	85.00
☐ **Model D2589 B,** same as above, but it had a bale (belt shank)	75.00	100.00	85.00
☐ **Model 1122,** three-blade medium size 3⅜", same except it did not have the caplifter-screwdriver, manufacturer's model number C2589B	75.00	100.00	85.00

An advertisement during the 1920s depicted a group of Scouts with the "Cattaraugus Scout, the Knife with the Compass." The author can find no evidence that this was an official knife of the Boy Scouts of America and believes it to be the knife of a rival group, The American Boy Scouts. The manufacturer's model was number 42209 B.

CAMILLUS CUTLERY COMPANY

Camillus Cutlery Company of Camillus, New York, is one of the giants of the American Knife business, but it did not make its first official Boy Scout Knife until the early 1940s.

	Current Price Range		P/Y Avg.

☐ **Model 1047,** three-blade, 3¹/₂″ whittler with white metal badge type shield, First-Class emblem, black plastic handle, manufactured from 1946–1950 . . . . 10.00 / 15.00 / 12.00

☐ **Model R1047,** three-blade, 3½″, whittler circle shield with Tenderfoot Emblem like current Ulster, black handle . . . . 10.00 / 15.00 / 12.00

☐ **Same as above,** with dark solid brown handle . . . . 9.00 / 14.00 / 12.00

☐ **Same as above,** with light brown delrin handle . . . . 8.00 / 12.00 / 12.00

☐ **Same as above,** but with ivory-color plastic handle, issued in 1900 . . . . 7.00 / 11.00 / 12.00

☐ **Model 1996,** four-blade standard 3¾″, black handle and white metal shield similar to the Imperial shield, issued 1946 . . . . 20.00 / 25.00 / 22.00

☐ **Model R1375,** single blade "Adventurer" folding sheath knife 4¾″ long with 3¾″ stainless steel blade, plastic simulated stag handle with hole for leather thong, no safety lock on knife, introduced in about 1973 and discontinued in 1979 . . . . 15.00 / 20.00 / 17.00

☐ **Model T1372,** same as above, but with safety lock and ivory-color handle with gold Tenderfoot emblem in dark blue oval, introduced in 1980 . . . . 15.00 / 20.00 / 17.00

Camillus also manufactured the five Cub Scout knives below:

☐ **Black handle,** raised white metal Cub emblem . . . . 9.00 / 14.00 / 9.50

	Current Price Range		P/Y Avg.
☐ **Black handle,** gold plastic inset Cub emblem	8.00	12.00	8.50
☐ **Blue handle,** gold metal raised Cub emblem	8.00	12.00	8.50
☐ **Ivory handle,** gold metal raised Cub emblem	6.00	10.00	6.50
☐ **Green handle,** gold plastic inset Cub emblem	20.00	30.00	25.00

IMPERIAL KNIFE COMPANY

Imperial Knife Company of Providence, Rhode Island, was a relative newcomer to the cutlery business. Beginning in 1916, they grew very rapidly and by the 1930s were producing 10,000 knives per day. Ten years later they were the largest cutlery company in the world.

As the decade of the 40s began, Universal, Cattaraugus and Ulster had discontinued Scout knives and Remington had sold out to Pal Company, which was phasing out the Scout knives to switch into war production. Imperial produced the vast majority of official pocket knives for the next thirty years, incorporating in 1947 with Ulster and Shrade. The surviving company is Imperial Knife Associated. This amalgamation may explain similarity in design after 1947.

☐ **Model 1996,** 3¾", four-blade, black handle with gray plastic shield. This was produced from 1942 until 1958, awls ranged in size from 1¹/₁₆" to 1⅞", produced until 1958	12.00	20.00	15.00
☐ **Same as above,** but with white metal shield same shape as gray plastic shield	12.00	20.00	15.90
☐ **Same as above,** but with imitation pearl handle and metal shield............................	40.00	50.00	42.50
☐ **Standard,** 3¾", four-blade reddish brown plastic handle simulated to look like stag with ''carved-in''			

	Current Price Range		P/Y Avg.

First-Class emblem, handle material ranged in color from dark brown to red. This is one of the most colorful Scout knives and was produced from 1958 until 1963 .... **15.00** **20.00** **17.00**

☐ **Model 1047,** three-blade 3½" whittler with black handle and gray plastic shield...................,, ... **12.00** **20.00** **13.60**

☐ **Same as above,** but raised white metal shield ....,,,. .. **12.00** **20.00** **16.00**

☐ **Model R1045,** economy standard four-blade 3¾", smooth black plastic handle with stamped white Tenderfoot emblem, produced from the early 1970s until 1980 .... **5.00** **10.00** **7.50**

☐ **Model T1045,** same as above, but with smooth ivory-colored plastic handle, began in 1980............. **5.00** **10.00** **5.25**

☐ **Model 1046,** five-blade deluxe, brown stratwood handle, fifth blade is the Phillips head screwdriver, 3½", no belt shackle, raised white metal shield **30.00** **40.00** **35.00**

☐ **Same as above,** but with black handle **20.00** **30.00** **25.00**

☐ **Same as above,** but with imitation mother-of-pearl handle, used as Scoutmaster presentation knife **30.00** **40.00** **35.00**

☐ **Same as above,** but with brown handle and round shield like late model Ulsters **20.00** **30.00** **25.00**

☐ **Folding Mess Kit Knife,** with early stamping "National Council" below First-Class emblem........... **4.00** **7.00** **5.00**

☐ **Same as above,** but with later

	Current Price Range		P/Y Avg.
stamping "Be Prepared" below Tenderfoot emblem...............	3.00	5.00	4.00
☐ **1967 World Jamboree Souvenir Knife**	19.00	20.00	15.00
☐ **Mess Kit Knives,** with current "Be Prepared" stamping under Tenderfoot emblem	2.00	4.00	3.00
☐ **Earlier Mess Kit Knife,** with "National Council" stamping under First-Class emblem	5.00	7.00	5.00
☐ **Cub Scout Knife,** black plastic handle with raised white metal shield	8.00	15.00	11.00
☐ **Cub Scout Knife,** black plastic handle with gray plastic recessed shield	8.00	15.00	11.00
☐ **Cub Scout Knife,** blue plastic handle with gold plastic recessed shield	8.00	15.00	11.00

SCHRADE CUTLERY

Schrade Cutlery, Walden, New York, is one of the currently best known knife companies in America. They have made only one official Scout knife pattern beginning in the early 1970s.

	Current Price Range		P/Y Avg.
☐ **Model R1043,** Leader's pocketknife model, two-blade 2¾", bonelike staglon handle, began in 1972 and apparently discontinued in 1981	8.00	10.00	8.00
☐ **Model 1066,** Leader's pocketknife, flat stainless steel with a cutting blade and a nail file, discontinued in 1972.............................	8.00	10.00	9.50

GEORGE SCHRADE KNIFE COMPANY

George Schrade had left the Schrade Cutlery Company of Bridgeport, Connecticut, in 1910, and formed his own company, basically to make switchblade knives. He went out of business in 1951.

From 1942 to 1946 he made folding spoon, fork, and knife sets for the Boy Scouts of America and the Girls Scouts of America. The Boy Scouts of America sets had red inserts and the Girls Scouts of America sets had green ones. They were called "Official Chow Kit," Boy Scouts of America number 1384.

	Current Price Range		P/Y Avg.
☐ **Complete Set**, knife, fork, and spoon in leather case..............	15.00	20.00	17.00
☐ **Knife Alone**	5.00	7.00	6.00

SHEATH KNIVES

What is more romantic to a young Scout than the thought of a gleaming sheath or hunting knife hanging from his belt? Safety considerations, however, have caused the Boy Scouts to emphasize the folding utility knife and more recently the lock-blade folding sheath knife. The author can find no record of an official sheath knife until the early 1930s, with the arrival of the Remington and the Marble Arms sheath knives. Both of these fine manufacturers had previously advertised in scouting publications, but their knives did not receive the official seal until about 1933.

Marble Arms and Manufacturing Company of Gladstone, Michigan produced two official sheath knives of very high quality.

☐ **Model 1562**, sport knife model, 4″ blade and buffed-leather ring handle, emblem etched on the blade and stamped on the leather sheath, produced from 1933 until 1941....	25.00	40.00	30.00
☐ **Model 1560**, woodcraft model, 4½″ blade, produced from about 1936 until 1941	25.00	40.00	30.00
☐ **Model 1559**, Remington R. H. 50, 4½″ blade, produced from 1933 until about 1941	35.00	40.00	40.00

	Current Price Range		P/Y Avg.
☐ **Model 1561,** Remington R. H. 51, 4″ blade, produced about 1941 ...	25.00	40.00	27.50

UNION CUTLERY COMPANY

Union Cutlery Company of Olean, New York, produced under the name KA-Bar. They produced two knives from mid-1937 until about 1940, when they began producing military knives.

☐ **Model 1553,** KA-Bar 5″ blade.....	25.00	40.00	27.50
☐ **Model 1554,** KA-Bar 3½″ blade	25.00	40.00	27.50
☐ **Model 1555,** KA-Bar also produced the official "Voyager" knife and marlin spike designed for use of Sea Scouts, produced for only a short time in the late 1930s	60.00	70.00	65.00
☐ **Model 1382,** although not a "sheath knife," KA-Bar also produced an official eating set consisting of a knife, fork, and spoon which could fit together in the shape of a pocketknife, produced for only a short time in 1940 and 1941	40.00	50.00	45.00

WESTERN CUTLERY COMPANY

Western Cutlery Company of Boulder, Colorado, has provided the official sheath knife from after World War II to the present.

☐ **Model 1378,** Western saber blade 4½″ with leather ring handle, produced until about 1970 with a leather handle	15.00	20.00	16.00
☐ **Model 1379,** Western grooved blade 5″ with leather ring handle, produced until about 1955.........	15.00	20.00	16.00

	Current Price Range		P/Y Avg.

☐ **Model 1381,** Western Frontiersman, with leather ring handle, produced from about 1955 to about 1970 ....

☐ **Model 1367,** Western 4½″ blade and a dark brown delrin plastic handle, produced from 1970 until 1974 ....   15.00   20.00   18.50

☐ **Model 1364,** Western 3½″ narrow blade and a dark brown delrin plastic handle, produced from 1970 until 1979... ....   10.00   15.00   11.00

JAMBOREE COLLECTIBLES

NATIONAL JAMBOREES

In 1913, Lord Robert S.S. Baden-Powell organized the Imperial Scout Exhibition held in the Exhibition Hall in Birmingham, England. Thousands of scouts had gathered and camped in nearby Perry Hall Park. It was a week-long public display of Scouting skills and games. Baden-Powell then decided that he would stage an international encampment since the exhibition was such a success. He used the word "Jamboree" to distinguish this encampment, which actually means "carousal, a spree of noisy merrymaking." The first Jamboree was planned for 1918, for Scouting's Tenth Anniversary, but World War I interrupted the plan for two years. In 1920, more than 6,000 Scouts from twenty-one nations gathered in London to attend the first World Jamboree. For the first and last time, a Jamboree was held indoors. The activities were extremely successful. Since that first Jamboree in London, Scouts around the world have gathered regularly for jamborees. The first jamborees were international, but soon Scouts in many countries realized that jamborees presented an opportunity to promote Scout ideals, spirit, and citizenship at home.

1935 NATIONAL JAMBOREE

The first Jamboree of the Boy Scouts of America was to be held in Washington, D.C., on an area of 300 acres provided by the national government in the shadow of the Washington monument. Each troop in the country was

1935 First National Jamboree Patch, *violet and yellow, Washington, D. C., $100.00–$150.00*

asked to pick one Scout to attend. Scheduled to have opened in 1935, this Jamboree was not actually held until 1937, because of a polio outbreak in the summer of 1935. The tragic news was reported by President Franklin Roosevelt over the radio. Jamboree collectibles were actually issued or available before the cancellation.

	Current Price Range		P/Y Avg.
☐ **Booklet,** highlights booklet........	45.00	50.00	47.50
☐ **Booklet,** How to Wear the National Jamboree Insignia	5.00	8.00	6.00
☐ **Booklet,** Invitation booklet and brochure	15.00	25.00	15.50
☐ **Booklet,** official equipment list, four pages	10.00	15.00	12.50
☐ **Booklet,** official guide book, foreword by West......................	10.00	20.00	15.00

	Current Price Range		P/Y Avg.
☐ **Booklet,** Pre-Jamboree Camp Training Manual	15.00	25.00	20.50
☐ **Booklet,** promotion brochure, four pages	5.00	8.00	5.50
☐ **Booklet,** promotion brochure, twenty pages	15.00	20.00	15.50
☐ **Flag,** troop flag	150.00	300.00	200.00
☐ **I.D. Card,** identification card	15.00	25.00	20.00
☐ **Neckerchief,** blue leader with red stripe, silk-screened Jamboree logo, 1935	70.00	125.00	95.00
☐ **Neckerchief,** red leader with blue stripe, silk-screened Jamboree logo, 1935	70.00	125.00	95.00
☐ **Pamphlet,** Earning Money for the Jamboree	10.00	15.00	10.50
☐ **Pamphlet,** tentative program	10.00	15.00	10.50
☐ **Ring,** silver, National Jamboree, 1935..................................	35.00	50.00	42.00
☐ **Seal,** paper pennant seal, silver, Twenty-fifth Anniversary, 8″	15.00	25.00	15.50
☐ **Seal,** scout in front of Capitol	7.00	10.00	7.50
☐ **Seal,** scout with staff	7.00	10.00	7.50
☐ **Seal,** National Jamboree, 1¾″ × 2½″, 1935	8.00	10.00	8.50
☐ **Songbook,** National Jamboree, 1935	6.00	8.00	6.50
☐ **Stationery,** official, National Jamboree, 1935........................	7.50	10.00	8.50
☐ **Sticker,** National Jamboree, 1935	8.00	10.00	8.50

1937 NATIONAL JAMBOREE (Prices remain stable because a lot of material was produced, and items are readily available in the marketplace.)

This was the first actual Jamboree, because the 1935 Jamboree was postponed. It was held in Washington, D.C., as originally planned. More than 30,000 Scouts participated, including 400 from foreign countries. This encampment was the greatest collection of boys ever brought together in the

1937 National Jamboree Patch

nation, and lasted ten days. Dan Beard, who was then eighty-seven years old, lit the campfire that opened this event. Scouts were there from every state of the nation and from remote corners of the world. Two Scouts had hiked 10,000 miles from Venezuela to Washington, through jungles and swamps. It took them two years to complete this incredible hike. Four more Scouts sent greetings and regrets that they couldn't attend because they had just recently established a Troop in a leper colony in the Phillipine Islands.

	Current Price Range		P/Y Avg.
☐ **Advertisement,** Coca-Cola ad, color	6.00	8.00	6.50
☐ **Advertisement,** Ad for Jamboree Journals, black and white	3.00	5.00	3.25
☐ **Advertisement,** Ad for Sweet-Orr Uniforms, black and white	3.00	5.00	3.25
☐ **Baggage Tags,** set of three, 3 colors	20.00	30.00	22.50
☐ **Booklet,** Boy Scouts of America preliminary program	8.00	12.00	8.50
☐ **Booklet,** Camp Fire Manual	25.00	30.00	27.50
☐ **Booklet,** Grand National Convocation, 45 pages	20.00	25.00	22.50
☐ **Booklet,** Jamboreeing in Washington	10.00	20.00	12.50
☐ **Booklet,** Journals, bound	50.00	75.00	70.00
☐ **Booklet,** Manual of Policy/Organization/Promotion	10.00	15.00	10.50
☐ **Booklet,** picture book, hard book, hard bound	30.00	45.00	32.50
☐ **Booklet,** Protestant Service	4.00	6.00	4.50
☐ **Booklet,** The Story of the Constitution	6.00	8.00	6.50
☐ **Booklet,** Songs and Jamboree Map	4.00	6.00	4.50
☐ **Booklet,** Trading Post Red book	8.00	12.00	8.50
☐ **Button,** "I'm Going," ⅞"	25.00	30.00	22.50
☐ **Flag,** troop	150.00	200.00	175.00
☐ **Magazine,** article in *Life*	10.00	14.00	10.50
☐ **Neckerchief,** blue, National Jamboree, 1937	60.00	100.00	95.00
☐ **Neckerchief,** red, National Jamboree, 1937	60.00	100.00	95.00
☐ **Neckerchief,** Jamboree Guide	200.00	300.00	250.00

	Current Price Range		P/Y Avg.
☐ **Neckerchief,** leader's, "Old Trails Jamboree"..........................	100.00	140.00	110.00
☐ **Patch,** Headquarters staff, red felt, half moon sectional................	100.00	125.00	105.00
☐ **Patch,** General Staff stripe, purple and gold, rare.....................	75.00	100.00	87.50
☐ **Patch,** World Staff stripe, red and gold, rare	200.00	250.00	225.00
☐ **Patch,** Sea Scout Staff stripe, black and white, very rare........	350.00	400.00	375.00
☐ **Patch,** original, National Jamboree, 1937	70.00	120.00	97.50
☐ **Patch,** Regional Staff stripe, yellow and green, rare.................	40.00	75.00	42.50
☐ **Patch,** shoulder tab, region 7	50.00	75.00	42.50
☐ **Same as above,** but region 1....	50.00	75.00	42.50
☐ **Same as above,** but region 2....	50.00	75.00	42.50
☐ **Same as above,** but region 3....	50.00	75.00	42.50
☐ **Same as above,** but region 4....	50.00	75.00	42.50
☐ **Same as above,** but region 5....	50.00	75.00	42.50
☐ **Same as above,** but region 6....	50.00	75.00	42.50
☐ **Same as above,** but region 9....	50.00	75.00	42.50
☐ **Same as above,** but region 10...	50.00	75.00	42.50
☐ **Same as above,** but region 11...	50.00	75.00	42.50
☐ **Ring,** silver, National Jamboree, 1937	35.00	50.00	42.50

1950 NATIONAL JAMBOREE

The second Jamboree was held in 1950, at Valley Forge, Pennsylvania. It was attended by over 47,000 Scouts, Explorers, and Leaders. Scouts were present from every state and 370 from twenty foreign nations. This Jamboree was opened by President Harry S. Truman, who reminded the boys in his message that Scouting was built on the ideal of brotherhood. He continued to say, "We must show them, over and over again, that fellowship is possible between men of different nations, different colors, and different creeds." This message was especially relevant since the United States had just ended World War II.

1950 Second National Jamboree Patch, *George Washington kneeling, yellow and blue, Valley Forge,* **$17.50–$30.00**

	Current Price Range		P/Y Avg.
☐ **Baggage Tag,** National Jamboree, 1950	6.00	8.00	8.50
☐ **Booklet,** Applicant and Personal Equipment Catalog	8.00	10.00	8.50
☐ **Booklet,** Guide for Unit Leaders	8.00	10.00	8.50
☐ **Booklet,** How to Publicize the Jamboree	4.00	5.00	4.25
☐ **Booklet,** Jamboree Adventure Book	6.00	8.00	6.50
☐ **Booklet,** Jamboree Training Manual	6.00	8.00	6.50

	Current Price Range		P/Y Avg.
☐ **Booklet,** Jamboreeing.............	4.00	5.00	4.25
☐ **Booklet,** Manual of Policies/Organization/Promotion	4.00	6.00	4.25
☐ **Booklet,** Patrol Duty Roster, 11" × 19"	4.00	6.00	4.25
☐ **Booklet,** Philadelphia Inquirer Book	5.00	7.00	5.25
☐ **Booklet,** Picture Book..............	12.00	18.00	12.50
☐ **Booklet,** Valley Forge Guidebook ..	8.00	10.00	8.50
☐ **Coin,** chrome, National Jamboree, 1950, reproduction................	3.00	5.00	3.25
☐ **Coin,** gold, National Jamboree, 1950	12.50	20.00	16.00
☐ **Decal,** National Jamboree, 1950....	5.00	7.00	5.50
☐ **Diary,** National Jamboree, 1950	9.00	12.00	9.50
☐ **Key Chain,** National Jamboree, 1950	14.00	17.00	14.50
☐ **Knife,** miniature sheath knife	10.00	15.00	10.50
☐ **Magazine,** article in *Life* magazine	5.00	7.00	5.25
☐ **Magazine,** article in *National Geographic*......................................	3.00	5.00	3.25
☐ **Map,** Pennsylvania R.R............	3.00	5.00	3.25
☐ **Map,** Sunoco Oil Co.	4.00	7.00	4.25
☐ **Neckerchief,** cotton, National Jamboree, 1950	20.00	35.00	32.50
☐ **Neckerchief,** silk, National Jamboree, 1950	20.00	40.00	27.50
☐ **Paperweight,** cannonballs	7.00	9.00	7.50
☐ **Paperweight,** covered wagon.....	7.00	9.00	7.50
☐ **Patch,** pocket, canvas.............	17.50	30.00	22.50
☐ **Patch,** pocket, embroidered.......	20.00	30.00	25.00
☐ **Photo,** aerial photo................	4.00	6.00	4.25
☐ **Plaque,** Jamboree logo	15.00	20.00	17.50
☐ **Ring,** silver, National Jamboree, 1950	25.00	35.00	27.50
☐ **Seal,** National Jamboree, 1950 ...	12.00	20.00	12.50
☐ **Shirt,** T-shirt......................	5.00	10.00	7.50

	Current Price Range		P/Y Avg.

	Current Price Range		P/Y Avg.
☐ **Tie Chain,** National Jamboree, 1950	6.00	8.00	6.50

1953 NATIONAL JAMBOREE

The third Jamboree took place in the summer of 1953 at Irvine Ranch in Southern California. It was attended by 45,000 boys with their leaders, who stayed in 30,000 tents on 3,000 acres. This National event was the greatest single peacetime rail movement of personnel, troops, or any other group in America's history. The statistics for this Jamboree are phenomenal; for example: ninety freight-car loads of food and supplies, plus ten freight-car loads of charcoal to do the cooking; 1,224 heads of steer to supply beef for the thousands of meals cooked by individual patrols; 60,000 quarts of milk; 34,694 pounds of butter; 175,000 loaves of bread, and 480,000 pancakes. Probably the most remembered event was that of the candle lighting ceremony, in which over 45,000 Scouts lit their candles and recited the Scout Oath.

	Current Price Range		P/Y Avg.
☐ **Advertisement,** for Swift meats, black and white...................	3.00	5.00	3.50
☐ **Armband,** G.H.Q. Service Troop-Alpha Phi Omega..................	30.00	40.00	32.50
☐ **Award,** Achievement Award, National Jamboree, 1953.............	5.00	7.50	4.50
☐ **Booklet,** "All Aboard Flyer"	4.00	5.00	4.50
☐ **Booklet,** Guide for Unit Leaders....	5.00	7.50	3.25
☐ **Booklet,** Guidebook to Jamboree Uniforms and Equipment..........	6.00	8.00	6.50
☐ **Booklet,** Jamboree book..........	12.00	15.00	12.50
☐ **Booklet,** Jamboree Equipment for Troop and Patrols	5.00	7.50	6.00
☐ **Booklet,** Information book, sixty pages	4.00	6.00	4.25
☐ **Booklet,** Manual of Policies/Organization.........................	5.00	7.50	4.25
☐ **Booklet,** On to the Jamboree	5.00	7.50	3.25

1953 Third National Jamboree Patch, *covered wagon, blue border, Irvine Ranch, California,* **$12.50–$20.00**

	Current Price Range		P/Y Avg.
☐ **Booklet,** On to the Pacific	5.00	7.50	3.25
☐ **Booklet,** picture book	12.00	15.00	12.50
☐ **Booklet,** Surf Bathing Report, fifty-two pages..........................	8.00	10.00	8.50
☐ **Booklet,** telephone pocket book....	5.00	10.00	5.50
☐ **Button,** "I'm Going"	12.00	15.00	12.50
☐ **Coin,** Circle B Roundup...........	5.00	7.00	5.25
☐ **Coin,** National Jamboree, 1953.....	10.00	14.00	11.00
☐ **Conservation Packet,** National Jamboree, 1953	18.00	22.00	18.50
☐ **Decal,** National Jamboree, 1953....	5.00	8.00	5.50
☐ **Diary,** National Jamboree, 1953	10.00	13.00	10.00
☐ **Flag,** troop flag, National Jamboree, 1953	75.00	100.00	80.00
☐ **Keychain Tab,** National Jamboree, 1953	7.00	10.00	7.50

	Current Price Range		P/Y Avg.
☐ **Magazine,** cover and article in *Scouting Magazine*............	3.00	5.00	3.25
☐ **Map,** Region 12, S.F. and L.A.....	3.00	4.00	3.25
☐ **Maps,** by L.A. Examiner, 13″ × 17″...........................	3.00	6.00	3.25
☐ **Medallion,** National Jamboree, 1953..............................	12.00	15.00	12.50
☐ **Neckerchief,** National Jamboree, 1953..............................	12.50	20.00	16.00
☐ **Neckerchief Slide,** wood and leather wagon....................	8.00	10.00	8.50
☐ **Patch,** back, National Jamboree, 1953..............................	70.00	80.00	72.00
☐ **Patch,** contingent, Region 5	12.50	17.50	14.00
☐ **Patch,** contingent, Region 12	15.00	18.00	15.50
☐ **Patch,** Aquatics Staff..............	100.00	150.00	125.00
☐ **Patch,** host, Region 12...........	11.00	15.00	11.50
☐ **Patch,** pocket, National Jamboree, 1953..............................	12.50	20.00	16.00
☐ **Pennant,** large, National Jamboree, 1953..........................	50.00	60.00	52.50
☐ **Scarf,** silk, woman's..............	15.00	25.00	20.00
☐ **Seal,** National Jamboree, 3½″, 1953..............................	4.00	6.00	4.25
☐ **Tags,** set of four pigeon racing tags................................	6.00	9.00	6.50

1957 NATIONAL JAMBOREE

This was the fourth National Jamboree, and it was held in the historic site of Valley Forge, Pennsylvania. An unbelievable 52,000 Scouts attended this camp. A special event was that of a visit by the then vice-president of the United States, Richard M. Nixon.

	Current Price Range		P/Y Avg.
☐ **Advertisement,** for 7-Up, color ...	5.00	6.00	5.25
☐ **Baggage Tags,** National Jamboree, 1957	3.00	5.00	3.25

1957 Fourth National Jamboree Patch, *George Washington kneeling, red trim, red embroidered letters, red and blue on white, Valley Forge, $10.00–$17.50*

	Current Price Range		P/Y Avg.
☐ **Belt Buckle,** two-piece, pewter "Noc"	12.50	14.00	13.00
☐ **Booklet,** Conservation Magic for Boy Scouts	4.00	6.00	2.25
☐ **Booklet,** Guidebook for Unit Leaders	6.00	8.00	6.50
☐ **Booklet,** Guidebook to Jamboree Uniforms and Equipment	5.00	8.00	5.50
☐ **Booklet,** Jamboree Book	9.00	11.00	9.50
☐ **Booklet,** Jamboree Equipment for Troop and Patrols	4.00	6.00	2.25

	Current Price Range		P/Y Avg.
☐ **Booklet,** Manual of Policies and Organization	5.00	8.00	5.25
☐ **Booklet,** picture book	7.00	12.00	7.50
☐ **Booklet,** promotional booklet, large	7.00	9.00	7.25
☐ **Booklet,** Section Leader's Guide-book	10.00	12.00	10.50
☐ **Booklet,** souvenir book	6.00	0.00	8.50
☐ **Booklet,** telephone book	4.00	6.00	4.25
☐ **Booklet,** Trading Post Services ...	4.00	5.00	1.00
☐ **Booklet,** WJ-Indaba-Moot Picture Log Book	18.00	22.00	18.50
☐ **Button,** pinback, Fourth Boy Scouts Jamboree	5.00	7.50	4.25
☐ **Button,** pinback, also ribbon and bell..............................	7.00	8.00	7.50
☐ **Cachet Cover,** National Jamboree cancellation, 1957	2.00	3.00	1.25
☐ **Certificate of Participation**	8.00	10.00	8.50
☐ **Charm,** brass, National Jamboree, 1957	9.00	11.00	9.50
☐ **China Cup,** small, National Jamboree, 1957.......................	5.00	7.50	4.25
☐ **Coin,** brass, National Jamboree, 1957	12.00	15.00	12.50
☐ **Coin,** gilt finish, National Jamboree, 1957	2.00	4.00	2.25
☐ **Decal,** National Jamboree, 1957....	5.00	6.00	5.25
☐ **Envelopes,** official logo	3.00	5.00	3.25
☐ **Flag,** troop flag, National Jamboree, 1957	75.00	100.00	80.00
☐ **Identification Bracelet,** silver, National Jamboree, 1957.............	15.00	18.00	15.75
☐ **Identification Card**	5.00	7.50	4.25
☐ **Map,** Atlantic Oil Co. map folder....	2.00	3.00	1.00
☐ **Map,** Boy Scouts of America/Freedoms Foundation—historic map of Valley Forge	4.00	6.00	4.25

	Current Price Range		P/Y Avg.
☐ **Map,** guide for Philadelphia Tour ...	2.00	4.00	1.25
☐ **Map,** Keystone Auto Club	3.00	4.00	3.25
☐ **Map,** Pennsylvania R.R. souvenir...	3.00	8.00	3.25
☐ **Map,** Sunoco, large	3.00	4.00	3.25
☐ **Map,** Sunoco, souvenir...........	4.00	5.00	4.25
☐ **Menus,** complete set	8.00	10.00	8.25
☐ **Movie,** Banners Over Valley Forge, 16mm..............................	175.00	225.00	190.00
☐ **Movie,** Let's Go to the Jamboree, 16mm..............................	125.00	175.00	145.00
☐ **Neckerchief,** Cub visitation day	30.00	40.00	32.50
☐ **Neckerchief,** National Jamboree, 1957	7.50	15.00	10.00
☐ **Newspaper,** Daily Papers, Journals, set	6.00	8.00	6.25
☐ **Newspaper,** scene newspaper....	2.00	4.00	2.25
☐ **Newspaper,** souvenir newspaper...	5.00	7.50	6.00
☐ **Patch,** back, National Jamboree, 1957	18.00	25.00	18.50
☐ **Patch,** leather, National Jamboree, 1957	17.50	35.00	17.50
☐ **Patch,** Nassau Council Contingent.................................	8.00	10.00	8.50
☐ **Patch,** pocket, National Jamboree, 1957	7.50	15.00	12.50
☐ **Patch,** Potawatomie Contingent	14.00	16.00	14.50
☐ **Patch,** Region 5	10.00	12.50	11.00
☐ **Same as above,** but Region 6 ...	10.00	15.00	12.00
☐ **Pennant,** large, National Jamboree, 1957	12.00	14.00	12.50
☐ **Pennant,** small, National Jamboree, 1957	9.00	10.00	9.50
☐ **Pin,** brass, lapel, National Jamboree, 1957	5.00	8.00	5.50
☐ **Pin,** octagon, lapel	15.00	20.00	15.50
☐ **Pin,** round, lapel	10.00	17.50	15.50
☐ **Postcard,** large, National Jamboree, 1957	1.00	3.00	1.25

	Current Price Range		P/Y Avg.
☐ **Postcard,** Pepsi-Cola, National Jamboree, 1957	2.00	3.00	2.25
☐ **Poster,** general program schedule poster	4.00	5.00	4.25
☐ **Poster,** National Jamboree, 13″ × 19″, 1957	20.00	25.00	20.00
☐ **Sardines,** National Jamboree, 1957	11.00	14.00	11.50
☐ **Scarf,** ladies', silk scarf	9.00	11.00	9.50
☐ **Seals,** set of four, Troop 37	3.00	5.00	0.25
☐ **Seals,** set of eight, National Jamboree, 1957	6.00	8.00	6.25
☐ **Seals,** set of six, in Esperanto	2.00	3.00	2.25
☐ **Shirt,** T-Shirt, National Jamboree, 1957	5.00	10.00	7.50
☐ **Tack,** walking stick, brass	4.00	6.00	4.25
☐ **Tie Bar,** National Jamboree, 1957	10.00	15.00	16.00
☐ **Tie Chain,** National Jamboree, 1957	4.00	6.00	4.25
☐ **Watch,** pocket, National Jamboree, 1957	10.00	25.00	16.00
☐ **Wooden Token,** money chip, National Jamboree, 1957.............	3.00	5.00	3.25

1960 NATIONAL JAMBOREE

The fifth National Jamboree was named the Golden Jubilee Jamboree to commemorate the Fiftieth Anniversary of Scouting in the United States. It was held on the "Reverse J. Diamond Ranch" in Colorado Springs, Colorado. Set right in the Rocky Mountains, this was the site for over 56,000 Scouts from every state and 650 foreign Scouts. The campsite covered four square miles with tents, and this became the fourth largest city in Colorado for one week. President Eisenhower visited the campsite and was named the honorary President of the Scouts. A great number of programs involved the Old West and the M.C. was "Marshall Matt Dillion" (James Arness) of Dodge City, and TV's "Gunsmoke." The attendance at this Jamboree was, and still remains, the largest encampment of Scouts in a single camp.

1960 Fiftieth Anniversary of B.S.A. Patch, Fifth National Jamboree, red on yellow, black embroidered letters, B.S.A. monogram in center, Colorado Springs, $6.00–$12.50

	Current Price Range		P/Y Avg.
☐ **Advertisement,** Chap Stick, black and white	3.00	4.00	3.25
☐ **Advertisement,** Scouts at religious service, color	3.00	4.00	3.25
☐ **Award,** Jamboree Adventure Award	5.00	10.00	6.00
☐ **Baggage Tag,** National Jamboree, 1960	2.00	3.00	2.25
☐ **Belt Slide,** souvenir National Jamboree, 1960........................	2.00	3.00	2.25
☐ **Booklet,** Camp Scenes	2.00	3.00	2.25

	Current Price Range		P/Y Avg.
☐ **Booklet,** Guide for Unit Leaders....	3.00	6.00	3.25
☐ **Booklet,** Information Manual......	4.00	6.00	4.25
☐ **Booklet,** An Invitation to the Seventh National Scout Jamboree	4.00	6.00	4.25
☐ **Booklet,** On to the Golden Jamboree	2.00	3.00	2.25
☐ **Booklet,** picture book, National Jamboree, 1960	6.00	10.00	6.50
☐ **Booklet,** Policies and Organization Manual	5.00	7.00	5.25
☐ **Booklet,** Pre-Jamboree Training Outline	5.00	7.00	5.25
☐ **Booklet,** Section Leader's Guide ...	6.00	8.00	6.50
☐ **Booklet,** souvenir book	6.00	8.00	6.50
☐ **Booklet,** Unit Guidebook..........	4.00	6.00	4.25
☐ **Cachet Envelope,** National Jamboree, 1960......................	3.00	5.00	3.15
☐ **Coin,** bronze, National Jamboree, 1960.............................	3.00	4.00	3.15
☐ **Coin,** gilt finish, National Jamboree, 1960	3.00	4.00	3.15
☐ **Decal,** National Jamboree, 1960....	4.00	6.00	4.25
☐ **Flag,** troop flag, National Jamboree, 1960	50.00	75.00	62.50
☐ **Key Chain,** token, Kewaunee, Wisconsin, National Jamboree, 1960	2.00	3.00	2.25
☐ **Magazine,** *Boy's Life* cover	5.00	7.00	5.25
☐ **Magazine,** *Saturday Evening Post* cover.................................	4.00	5.00	4.15
☐ **Map,** Carter (Humble) Oil Co., souvenir	2.00	4.00	2.25
☐ **Map,** Conoco	3.00	4.00	3.15
☐ **Map,** framed, Adventure Award, 18″ x 22″..........................	6.00	8.00	6.50
☐ **Monkey Clip,** National Jamboree, 1960	7.00	9.00	7.50

	Current Price Range		P/Y Avg.
☐ **Neckerchief,** Covered Wagon Council Contingent	7.50	15.00	10.00
☐ **Neckerchief,** National Jamboree, 1960	7.50	12.50	10.00
☐ **Newspaper,** daily papers, complete set	12.00	15.00	12.50
☐ **Newspaper,** *Scene* magazine	3.00	5.00	3.25
☐ **Patch,** back, National Jamboree, 1960	15.00	30.00	15.50
☐ **Patch,** Crossroads of America Council Contingent, National Jamboree, 1960	12.00	16.00	12.50
☐ **Patch,** hat, National Jamboree, 1960	5.00	10.00	7.00
☐ **Patch,** pocket, Jamboree	4.00	6.00	5.00
☐ **Patch,** pocket, Field Day	8.00	10.00	9.00
☐ **Patch,** Rifle Shooting Winner	50.00	75.00	62.50
☐ **Patch,** Region Nine Contingent, National Jamboree, 1960	10.00	15.00	12.50
☐ **Pennant,** National Jamboree, 1960, 9″ × 26″	15.00	20.00	17.00
☐ **Photo,** aerial, 8″ × 10″	2.00	4.00	3.00
☐ **Pin,** bucking bronco, National Jamboree, 1960	6.00	12.50	9.00
☐ **Pin,** lapel, gilt finish	5.00	10.00	7.00
☐ **Ring,** silver, adjustable, National Jamboree, 1960	20.00	30.00	25.00
☐ **Sardines,** National Jamboree, 1960	7.00	10.00	7.50
☐ **Shirt,** T-shirt	5.00	10.00	6.25
☐ **Stationery,** National Jamboree, 1960	1.00	2.00	1.25

1964 NATIONAL JAMBOREE

The 1964 Jamboree was held, once again, at Valley Forge, Pennsylvania. This site hosted some 53,000 Scouts from every state. The Scouts were honored to have President Lyndon B. Johnson attend and give a closing speech. A special moment came when Lady Baden-Powell called on the

1904 Sixth National Jamboree Patch, *red white, and blue, Valley Forge, $6.00–$9.00*

boys to "go deeper into the well of the spirit of Scouting." She received a five-minute standing ovation.

	Current Price Range		P/Y Avg.
☐ **Advertisement,** shows back patch and neckerchief, color	3.00	4.00	3.25
☐ **Advertisement,** shows neckerchief and Coke bottle, color	3.00	5.00	3.50
☐ **Advertisement,** Seven-Up color	3.00	4.00	3.25
☐ **Advertisement,** "Super Camp Cookery," Campbell's	1.00	2.00	1.25
☐ **Baggage Tag,** blue, Jamboree, 1964	3.00	5.00	4.00
☐ **Belt Buckle,** Max Silber	50.00	65.00	62.50
☐ **Belt Buckle,** hinged loop	10.00	15.00	12.50
☐ **Booklet,** Administrative Manual	4.00	5.00	4.25
☐ **Booklet,** Guide for Troop Leaders	4.00	6.00	4.25
☐ **Booklet,** Handbook and Diary	2.50	5.00	2.15
☐ **Booklet,** Information and Policies Manual	4.00	6.00	4.25

	Current Price Range		P/Y Avg.
☐ **Booklet,** Personal Equipment Catalog	4.00	5.00	4.15
☐ **Booklet,** picture book, National Jamboree, 1964	6.00	8.00	6.25
☐ **Booklet,** Section Leader's Guide ...	3.00	5.00	2.15
☐ **Booklet,** Sixth National Jamboree, 44 pages, color	5.00	6.00	5.25
☐ **Booklet,** souvenir book	4.00	6.00	4.25
☐ **Cap,** National Jamboree, 1964	5.00	7.00	5.15
☐ **Coin,** brass, National Jamboree, 1964	3.00	5.00	3.15
☐ **Coin,** bronze, National Jamboree, 1964	8.00	9.50	9.00
☐ **Coin,** Continental Currency, National Jamboree, 1964	2.00	6.00	2.50
☐ **Decal,** National Jamboree, 1964....	3.00	4.00	3.15
☐ **Diary,** National Jamboree, 1964	5.00	7.00	5.25
☐ **Flag,** troop, National Jamboree, 1964	50.00	75.00	62.50
☐ **Litter Bag,** National Jamboree, 1964	2.00	3.00	2.15
☐ **Magazine,** *Boy's Life* article	3.00	4.00	3.15
☐ **Map,** Atlantic Oil Co	3.00	5.00	3.15
☐ **Map,** historic Valley Forge map.....	1.00	3.00	1.10
☐ **Map,** Sunoco, National Jamboree, 1964	2.00	4.00	2.10
☐ **Menus,** booklet of meals, National Jamboree, 1964	5.00	7.00	5.50
☐ **Mug,** National Jamboree, 1964 ...			
☐ **Neckerchief,** National Jamboree, 1964	30.00	40.00	35.00
☐ **Neckerchief,** red with black emblem, rare...........................	15.00	20.00	15.50
☐ **Neckerchief,** souvenir, National Jamboree, 1964	10.00	12.00	9.00
☐ **Neckerchief Slide,** enameled, National Jamboree, 1964	4.00	6.00	4.15

	Current Price Range		P/Y Avg.
☐ **Neckerchief Slide,** Region 2 Contingent, enameled	4.00	6.00	4.15
☐ **Neckerchief Slide,** Region 12 Contingent, black bull	7.50	15.00	5.25
☐ **Newspaper,** Journals, set of eight	7.00	9.00	7.25
☐ **Newspaper,** scenes, National Jamboree, 1964	2.00	3.00	2.15
☐ **Paperweight,** lucite, National Jamboree, 1964	5.00	7.00	5.25
☐ **Patch,** .22 Caliber shotgun	50.00	75.00	62.50
☐ **Patch,** contingent patch, Region 5	8.00	10.00	8.50
☐ **Same as above,** but Region 6 ...	5.00	7.00	5.25
☐ **Same as above,** but Region 12 ..	8.00	12.00	8.25
☐ **Patch,** Rifle shooting	50.00	75.00	62.50
☐ **Patch,** jacket, National Jamboree, 1964	12.00	15.00	12.50
☐ **Patch,** pocket, embroidered, white or blue back, National Jamboree, 1964	5.00	10.00	7.00
☐ **Patch,** leather, small, National Jamboree, 1964	8.00	10.00	8.50
☐ **Same as above,** but large	12.00	15.00	12.50
☐ **Patch,** pocket woven	7.50	10.00	8.00
☐ **Pencil,** National Jamboree, 1964 ...	1.00	2.00	1.25
☐ **Pennant,** small, National Jamboree, 1964	5.00	7.00	5.25
☐ **Pennant,** large, National Jamboree, 1964, 9″ x 26″	18.00	22.00	18.50
☐ **Pin,** enameled, National Jamboree, 1964	4.00	5.00	4.25
☐ **Sardines,** National Jamboree, 1964	7.00	9.00	7.25
☐ **Scarf,** ladies', silk, National Jamboree, 1964	7.50	10.00	8.50
☐ **Seeds,** dogwood seeds, National Jamboree, 1964	2.00	3.00	2.15

	Current Price Range		P/Y Avg.
☐ **Shirt,** T-Shirt, National Jamboree, 1964	4.00	6.00	4.25
☐ **Stationery,** sheet, National Jamboree, 1964........................	2.00	3.00	2.15
☐ **Tie Bar,** small brass, National Jamboree, 1964	4.00	5.00	4.15
☐ **Tie Bar,** enameled, National Jamboree, 1964........................	5.00	7.00	5.25

1969 NATIONAL JAMBOREE

The seventh National Scout Jamboree took place at the beautiful Farragut State Park in Idaho. The park was nicknamed "tent city." Over 35,000 Scouts were in attendance at this jamboree.

This was a period of turmoil and unrest among the youth of America, but none of this was present at the National Jamboree, where Scout Spirit was ever-present as an example for the rest of the country.

☐ **Ashtray,** ceramic, round, 14 cm.	2.00	3.00	2.15
☐ **Baggage Tag,** many varieties.....	2.00	4.00	3.00
☐ **Belt,** leather with buckle	5.00	10.00	7.00
☐ **Brochure,** "An Invitation to the Seventh National Jamboree"......	3.00	4.00	3.25
☐ **Brochure,** State Park information, postcard size	2.00	3.00	2.15
☐ **Brochure,** "Outdoor Fish Cookery".................................	2.00	3.00	2.50
☐ **Brochure,** "Welcome to Idaho"	2.00	3.00	2.50
☐ **Book,** Camp Leader's Manual	4.00	5.00	4.50
☐ **Book,** Conservation Book	5.00	6.00	5.10
☐ **Book,** Jamboree Picture Book	6.00	7.00	6.15
☐ **Book,** Pre-Jamboree Training Manual...............................	4.00	6.00	5.00
☐ **Book,** Program Guide Book.......	5.00	6.00	5.10
☐ **Book,** Promotion Guide Book	3.00	4.00	3.15
☐ **Book,** Service Manual.............	3.00	4.00	3.15

1969 Seventh National Jamboree Patch, embroidered deer in center, gold B.S.A. monogram, Idaho, $8.00–$10.00

	Current Price Range		P/Y Avg.
☐ **Book,** Souvenir Book.............	6.00	7.00	6.15
☐ **Cards,** D. and S. Building to Serve cards, two types	2.00	3.00	2.10
☐ **Coin,** brass, National Jamboree, 1969	3.00	4.00	3.15
☐ **Coin,** bronze, National Jamboree, 1969	7.00	8.00	6.50

	Current Price Range		P/Y Avg.
☐ **Coin,** wooden nickel, N. Idaho lumbering industry	1.00	2.00	.75
☐ **Cup,** coffee	4.00	6.00	5.15
☐ **Decal,** National Jamboree, 1969	1.00	2.00	2.15
☐ **Decal,** Cabinet Gorge Dam	2.00	3.00	2.15
☐ **Diary,** Jamboree Issue	3.00	5.00	4.00
☐ **Emblem,** metal emblem for hiking staff	3.00	4.00	3.25
☐ **Flag,** Troop	50.00	75.00	62.50
☐ **Jewelry,** Bolo tie	3.00	4.00	3.15
☐ **Jewelry,** brass clutch pin	3.00	4.00	3.15
☐ **Jewelry,** cuff links	3.00	4.00	3.15
☐ **Jewelry,** enameled clutch pin	4.00	5.00	4.15
☐ **Jewelry,** enameled fob	1.00	2.00	1.15
☐ **Jewelry,** enameled sweater clip, no chain	2.00	3.00	2.25
☐ **Jewelry,** lapel pin, gilt finish	2.00	3.00	2.15
☐ **Jewelry,** tie tack	3.00	4.00	3.15
☐ **Magazine,** *Boy's Life* issue	3.00	5.00	4.10
☐ **Magazine,** *Scouting* issue	2.00	3.00	2.15
☐ **Map,** Seventh National Jamboree, 1969, 96 pages	4.00	5.00	4.50
☐ **Map,** hiking trails	2.00	3.00	2.50
☐ **Map,** Pepsi-Cola, souvenir	2.00	3.00	2.50
☐ **Map,** Pop-up	3.00	4.00	3.15
☐ **Neckerchief,** Trading post staff, A, B, C, or D	20.00	25.00	22.50
☐ **Neckerchief,** Trading post staff	20.00	25.00	22.50
☐ **Neckerchief Slide,** Regional	3.00	5.00	4.25
☐ **Newspaper,** National Jamboree Journal, set of 9, 1969	8.00	9.00	8.25
☐ **Patch,** Building to serve, segment	10.00	15.00	12.50
☐ **Patch,** jacket emblem	7.50	12.50	9.50
☐ **Patch,** large, black, leather	7.50	12.50	12.50
☐ **Patch,** pocket emblem	4.00	6.00	5.25
☐ **Patch,** small, black, leather	7.00	9.00	7.50
☐ **Pennant,** large	7.50	12.50	10.00
☐ **Pennant,** small	5.00	10.00	7.00

	Current Price Range		P/Y Avg.
☐ **Postcards,** set of seven...........	9.00	11.00	9.50
☐ **Spoon**	10.00	15.00	12.50
☐ **Stationery Sheet,** many various types...............................	2.00	3.00	2.15
☐ **Totem Pole,** 7″	2.00	3.00	2.15

1973 NATIONAL JAMBOREE

The eighth National Jamboree was the first ever dual Jamboree. Jamboree West was held at Farragut State Park, Idaho, and Jamboree East was at Moraine State Park, Pennsylvania. This Jamboree touched the lives of 72,000 Scouts; 28,000 at West and 44,000 at East. The old saying of "A troop travels on its stomach" applied here. The Scouts used 136,000 loaves of bread, 714,000 quarts of milk, 72,000 trout, 204,000 chickens, 425,000 eggs, 3,500 beef cattle on the hoof, and 340 tons of charcoal to cook it all.

☐ **Armband,** Order of the Arrow Service Corps	10.00	15.00	12.50
☐ **Baggage Tag,** several variations ...	1.00	2.00	1.15
☐ **Band Aid Holder,** National Jamboree, 1973	4.00	5.00	4.15
☐ **Belt,** leather with buckle	7.50	10.00	9.50
☐ **Belt Buckle,** Max Silbur issue	30.00	35.00	32.50
☐ **Belt Buckle,** National Jamboree, 1973	4.00	5.00	4.25
☐ **Booklet,** Scout Information Guide and Diary	2.00	3.00	2.15
☐ **Brochure,** "Your Invitation to Attend"	1.00	2.00	.75
☐ **Button,** fishing permit, celluloid ...	4.00	5.00	4.50
☐ **Card,** wallet.........................	1.00	2.00	.75
☐ **Coin,** brass	2.00	3.00	2.15
☐ **Coin,** gilt finish	2.00	3.00	2.15
☐ **Coin,** silver gilt	7.00	8.00	7.25
☐ **Coin,** souvenir set.................	11.00	13.00	11.50
☐ **Coin,** Troop 101, bronze	3.00	4.00	3.25

1973 National Scout Jamboree, $3.00–$4.00

	Current Price Range		P/Y Avg.
☐ **Coin,** Troop 101, silver	12.00	14.00	12.50
☐ **Coin,** wooden nickel, Philadelphia Council	1.00	2.00	1.10
☐ **Decal,** National Jamboree, 1973....	1.00	2.00	1.50
☐ **Directions,** National Jamboree Directions, staff, set of three, 1973....	3.00	4.00	3.25
☐ **Emblem,** small metal, gummed	2.00	3.00	2.25
☐ **Envelope,** official..................	1.00	2.00	.75
☐ **Flag,** Jamboree troop	50.00	75.00	62.50
☐ **Folder,** West Welcome............	1.00	2.00	.75
☐ **Folder,** Woodbadge Conclave	4.00	5.00	4.25
☐ **Handkerchief,** official	3.00	4.00	3.25
☐ **Jewelry,** bolo tie	3.00	5.00	4.00
☐ **Jewelry,** brass lapel pin...........	3.00	5.00	2.10

	Current Price Range		P/Y Avg.
☐ **Jewelry,** enameled cuff-links......	3.00	4.00	3.25
☐ **Jewelry,** enameled hatpin.........	2.00	3.00	2.10
☐ **Jewelry,** enameled tie tack	2.00	3.00	2.10
☐ **Jewelry,** enameled tie tack with chain.............................	2.00	3.00	2.10
☐ **Jewelry,** gilt-finished lapel pin	2.00	3.00	2.10
☐ **Jewelry,** horseshoe bolo tie.......	10.00	12.50	11.00
☐ **Jewelry,** pewter fob type, key-chain................................	3.00	4.00	3.25
☐ **Knife,** pen knife/money clip	4.00	5.00	4.25
☐ **Lost and Found,** L. F. Center, "Urgent Notice"	1.00	2.00	1.15
☐ **Lost and Found,** "Item Located" notice	1.00	2.00	1.15
☐ **Lost and Found,** "Visitors/Participant Inquiry for Lost Item"........	1.00	2.00	1.15
☐ **Map,** National Jamboree, 1973....	1.00	2.00	1.15
☐ **Map,** Exxon Company souvenir map.................................	1.00	2.00	1.15
☐ **Mug,** National Jamboree, 1973 ...	3.00	4.00	3.15
☐ **Neckerchief,** Trading post services staff, A, B, C, or D..........	20.00	25.00	22.50
☐ **Neckerchief,** Trading post services staff............................	20.00	25.00	22.50
☐ **Neckerchief,** National Jamboree, souvenir, 1973.....................	2.00	3.00	2.25
☐ **Neckerchief Slide,** metal, pewter color	3.00	4.00	3.50
☐ **Neckerchief Slide,** plastic	2.00	3.00	2.50
☐ **Newspaper,** *National Jamboree Journal,* set, 1973..................	5.00	8.00	5.50
☐ **Parking Pass,** visitors, two-dollar pass	1.00	2.00	1.25
☐ **Patch,** Kybo patrol	20.00	30.00	25.00
☐ **Patch,** back, Trading Post C	15.00	20.00	15.00
☐ **Patch,** jacket	3.00	4.00	3.25
☐ **Patch,** Aquatic staff	30.00	40.00	35.00
☐ **Patch,** Service corps, OA	25.00	30.00	27.50

	Current Price Range		P/Y Avg.
☐ **Patch,** wide game strip............	4.00	5.00	4.25
☐ **Patch,** World Friendship game strip.................................	6.00	8.00	6.25
☐ **Pennant,** large, National Jamboree, 1973	6.00	7.00	6.50
☐ **Postcard,** picture, sold at Jamboree	1.00	2.00	.75
☐ **Shirt,** men's large, new	5.00	7.50	6.05
☐ **Stationery Set,** official issue......	2.00	3.00	2.25
☐ **Towel,** hand.......................	3.00	4.00	3.15
☐ **Wall Tile,** colorful ceramic tile, 6″ x 6″	4.00	5.00	4.50

1977 NATIONAL JAMBOREE

The 1977 National Jamboree took place at Moraine State Park, Pennsylvania, which the Scouts nicknamed "More Rain" because of the rain-soaked grounds. 28,000 Scouts attended this event.

In 1907, the world's first Scouts were in camp on the small island of Brownsea off the coast of England. That first camp had twenty-one boys and two adults. One of the leaders was Robert S.S. Baden-Powell, the founder of Scouting. The Brownsea Island camp was recreated at the 1977 National Scout Jamboree. Twenty-one Scouts and two leaders played the games, practiced the skills, and wore the makeshift clothing worn by the world's first Scouts in August, 1907. If Baden-Powell, who died in 1941, could have seen his recreated Scout camp and the gigantic encampment that surrounded it, he would have been astonished and delighted.

	Current Price Range		P/Y Avg.
☐ **Ashtray,** Jamboree inscribed	2.00	3.00	2.15
☐ **Baggage Tags,** six different, color, region.............................	9.00	10.00	9.25
☐ **Baggage Tags,** Headquarter, subcamps 31–35	4.00	6.00	5.00
☐ **Belt,** leather, with buckle..........	7.00	8.00	7.25
☐ **Belt Buckle........................**	5.00	7.50	6.00

1977 Ninth National Jamboree Patch, *red, white, and blue with gold B.S.A. monogram, $2.00–$3.00*

	Current Price Range		P/Y Avg.
☐ **Belt Buckle,** Max Silber...........	15.00	20.00	17.00
☐ **Book,** Administrative Guide	1.00	2.00	.75
☐ **Book,** Administrative Guidebook ..	2.00	3.00	2.15
☐ **Book,** *Boy's Life* Jamboree Guidebook	2.00	3.00	2.15
☐ **Book,** Coca-Cola Guidebook	2.00	4.00	3.15
☐ **Book,** Pre-Jamboree Training	1.00	2.00	.75
☐ **Book,** Program Guide	1.00	2.00	.75
☐ **Book,** Promotion Tips Information Packet	1.00	2.00	.75
☐ **Book,** Troop Leader's Guide	2.00	3.00	2.10
☐ **Book,** Visitors Guide	1.00	2.00	.75

	Current Price Range		P/Y Avg.
☐ **Brochure,** Your Invitation to Attend.............................	1.00	2.00	.75
☐ **Brochure,** Official Order Form for Patches............................	1.00	2.00	.75
☐ **Brochure,** Management Bulletin, 1–8, staff...........................	10.00	12.00	10.50
☐ **Card,** butterfly key, Chaplain......	1.00	2.00	.75
☐ **Card,** daily activity tags, various colors	1.00	2.00	1.10
☐ **Card,** fishing permit	1.00	2.00	.75
☐ **Card,** ham radio, KZBSA/3........	5.00	7.50	6.00
☐ **Card,** marksmanship, individual competition score card	1.00	2.00	.75
☐ **Coin,** plastic, "Azimuth Trail".....	2.00	3.00	2.15
☐ **Coin,** gilt finish	2.00	3.00	2.15
☐ **Coin,** silver finish.................	2.00	3.00	2.15
☐ **Decal,** National Jamboree, colorful, 1977	1.00	2.00	.75
☐ **Decal,** self-adhesive, metal emblem	2.00	4.00	3.15
☐ **Emblem,** North East Region, metal, desk	4.00	5.00	4.15
☐ **Envelope,** official letter-size envelope	1.00	2.00	.75
☐ **Flag,** Jamboree troop	50.00	75.00	62.50
☐ **Form,** Jamboree Journal subscription.............................	1.00	2.00	.75
☐ **Form,** largest fish, length, certificate	4.00	5.00	4.25
☐ **Form,** largest fish, weight, certificate................................	4.00	5.00	4.25
☐ **Form,** shareholder certificate	2.00	3.00	2.15
☐ **Form,** troop inspection scoresheet................................	1.00	2.00	.75
☐ **Form,** troop leader application	1.00	2.00	.75
☐ **Hat,** green with patch	5.00	7.50	6.00
☐ **Identification Card**................	2.00	3.00	2.15

1977 National Jamboree Belt Buckle, $3.50–$6.00

	Current Price Range		P/Y Avg.
☐ **Jewelry,** bolo clasp, "1977 Order of the Arrow Service Corps," metal...	4.00	5.00	4.15
☐ **Jewelry,** bolo tie, horseshoe type	6.00	9.00	6.50
☐ **Jewelry,** bolo tie, medallion plaque ...	4.00	6.00	4.25
☐ **Jewelry,** charm...	1.00	2.00	1.10
☐ **Jewelry,** enameled tie bar, long bar type...	3.00	4.00	3.15
☐ **Jewelry,** enameled tie bar, short bar type...	2.00	3.00	2.10
☐ **Jewelry,** key ring with plastic fob...	1.00	2.00	1.10
☐ **Jewelry,** lapel pin, enameled finish...	2.00	3.00	2.15

1977 National Jamboree Ceramic Mug, $3.00–$5.00

	Current Price Range		P/Y Avg.
☐ **Jewelry,** lapel pin, silver finish....	2.00	3.00	2.15
☐ **Jewelry,** pin, Handicapped Awareness Trail	3.00	5.00	4.00
☐ **Magazine,** *Boy's Life,* National Jamboree issue, 1977	2.00	3.00	2.15
☐ **Map,** Exxon, souvenir	1.00	2.00	1.10

	Current Price Range		P/Y Avg.
☐ **Mug,** National Jamboree, ceramic, 1977	2.00	3.00	2.15
☐ **Newspaper,** *National Jamboree Journal,* set of nine, 1977	5.00	8.00	5.50
☐ **Neckerchief,** National Jamboree, official, 1977	3.00	4.00	3.25
☐ **Neckerchief,** Trading post services	20.00	25.00	22.50
☐ **Neckerchief,** Trading post services staff	20.00	25.00	22.50
☐ **Patch,** Aquatic staff	20.00	25.00	22.50
☐ **Patch,** Environmental conservation staff	50.00	75.00	62.50
☐ **Patch,** Exhibits	20.00	25.00	22.50
☐ **Patch,** (Order of the Arrow Service Corps, round)	20.00	25.00	22.50
☐ **Patch,** Youth service corp.	20.00	25.00	22.50
☐ **Patch,** Medical health	20.00	25.00	22.50
☐ **Patch,** Order of the Arrow Service Corps, flap	25.00	30.00	27.50
☐ **Patch,** Region	1.00	2.00	.75
☐ **Patch,** various contingents	5.00	20.00	7.50
☐ **Parking Pass,** various kinds	1.00	2.00	.75
☐ **Pennant,** desk flag	2.00	3.00	2.15
☐ **Pennant,** National Jamboree, 1977	3.00	4.00	3.15
☐ **Plate,** metal and ceramic	8.00	10.00	8.50
☐ **Sardines,** National Jamboree, 1977	2.00	3.00	2.15
☐ **Shirt,** men's large, new	6.00	7.00	6.25
☐ **Stationery,** news letterhead	1.00	2.00	1.10
☐ **Stationery,** unopened package	2.00	3.00	2.15
☐ **Trivet,** ceramic and metal	3.00	4.00	3.15

1981 NATIONAL JAMBOREE

"Scouting's Reunion with History" came to life as 31,000 Scouts and Scouters followed in the footsteps of America's Heritage 200 years after the last major battle of the American Revolution. The site was Fort A. P. Hill, Virginia.

For the first time, advance scheduling of all program activities was determined by computer. Each troop received a computer printout showing each patrol's scheduled activities. Nearly 40,000 individual activity tickets were printed and 22,600 patrol tickets distributed to the 2,660 patrols.

The opening show, "America's Heritage," presented a musical rendition of historical events from colonial times to the present. Other events included Brownsea Island Camp, Merit Badge Midway, National Exhibits, and the Patrol Challenge Trail. The "World's Largest Harmonica Band"—1,700-strong—entertained.

A staff of 432 volunteers packaged food and supplies for distribution. Among the interesting supply distributions were: 1.8 million slices of bread, a mile-high tower of pancakes, 1.7 million pounds of charcoal, 563,731 paper plates, 869,204 napkins, and 8,000,000 yards of toilet tissue.

In addition, nearly five tons of fireworks were used in the closing show.

	Current Price Range		P/Y Avg.
☐ **Belt,** leather with embossed emblem	7.50	10.00	8.50
☐ **Belt,** leather name belt	7.50	10.00	8.50
☐ **Belt Buckle,** official	5.00	7.00	5.50
☐ **Belt Buckle,** souvenir coin	5.00	7.00	5.25
☐ **Bolo Tie,** silver emblem on black cord	4.00	5.00	4.25
☐ **Buckle,** brass, stamped with Jamboree emblem	5.00	7.50	6.50
☐ **Bumper Sticker,** official Jamboree emblem and six stickers	1.00	2.00	1.10
☐ **Button,** pinback, Baptist Association	4.00	5.00	4.25
☐ **Button,** pinback, Life to Eagle meeting	5.00	6.00	5.25
☐ **Car Pass**	2.00	3.00	2.50
☐ **Card,** health alert notice	1.00	2.00	.75

1981 National Scout Jamboree, $3.00–$4.00

	Current Price Range		P/Y Avg.
☐ **Clocks,** special National Jamboree clock	12.50	20.00	16.00
☐ **Coin,** official, silver antiqued finish, 1½″ diameter	2.00	3.00	2.25
☐ **Coin,** subcamp, wooden	1.00	2.00	1.50
☐ **Coin Paper Weight,** official, coin in clear plastic	15.00	17.00	15.50
☐ **Decal,** pressure-sensitive, 3″ × 3½″	1.00	2.00	.75
☐ **Decals,** set of six	2.00	3.00	2.25
☐ **Decal,** T-shirt iron-on	2.00	3.00	2.25
☐ **Flag,** Jamboree troop	40.00	50.00	45.00
☐ **Envelope,** set of Jamboree stamped 7/29/83	4.50	6.00	4.75
☐ **Flag cards,** British Union Jack, set of eighteen	5.00	6.00	5.25

	Current Price Range		P/Y Avg.
☐ **Guidebook**, *Boy's Life* Jamboree ..	1.00	2.00	1.25
☐ **Guidebook**, Jamboree Scout Guide	1.00	2.00	.75
☐ **Journals**, *Jamboree Journals*, set of eight	6.00	8.00	6.50
☐ **Money**, packs of shredded money distributed by Jamboree bank.....	2.00	3.00	2.15
☐ **Mug**, official, dairy style	3.00	4.00	3.25
☐ **Mug**, plastic, thermo	3.00	4.00	3.25
☐ **Nametag**, Trading Post	6.00	7.50	8.50
☐ **Neckerchief**, official, Jamboree...	3.00	4.00	3.25
☐ **Neckerchief Slide**, silver medal with Jamboree emblem...........	2.00	3.00	2.25
☐ **Patch**, BSA, navy	7.50	10.00	8.50
☐ **Patch**, camp.......................	10.00	12.00	10.50
☐ **Patch**, Aquatic staff	20.00	25.00	22.50
☐ **Patch**, 40 mm square, Olympic Trail, Handicap Awareness, Orienteering, Obstacle Course, Electronic Orienteering, Heritage Trail, Action Archery & Patrol Challenge	8.00	10.00	9.00
☐ **Patch**, 18 subcamp flags, each ...	12.00	15.00	12.50
☐ **Patch**, Scouting's Reunion with History, segment, solid	10.00	15.00	12.50
☐ **Patch**, Scouting's reunion with history, segment, twill	40.00	50.00	45.00
☐ **Patch**, pocket, twill	40.00	50.00	45.00
☐ **Patch**, jacket, 5″ round, twill	40.00	50.00	45.00
☐ **Patch**, confidence course	7.50	10.00	7.25
☐ **Patch**, leather emblem, 4″ circle ...	1.00	3.00	1.50
☐ **Patch**, OA Service Corps	15.00	18.00	15.75
☐ **Patch**, pocket, solid	3.00	4.00	4.50
☐ **Patch**, round, back, 5″ diameter, solid.................	3.00	4.00	3.15
☐ **Patch**, Regional Jamboree........	3.00	4.00	3.15
☐ **Patch**, shoulder, Calcasieu Area Council	5.00	10.00	7.00

	Current Price Range		P/Y Avg.
☐ **Patch,** shoulder, Audubon Council	5.00	10.00	7.00
☐ **Patch,** shoulder, Jamboree	5.00	7.50	6.00
☐ **Patch,** shoulder, Northwest Suburban	5.00	12.50	9.50
☐ **Patch,** Southeast region	3.00	4.00	3.25
☐ **Patch,** 18 subcamp Flags, each	12.00	15.00	12.50
☐ **Patches,** subcamp, set of eighteen	350.00	400.00	350.00
☐ **Pillbox,** compartmented with hinged lid	5.00	10.00	7.00
☐ **Pin,** archery course	2.00	3.00	2.15
☐ **Plate,** pewter, Jamboree souvenir	8.00	11.00	8.50
☐ **Sardines,** can from Maine	1.00	2.00	1.15
☐ **Segment,** Trading post staff	15.00	17.00	15.50
☐ **Shakers,** ceramic salt and pepper set	3.00	4.00	3.25
☐ **Shirt,** Jamboree T-shirt	6.00	8.00	6.50
☐ **Staff strip**	12.00	15.00	12.50
☐ **Stamps,** Commemorative Covers honoring the visit of King Carl XVI Gustaf of Sweden	2.00	3.00	2.15
☐ **Sun Glasses,** official, Jamboree	7.00	9.00	7.50
☐ **Sun Visor,** red with Jamboree design in white	4.00	5.00	4.25
☐ **Tag,** subcamp baggage	1.00	2.00	1.25
☐ **Telephone calling instructions**	1.00	2.00	.75
☐ **Ticket Strip,** Trading post	1.00	2.00	.75
☐ **Token,** wooden, various	1.00	2.00	.75
☐ **Visor,** CPA	4.00	5.00	4.25

1985 NATIONAL SCOUT JAMBOREE

The Boy Scouts' anniversary theme, ''Pride in the Past . . . Footsteps to the Future,'' led various councils throughout the country to initiate exciting events all through 1985 in celebration of the Seventy-fifth Anniversary of the Boy Scouts of America. The highlight of the year took place during the week of July 24–30, when more than 32,000 Scouts and leaders converged on Fort A.P. Hill, Virginia, for the 1985 National Scout Jamboree.

Scouts gathered to greet one another, share ideas, renew old acquaintances, and reaffirm the challenges involved in scouting. Excitement prevailed as celebrities appeared on the scene. First Lady Nancy Reagan was a special visitor. Music from the Oak Ridge Boys, not to be outdone by the Beach Boys, drifted across the acres and acres of land, covered with huge Army tents, large enough to sleep sixteen. Dr. Ralph Armstrong from LA lifted his hot-air balloon into the sky again and again; an impressive Art and Science Show provided excellent examples of studio art; an amateur radio station operated throughout the eight days and nights.

During May, June, and July, the BSA lit a Heritage Campfire outside every state capitol. Campfire ashes from these fires were added to a Heritage Campfire Caravan that traveled from Washington State 7,600 miles across the country, through forty state capitals. After three months on the road, it arrived at the A. P. Hill campsite during the Jamboree.

Ben H. Love became the BSA's eighth Chief Scout Executive; a BSA history book entitled *The Boy Scouts, An American Adventure,* was printed in cooperation with Robert W. Peterson, author, and the American Heritage Publishing Company. Youth membership increased for the sixth consecutive year, registering a 2.7 percent gain over 1984. Cub Scouting introduced a new emphasis on Cub Scout Sports. The Order of the Arrow presented 104 camperships, totaling more than $4,000, to Native American Boy Scouts. Membership in the Order of the Arrow increased significantly. The BSA Scouting for the Handicapped Program was cited for its innovative approaches in serving the handicapped. Its members received the 1985 National Organization on Disability Award. Membership totals 73,639,425.

	Current Price Range		P/Y Avg.
☐ **Neckerchief,** Trading post staff C	15.00	25.00	20.00
☐ **Newspaper,** set of seven, *Jamboree Journal*	7.00	9.00	8.00
☐ **Patch,** Youth services	10.00	15.00	12.50
☐ **Patch,** Order of the Arrow Service Corps, flap	20.00	30.00	25.00
☐ **Patch,** pocket	3.00	5.00	4.00
☐ **Patch,** jacket, 6″ round	6.00	10.00	7.00
☐ **Patch,** leather	5.00	7.00	6.00
☐ **Patch,** Seventy-fifth Anniversary, segment	5.00	7.00	6.00
☐ **Patch,** various contingents	4.00	6.00	5.00

	Current Price Range		P/Y Avg.
☐ **Patch**, Western Region contingent	5.00	7.00	6.00
☐ **Patch**, Western Region contingent, gold mylar edge	25.00	30.00	27.50
☐ **Pens**, six different colors	1.00	2.00	1.50
☐ **Pins**, Sub-camp	3.00	4.00	3.50
☐ **Pins**, Commemorative set	75.00	125.00	100.00
☐ **Pin**, official blue	10.00	15.00	12.50
☐ **Pin**, official red	15.00	20.00	17.50
☐ **Pin**, official white	15.00	20.00	17.50
☐ **Pins**, contingent	2.00	4.00	3.00
☐ **Pins**, staff	4.00	6.00	5.00
☐ **Salt & pepper shakers**	8.00	10.00	9.00
☐ **Shirt**, T-shirt	10.00	12.00	11.00
☐ **Soft drink**, insulated holder	1.00	2.00	1.50
☐ **Ticket strip**, trading post	1.00	2.00	1.50
☐ **Tile**	3.00	5.00	4.00
☐ **Token**	1.00	2.00	1.50
☐ **Towel**, beach	10.00	12.00	11.00
☐ **Towel**, small	4.00	6.00	5.00
☐ **Vase**, ceramic	4.00	6.00	5.00
☐ **Vase**, ceramic western boot	4.00	6.00	5.00

COLLECTIBLES (Official 1985 Scout Jamboree collectibles. All carry the 1985 Scout Jamboree Logo.)

☐ **Ashtray**, Jamboree emblem	3.00	5.00	4.00
☐ **Baggage tags**	1.00	2.00	1.50
☐ **Buckle**, belt, official	8.00	10.00	9.00
☐ **Buckle**, Max I. Silber	25.00	50.00	37.50
☐ **Box**, ceramic heart	4.00	6.00	5.00
☐ **Card**, Jamboree identification	5.00	7.00	6.00
☐ **Clock**, staff appreciation	10.00	15.00	12.50
☐ **Decal**, sticker sheet	2.00	3.00	2.50
☐ **Flag**, desk	10.00	12.00	11.00

1910–1985—The Spirit Lives On

	Current Price Range		P/Y Avg.
☐ **Flag,** troop........................	50.00	75.00	62.50
☐ **Hat,** staff, with official emblem	10.00	15.00	12.50
☐ **Map,** topographical................	5.00	7.00	6.00
☐ **Mug,** ceramic coffee...............	2.00	3.00	2.50
☐ **Mug,** plastic coffee	2.00	3.00	2.50
☐ **Name tag,** trading post...........	10.00	15.00	12.50
☐ **Neckerchief**	5.00	7.00	6.00
☐ **Neckerchief,** Trading post staff A	15.00	25.00	20.00
☐ **Neckerchief,** Trading post staff B	15.00	25.00	20.00

WORLD JAMBOREES

Inside Bingley Hall in 1913, the first Imperial Scout Exhibition was in progress. Excitement was in the air, both for the townspeople and the Scouts. Scouts from twelve countries came to participate. Lord Baden-Powell directed this week-long display of Scouting demonstrations, and it was he who envisioned an international encampment to promote friendship, encourage outdoor skills, and build citizenship. Baden-Powell was quoted as saying, "When a gang of Scouts get together, it ought to be a noisy merrymaking;" therefore he struck upon the word "jamboree." Before the exhibition was over in 1913, he decided that there would be an international Jamboree in 1918, since the exhibition went so well and city residents were interested also. Plans were made, but the Jamboree was interrupted because of World War I and was therefore held in 1920. Over 6,000 Scouts came to this first World Jamboree. Since then, World Jamborees have been held in thirteen different countries, and three times in England.

1920 WORLD JAMBOREE

Over 6,000 Scouts attended this first World Jamboree, including 301 Scouts from the United States. Scouts were present from thirty-two of the fifty-two countries with Scouting programs. The entire Jamboree that year was held inside, with all kinds of displays and competitions, including such things as fire-fighting and gymnastics. Obstacle races and tug-of-wars were even held in the large glass-roofed Olympia Exhibition Hall in London, England. The Jamboree activities were tremendously successful. Every day for an entire week, newspapers of many countries carried lengthy stories and reports on this international encampment. A special moment came as Baden-Powell rose to make his farewell speech. An unknown Scout rose and shouted, "We, the Scouts of the World, salute you, Sir Robert Baden-Powell—Chief Scout of the World." Then, in unison, the standard bearers of all nations dipped their flags in salute. Baden-Powell went on to speak of world peace and happiness, and asked the Scouts to pledge this endeavor.

	Current Price Range		P/Y Avg.
☐ **Baggage Tags,** Army issue; U.S. contingent on battleship Pocahontas	15.00	20.00	15.50

Basic Pocket Patches Issued for all the World Jamborees, 1924–1983

	Current Price Range		P/Y Avg.
☐ **Book,** The Jamboree Book, green, hard cover	25.00	35.00	27.50
☐ **Booklet,** instruction pamphlet, Boy Scouts of America contingent	15.00	20.00	15.50
☐ **Newspaper,** August 5, 1920, printed at Jamboree	15.00	25.00	15.50
☐ **Patch,** U.S. contingent	30.00	40.00	35.00

1924 WORLD JAMBOREE

The second World Jamboree was held in Copenhagen, Denmark. A United States delegation of fifty-six Scouts was in attendance for this Nordic Jamboree. Unlike the first World Jamboree, this was not held inside an exhibition hall, but was held outside, setting the trend for all future Jamborees. Because of World War I, only sixty countries attended. The most valuable collectible items are the patches, which were made of silk.

☐ **Book,** The Imperial Jamboree 1924, green, hard back............	20.00	30.00	22.50
☐ **Patch,** silk	2000.00	3000.00	2500.00
☐ **Patch,** U.S. contingent	360.00	400.00	350.00
☐ **Seal,** Jamboree, 1924	22.00	27.00	22.50

1929 WORLD JAMBOREE

Birkenhead, England, was the site of the third World Jamboree, which hosted some 50,000 Scouts. The United States was represented by 1,300 Scouts. A total of seventy-three lands was represented in the Jamboree.

☐ **Book,** church service bulletin, eight pages	14.00	16.00	14.50
☐ **Book,** Daily Telegraph Scouts, Jamboree supplement..............	14.00	18.00	14.50
☐ **Book,** picture storybook	30.00	40.00	32.50
☐ **Book,** program and guide book ...	20.00	35.00	22.50

	Current Price Range		P/Y Avg.
☐ **Book,** Scouts' Own...............	8.00	10.00	8.50
☐ **Book,** Scouts' Thanksgiving Service, program......................	12.00	14.00	12.50
☐ **Book,** The Daily Arrow, bound volume............................	60.00	100.00	72.50
☐ **Book,** The Scout Jamboree Book, Putnam	10.00	20.00	12.50
☐ **Book,** The World Jamboree, 1929, brown, hard back.................	15.00	35.00	16.50
☐ **Book,** Universal Indian Sign Language, Eastern	6.00	17.00	6.50
☐ **Christmas Card,** Rhodesian contingent	5.00	10.00	5.50
☐ **Newsletter,** United States contingent................................	10.00	14.00	10.50
☐ **Patch,** Official 1929 Jamboree	150.00	300.00	225.00
☐ **Patch,** U.S. Contingent...........	100.00	200.00	150.00

1933 WORLD JAMBOREE

Twenty-one thousand Scouts attended the fourth World Jamboree in Godollo, Hungary. A contingent of 406 was present from the United States. Forty-six countries were represented by Scouts.

☐ **Book,** Scout Jamboree book, by West and Hillcourt.................	18.00	25.00	18.50
☐ **Booklet,** Jamboree Camping Guide	20.00	40.00	21.50
☐ **Calendar,** calendar and program of the European Tour, United States contingent	18.00	22.00	18.50
☐ **Magazine Article,** *National Geographic,* May 1934.................	7.00	9.00	7.50
☐ **Patch,** Jamboree, 1933	300.00	400.00	350.00
☐ **Patch,** U.S. contingent	100.00	200.00	150.00

	Current Price Range		P/Y Avg.
☐ **Souvenir Neckerchief Slide,** replica	2.00	3.00	2.25

1937 WORLD JAMBOREE

The World Jamboree took place in Vogelenzang, Holland. The United States sent a contingent of 814, which was a large number considering that the United States was also holding its first National Jamboree in Washington, D.C., in the same year.

☐ **Book,** The National and World Jamboree of America 1937, hard back	30.00	45.00	32.50
☐ **Booklet,** Campbook	8.00	12.00	8.50
☐ **Booklet,** Daily Telegraph, supplement, sixteen pages	18.00	22.00	18.50
☐ **Booklet,** program for visit to Den Helder	10.00	12.00	10.50
☐ **Magazine,** *Scouting Magazine,* March 1937	5.00	7.50	6.00
☐ **Patch,** pocket	200.00	350.00	250.00
☐ **Seal,** Jamboree, 1937	9.00	11.00	9.50
☐ **Songbook,** Jamboree, 1937	8.00	10.00	8.50

1947 WORLD JAMBOREE

This World Jamboree was held in Moisson, France, where 32,000 Scouts gathered for the international encampment. The Scouts came from all over the world, representing thirty-eight countries. The United States was represented by 1,151 Scouts.

☐ **Booklet,** menu book	14.00	16.00	14.50
☐ **Diary,** Jamboree, 1947	12.00	14.00	12.50
☐ **Mug,** Jamboree, 1947	6.00	9.00	6.50

	Current Price Range		P/Y Avg.
☐ **Neckerchief,** Boy Scouts of America contingent, blue silk–screened emblem on yellow	40.00	75.00	55.00
☐ **Patch,** Jamboree, 1947, various subcamps...........................	200.00	450.00	310.00
☐ **Patch,** United States contingent ..	20.00	40.00	25.00
☐ **Pin,** Jamboree, 1947	35.00	50.00	40.00
☐ **Postcards,** set of twelve, French country scenes	40.00	75.00	55.00

1951 WORLD JAMBOREE

The seventh Jamboree was held in Bad Ischl, Austria. Some 13,000 Scouts from fifty-nine countries were present with 700 Explorers.

☐ **Booklet,** guide book for Leaders ...	15.00	25.00	22.50
☐ **Booklet,** public relation book	12.50	17.50	15.00
☐ **Bulletin,** two Boy Scouts of America bulletins........................	3.00	5.00	3.25
☐ **Neckerchief,** United States contingent	15.00	22.50	17.00
☐ **Patch,** leather	40.00	75.00	50.00
☐ **Patch,** pocket	60.00	65.00	50.00
☐ **Patch,** reissue patch	20.00	50.00	25.00

1955 WORLD JAMBOREE

Ontario, Canada, was the area designated for the "Niagara on the Lake" World Jamboree. Over 15,000 Scouts from sixty-three nations gathered for this eighth World Jamboree. Also present were 1,500 Explorers from the Boy Scouts of America.

☐ **Belt Buckle,** Max I. Silber.........	100.00	125.00	110.00
☐ **Booklet,** Region 7 Rail Travel Guide, Out The Window...........	4.00	7.50	2.25

	Current Price Range		P/Y Avg.
☐ **Newspaper**, Jamboree 1955	4.00	6.00	4.25
☐ **Patch**, jacket	35.00	60.00	45.00
☐ **Patch**, pocket woven	25.00	30.00	27.50
☐ **Patch**, United States contingent ..	12.50	20.00	15.00
☐ **Patch**, visitor's	5.00	7.00	5.25
☐ **Pennant**, black	14.00	17.00	14.50

1957 WORLD JAMBOREE

For this ninth World Jamboree, over 35,000 Scouts gathered in Birmingham, England. Scouts from eighty-two nations took part in the festive activities. They came from all parts of the world to celebrate the centennial of Lord Baden-Powell's birthday and the Fiftieth Anniversary of the Boy Scout movement. Seventeen thousand Explorers from the Boy Scouts of America took part in this Jamboree even though the United States was involved in its fourth National Jamboree in Valley Forge, Pennsylvania that summer.

☐ **Book**, For Meal Time	4.00	6.00	4.25
☐ **Book**, Moot Handbook and Diary	10.00	12.00	10.50
☐ **Book**, picture	8.00	10.00	8.25
☐ **Neckerchief**, Boy Scouts of America Foreign Travel	18.00	20.00	18.50
☐ **Neckerchief**, bronze metal	12.00	16.00	12.50
☐ **Neckerchief**, leather	8.00	12.00	8.50
☐ **Neckerchief**, United States contingent	15.00	20.00	17.00
☐ **Neckerchief Slide**, silver metal ...	12.00	16.00	12.50
☐ **Newspaper**, daily papers, full set	20.00	30.00	22.50
☐ **Patch**, United States contingent ..	7.50	15.00	8.50
☐ **Patch**, World Jamboree	45.00	60.00	42.50
☐ **Souvenir Newspaper**, evening news	5.00	8.00	5.50

1959 WORLD JAMBOREE

The tenth World Jamboree was held in the Phillipines.

	Current Price Range		P/Y Avg.
☐ **Booklet,** Here's How Folder	1.00	2.00	1.25
☐ **Buckle,** Phillipines metal belt buckle...............................	5.00	7.50	5.50
☐ **Buckle,** World Jamboree, belt buckle, 1959...........................	10.00	17.50	7.25
☐ **Card,** picture card of Scouts of Jamboree	1.00	2.00	.75
☐ **Hat,** straw with official emblem....	35.00	40.00	37.50
☐ **Mondial,** official, red enamel......	20.00	25.00	22.50
☐ **Neckerchief,** United States contingent	12.50	17.50	15.50
☐ **Neckerchief,** World Jamboree, 1959	30.00	40.00	32.50
☐ **Newspaper,** one of the daily papers	4.00	7.00	4.25
☐ **Patch,** pocket, Chinese contingent.................................	8.00	12.00	4.50
☐ **Patch,** pocket, United States contingent	12.00	16.00	12.50
☐ **Patch,** pocket, World Jamboree, 1959	25.00	35.00	24.50
☐ **Pennant,** Chinese contingent	4.00	8.00	4.50
☐ **Pin,** enameled, Jamboree, 1959 ..	15.00	25.00	5.50

1963 WORLD JAMBOREE

The eleventh World Jamboree was held in beautiful Marathon, Greece, on the banks of the Aegean Sea. There were 621 Scouts from the United States in attendance. There were no official patches or brass and silver pass official items.

☐ **Book,** Golden Leaces of Marathon	10.00	15.00	12.50

World Jamboree Paperweight, 1963, silver, 2¹⁄₂″ × 3¹⁄₈″,
$15.00–$25.00

		Current Price Range		P/Y Avg.
☐	**Booklet,** Guide for Leaders	6.00	9.00	6.50
☐	**Boy's Life,** July 1963	3.00	4.00	3.25
☐	**Boy's Life,** December 1963.......	3.00	4.00	3.25
☐	**Coin,** brass	10.00	17.50	9.50
☐	**Coin,** Higher and Wilder	8.00	10.00	8.25
☐	**Decal,** small, blue	5.00	6.00	5.25
☐	**Decal,** large, blue	8.00	10.00	8.25
☐	**Decal,** brown	4.00	6.00	4.25
☐	**Letter Opener,** plastic with mon- dial...................................	6.00	8.00	6.25
☐	**Mirror,** blue-backed	8.00	10.00	8.25
☐	**Mondial,** small, brass	12.00	30.00	12.50

	Current Price Range		P/Y Avg.
☐ **Mondial,** large, brass..............	35.00	45.00	37.50
☐ **Mondial,** large, silver, Leader's ...	35.00	50.00	60.00
☐ **Neckerchief,** orange, staff	30.00	60.00	32.50
☐ **Neckerchief,** silk-screened with mondial	15.00	20.00	15.50
☐ **Neckerchief,** red with black.......	10.00	12.00	10.00
☐ **Patch,** large, square, silk..........	10.00	17.00	12.50
☐ **Patch,** large, white, woven	8.00	12.00	8.50
☐ **Patch,** small, silk, canvas back ...	9.00	15.00	9.50
☐ **Patch,** small, silk in black lettering	19.00	20.00	18.50
☐ **Patch,** small, white, woven........	8.00	12.00	8.50
☐ **Pennant,** blue	8.00	12.00	8.50
☐ **Pin,** large, bronze	15.00	35.00	20.00
☐ **Pin,** large, silver	30.00	70.00	40.00
☐ **Pin,** small, bronze	8.00	15.00	8.50
☐ **Souvenir Belt Slide,** Jamboree, 1963	3.00	5.00	3.50
☐ **Souvenir Book,** Jamboree, 1963	12.00	16.00	12.50

1967 WORLD JAMBOREE

The United States hosted the twelfth World Jamboree at Farragut State Park in Idaho. Over 12,000 Scouts assembled for the theme "For Friendship." One hundred seven countries were represented, making this the most delegated Jamboree to date. A program called "The Wide Game" gave the Scouts an opportunity to meet Scouts of other lands and to make new friends. A special Brownsea Island exhibit was set up, and the Jamboree was visited by Lady Baden-Powell.

☐ **Belt,** leather with two-piece buckle, official	10.00	13.00	10.50
☐ **Belt Buckle,** limited edition, brass and magnesium	17.00	21.00	17.50
☐ **Belt Buckle,** max silver, brass	35.00	40.00	37.50
☐ **Belt Slide,** Jamboree, 1967	1.00	2.00	1.10

	Current Price Range		P/Y Avg.
☐ **Book,** Jamboree book............	4.00	6.00	4.25
☐ **Book,** picture book	7.00	9.00	7.50
☐ **Booklet,** Couer D'Alene Rodeo, Rockwell cover	3.00	5.00	3.25
☐ **Booklet,** fact sheet, Jamboree, 1967	1.00	2.00	1.10
☐ **Booklet,** program guide book	2.00	3.00	2.25
☐ **Booklet,** scenes booklet, Coca-Cola..............	4.00	6.00	4.25
☐ **Booklet,** Troop Leader Guidebook	2.00	3.00	2.25
☐ **Booklet,** Welcome to Idaho, brochure	2.00	3.00	2.25
☐ **Certificate,** Farragut Silver M	2.00	3.00	2.25
☐ **Coin,** brass	5.00	7.00	5.25
☐ **Coin,** bronze.....................	8.00	9.00	8.50
☐ **Coin,** rectangular	8.00	11.00	8.25
☐ **Coin,** round....................	8.00	11.00	8.25
☐ **Coin,** silver	4.00	8.00	4.25
☐ **Decal,** Jamboree, 1967	2.00	3.00	2.25
☐ **Decal,** Union Oil.................	1.00	2.00	1.10
☐ **Diary and Guidebook**............	3.00	8.00	3.25
☐ **Fob,** plastic disk, I am Indian Tea, 1¾"	2.00	3.00	1.75
☐ **Folder,** Commemorative postal card, ceremony folder	2.00	3.00	2.15
☐ **Hat,** field, with patch	7.00	9.00	7.25
☐ **Hat,** purple, field, patch, host corps strip....................	10.00	15.00	10.50
☐ **Hat Patch,** purple on white........	6.00	9.00	6.50
☐ **Hot Plate,** ceramic tile	6.00	9.00	6.50
☐ **Journals,** complete set, Jamboree Journals	10.00	12.00	10.25
☐ **Key Chain,** plastic, Jamboree, 1967	1.00	3.00	.75
☐ **Magazine,** World Jamboree Scenes...........................	2.00	3.00	1.75
☐ **Map,** Conoco souvenir	1.00	2.00	.75

	Current Price Range		P/Y Avg.
☐ **Map,** Idaho, Jamboree, 1967	2.00	3.00	2.25
☐ **Map,** official, Jamboree, 1967	3.00	5.00	3.25
☐ **Map,** Pepsi-Cola souvenir	2.00	3.00	2.25
☐ **Map,** United States Department Interior Geological	5.00	7.50	6.00
☐ **Mug,** Jamboree, 1967	5.00	7.50	6.00
☐ **Neckerchief,** Fisherman Award . . .	20.00	40.00	25.00
☐ **Neckerchief,** Jamboree, 1967	7.00	15.00	7.50
☐ **Neckerchief,** Japan, Tokyo contingent	3.00	5.00	3.25
☐ **Neckerchief,** Region 1 contingent	8.00	11.00	8.50
☐ **Neckerchief,** Region 3 contingent	6.00	8.00	6.25
☐ **Neckerchief,** Region 9 contingent	8.00	11.00	8.50
☐ **Neckerchief,** St. Louis, Mo., contingent, red and white	3.00	4.00	3.25
☐ **Neckerchief Slide,** brass	4.00	7.00	4.25
☐ **Neckerchief Slide,** colored slate	2.00	4.00	2.25
☐ **Neckerchief Slide,** JW USA contingent	7.00	9.00	7.50
☐ **Neckerchief Slide,** metal	4.00	6.00	4.25
☐ **Paperweight,** For Friendship, Irving J. Feist, President, Boy Scouts of America	9.00	11.00	9.50
☐ **Paperweight,** 3½″, aluminum	12.00	16.00	12.50
☐ **Paperweight,** In Appreciation, Boy Scouts of America	12.00	16.00	12.50
☐ **Patch,** back	10.00	12.50	8.50
☐ **Patch,** For Friendship, segment, rare	10.00	15.00	12.00
☐ **Patch,** Idaho Panhandle Council contingent	6.00	8.00	6.25
☐ **Patch,** large, design as shirt patch, 3″ × 4″	5.00	8.00	5.50
☐ **Patch,** large, leather	9.00	12.00	9.50
☐ **Patch,** physician	35.00	45.00	37.50
☐ **Patch,** pocket, white or blue back . .	7.00	12.00	8.00
☐ **Patch,** South African contingent . .	10.00	12.00	10.50

	Current Price Range		P/Y Avg.
☐ **Patch,** World Jamboree, reissue, used as subcamp item, 1951	12.00	16.00	12.50
☐ **Pencil,** lead, Jamboree, 1967	1.00	2.00	2.25
☐ **Pennant,** large, Jamboree, 1967 ...	5.00	8.00	6.00
☐ **Pennant,** small, blue, felt	5.00	10.00	7.50
☐ **Pin,** lapel, enamel finish...........	4.00	6.00	4.25
☐ **Postcard,** Idaho, gemstone state ...	2.00	3.00	2.50
☐ **Postcard, United States,** 6¢, First Day Cover	1.00	2.00	1.10
☐ **Postcard,** World Jamboree emblem	2.00	3.00	2.25
☐ **Postcard,** World Jamboree, Mc-Donald's	2.00	3.00	2.25
☐ **Record,** LP, For Friendship	5.00	7.00	5.25
☐ **Scarf,** women's, silk...............	7.50	12.50	10.50
☐ **Seals,** full sheet, Jamboree, 1967 ..	1.00	3.00	1.10
☐ **Songbook,** with Mickey	3.00	6.00	3.25
☐ **Songbook,** Songs for Friendship ...	2.00	4.00	2.25
☐ **Souvenir Newspaper,** Couer D'Alene Press, August 1967	2.00	4.00	2.25
☐ **Stationery,** Scouts badges of the world................................	2.00	3.00	2.25
☐ **Sticker,** Subcamp Bad Ischl	1.00	2.00	1.10
☐ **Sticker,** Watch the World Jamboree on ABC-TV, 3½"	1.00	2.00	1.10
☐ **Tickets,** 5 trading post tickets	1.00	2.00	1.10
☐ **Tie Bar,** enameled	5.00	7.50	7.25
☐ **Wallet Card,** Jamboree, 1967.....	1.00	2.00	1.10

1971 WORLD JAMBOREE

This Jamboree was held at the foothills of Mt. Fuji in Shizuoka Prefecture, Japan.

☐ **Badge,** admission badge, multicolored metal	6.00	8.00	6.25

	Current Price Range		P/Y Avg.
☐ **Banner**, fringed...................	5.00	7.00	5.50
☐ **Belt Slide**, Okinawa contingent ...	2.00	3.00	2.25
☐ **Belt Slide**, Region 13	4.00	6.00	4.25
☐ **Bolo Tie**, custom leather, Jamboree, 1971	15.00	20.00	15.50
☐ **Bolo Tie**, leather, blue enamel pin	7.50	10.00	8.00
☐ **Bolo Tie**, with slide, Jamboree 1971	3.00	5.00	3.50
☐ **Booklet**, Tour Guide	5.00	10.00	5.50
☐ **Booklet**, General Guidebook......	5.00	10.00	7.50
☐ **Booklet**, Training Course book ...	5.00	10.00	9.00
☐ **Booklet**, souvenir book	6.00	8.00	7.50
☐ **Booklet**, Welcome Folder, Jamboree	1.00	3.00	1.10
☐ **Bulletins**, United States, Journal, set of five	14.00	17.00	14.50
☐ **Coat**, Happi or Kimona.............	7.00	9.00	7.25
☐ **Coin**, bronze......................	5.00	7.00	5.50
☐ **Coin**, bronze, plastic case........	7.00	9.00	7.25
☐ **Coin**, copper, Jamboree, 1971	3.00	6.00	3.50
☐ **Coin**, gold, 24K, 12 grams	200.00	300.00	225.00
☐ **Cuff Links**, with tie bar in box	7.00	10.00	7.50
☐ **Decal**, Jamboree, 4¾" round, 1971	1.00	3.00	1.10
☐ **Handkerchief**, cotton, Jamboree, 1971	3.00	4.00	3.75
☐ **Key Case**, leather, Jamboree, 1971	2.00	3.00	2.25
☐ **Key Chain**, enameled, Jamboree, 1971	3.00	5.00	4.25
☐ **Map**, Coca-Cola, map and guide ...	3.00	5.00	3.25
☐ **Map**, Official 20" × 28"	5.00	7.50	7.00
☐ **Medal**, brass in plastic case	10.00	12.50	11.00
☐ **Medallion**, set in plastic frame....	3.00	5.00	3.25
☐ **Mug**, Jamboree, 1971	4.00	6.00	4.25
☐ **Neckerchief**, blue, World Jamboree	8.00	12.00	8.50

	Current Price Range		P/Y Avg.
☐ **Neckerchief**, orange, World Jamboree	12.00	16.00	12.50
☐ **Neckerchief**, United States contingent	5.00	8.00	5.50
☐ **Neckerchief Slide**, leather with enamel pin	3.00	5.00	4.25
☐ **Neckerchief Slide**, blue, enameled	3.00	5.00	4.25
☐ **Neckerchief Slide**, metal slide, United States contingent	3.00	8.00	3.25
☐ **Neckerchief Slide**, metal slide, world emblem	4.00	5.00	4.50
☐ **Newspaper**, daily papers, complete set	8.00	10.00	8.25
☐ **Newspaper**, Mainichi Daily News, Japan, August 1971	2.00	4.00	2.15
☐ **Patch**, back	8.00	10.00	8.50
☐ **Patch**, official, large, jacket	12.00	17.50	14.00
☐ **Patch**, official, blue	12.50	15.00	13.00
☐ **Patch**, pocket, shield type, red felt	8.00	10.00	8.50
☐ **Patch**, pocket, woven or embroidered	7.00	9.00	7.50
☐ **Patch**, Region 7, Boy Scouts of America	5.00	7.00	5.25
☐ **Patch**, United States contingent, back	10.00	12.00	10.50
☐ **Patch**, United States contingent, pocket	5.00	8.00	5.50
☐ **Pennant**, felt, Jamboree, 1971	4.00	6.00	4.25
☐ **Pennant**, fish, windbag, blue	6.00	8.00	6.50
☐ **Pennant**, fish, windbag, red	6.00	8.00	6.50
☐ **Pin**, hat, enameled	4.00	6.00	4.50
☐ **Pin**, enameled, pinback, emblem, 1½"	9.00	12.00	9.50
☐ **Pin**, For Understanding, wide game	25.00	30.00	27.50
☐ **Postcards**, set of ten	4.00	6.00	4.25

	Current Price Range		P/Y Avg.
☐ **Purse,** change purse with logo....	4.00	6.00	4.25
☐ **Seal,** sheet of ten	2.00	4.00	2.25
☐ **Seal,** Hong Kong contingent	1.00	2.00	1.10
☐ **Sticker,** small, red................	1.00	2.00	1.10
☐ **Ticket,** meal	1.00	3.00	1.10
☐ **Tie Bar,** enameled, Jamboree, 1971	2.00	4.00	2.25

1975 WORLD JAMBOREE

This Jamboree was called "Nordjamb" and was held near Lake Mjosa, Norway, which is located 120 miles north of Oslo. Fifteen thousand Scouts from ninety-one countries assembled for this fourteenth World Jamboree. The symbol of the Jamboree was a hand with five fingers outward symbolizing the five Nordic countries who jointly hosted the Jamboree.

	Current Price Range		P/Y Avg.
☐ **Badge,** conservation	4.00	5.00	4.25
☐ **Belt Loop,** Jamboree, 1975.......	5.00	8.00	5.50
☐ **Booklet,** fourteenth World Jamboree, uniform requirements and order form	8.00	10.00	8.50
☐ **Booklet,** Official Guidebook.......	6.00	10.00	8.50
☐ **Booklet,** welcome brochure.......	1.00	2.00	.75
☐ **Boys' Life,** Jamboree issue, February 1976	1.00	2.00	1.10
☐ **Coin,** purple, Jamboree 1975	3.00	4.00	3.25
☐ **Decal,** Jamboree, 1975	1.00	2.00	1.10
☐ **Mug,** Jamboree, 1975	5.00	7.00	5.25
☐ **Napkin,** paper, Jambo emblem, staff use	1.00	3.00	1.10
☐ **Neckerchief,** Subcamp Trelleborg	20.00	30.00	22.50
☐ **Neckerchief,** United States contingent	4.00	6.00	4.25
☐ **Notebooks,** Nordjamb books #1 and #2.............................	2.00	3.00	2.25

Max I. Silber World Jamboree Belt Buckle, 1975, $30.00–$50.00

	Current Price Range		P/Y Avg.
☐ **Patch,** back, United States contingent	5.00	10.00	5.50
☐ **Patch,** blue silk	12.50	17.50	14.00
☐ **Patch,** Friendship Tour	5.00	10.00	7.00
☐ **Patch,** Join-In Jambo, woven	4.00	6.00	4.25
☐ **Patch,** official, blue twill	10.00	12.50	11.00
☐ **Patch,** pocket, Canadian contingent	7.00	10.00	7.50
☐ **Patch,** pocket, embroidered, round	5.00	8.00	5.50
☐ **Patch,** pocket, United States contingent	5.00	8.00	5.50

	Current Price Range		P/Y Avg.
☐ **Plaque,** copper, hiking staff	4.00	6.00	4.50
☐ **Pennant,** white with emblem, 14″ . .	4.00	6.00	4.25
☐ **Postcard,** official, Jamboree, 1975	1.00	3.00	1.10
☐ **Poster,** folder, 20″ × 26″	4.00	6.00	4.25

1979 WORLD JAMBOREE

The fifteenth World Jamboree, scheduled to be held in Iran, was cancelled because of political uncertainties. The Swedish National Jamboree called "Dalajamb," hosted some of the contingents.

☐ **Application,** for Jamboree	3.00	4.00	3.25
☐ **Belt Buckle,** official, brass	60.00	75.00	62.50
☐ **Booklet,** campfire camp	6.00	8.00	6.50
☐ **Booklet,** Camp Guide Book	4.00	6.00	4.25
☐ **Booklet,** Lager book Campguide . . .	8.00	10.00	8.50
☐ **Brochure,** Your Invitation to Iran . . .	4.00	6.00	4.25
☐ **Buckle,** Jamboree, 1979	12.00	15.00	12.50
☐ **Cachet Covers,** various types	3.00	5.00	3.25
☐ **Decal,** official	12.00	15.00	12.50
☐ **Map,** Jamboree	5.00	6.00	5.25
☐ **Milk Carton,** with official Jambo emblem	15.00	20.00	15.50
☐ **Neckerchief,** United States contingent	24.00	30.00	24.50
☐ **Neckerchief,** World Jamboree	40.00	55.00	42.50
☐ **Neckerchief Slide,** United States contingent	6.00	8.00	6.25
☐ **Patch,** back, United States contingent	25.00	30.00	27.50
☐ **Patch,** Canadian-Iranian contingent	25.00	30.00	27.50
☐ **Patch,** Hiking trail, woven	30.00	40.00	32.50
☐ **Patch,** Iran, rare, never used	85.00	100.00	87.50

	Current Price Range		P/Y Avg.
☐ **Patch,** Iran, United States contingent	40.00	75.00	50.00
☐ **Patch,** jacket, Swedish contingent	25.00	30.00	27.50
☐ **Patch,** jacket, United States contingent	22.00	27.00	22.50
☐ **Patch,** Join-In Jambo	20.00	25.00	22.50
☐ **Patch,** Join-In Jambo, Canadian contingent	6.00	8.00	6.25
☐ **Patch,** Join-In Jambo, Iran, silk	5.00	6.00	5.25
☐ **Patch,** official, embroidered	25.00	00	27.50
☐ **Patch,** official, silk	40.00	50.00	42.50
☐ **Patch,** pocket, Canadian contingent	8.00	12.00	8.50
☐ **Patch,** pocket, Swedish contingent	25.00	30.00	27.50
☐ **Patch,** service corps, United States contingent	40.00	50.00	42.50
☐ **Patch,** special hike, blue and white	20.00	25.00	20.50
☐ **Patch,** pocket, United States contingent	25.00	30.00	27.50
☐ **Patch,** United States contingent, small	17.50	23.00	18.00
☐ **Patch,** pocket, World Jamboree	45.00	50.00	47.50
☐ **Postcard,** official, with Jambo cancellation	3.00	5.00	3.25
☐ **Songbook,** Songs for Protestant Worship	2.00	4.00	2.25
☐ **Stationery,** official, headquarter staff sheet, white	2.00	3.00	2.25
☐ **Stationery,** official, headquarter staff sheet, yellow	2.00	3.00	2.25
☐ **Stationery,** Swedish contingent, sheets	3.00	4.00	3.25
☐ **Sticker,** sheet	8.00	10.00	8.25
☐ **Woggle,** wrap around and snaps	4.00	6.00	4.25

1983 WORLD JAMBOREE

Officially, this great gathering of 15,483 Scouts was the Fifteenth World Jamboree due to the cancellation of the 1979 Jamboree, which was to be hosted by Iran. For the first time in the history of this event, girls, 984 of them to be exact, were official delegates in beautiful Alberta, Canada. The foothills of the Rocky Mountains provided a breathtaking setting for the exciting activities which brought together Scouts from 101 countries.

Among the many outstanding events was a raft trip down the white water rapids of the Kananaskis River, a rodeo known as the Calgary Stampede, and a wide friendship game that broke all records for continuing international Scouting.

	Current Price Range		P/Y Avg.
☐ **Badge,** printed cloth...............	1.00	2.00	.50
☐ **Badge,** woven cloth	1.00	2.00	.50
☐ **Belt Buckle**........................	15.00	17.00	15.50
☐ **Buckle,** Max Silber................	50.00	60.00	55.00
☐ **Card,** Lawrence L. Lee Museum, first day of issue...................	1.25	2.25	.75
☐ **Decal**	1.00	2.00	.75
☐ **Diary,** Jamboree....................	1.00	2.00	.75
☐ **Envelope,** Lawrence L. Lee Museum, first day of issue............	1.50	2.50	1.25
☐ **Frisbee,** Jamboree	5.00	7.50	6.00
☐ **Journals,** Jamboree...............	8.00	10.00	8.50
☐ **Manual,** troop	2.00	3.00	1.75
☐ **Matches,** box of fifty books	15.00	18.00	15.50
☐ **Patch,** back	25.00	40.00	30.00
☐ **Patch,** back, commemorative, limited edition of 1000	200.00	300.00	175.00
☐ **Patch,** Buffalo subcamp...........	10.00	12.00	10.50
☐ **Patch,** leather.....................	12.00	14.00	12.50
☐ **Patch,** medical staff	25.00	30.00	27.50
☐ **Patch,** shirt, embroidered	15.00	18.00	15.50
☐ **Pin,** hat, green	5.00	7.50	6.00
☐ **Poster,** Jamboree, full color.......	15.00	17.00	15.50
☐ **Program,** Scout's	1.00	2.00	1.25
☐ **Stickers,** screen-printed vinyl	1.00	2.00	.50

	Current Price Range		P/Y Avg.
☐ **Sticker**, Sixteenth World Jamboree	10.00	12.00	10.50
☐ **T-shirt**	10.00	12.00	8.50
☐ **Tile**, World Jamboree Crest	10.00	12.00	10.00
☐ **Tote bag**, Jamboree seal	10.00	12.00	10.50
☐ **Wide game cards**, set of eleven....	9.00	10.00	9.25

ORDER OF THE ARROW

One of the finest traditions of the Boy Scouts of America is the honor camper association named The Order of the Arrow. It is the brotherhood of cheerful service in Scouting. A Scout-run organization, it requires candidates to possess certain advancement status, camping experience, and Scouting ideals. The members are elected on a troop basis by fellow Scouts who are not necessarily members.

The candidates must complete a meaningful initiation called the Ordeal Ceremony. A Scout may pass from an "Ordeal Member" to a "Brotherhood Member" status upon completion of certain requirements. The highest honor status is "The Vigil Honor," which may be presented in recognition of outstanding service to the local lodge and Council.

The Order of the Arrow was founded in 1915 at the Philadelphia Council's Camp Treasure Island. The Camp director, Dr. E. Urner Goodman, and his assistant Carroll A. Edison, created the brotherhood based on the legends and traditions of the Delaware Indians. It was an immediate success and spread to other Scout camps.

The O. A. became an official experiment of the B.S.A. in 1922, and on June 2, 1934, the National Council officially approved it as part of the program. The O. A. continued to operate as a separate program within Scouting until May, 1948, when it was completely integrated and the separate National Lodge was dissolved.

Annual conventions of the National Lodge began in 1921 and became semi-annual after 1927. Over 5,000 members participate in the annual conventions.

Each Scout Council has its own O. A. lodge, which is grouped into geographic sections with the sections grouped into six National regions. Each lodge has a separate number and Indian name.

O. A. members are great collectors of Scouting memorabilia, particularly patches. Many of the older patches and patches of obsolete or merged lodges are rare and in great demand. As a result of counterfeiting, in 1975 National headquarters began to require that every O. A. patch contain the emblems "Boy Scouts of America" or "B.S.A." in order to utilize the copyright laws to help stamp out the counterfeits.

There are literally thousands of variations of lodge and area Conference patches and other collectibles. A tremendous study of these is presented in *Arapaho II, A History of the Order of the Arrow through Insignia.* This outstanding pictorial history was coauthored by Albertus Hoogeveen, Rick Breithaupt, Jr., and Dave C. Leubitz. Information on the current purchase of *Arapaho II* may be obtained through Arapaho, P. O. Box 8454, Universal City, California 91608.

A smaller but more available study entitled *O. A. Illustrated Lodge Patch Handbook* has been prepared by Bill Price and is available through regional distributors. To find the current price and information on obtaining the booklet, contact Bill Price, 14306 Waterville Way, Houston, Texas 77015.

In view of the overwhelming variety of lodge and area collectibles, we are attempting only a listing of the nationally issued memorabilia consisting of National Conference patches and neckerchiefs, sashes, handbooks, and ceremony books.

We in the Order of the Arrow often get so involved with patches, neckerchiefs, and sashes, we tend to overlook the opportunity to develop a worthwhile collection of O. A. literature, which is available at very reasonable prices or trades. This literature consists of many items, but a particularly attractive collecting field is the Handbooks or Ceremony Guidebooks.

NATIONAL O. A. CONFERENCE PATCHES

National Conferences began in 1921, but patches were not issued until 1940.

1940—LIGONIER, PA	Current Price Range		P/Y Avg.
☐ **Patch,** red felt Arrowhead with white "C.T.E." letters. It is thought these were from a Scout camp....	200.00	300.00	175.00
☐ **Delegate Medal**	300.00	400.00	375.00
☐ **Staff Neckerchief**	100.00	150.00	110.00

Order of the Arrow Handbook, Fiftieth Anniversary Edition, 1965 revision, green, blue and gray cover, $5.00–$7.00

	Current Price Range		P/Y Avg.
1946—CHANUTE FIELD, IL			
☐ **Patch,** white felt with red lettering, round	75.00	125.00	90.00
1948—BLOOMINGTON, IN			
☐ **Patch,** small round white felt with red silk-screened lettering, first National Conference after integration as B.S.A. official program	50.00	100.00	65.00
1950—BLOOMINGTON, IN			
☐ **Patch,** white twill oval with grey and red embroidery	40.00	60.00	50.00
1952—OXFORD, OH, 2,200 delegates			
☐ **Patch,** red twill with yellow, black and white	40.00	60.00	50.00

	Current Price Range		P/Y Avg.

1954—LARAMIE, WY, 1,300 delegates

☐ **Patch,** white twill with yellow, blue and red	25.00	50.00	35.00

1956—BLOOMINGTON, IN, 2,201 delegates

☐ **Patch,** white twill with many colors	25.00	50.00	35.00
☐ **Neckerchief**	30.00	35.00	30.50

1958—LAWRENCE, KS, 2,368 delegates

☐ **Patch,** white twill with yellow, red and blue	25.00	50.00	35.00
☐ **Staff Neckerchief**	30.00	50.00	42.00

1961—BLOOMINGTON, IN, 2,800 delegates

☐ **Patch,** white twill with red, yellow and black	20.00	35.00	27.00
☐ **Delegate Neckerchief**	17.50	30.00	27.00
☐ **Committee Neckerchief**	30.00	40.00	32.50

1963—CHAMPAIGN, IL, 3,105 delegates

☐ **Patch,** multicolored, fully embroidered	17.50	30.00	22.00
☐ **Delegate Neckerchief**	15.00	25.00	20.00
☐ **Committee Neckerchief**	35.00	40.00	37.00

1965—BLOOMINGTON, IN, 4,200 delegates

☐ **Patch,** grey twill with many colors	15.00	25.00	22.50
☐ **Delegate Neckerchief**	12.50	20.00	15.50
☐ **Committee Neckerchief**	20.00	25.00	20.50

1967—LINCOLN, NE, 4,158 delegates

☐ **Patch,** multicolored, fully embroidered	12.50	17.50	14.00
☐ **Delegate Neckerchief**	12.00	16.00	12.50

	Current Price Range		P/Y Avg.
☐ **Committee Neckerchief**	17.50	25.00	15.50

1969—BLOOMINGTON, IN, 4,421 delegates

☐ **Patch,** multicolored, fully embroidered	12.50	15.00	15.50
☐ **Delegate Neckerchief**	10.00	12.00	10.50
☐ **Staff Neckerchief**	15.00	25.00	15.50

1971—CHAMPAIGN, IL, 5,200 delegates

☐ **Patch,** multicolored, fully embroidered	8.00	10.00	8.50
☐ **Delegate Neckerchief**	8.00	10.00	8.50
☐ **Committee Neckerchief**	15.00	20.00	16.00

1973—SANTA BARBARA, CA, 4,400 delegates

☐ **Patch,** white twill with many colors, six-sided, also a back patch	6.50	9.00	7.50
☐ **Delegate Neckerchief**	7.50	10.00	8.50

1975—OXFORD, OH, 3,700 delegates

☐ **Patch,** six-sided, diamond-shaped	6.50	9.00	8.50
☐ **Delegate Neckerchief**	7.50	10.00	8.50

1977—KNOXVILLE, TN, 3,500 delegates

☐ **Patch,** pocket	6.00	8.00	7.00
☐ **Patch,** jacket	7.00	10.00	8.00

1979—FT. COLLINS, CO, 5,000 delegates

☐ **Patch,** diamond-shaped	6.00	8.00	7.50
☐ **Patch,** jacket	7.00	10.00	8.00

1981—NEW BRUNSWICK, NJ, RUTGERS UNIVERSITY, 3,600 delegates

☐ **Patch,** pocket	5.00	7.00	6.00

	Current Price Range		P/Y Avg.
☐ **Patch,** jacket	7.00	10.00	8.00
☐ **Neckerchief**	5.00	7.00	6.00

Note: The Boy Scouts of America released a souvenir set of National O.A. Conference patches (1948–1973) in 1975. These are plastic-backed, but there is a process for removing the plastic—so beware.

SASHES

The original 1915 sashes were black with a white felt arrow, but none of these are known to exist today.

☐ **Ordeal Sash,** white sateen sash with red sateen arrow, 1918 to mid 1920s	200.00	250.00	205.00
☐ **Vigil Sash,** arrows counter-clockwise.................................	300.00	400.00	310.00
☐ **Ordeal Sash,** white twill sash with red felt arrow, mid 1920s to about 1927	200.00	250.00	205.00
☐ **Ordeal Sash,** white felt with red felt arrow, 1928 to 1948	50.00	65.00	51.00
☐ **Vigil Sash,** triangle is sewn to band, 1934, felt....................	175.00	225.00	180.00
☐ **Ordeal Sash,** white felt with red printed or "flocked" arrow, 1948 to 1955	18.00	22.00	18.50
☐ **Brotherhood Sash,** begins, felt...	20.00	40.00	37.00
☐ **Vigil Sash,** felt	50.00	125.00	60.00
☐ **Ordered Sash,** white twill band with red embroidered arrow, 1955	7.50	12.50	10.00
☐ **Brotherhood Sash**	8.00	15.00	10.00
☐ **Vigil Sash,** arrows remained counter-clockwise until about 1978	7.50	15.00	10.00

HANDBOOKS

Prior to 1948, regulations were distributed to the lodges in pamphlet form. The first complete handbook was introduced in 1948 and there were three variations of this edition.

1948 HANDBOOK VARIATIONS

	Current Price Range		P/Y Avg.
☐ **Dark hard cover**	35.00	65.00	36.00
☐ **White with "Handbook" at top** ...	30.00	50.00	31.00
☐ **Same without "Handbook"**	30.00	50.00	31.00
☐ **1950 handbook,** Arrow across red cover	15.00	25.00	20.50
☐ **1956 handbook,** Red Indian on white	15.00	20.00	15.50
☐ **1961 handbook,** White cover with Indian head	5.00	7.00	5.50
☐ **1965 handbook,** Gold with Indian head, Fiftieth Anniversary Edition ...	5.00	7.00	5.50
☐ **1973 handbook,** Dancing Indian on white	3.00	4.00	3.10
☐ **1975 handbook,** Abstract Indian in silver	2.00	3.00	2.10
☐ **1977 handbook,** Abstract Indian in black	1.00	2.00	1.10

CEREMONY GUIDEBOOKS

1930s CEREMONY GUIDEBOOK

☐ **Ordeal,** early 1930s	35.00	40.00	36.00
☐ **Brotherhood,** early 1930s	40.00	50.00	41.00
☐ **Vigil,** late 1930s	50.00	65.00	52.00

MID-1930s GUIDEBOOKS

☐ **Ordeal,** 1935	20.00	30.00	20.50
☐ **Brotherhood,** 1936...............	25.00	35.00	25.50

	Current Price Range		P/Y Avg.
☐ Vigil, 1940	30.00	40.00	30.50

LATE 1940s GUIDEBOOKS

☐ Ordeal, 1948	15.00	27.50	20.00
☐ Brotherhood, 1949	17.50	30.00	20.00
☐ Vigil, 1949	20.00	30.00	22.00

1960s GUIDEBOOKS

☐ Ordeal, 1960	5.00	7.00	5.50
☐ Brotherhood, 1960	6.00	8.00	6.50
☐ Vigil, early 1960s	10.00	12.00	10.50

LATE 1960s GUIDEBOOKS

☐ Ordeal, 1968	3.00	4.00	3.10
☐ Brotherhood, 1968	3.00	4.00	3.10
☐ Vigil, 1968	5.00	7.50	4.50

1971 GUIDEBOOKS

☐ Ordeal, 1971	3.00	4.00	3.10
☐ Brotherhood, 1971	3.00	4.00	3.10
☐ Vigil, 1971	4.00	6.00	4.50

1977 GUIDEBOOKS

☐ Ordeal, 1977	1.00	2.00	1.10
☐ Brotherhood, 1977	1.00	2.00	1.10
☐ Vigil, 1977	2.00	3.00	2.10

PERIODICALS

ANNUAL REPORTS TO CONGRESS

In March, 1916, the Congress of the United States of America chartered the Boy Scouts of America in order to give it protection against less worthy organizations which were attempting to profit by its steadily gaining reputation and good will.

A portion of House Bill 755 required the following:

"That on or before the first day of April of each year the said Boy Scouts of America shall make and transmit to Congress a report of its proceedings for the year ending December thirty-first preceding, including a full, completed, and itemized report of receipts and expenditures, of whatever kind."

As a result of this requirement, the Annual Reports to Congress have always presented an extremely complete and detailed picture of yearly scouting activity. A true scholar of scouting will find a great mountain of information within these reports.

From 1917 through 1920, the Annual Reports were contained in the Spring issue of *Scouting,* a magazine for professional scouters. Beginning in 1921, the reports have been printed by the U.S. Government Bureau of Printing.

	Current Price Range		P/Y Avg.
☐ 1914–1925	20.00	25.00	20.50
☐ 1915–1925	20.00	25.00	20.50
☐ 1917, *Scouting* magazine	25.00	35.00	27.00
☐ 1918, *Scouting* magazine	25.00	30.00	25.50
☐ 1919, *Scouting* magazine	25.00	30.00	25.50
☐ 1920, *Scouting* magazine	20.00	25.00	20.50
☐ 1921, U.S. Government printing office, scarce	30.00	40.00	33.00
☐ 1922, U.S. Government printing office, scarce	30.00	40.00	33.00
☐ 1923, U.S. Government printing office, scarce	30.00	40.00	33.00
☐ 1924, U.S. Government printing office, scarce	30.00	40.00	33.00
☐ 1925, U.S. Government printing office, scarce	30.00	40.00	33.00
☐ 1926, U.S. Government printing office, scarce	30.00	40.00	33.00
☐ 1927, U.S. Government printing office, scarce	30.00	40.00	33.00
☐ 1928, U.S. Government printing office, scarce	30.00	40.00	33.00

	Current Price Range		P/Y Avg.
☐ **1929,** U.S. Government printing office, scarce	30.00	40.00	33.00
☐ **1930,** U.S. Government printing office, scarce	15.00	20.00	15.50
☐ **1931,** U.S. Government printing office, scarce	15.00	20.00	15.50
☐ **1932,** U.S. Government printing office, scarce	15.00	20.00	15.50
☐ **1933,** U.S. Government printing office, scarce	15.00	20.00	15.50
☐ **1934,** U.S. Government printing office, scarce	15.00	20.00	15.50
☐ **1935,** U.S. Government printing office, scarce	15.00	20.00	15.50
☐ **1936,** U.S. Government printing office, scarce	15.00	20.00	15.50
☐ **1937,** U.S. Government printing office, scarce	15.00	20.00	15.50
☐ **1938,** U.S. Government printing office, scarce	15.00	20.00	15.50
☐ **1939,** U.S. Government printing office, scarce	10.00	12.00	10.50
☐ **1940,** U.S. Government printing office, scarce	10.00	12.00	10.50
☐ **1941,** U.S. Government printing office, scarce	10.00	12.00	10.50
☐ **1942,** U.S. Government printing office, scarce	10.00	12.00	10.50
☐ **1943,** U.S. Government printing office, scarce	9.00	11.00	9.50
☐ **1944,** U.S. Government printing office, scarce	9.00	11.00	9.50
☐ **1945,** U.S. Government printing office, scarce	9.00	11.00	9.50
☐ **1946,** U.S. Government printing office, scarce	8.00	10.00	8.50

	Current Price Range		P/Y Avg.
☐ **1947,** U.S. Government printing office, scarce	8.00	10.00	8.50
☐ **1948,** U.S. Government printing office, scarce	8.00	10.00	8.50
☐ **1949,** U.S. Government printing office, scarce	8.00	10.00	8.50
☐ **1950,** U.S. Government printing office, scarce	8.00	10.00	8.50
☐ **1951,** U.S. Government printing office, scarce	7.00	9.00	7.50
☐ **1952,** U.S. Government printing office, scarce	7.00	9.00	7.50
☐ **1953,** U.S. Government printing office, scarce	7.00	9.00	7.50
☐ **1954,** U.S. Government printing office, scarce	7.00	9.00	7.50
☐ **1955,** U.S. Government printing office, scarce	7.00	9.00	7.50
☐ **1956,** U.S. Government printing office, scarce	6.00	8.00	6.50
☐ **1957,** U.S. Government printing office, scarce	6.00	8.00	6.50
☐ **1958,** U.S. Government printing office, scarce	6.00	8.00	6.50
☐ **1959,** U.S. Government printing office, scarce	6.00	8.00	6.50
☐ **1960,** U.S. Government printing office, scarce	5.00	7.00	5.50
☐ **1961,** U.S. Government printing office, scarce	5.00	7.00	5.50
☐ **1962,** U.S. Government printing office, scarce	5.00	7.00	5.50
☐ **1963,** U.S. Government printing office, scarce	5.00	7.00	5.50

	Current Price Range		P/Y Avg.
☐ **1964,** U.S. Government printing office, scarce	5.00	7.00	5.50
☐ **1965,** U.S. Government printing office, scarce	5.00	7.00	5.50
☐ **1966,** U.S. Government printing office, scarce	4.00	5.00	4.50
☐ **1967,** U.S. Government printing office, scarce ....,......	4.00	5.00	4.50
☐ **1968,** U.S. Government printing office, scarce	4.00	5.00	4.50
☐ **1969,** U.S. Government printing office, scarce	4.00	5.00	4.50
☐ **1970,** U.S. Government printing office, scarce	4.00	5.00	4.50
☐ **1971 to 1981,** U.S. Government printing office, scarce..............	4.00	5.00	4.50

BOY'S LIFE

The fascinating history of *Boy's Life* magazine begins a few months after the 1910 organization of the Boy Scouts of America. An eighteen-year-old boy, Joe Lane, from Providence, R.I., created the magazine and published it without authorization from the Boy Scouts of America. His first edition of January 1, 1911, indicated that it was *Boy's and Boy Scout's* magazine. The cover of subsequent issues carried the legend, "The Semi-Official Publication of the Boy Scouts of America." Actually, the B.S.A. had no connection with the magazine, but were not displeased with it because Joe Lane proved to be a good editor in spite of his youth, and he portrayed an accurate picture of the then current Scouting activities.

The National Executive Committee was concerned however that future editions of *Boy's Life* would not continue to accurately portray the principles of Scouting. Negotiations began in 1912 for the full purchase of the publication rights. The final purchase price agreed upon was $1.00 per subscription, and there were then 6,100 outstanding subscriptions. The purchase price of $6,100.00 was a princely sum for the twenty-year-old Joe Lane in 1913.

The July, 1913, edition of *Boy's Life* magazine was the first fully official copy, and it has continued to grow from that point to its current status as the world's leading magazine for boys.

The first editor of *Boy's Life* under the ownership of Boy Scouts of America was W.P. McGuire. McGuire was impressed with the materials submitted by a young unknown artist, and within a month or two after the purchase of *Boy's Life,* McGuire hired the young artist at seventy-four dollars a month to do the magazine covers plus the illustrations for two articles in each issue. The young artist was Norman Rockwell. Norman Rockwell, of course, went on to greater accomplishment and recognition throughout his lifetime, but he always continued his loyalty to the Boy Scouts of America, producing over fifty highly valued covers for *Boy's Life* over the next sixty-year period.

Many of the great personalities of the past seventy years have contributed articles, including presidents, admirals, generals, senators, noted conservationists, outdoorsmen, and outstanding athletes from every imaginable sport. Virtually every activity of interest to the American boy has been presented on the pages of *Boy's Life* magazine in an accurate but colorful manner. Millions of boys have participated in exciting adventure, which has always been prepared for them with absolute good taste. Sex, violence, discrimination, immorality, brutality and the advertisement of any products not beneficial to youth have been scrupulously avoided.

Boy's Life is available to all boys regardless of their registration in Scouting. It is published monthly at an annual subscription cost of $8.40 per year through Boy's Life, 1325 Walnut Hill Lane, Iving, Texas 75062. Outside the U.S., add $4.00 per year for postage.

The market value of *Boy's Life* is determined to a great degree by its age. Higher prices are accorded original copies with Norman Rockwell cover illustrations, and moderately higher prices placed on valued "Jamboree" issues. On the whole, prices remain stable because more and more issues are appearing.

	Current Price Range		P/Y Avg.
☐ **Pre-Boy Scouts of America,** issues from January 1, 1911, until June, 1913	45.00	60.00	47.00
☐ **July, 1913**	75.00	90.00	77.00
☐ **August, 1913**	40.00	50.00	41.00
☐ **September, 1913,** first Norman Rockwell cover	80.00	100.00	85.00

	Current Price Range		P/Y Avg.
☐ **October, 1913,** Norman Rockwell cover..................................	40.00	50.00	41.00
☐ **November, 1913,** Norman Rockwell cover............................	35.00	40.00	35.50
☐ **December, 1913,** Norman Rockwell cover............................	35.00	40.00	35.50
☐ **January, February, March, April, June and December, 1914,** Norman Rockwell Covers	25.00	30.00	25.50
☐ **Other 1914 issues**	12.00	18.00	12.50
☐ **May and August, 1915,** Norman Rockwell	20.00	25.00	20.50
☐ **Other 1915 issues**	12.00	18.00	12.50
☐ **1916 issues**	10.00	15.00	10.50
☐ **1917 issues**	10.00	15.00	10.50
☐ **1918 issues**	10.00	15.00	10.50
☐ **February, July, and August, 1919,** Norman Rockwell............	20.00	25.00	20.50
☐ **Other 1919 issues**	10.00	15.00	10.50
☐ **June, 1920,** Sea Scout Number ..	10.00	14.00	10.50
☐ **Other 1920 issues**	8.00	12.00	8.50
☐ **July, 1921,** Norman Rockwell cover..................................	15.00	20.00	15.50
☐ **Other 1921 issues**	7.00	10.00	7.50
☐ **1922 issues**	7.00	10.00	7.50
☐ **1923 issues**	7.00	10.00	7.50
☐ **1924 issues**	7.00	10.00	7.50
☐ **1925 issues**	7.00	10.00	7.50
☐ **February, 1926,** Norman Rockwell cover..................................	15.00	18.00	15.50
☐ **Other 1926 issues**	7.00	10.00	7.50
☐ **February, 1927,** Norman Rockwell cover..................................	15.00	18.00	15.50
☐ **Other 1927 issues**	7.00	10.00	7.50
☐ **Other 1928 issues**	6.00	9.00	6.50
☐ **February, 1929,** Norman Rockwell cover..................................	15.00	18.00	15.50

	Current Price Range		P/Y Avg.
☐ August, 1929, Passed out at World Jamboree	10.00	12.00	10.50
☐ Other 1929 issues	6.00	9.00	6.50
☐ 1930 issues	6.00	9.00	6.50
☐ February, 1931, Norman Rockwell cover	15.00	18.00	15.50
☐ Other 1931 issues			
☐ February, 1932, Norman Rockwell cover	13.00	15.00	13.50
☐ Other 1932 issues	5.00	8.00	5.50
☐ February, 1933, Norman Rockwell cover	13.00	15.00	13.50
☐ Other 1933 issues	5.00	8.00	5.50
☐ April, 1934, Norman Rockwell cover	13.00	15.00	13.50
☐ Other 1934 issues	13.00	15.00	13.50
☐ February and July, 1935, Norman Rockwell cover	13.00	15.00	13.50
☐ Other 1935 issues	5.00	8.00	5.50
☐ February, 1936, Norman Rockwell cover	13.00	15.00	13.50
☐ Other 1936 issues	5.00	8.00	5.50
☐ February, 1937, Norman Rockwell cover	13.00	15.00	13.50
☐ Other 1937 issues	5.00	8.00	5.50
☐ February, 1938, Norman Rockwell cover	13.00	15.00	13.50
☐ Other 1938 issues	5.00	8.00	5.50
☐ February, 1939, Norman Rockwell cover	13.00	15.00	13.50
☐ May, 1939, New York World's Fair and Golden Gate Expo issue	8.00	12.00	8.50
☐ Other 1939 issues	5.00	8.00	5.50
☐ February, 1940, Norman Rockwell cover	10.00	15.00	13.50
☐ Other 1940 issues	5.00	8.00	5.50
☐ 1941, Norman Rockwell cover	10.00	15.00	13.50
☐ Other 1941 issues	5.00	8.00	5.50

	Current Price Range		P/Y Avg.
☐ **February, 1942,** Norman Rockwell cover...............................	10.00	15.00	13.50
☐ **Other 1942 issues**	5.00	8.00	5.50
☐ **1943 issues**	5.00	8.00	5.50
☐ **February, 1944,** Norman Rockwell cover...............................	10.00	15.00	13.50
☐ **Other 1944 issues**	5.00	8.00	5.50
☐ **1945 and 1946 issues**	5.00	8.00	5.50
☐ **February, 1947,** Norman Rockwell cover...............................	9.00	12.50	10.00
☐ **Other 1947 issues**	4.00	5.00	4.10
☐ **February, 1948,** Norman Rockwell cover...............................	9.00	12.50	10.00
☐ **Other 1948 issues**	4.00	5.00	4.10
☐ **1949 issues**	4.00	5.00	4.10
☐ **February, 1950,** Norman Rockwell cover...............................	7.50	10.00	8.00
☐ **Other 1950 issues**	3.00	4.00	3.10
☐ **February, 1951,** Norman Rockwell cover...............................	7.50	10.00	8.00
☐ **Other 1951 issues**	3.00	4.00	3.10
☐ **February, 1952,** Norman Rockwell cover...............................	7.50	10.00	8.00
☐ **Other 1952 issues**	3.00	4.00	3.10
☐ **February, 1953,** Norman Rockwell cover...............................	7.50	10.00	8.00
☐ **Other 1953 issues**	3.00	4.00	3.10
☐ **1954 issues**	3.00	4.00	3.10
☐ **February, 1955,** Norman Rockwell cover...............................	6.00	10.00	8.00
☐ **Other 1955 issues**	3.00	4.00	3.10
☐ **February, 1956,** Norman Rockwell cover...............................	6.00	10.00	8.00
☐ **Other 1956 issues**	3.00	4.00	3.10
☐ **June, 1957,** Norman Rockwell cover...............................	6.00	10.00	8.00
☐ **February, 1957,** Fiftieth Anniversary of Scouting issue.............	4.00	5.00	4.50

	Current Price Range		P/Y Avg.
☐ **Other 1957 issues**	4.00	7.00	4.50
☐ **February, 1958,** Norman Rockwell cover.................................	6.00	9.00	7.00
☐ **Other 1958 issues**	2.00	3.00	2.10
☐ **February, 1959,** Norman Rockwell cover.................................	6.00	9.00	7.00
☐ **Other 1959 issues**	2.00	3.00	2.10
☐ **January, 1960,** composite cover of twelve of Norman Rockwell's previous covers	6.00	9.00	7.00
☐ **February, 1961,** Norman Rockwell cover.................................	6.00	9.00	7.00
☐ **February, 1962,** Norman Rockwell cover.................................	6.00	9.00	7.00
☐ **October, 1962,** Philmont Scout Ranch issue	4.00	5.00	4.10
☐ **February, 1963,** Norman Rockwell cover.................................	5.00	7.50	6.00
☐ **July, 1963,** World Jamboree Patches in color	4.00	5.00	4.10
☐ **February, 1964,** Norman Rockwell cover.................................	5.00	7.50	6.00
☐ **July, 1964,** National Jamboree Guide	4.00	5.00	4.10
☐ **October, 1964,** National Jamboree issue...........................	4.00	5.00	4.10
☐ **February, 1965,** Norman Rockwell cover.................................	5.00	7.50	6.00
☐ **March, 1969,** reprint of March 1, 1911, cover	3.00	4.00	3.10
☐ **July, 1969,** National Jamboree edition	3.00	4.00	3.10
☐ **Other 1960, 1970, and 1980 issues**	1.00	3.00	1.50
☐ **March, 1971,** last original Norman Rockwell cover for Sixtieth Anniversary.............................	5.00	7.50	6.00

	Current Price Range		P/Y Avg.
☐ **September, 1976,** thirty-two Hiking Trail patches in color	3.00	4.00	3.10
☐ **July, 1977,** National Jamboree issue	3.00	4.00	3.10

MISCELLANEOUS

☐ **Armband,** khaki, now uniform use, 1925	12.00	16.00	12.50
☐ **Armband,** emergency service armband, BSA 1940s	10.00	15.00	10.50
☐ **Ashtray,** Gilwell Park, brass	5.00	7.00	5.25
☐ **Ashtray,** Kit Carson House, Philmont, 1950........................	4.00	5.00	4.10
☐ **Bank,** cast iron, Scout saluting, 3″	14.00	18.00	14.50
☐ **Bank,** cast iron, standing figure, slot in knapsack, original has enameled coating, c. 1915	75.00	90.00	77.00
☐ **Bank,** same as above, but made in Taiwan, slightly smaller and light bronze finish, 1970s	10.00	15.00	10.50
☐ **Bank,** celluloid pocket bank, "A Scout Is Thrifty"....................	8.00	10.00	8.50
☐ **Bank,** Conn., has another Scout behind kettle, 1915	200.00	300.00	210.00
☐ **Bank,** mechanical, coin drops and Scout raises flag, Taiwan..........	25.00	30.00	26.00
☐ **Bank,** same as above, but made by J&E Stevens Co., Cornwall	25.00	30.00	26.00
☐ **Bank,** plaster Scout (or Cub) bank, 1960s	10.00	12.00	10.50
☐ **Bank,** Scout, tin coin building, 3½″	30.00	40.00	30.50
☐ **Bank,** shape of small book, BSA-approved, 1920	25.00	40.00	25.50
☐ **Bank,** tin, lithographed scout, 1912	25.00	30.00	25.50

	Current Price Range		P/Y Avg.
☐ **Belt,** belt and buckle, gun metal, 1930s	8.00	10.00	8.25
☐ **Belt,** buckle, c. 1928	7.00	10.00	7.50
☐ **Belt,** dress, for civilian wear, 1940			
☐ **Belt,** "Expanso," tan or black			
☐ **Binoculars,** brass with leather, official BSA, 1930s	60.00	75.00	61.00
☐ **Binoculars,** tan leather, 1920s	50.00	70.00	52.00
☐ **Blotter,** BSA "America's Future Lies in Its Youth"	4.00	5.00	4.10
☐ **Blotter,** BSA "Boys Today, Men of Leadership Tomorrow"	4.00	5.00	4.10
☐ **Blotter,** BSA/Coca-cola, "Be Prepared, Be Refreshed"	5.00	7.00	5.25
☐ **Blotter,** BSA, "Onward for God and My Country"	4.00	5.00	4.10
☐ **Blotter,** BSA, "Vacation Has Just Begun for the Boy Scouts," 1922	4.00	6.00	4.10
☐ **Bookends,** metal, First-Class emblem 6″ × 6″	20.00	30.00	20.50
☐ **Bookends,** Sea Scout, heavy metal, Sea Scout emblem	25.00	35.00	27.00
☐ **Bookmark,** green and gold, First-Class emblem, BSA National Council	4.00	5.00	4.10
☐ **Bookmark,** metal, Scout emblem, no enamel, BSA National Council	1.00	1.50	1.05
☐ **Bookmark,** metal, Scout emblem, enameled	2.00	2.50	2.05
☐ **Books,** Holy Bible, early BSA seal on cover	40.00	50.00	47.00
☐ **Bow Pin,** BSA Spencer Award	3.00	4.50	3.50
☐ **Cachet Cover,** Boy Scout stamp club, 1932	10.00	12.00	10.50
☐ **Cachet Cover,** Boy Scouts/Lincoln/Washington, 1933	4.00	5.00	4.10
☐ **Calendar,** Norman Rockwell, 16″ × 32″, Scouting Trail, 1939	25.00	28.00	26.00

	Current Price Range		P/Y Avg.
☐ **Calendar,** Norman Rockwell, 16″ × 32″, Scout Is Reverent, 1940.......	25.00	28.00	26.00
☐ **Calendar,** Norman Rockwell, 16″ × 32″, Scout Is Helpful, 1941.........	25.00	28.00	26.00
☐ **Calendar,** Norman Rockwell, 16″ × 32″, Scout Is Loyal, 1942..........	25.00	28.00	26.00
☐ **Calendar,** Norman Rockwell, 16″ × 32″, All Together, 1947.............	25.00	28.00	26.00
☐ **Camera,** Official seven-piece flash camera kit	14.00	17.00	14.50
☐ **Camera,** Seneca #2a with box, smaller than 3a....................	40.00	60.00	42.00
☐ **Camera,** Seneca #3, foldable, 1915	80.00	90.00	80.50
☐ **Camera,** Seneca #3a with box	50.00	60.00	50.50
☐ **Campaign hat,** brown, size 7, silk band with Japanese BS insignia ..	20.00	25.00	23.00
☐ **Canteen,** Wearever seamless, felt cover, 1930s.......................	15.00	20.00	15.50
☐ **Cap,** red visor with 1981 patch on hat	5.00	6.00	5.50
☐ **Cards,** sixteen different job description cards, 1950	3.00	5.00	3.25
☐ **Cards,** cigarette card album, scout figures on leather...................	20.00	30.00	21.00
☐ **Cards,** fifty CWS cigarette cards, Boy Scout badges, 1939	38.00	50.00	40.00
☐ **Cards,** 100 Gallager cigarette cards, Boy Scout series, 1922.....	90.00	110.00	92.00
☐ **Cards,** Gouday gum cards, Boy Scout series	60.00	75.00	62.00
☐ **Cards,** fifty Ogden's cigarette cards, Boy Scout series, 1929.....	3 8.00	50.00	40.00
☐ **Cards,** Scout bugler, printed card, 3½″ × 5″, 1920...................	3.50	7.00	3.75
☐ **Cards,** Scout playing cards	2.00	3.00	2.10
☐ **Cards,** Scouts of different countries, boxed, set of 111, color	15.00	20.00	15.50

historical Scout plates & mug

Porcelain Plates, 6⅝", with gold rim and mug, manufactured by Dresden between 1915 and 1920. Uniforms suggest Scouts from Europe.

	Current Price Range		P/Y Avg.
☐ **Ceramics,** Dresden China Plates, color, gold rim, 1915...............	50.00	75.00	52.00
☐ **Ceramics,** American Boy Scout cup, china, color, scouts	40.00	50.00	41.00
☐ **Ceramics,** Boy Scout in color on a cream pitcher, china..............	60.00	75.00	62.00
☐ **Cigarette Lighter,** World Bureau	7.50	8.50	8.00
☐ **Coin,** silver color, Get Out the Vote, 1952	5.00	6.50	6.00
☐ **Coin,** Bicentennial, Be Prepared,.................................	2.50	4.00	3.25
☐ **Coin,** Blackhawk Council, US Grant, 1972........................	10.00	12.50	11.00
☐ **Coin,** BSA Fiftieth Anniversary, 1960	8.00	9.00	8.50
☐ **Collector Plate,** Norman Rockwell, Beyond the Easel	35.00	45.00	40.00
☐ **Compass,** round, 1st Class in center....................	20.00	28.00	25.00
☐ **Compass,** Official BSA, eight-sided.................................	2.00	4.00	2.50
☐ **Compass,** Official, shaped like pocket watch, silver	12.00	17.00	12.50
☐ **Compass,** Sylva pathfinder, BSA...	1.00	3.00	1.50
☐ **Container,** BSA tin cup, collapsible, BSA, 1916	8.00	10.00	8.50
☐ **Container,** complete marshmallow tin, Scout scene on cover	18.00	22.00	18.50
☐ **Container,** same as 1940s........	6.00	8.00	6.25
☐ **Contest Cups,** 10″ high, 1930s	20.00	27.00	20.50
☐ **Cut-Outs,** Camping with the Scouts, gummed paper in book form, 1930s.........................	20.00	25.00	20.50
☐ **Cut-Outs,** *Women's Home Companion* Scout paper doll, 1920	6.00	9.00	6.25
☐ **Cut-Outs,** *Women's Home Companion* Scout paper doll, 1923	6.00	9.00	6.50

	Current Price Range		P/Y Avg.
☐ **Cut-Outs,** BSA, wood rims, metal, BSA flag	75.00	100.00	75.50
☐ **Decal,** Tenderfoot emblem in color	2.00	3.00	2.50
☐ **Decal,** 8½″ × 11″, Scouting/ USA–gummed	2.00	3.00	2.50
☐ **Drum,** "Boy Scout Drum" tin, 6″ round, 3½″ high, 1908.............	30.00	50.00	32.00
☐ **Drum,** Boy Scouts with guns and bows, 7″ high, 10″ dia., 1912.....	25.00	35.00	27.00
☐ **Drum,** Boy Scout Official, bass, 8″ high, 24″ dia......................	50.00	75.00	55.00
☐ **Dye,** Uniform Soap Dye, 1920	12.00	15.00	12.50
☐ **Figurine,** cast iron Scout saluting, 3″ tall	14.00	17.00	14.50
☐ **Figurine,** casting set makes five small lead Scout figures...........	40.00	70.00	45.00
☐ **Figurine,** ceramic Scout knee-up, 3–4″	2.00	4.00	2.50
☐ **Figurine,** ceramic Scout saluting, 3–4″	3.00	4.00	3.50
☐ **Figurine,** ceramic Scout seated, 3– 4″	3.00	4.00	3.50
☐ **Figurine,** Head Scout, fire maker, unpainted	3.00	5.00	3.50
☐ **Figurine,** Head Scout, signaller, 4″	8.00	12.00	8.50
☐ **Figurine,** Head Scout, signaller, arms move, 2″.....................	15.00	22.00	15.50
☐ **Figurine,** Head Scout, tuba player, arms move, 4″.....................	10.00	15.00	10.50
☐ **Figurine,** iron Scout hiking, 3″	9.00	12.00	9.50
☐ **Figurine,** iron Scout hiker with canteen, 3″	6.00	8.00	6.50
☐ **Figurine,** iron Scout saluting, 3″ ...	6.00	8.00	6.50
☐ **Figurine,** Kenner doll, Craig Cub Scout	12.00	18.00	12.50

	Current Price Range		P/Y Avg.
☐ **Figurine,** Kenner doll, Steve Scout	12.00	18.00	12.50
☐ **Figurine,** Scout with gun, 9″ high, cardboard	9.00	11.00	9.50
☐ **Figurine,** Scout with gun, 6″ high, cardboard, 1915	5.00	7.00	5.50
☐ **Figurine,** Scout with pack and rifle, cardboard, 6″ high	4.00	5.00	4.25
☐ **Figurine,** Scout with staff and flag, cardboard, 9″ high	9.00	11.00	9.50
☐ **Figurine,** Lead Scout kneeling, frying eggs	10.00	12.00	10.50
☐ **Figurine,** Lead Scout hiker with staff, 3″	6.00	8.00	6.50
☐ **Figurine,** Lead Scout saluting, 3″	6.00	8.00	6.50
☐ **Figurine,** McKenzie Scout, 4¼″ on 3″ base	14.00	17.00	14.50
☐ **Figurine,** McKenzie Scout, bronze, 8½″	25.00	35.00	26.00
☐ **Figurine,** McKenzie Scout, mahogany base, 11″ high	15.00	25.00	16.00
☐ **Figurine,** copper finish, McKenzie Scout, plaster, 17″ high	25.00	35.00	26.00
☐ **Figurine,** plastic Scout bugler, 2″	4.00	6.00	4.50
☐ **Figurine,** plastic seated Scout, green, 2½″	2.00	3.00	2.00
☐ **Figurine,** plastic hiker w/ camera and staff, 2″	4.00	6.00	4.50
☐ **Figurine,** Scout plastic figure, tree and flagpole, 3″	7.00	10.00	7.50
☐ **Figurine,** Scout standing with rifle and pack, cardboard	5.00	8.00	5.50
☐ **Figurine,** Scout with rifle, cardboard on wood, 1910	15.00	22.00	15.50
☐ **First Aid Kit,** Bauer and Black, gray, oval belt loop kit, rare, 1932	15.00	25.00	16.00
☐ **First Aid Kit,** Bauer and Black, rectangular, 1933	12.00	20.00	13.00

	Current Price Range		P/Y Avg.
☐ **First Aid Kit,** Bauer and Black, tin box in canvas, 1926	25.00	35.00	26.00
☐ **First Aid Kit,** Johnson and Johnson, snap lid, late 1940s	9.00	14.00	9.50
☐ **First Aid Kit,** Johnson and Johnson, swing clasp, 1942	12.00	20.00	13.00
☐ **Flag,** set, US and BSA, c. 1940s ...	12.00	15.00	12.50
☐ **Flashlight,** Boy Scout L-shaped, metal, First-Class emblem....	5.00	8.00	5.50
☐ **Flashlight,** Boy Scout L-shaped, plastic, brown...............	3.00	5.00	3.25
☐ **Flashlight,** Eveready L-shaped, khaki, brass, BSA Ed.............	10.00	12.00	10.50
☐ **Flint and Steel,** Official BSA, set ...	1.00	2.50	1.10
☐ **Gadget Box,** BSA "Be Prepared, Do a Good Turn Daily," wood, 3″ × 4″	5.00	7.00	5.50
☐ **Gadget Box,** imitation wood, Cub, Scout, and Explorer emblems	3.00	5.00	3.50
☐ **Gadget Box,** Official BSA Gadget bag	4.00	7.00	4.50
☐ **Game,** American Boy Game by Milton Bradley, 1912..............	60.00	100.00	65.00
☐ **Game,** Boy Scouts Ten Pins, Milton Bradley Co....................	70.00	90.00	75.00
☐ **Game,** BSA/Burger King Frisbee ...	2.00	4.00	2.50
☐ **Game,** BSA punchboard, pass game to each boy to punch. He must then answer or do stunt, 1929	25.00	50.00	27.00
☐ **Game,** game of Scouting by Milton Bradley, 1920s...................	60.00	100.00	65.00
☐ **Game,** Scout picture puzzle, Brown and Bigelow, Norman Rockwell, "An Army of Friendship," 1933 ...	20.00	40.00	22.00

Scouting Game, *made by Milton Bradley and Company between 1916–1920*

	Current Price Range		P/Y Avg.
☐ **Game,** "Sunny Andy" Kiddie Kampers, Tin action game, Scouts saw wood, chop, and Girl Scouts use signal flag..........................	80.00	115.00	85.00
☐ **Game,** target ball game, Miller Co., spring tosses ball in air to land in circles, scouts w/ rifles	50.00	75.00	53.00

	Current Price Range		P/Y Avg.
☐ **Game,** target ball game, uses three marbles, like tiddlywinks, Boy Scout target shooting scene.......	40.00	60.00	45.00
☐ **Game,** The Boy Scouts Progress Game, Parker Bros., 1924........	60.00	80.00	65.00
☐ **Game,** The Game of Boy Scouts, Parker Bros., 1912	50.00	75.00	54.00
☐ **Handkerchief,** Boy Scout, printed, olive green/red....................	7.50	8.50	8.00
☐ **Hymn & Song Book for Scouts,** breast pocket, England, 1924	7.50	8.50	8.00
☐ **Label Pin,** Wonderful World of Scouting, clutch back..............	2.50	3.50	3.00
☐ **Large paperclip paper holder,** 1973, "Be A Winner"...............	3.00	4.00	3.50
☐ **Membership Cards,** BSA three-fold, 1919.........................	6.00	7.00	6.50
☐ **Membership Cards,** BSA three-fold, 1920.........................	6.00	7.00	6.50
☐ **Membership Cards,** BSA three-fold, 1921.........................	6.00	7.00	6.50
☐ **Membership Cards,** BSA three-fold, 1922.........................	6.00	7.00	6.50
☐ **Membership Cards,** BSA three-fold, 1923.........................	6.00	7.00	6.50
☐ **Membership Card,** BSA Rover, three-fold, 1939....................	7.50	8.50	8.00
☐ **Membership 15-year veteran card,** BSA, three-fold, 1932	4.00	5.00	4.50
☐ **Membership 5-year veteran card,** BSA, three-fold, 1922..............	5.00	6.00	5.50
☐ **Money Clip,** pewter color, Commissioner emblem	4.00	5.00	4.50
☐ **Neckerchief,** square, BSA, gray on red violet, First-Class emblem, earliest variety	40.00	50.00	45.00
☐ **Neckerchief,** square, BSA, yellow on red, emblem...................	4.00	5.50	4.50

	Current Price Range		P/Y Avg.
☐ **Neckerchief Slide,** brass, Strengthen the Arm of Liberty.....	4.00	5.00	4.50
☐ **Pamphlet,** khaki leggings with instructions, How to Wear Your Leggings.................................	8.00	9.00	8.50
☐ **Paperweight,** campaign hat, painted, iron, 3″	2.00	4.00	2.25
☐ **Paperweight,** contains large Fiftieth Anniv. medal, Lucite	20.00	25.00	20.50
☐ **Paperweight,** National Camp School, Lucite	4.00	5.00	4.25
☐ **Paperweight,** Tenderfoot emblem, metal, silver, 3¼″	6.00	8.00	6.50
☐ **Paperweight,** "Safety Good Turn 1958," Tenderfoot emblem, Lucite ..	8.00	10.00	8.50
☐ **Paperweight,** Scout key in Lucite...	8.00	10.00	8.50
☐ **Paperweight,** white marble, 2″ square	5.00	7.00	5.25
☐ **Pedometer,** BSA New Haven	10.00	14.00	10.50
☐ **Pedometer,** Official BSA	8.00	12.00	8.50
☐ **Pedometer,** Scouts hike-meter, also a compass....................	7.00	12.00	7.50
☐ **Pennant,** 23″, Be Prepared, BSA Headquarters, NY	10.00	12.00	10.50
☐ **Pennants,** various, felt	4.00	7.00	4.50
☐ **Pin,** "Boy Scout #1"	2.00	4.00	2.25
☐ **Pin,** Cub scout on red, white and blue..................................	1.00	3.00	1.50
☐ **Pin,** "I Gave, Scout"	1.00	1.50	1.05
☐ **Pin,** "I'm A Camper," pictures tent Scout and fire, 1″ button	1.00	4.00	1.50
☐ **Pin,** "I'm Selling Scouting"	1.00	1.50	1.05
☐ **Pin,** "I Recruited One BSA"	1.00	1.50	1.05
☐ **Pin,** Scout, "Strengthen the Arm of Liberty".............................	1.00	3.00	1.50
☐ **Plaque,** Boy Scout Creed, c. 1920	20.00	30.00	21.00

	Current Price Range		P/Y Avg.
☐ **Plaque,** imitation wood, first class emblem on shield, 3½″ × 5″	4.50	7.00	5.00
☐ **Plaque,** wood shield with bronzed plaster Scout head, 1930s.........	25.00	35.00	26.00
☐ **Postcard,** BSA World War I, Liberty Loan	3.00	5.00	3.50
☐ **Postcard,** W.D. Boyce monument	2.00	4.00	2.50
☐ **Postcard,** Official BSA, thirteen cartoon camp scenes, 1957 issue ...	10.00	15.00	10.50
☐ **Postcards,** twelve Scout law postcards, 1917	50.00	75.00	55.00
☐ **Postcards,** 111 full-color, Scouts of the world in uniform	20.00	25.00	20.50
☐ **Poster,** Bauer and Black Scout first aid chart, 20″ × 32″, 1920s	5.00	8.00	5.50
☐ **Poster,** Boy Scout Week, color, President Wilson's proclamation on back, signed by artist Victor C. Anderson, 9½″ × 12½″, 1919	20.00	25.00	20.50
☐ **Poster** *Boy's Life,* cardboard, 1932	6.00	8.00	6.50
☐ **Poster,** BSA Forty-ninth Anniversary, 9″ × 14″, 1959..............	2.00	3.00	2.10
☐ **Poster,** "Follow the Rugged Road," large, 28″ × 40″..........	5.00	7.00	5.50
☐ **Poster,** "Henry Aldrich, Boy Scout," 11″ × 4″, 1944...........	30.00	40.00	30.50
☐ **Poster,** "How to Tie Knots," splices, lashings, etc., Carte-Scope Co., set of twenty-five photographic, 14″ × 18″, 1923.........	70.00	85.00	71.00
☐ **Poster,** "Is God Calling Me," Catholic Committee on Scouting, 14″ × 10″, 1946	3.50	5.00	3.75
☐ **Poster,** "Just Listen and Obey and You'll Command Some Day," canvas, Scoutmaster and Scout with bicycle, World War I, 26″ × 38″....	60.00	75.00	62.00

Official Boy Scouts of America Commemorative Plate, *Norman Rockwell and four scouts, one in a set of nine, Thorsen's Museum, Florida*

	Current Price Range		P/Y Avg.
☐ **Poster,** ''Lend to your Uncle,'' Buy a Victory Bond, 1917	45.00	60.00	47.00
☐ **Poster,** Leyendecker/BSA, World War I Liberty Loan	70.00	90.00	75.00
☐ **Poster,** Scout Week, cardboard, 1963	3.50	5.00	3.75

	Current Price Range		P/Y Avg.
☐ **Poster,** Scouts of Today, Men of Leadership Tomorrow, 13½″ × 19½″, c. 1925	12.00	16.00	12.50
☐ **Poster,** Scouters key, cardboard....	3.50	5.00	3.75
☐ **Poster,** Scouting Can Make a Difference, cardboard	3.50	5.00	3.75
☐ **Poster,** "Scouting Needs Money," Remington-Schuyler illustration, framed under glass, 17″ × 26″, 1920s	45.00	60.00	50.00
☐ **Poster,** religious awards, heavy cardboard, easel back, set of 8, 14″ × 20″	12.00	15.00	12.50
☐ **Poster,** "Tex Ritter Rides with the Boy Scouts," 11″ × 14″, 1937 ...	30.00	40.00	30.50
☐ **Poster,** Three hiking Scouts, Goodrich Sports Shoes, stand-up, 15″ high	15.00	20.00	15.50
☐ **Poster,** Twenty-fifth Anniversary, cardboard, 1935	6.00	8.00	6.50
☐ **Poster,** "Wanted—A Million Men and Women Associate Members," Boy Scout Week color poster, signed by artist Victor C. Anderson, 9½″ × 12½″, 1919	20.00	30.00	21.00
☐ **Poster,** "We'll help You to Win the War, Dad," World War I, Scout and soldier, framed under glass, 12″ × 18″	60.00	75.00	65.00
☐ **Railroad Car,** "Salute the Boy Scouts"	50.00	70.00	54.00
☐ **Record,** "Boy Recruiting"	2.00	3.00	2.10
☐ **Record,** Boy Scout in Switzerland, Fox Trot, Raymond Scott Quartet, Brunswick, 10″, 78 rpm	10.00	15.00	10.50
☐ **Record,** Brunswick label, two marches played by Boy Scout Band, 10″, 78 rpm	10.00	15.00	8.50

	Current Price Range		P/Y Avg.
☐ **Record,** BSA, "Follow the Rugged Road," cardboard phonograph type	1.00	2.00	1.10
☐ **Record,** BSA radio spots on Boy Recruiting, 7"	1.00	2.00	1.10
☐ **Record,** BSA, "Message from Gus Grissom," cardboard phonograph type	1.00	2.00	1.10
☐ **Record,** BSA, "Message from John Glenn," cardboard phonograph type	1.00	2.00	1.10
☐ **Record,** BSA, "Scouting Do All OK," cardboard phonograph type	1.00	2.00	1.10
☐ **Record,** bugle calls, official BSA, 10", 78 rpm	12.00	16.00	12.50
☐ **Record,** Edison cylinder record of Sousa's "Boy Scouts of America March"	30.00	50.00	35.00
☐ **Record,** "Learning International Morse Code," two-record set, 10", 78 rpm	10.00	15.00	10.50
☐ **Record,** little tot's album, patriotic songs, four Scouts saluting on cover, 4–7"	15.00	22.00	16.00
☐ **Record,** plastic, song of Thirteenth World Jamboree	1.00	2.50	1.25
☐ **Record,** "Rugged Road Round-up"	2.00	3.00	2.10
☐ **Record,** "Support Scouting/United Way"	2.00	3.00	2.10
☐ **Record,** "The Explorers March," 45 rpm, 1950s	4.00	6.00	4.50
☐ **Record,** "The Scout March," 45 rpm, 1950s	4.00	6.00	4.50
☐ **Record,** Victor Military Band playing Sousa's "Boy Scouts of America March," 10", 78 rpm	12.00	15.00	12.50

	Current Price Range		P/Y Avg.
☐ **Ring,** "Cubs-BSA," sterling, 1930s	7.00	10.00	7.50
☐ **Ring,** Eagle, silver with red, white, and blue enameled background, c. 1920s	60.00	75.00	63.00
☐ **Ring,** Eagle, square ribbed with enamel, 1940s	35.00	45.00	37.00
☐ **Ring,** First-Class, scroll, no knots, c. 1919	20.00	30.00	21.00
☐ **Ring,** First-Class, Scout, silver, oval, 1930s	9.00	13.00	9.50
☐ **Ring,** First-Class, Scout, silver, square, 1970s	7.00	12.00	7.50
☐ **Ring,** First-Class, square on black enamel, 1930s	12.00	15.00	12.50
☐ **Ring,** Eagle, gold ring, 1970s	100.00	120.00	105.00
☐ **Ring,** life, square ribbed with enamel, 1940s	45.00	55.00	46.00
☐ **Ring,** Lone Scout "BSA"	40.00	50.00	41.00
☐ **Ring,** recessed First-Class emblem, sterling c. 1920s	15.00	18.00	15.50
☐ **Ring,** Sea Scout oval, sterling silver, 1930s	30.00	45.00	32.00
☐ **Ring,** star, square ribbed with enamel, 1940s	35.00	45.00	35.50
☐ **School Supplies,** Boy Scout painting book, Thompson Co., 1918	28.00	32.00	28.50
☐ **School Supplies,** chalk, Scout brand, Scout scene on box	10.00	15.00	10.50
☐ **School Supplies,** tin pencil box, mfg. by Wallace Pencil Co., Boy Scout scene in color	20.00	30.00	20.50
☐ **School Supplies,** wood ruler, "Boy Scout, Best Syrup Out," 6″	5.00	7.00	5.50
☐ **Seal,** Every Scout in Camp, black/orange	2.00	3.00	2.50
☐ **Seal,** Squanto Council, 1969	1.00	2.00	1.50
☐ **Seal,** BSA Fiftieth Anniversary	2.00	3.00	2.50

	Current Price Range		P/Y Avg.
☐ **Sheet Music,** "A Day with the Scouts," Rovanger, 1929..........	8.00	12.00	8.50
☐ **Sheet Music,** "America Salutes You," Thabes/Olson, 1951	3.00	5.00	3.50
☐ **Sheet Music,** "Be A Good Scout," Murphy, 1912......................	14.00	20.00	14.50
☐ **Sheet Music,** "Be Prepared," Prey/Herbert, 1946	4.00	7.00	4.50
☐ **Sheet Music,** Boy Scout March, Macy, 1911	12.00	15.00	12.50
☐ **Sheet Music,** Boy Scouts' March, Hopkins, 1937	6.00	10.00	6.50
☐ **Sheet Music,** Boy Scouts of America, Haimsohn, 1934..............	6.00	10.00	6.50
☐ **Sheet Music,** "Boy Scouts of America March," Sousa, 1916	12.00	18.00	10.50
☐ **Sheet Music,** "Boy Scouts of America, Young American on Parade," 1934......................	6.00	8.00	6.50
☐ **Sheet Music,** "Boy Scouts on Parade," Martin, 1930................	6.00	10.00	6.50
☐ **Sheet Music,** "Boy Scouts' Parade March," Johnson, 1917......	12.00	18.00	12.50
☐ **Sheet Music,** "BSA March and Two-Step," Ruhe, 1911	16.00	20.00	16.50
☐ **Sheet Music,** "Ever Onward," Manuscript, Little, 1960............	3.00	5.00	3.50
☐ **Sheet Music,** "Follow the Rugged Road," 1965......................	1.00	3.00	1.50
☐ **Sheet Music,** "Hoe Your Little Bit in Your Own Back Yard," 1917 ...	10.00	16.00	11.00
☐ **Sheet Music,** "I Belong," Reader, 1962	3.00	5.00	3.50
☐ **Sheet Music,** "Let's All Be Good Scouts Together," Penner/Raynor, 1938	7.00	9.00	7.50
☐ **Sheet Music,** "March of the Boy Scouts," Grant/Schaefer, 1913....	12.00	18.00	12.50

	Current Price Range		P/Y Avg.
☐ **Sheet Music**, 'March of the Boy Scouts," Kocian, 1912	10.00	14.00	10.50
☐ **Sheet Music**, "March of the Boy Scouts," Martin, 1912	12.00	18.00	12.50
☐ **Sheet Music**, "Off to Camp March," Anthony, 1921............	15.00	18.00	15.50
☐ **Sheet Music**, 101 Best songs of 1922, contains Boy Scout March....	6.00	10.00	6.50
☐ **Sheet Music**, "Onward for God and My Country," Waring/Dolph, 1065	3.00	5.00	3.50
☐ **Sheet Music**, "Scouting in the USA—Scout March," Bartlett, 1917	10.00	17.00	10.50
☐ **Sheet Music**, "The Boy Scout Anthem," Wright/Mitchell, 1954 ......-	3.00	5.00	3.50
☐ **Sheet Music**, "The Boy Scout Dream," Jones, 1915..............	14.00	17.00	14.50
☐ **Sheet Music**, "The Boy Scout's March," Herman, 1911	12.00	18.00	12.50
☐ **Sheet Music**, "Tomorrow's America," 1949	5.00	7.00	5.50
☐ **Sheet Music**, "Tomorrow's America," Edwards/Bratton, 1949	4.00	6.00	4.50
☐ **Sheet Music**, "Tough-Up, Buckle Down," Mals Music, 1943	10.00	14.00	11.00
☐ **Signals**, BSA Signaller, 1937	12.00	15.00	12.50
☐ **Signals**, set, Morse flags..........	6.00	8.00	6.50
☐ **Signals**, set, semaphore flags	6.00	8.00	6.50
☐ **Signals**, disk, pocket-size, 1914 ..	4.00	6.00	6.50
☐ **Signals**, triple signal set, battery operated, Ryan and Co., 1932	14.00	20.00	14.50
☐ **Supply Service Box**, National BSA, 1' x 2.3', 1938..............	5.00	6.00	5.50
☐ **Tie Bar**, silver with red enameled emblem in BSA circle	4.00	5.00	4.50
☐ **Tie Bar**, local council staff	4.00	5.00	4.50

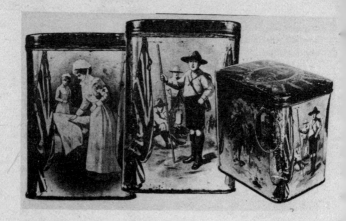

Ridgeway's Tea World War I Souvenir, 5⅛" × 3½" × 5",
Thorsen's Museum, Florida

	Current Price Range		P/Y Avg.
☐ **Tie Bar,** Boy Scouts of America, silver with red & silver universal emblem	3.00	4.00	3.50
☐ **Tie Bars,** Cub Scout, wood	2.00	4.00	2.50
☐ **Tie Rack,** imitation wood, swinging wire hangers, 1950s	5.00	7.00	5.50
☐ **Tie Rack,** pressed wood, First-Class emblem and camp scenes, c. 1937	8.00	12.00	8.50
☐ **Tie Rack,** same as above, but 1941 issue	8.00	12.00	8.50

	Current Price Range		P/Y Avg.
☐ **Tie Tack,** Local Council Staff	4.00	5.00	4.50
☐ **Toilet Kit,** Official BSA............	1.00	3.00	1.50
☐ **Tray,** metal Scout law and smiling Scout, 12″ × 18″	10.00	15.00	10.50
☐ **Tray,** tin, World War II, hinged lid showing Boy Scouts and British military leaders, 4″ × 5″ × 5″ ...	20.00	30.00	21.00
☐ **Viewing Material,** Corte-Scope Co., authorized by BSA, trail signs, hiking, backpacking and estimation with stereo viewer and twenty-five stereo cards, 1923	120.00	160.00	125.00
☐ **Viewing Material,** Keptone stereopticon cards showing Boy Scouts in various activities	4.00	5.00	4.50
☐ **Viewing Material,** glass lantern slides of Scouts, set of eight, color, 1917	40.00	60.00	45.00
☐ **Viewing Material,** glass lantern slides, Scout Oath, Scout Law, set of fourteen, color	100.00	150.00	105.00
☐ **Wallet,** Official BSA, cowhide	1.00	2.50	1.50
☐ **Watch,** BSA wrist watch	75.00	90.00	80.00
☐ **Watch,** Ingersol pocket watch, color Scout scene and law on face, 1933	80.00	120.00	85.00
☐ **Watch,** Ingersol wrist watch, color Scout scene and Scout law on face, rare—made only in 1933	75.00	100.00	80.00
☐ **Watch,** New Haven wrist, BSA seal on dial, 1937......................	15.00	30.00	17.00
☐ **Watch,** Official BSA, sun watch, 1921	50.00	75.00	13.50
☐ **Watch,** Official BSA, Timex, First-Class emblem on face, expansion band	13.00	18.00	13.50

	Current Price Range		P/Y Avg.
☐ **Watch,** pocket style, crossed signal flags on face, Scouts signalling, hiking on back, 1912–1915 ...	85.00	100.00	87.00
☐ **Watch Fob,** American Boy Scout bugling.............................	20.00	30.00	22.00
☐ **Watch Fob,** American Boy Scout kneeling.............................	20.00	30.00	22.00
☐ **Watch Fob,** American Boy Scout saluting	20.00	30.00	22.00
☐ **Watch Fob,** blue ribbon, brass color, standing Scout with staff....	30.00	50.00	33.00

SENIOR SCOUT AND EXPLORER PROGRAMS

Lord Baden-Powell announced the Sea Scout program in early 1910, and his older brother, Warrington, prepared the first manual, entitled *Sea Scouting for Boys,* in 1912. Sea Scouting was enthusiastically received and spread rapidly in England.

The first manual for Sea Scouts in the U.S.A. was prepared by Arthur A. Carey in 1912. It was actually a twenty-four-page pamphlet that helped launch the program. Sea Scouting spread slowly until America's entry into World War I, which spurred a great interest in the program. James Austin Wilder became the first Chief Sea Scout and prepared the first complete manual in 1920. The Sea Scouting Service of the B.S.A. became the Senior Scouting Service in 1935; a fifteen-year-old scout was given the option of either remaining in his troop or becoming a Sea Scout or an Explorer Scout.

In 1941, as interest in aviation increased due to the outbreak of World War II, Air Scouting was established as a separate branch of the Senior Scouting Service.

A continuing study of the needs and interests of the older boy resulted in a revised Explorer Program in 1959 that offered a wide range of activities for Explorer-aged boys. Sea Explorer and Air Explorer programs remained unchanged.

Twenty-five percent of Scouting collectors do something within this area. Items are available; some more valuable than others. Prices fluctuate according to demands of the marketplace.

SENIOR SCOUTS (1938–1946)

BADGES—SENIOR SCOUT RATINGS (Titles)

	Current Price Range		P/Y Avg.
☐ **Scout Airman**, blue background....	20.00	40.00	30.00
☐ **Scout Artist**, light green and dark green	10.00	30.00	20.00
☐ **Scout Seaman**, light and dark green	10.00	30.00	20.00
☐ **Scout Naturalist**, light green and dark green	10.00	40.00	25.00
☐ **Scout Artisan**, light green and dark green	10.00	40.00	25.00
☐ **Scout Sportsman**, light green and dark green	10.00	40.00	25.00
☐ **Scout Gardener**, light green and dark green	10.00	40.00	25.00
☐ **Scout Journalist**, light green and dark green	10.00	40.00	25.00
☐ **Scout Radioman**, light green and dark green	10.00	40.00	25.00
☐ **Scout Citizen**, light green and dark green	10.00	40.00	25.00
☐ **Scout Craftsman**, light green and dark green	10.00	40.00	25.00
☐ **Scout Forester**, light green and dark green	10.00	40.00	25.00
☐ **Scout Livestockman**, light green and dark green	10.00	40.00	20.00
☐ **Scout Conservationist**, light green and dark green	10.00	40.00	20.00
☐ **Scout Farm Manager**, light green and dark green	10.00	40.00	20.00
☐ **Scout Dairyman**, light green and dark green	10.00	40.00	20.00
☐ **Scout Poultryman**, light green and dark green	10.00	40.00	20.00

	Current Price Range		P/Y Avg.

CHEVRONS

☐ **Chevron,** Explorer Patrol Leader, one green bar	20.00	40.00	30.00
☐ **Chevron,** Explorer Patrol Leader, with First Honors, two green bars.................................	20.00	40.00	30.00
☐ **Chevron,** Explorer Patrol Leader, with Second Honors, three green bars.........................	20.00	40.00	30.00
☐ **Chevron,** Explorer with First Honors, two long green bars...........	20.00	40.00	30.00
☐ **Chevron,** Explorer with Second Honors, three long green bars	20.00	40.00	30.00

EXPLORING SCOUTS (Branch of Senior Scouts, 1942–1949)

PATCHES

☐ **Patch,** Explorer Scout Advisor, dark green	30.00	50.00	40.00
☐ **Patch,** Explorer Scout Advisor, light green	30.00	50.00	40.00
☐ **Patch,** Explorer Scout Assistant Advisor, dark green................	30.00	50.00	40.00
☐ **Patch,** Explorer Scout Assistant Advisor, light green................	30.00	50.00	40.00
☐ **Patch,** Explorer Scout, small, light green	12.00	25.00	15.00
☐ **Patch,** Explorer Scout, small, dark green	12.00	25.00	15.00
☐ **Patch,** Explorer Scout, Hat........	20.00	30.00	15.00
☐ **Patch,** Explorer Scout Post Guide ..	25.00	50.00	30.00
☐ **Patch,** Explorer Scout Assistant Guide	25.00	50.00	30.00
☐ **Patch,** Explorer Scout Crew Leader	25.00	50.00	30.00

	Current Price Range		P/Y Avg.
☐ **Patch,** Explorer Scout Assistant Crew Leader........................	25.00	50.00	30.00
☐ **Patch,** Explorer Scout Post Secretary	50.00	100.00	65.00
☐ **Patch,** Explorer Scout Apprentice ...	15.00	25.00	18.00
☐ **Patch,** Explorer Scout Woodsman ..	25.00	40.00	30.00
☐ **Patch,** Explorer Scout Frontiersman..................................	35.00	60.00	45.00
☐ **Patch,** Explorer Scout Ranger	50.00	100.00	65.00

MEDALLION

☐ **Leader's Medallion,** Explorer Scout Universal, with white embroidered edge	35.00	50.00	45.00

SHIRT STRIPS

☐ **Shirt Strip,** Explorer Scout, BSA, green	5.00	15.00	10.00
☐ **Shirt Strip,** Explorer Scout, BSA, khaki...............................	5.00	15.00	10.00
☐ **Shirt Strip,** Senior Scout, BSA, khaki...............................	10.00	20.00	15.00

MEDAL

☐ **Medal,** Explorer Scout Ranger	400.00	700.00	350.00

KNOTS

☐ **Knot,** Explorer Scout, green	75.00	125.00	90.00
☐ **Knot,** Explorer Scout, khaki.......	75.00	125.00	90.00

PINS

☐ **Pin,** Explorer Scout Advisor, ⅞" & ⅝"	40.00	75.00	60.00
☐ **Pin,** Explorer Scout Assistant Advisor, ⅞" & ⅝"......................	40.00	75.00	60.00

	Current Price Range		P/Y Avg.
☐ **Pin,** Explorer Scout Universal, ⅞" & ⅝"	15.00	30.00	20.00

EXPLORERS (1949–1958)

SHIRT STRIPS

☐ **Shirt Strip,** Explorers BSA, green...	3.00	5.00	4.00
☐ **Shirt Strip,** Explorers BSA, khaki ...	3.00	5.00	4.00

PATCHES

☐ **Patch,** Local Standard Explorer Unit	1.00	3.00	2.00
☐ **Patch,** Regional Standard Explorer Unit	1.00	3.00	2.00
☐ **Patch,** National Standard Explorer Unit	2.00	4.00	3.00
☐ **Patch,** Local Standard Senior Scout Unit	5.00	15.00	7.00
☐ **Patch,** Regional Standard Senior Scout Unit	5.00	15.00	7.00
☐ **Patch,** National Standard Senior Scout Unit	5.00	15.00	7.00
☐ **Patch,** Explorer Silver Award, Flying Eagle, Type II..............	40.00	75.00	55.00

COMPASS-ANCHOR-WINGS DESIGN

☐ **Patch,** Universal, blue.............	2.00	6.00	4.00
☐ **Patch,** Universal, green	1.00	4.00	3.00
☐ **Patch,** Universal, red..............	1.00	2.00	1.50
☐ **Patch,** Universal, small, red.......	5.00	10.00	7.00
☐ **Patch,** Hat.......................	5.00	10.00	7.00

BLUE

☐ **Patch,** Explorer Outfit Guide, 3 bars.................................	10.00	25.00	15.00
☐ **Patch,** Explorer Outfit Assistant Guide, 2½ bars	25.00	50.00	35.00

	Current Price Range		P/Y Avg.
☐ **Patch**, Explorer Outfit Crew Leader, 2 bars	10.00	25.00	15.00
☐ **Patch**, Explorer Outfit Assistant Crew Leader, 1 bar	10.00	25.00	15.00
☐ **Patch**, Explorer Outfit, Secretary	15.00	30.00	20.00

GREEN (WITH AND WITHOUT EMBROIDERED EDGE)

☐ **Patch**, Explorer Post Assistant Senior Crew Leader	8.00	18.00	12.00
☐ **Patch**, Explorer Post Crew Leader	8.00	18.00	12.00
☐ **Patch**, Explorer Post Assistant Crew Leader	7.00	17.00	10.00
☐ **Patch**, Explorer Post Secretary	10.00	30.00	20.00

BLUE AND GREEN (ROUND)

☐ **Patch**, Explorer Advisor	5.00	15.00	7.00
☐ **Patch**, Explorer Assistant Advisor	5.00	15.00	7.00
☐ **Patch**, Explorer Senior Crew Leader	5.00	15.00	7.00

BLUE AND RED

☐ **Patch**, Explorer Apprentice	2.00	7.00	4.00
☐ **Patch**, Explorer Bronze Award	10.00	20.00	15.00
☐ **Patch**, Explorer Gold Award	15.00	30.00	20.00
☐ **Patch**, Explorer Silver Award, Type I	45.00	100.00	60.00

POSITION STRIPS, RED AND GREEN

☐ **Position Strip**, Advisor	.50	1.00	.75
☐ **Position Strip**, Associate Advisor	.50	1.00	.75
☐ **Position Strip**, Secretary	.50	1.00	.75
☐ **Position Strip**, Treasurer	.50	1.00	.75
☐ **Position Strip**, Vice President	.50	1.00	.75
☐ **Position Strip**, President	.50	1.00	.75

	Current Price Range		P/Y Avg.
☐ **Position Strip,** Quartermaster	.50	1.00	.75
☐ **Position Strip,** Post Committee...	.50	1.00	.75
☐ **Position Strip,** Cabinet Officer....	.50	1.00	.75
☐ **Position Strip,** Cabinet Advisor	.50	1.00	.75
☐ **Position Strip,** Representative....	.50	1.00	.75

NUMERALS, GREEN & BROWN

☐ 1 through 9	.50	1.50	.75

RATINGS (Titles—Outdoor Skills)

☐ **Aviation**	3.00	4.00	2.00
☐ **Craft Skills**	3.00	4.00	2.00
☐ **Navigation**	3.00	4.00	2.00
☐ **Physical Fitness**	3.00	4.00	2.00
☐ **Vocational Exploration**	3.00	4.00	2.00
☐ **Communications**..................	3.00	4.00	2.00
☐ **Emergency Skills**	3.00	4.00	2.00
☐ **Seamanship**......................	3.00	4.00	2.00

MEDALS

☐ **Medal,** Explorer Silver Award, Type I, with red & yellow ribbon.........	300.00	800.00	400.00
☐ **Medal,** Explorer Silver Award, Type II, with red, white and blue ribbon ...	150.00	300.00	200.00

KNOTS

☐ **Knot,** Explorer Silver Award, blue with red & yellow strands..........	25.00	75.00	45.00
☐ **Knot,** Explorer Silver Award, red, white & blue	2.00	8.00	4.00

PINS

☐ **Pin,** Miniature, Explorer Silver Award, Type I.....................	40.00	75.00	50.00
☐ **Pin,** Miniature, Explorer Silver Award, Type II	30.00	75.00	40.00

	Current Price Range		P/Y Avg.

☐ **Pin,** Explorer Adviser, blue & white, 7/8″	18.00	30.00	22.00
☐ **Pin,** Explorer Advisor, blue & white, 5/8″	18.00	30.00	20.00
☐ **Pin,** Explorer Assistant Advisor, gold, 7/8″	18.00	30.00	20.00
☐ **Pin,** Explorer Assistant Advisor, gold, 5/8″	18.00	30.00	20.00
☐ **Pin,** Explorer Universal, red, 5/8″ & 7/8″	10.00	25.00	15.00

AIR SCOUTS/EXPLORERS (1942–1949)

SHIRT STRIPS

☐ **Shirt Strip,** Air Scout, BSA, blue	10.00	20.00	15.00
☐ **Shirt Strip,** Senior Scout, BSA, blue	10.00	20.00	15.00

MEDAL

☐ **Medal,** Air Scout Ace	700.00	1200.00	900.00

KNOT

☐ **Knot,** Air Scout Ace	100.00	200.00	150.00

PINS

☐ **Pin,** Air Scout Ace Miniature	50.00	150.00	75.00
☐ **Pin,** Air Scout Universal, wings (Leaders Collar Emblem)	20.00	50.00	30.00

PATCHES

☐ **Patch,** Air Scout Universal, Type I	10.00	40.00	20.00
☐ **Patch,** Air Scout Universal, Type II	8.00	18.00	12.00
☐ **Patch,** Air Scout Hat	10.00	30.00	20.00
☐ **Patch,** Air Scout Scribe, blue	15.00	35.00	20.00

	Current Price Range		P/Y Avg.
☐ **Patch,** Air Scout Assistant Flight Pilot.................................	15.00	40.00	30.00
☐ **Patch,** Air Scout Flight Pilot.......	15.00	40.00	30.00
☐ **Patch,** Air Scout Assistant Squadron Pilot.................................	15.00	40.00	30.00
☐ **Patch,** Air Scout Squadron Pilot ..	15.00	40.00	30.00
☐ **Patch,** Air Scout Assistant Squadron Leader...........................	15.00	40.00	30.00
☐ **Patch,** Air Scout Squadron Leader...................................	15.00	40.00	30.00
☐ **Patch,** Air Scout Apprentice.......	12.00	25.00	18.00
☐ **Patch,** Air Scout Apprentice, no words	20.00	40.00	30.00
☐ **Patch,** Air Scout Observer	25.00	50.00	30.00
☐ **Patch,** Air Scout Observer, no words	25.00	50.00	30.00
☐ **Patch,** Air Scout Craftsman	40.00	60.00	50.00
☐ **Patch,** Air Scout Craftsman, no words	40.00	100.00	60.00
☐ **Patch,** Air Scout Ace	50.00	125.00	75.00
☐ **Patch,** Tenderfoot Air Scout Candidate	10.00	20.00	15.00
☐ **Patch,** Second-Class Air Scout Candidate...........................	10.00	20.00	15.00
☐ **Patch,** First-Class Air Scout Candidate	10.00	20.00	15.00
☐ **Patch,** Air Explorer Apprentice....	25.00	60.00	45.00
☐ **Patch,** Air Explorer Observer	35.00	75.00	50.00
☐ **Patch,** Air Explorer Craftsman	40.00	100.00	85.00
☐ **Patch,** Air Explorer Ace	55.00	125.00	100.00

RATINGS (Titles)

☐ **Explorer Specialist Ratings,** Each title came in:			
☐ Observer, no wings	15.00	25.00	20.00
☐ Craftsman, one wing...........	20.00	35.00	25.00
☐ Ace, two wings.................	25.00	45.00	35.00

	Current Price Range		P/Y Avg.

Titles:
  Outdoorsman
  Navigator
  Airman
  Mechanic
  Builder
  Communicator

MEDAL

☐ Medal, Air Explorer Ace	700.00	1200.00	900.00

KNOT

☐ Knot, Air Explorer Ace (same as Air Scout)	100.00	200.00	150.00

PINS

☐ Pin, Air Scout Ace Miniature	50.00	150.00	110.00
☐ Pin, Air Scout Universal, wings (Leaders Collar Emblem)	20.00	50.00	30.00
☐ Pin, Basic Aeronautics	40.00	100.00	60.00
☐ Pin, Advanced Aeronautics	40.00	100.00	60.00

NUMERALS, BLUE

☐ 1 through 9	8.00	15.00	10.00

EMERGENCY SERVICE CORPS.

PATCHES

☐ Patch, Emergency Service Corps.	8.00	20.00	12.00
☐ Patch, Emergency Service Apprentice	8.00	20.00	12.00
☐ Patch, Emergency Service Explorer	3.00	8.00	5.00

ARMBANDS

ARMBANDS	Current Price Range		P/Y Avg.
☐ **Armband,** BSA with lightning bolt, wrap-around	5.00	20.00	12.00
☐ **Armband,** First-Class with lightning bolt, wrap-around	5.00	20.00	12.00
☐ **Armband,** First-Class with lightning bolt, oval	15.00	50.00	36.00
☐ **Armband,** Emergency Service, wrap-around	3.00	8.00	5.50
☐ **Armband,** Emergency Service, oval, white letters	3.00	8.00	5.50
☐ **Armband,** Emergency Services Explorer, oval, black letters	3.00	8.00	5.50
☐ **Armband,** Explorer Ready	1.00	5.00	3.00
☐ **Armband,** Emergency Service "E"	1.00	5.00	3.00

SEA SCOUTS/EXPLORERS

SEA SCOUTS

SHIRT STRIPS	Current Price Range		P/Y Avg.
☐ **Shirt Strip,** Sea Scout, BSA, blue	8.00	15.00	10.00
☐ **Shirt Strip,** Sea Scout, BSA, white	8.00	15.00	10.00

PATCHES, BLUE AND WHITE

☐ **Patch,** Sea Scout, oval	15.00	30.00	20.00
☐ **Patch,** Sea Scout Apprentice	10.00	20.00	15.00
☐ **Patch,** Sea Scout Ordinary	15.00	25.00	20.00
☐ **Patch,** Sea Scout Able	20.00	40.00	30.00

SEA EXPLORERS

	Current Price Range		P/Y Avg.

SHIRT STRIPS

	Current		P/Y
☐ **Shirt Strip**, Sea Explorer, BSA, white	1.00	5.00	3.00
☐ **Shirt Strip**, Sea Explorer, BSA, blue	1.00	5.00	3.00
☐ **Shirt Strip**, Sea Explorer, BSA, khaki	1.00	5.00	3.00

PATCHES

☐ **Patch**, Sea Explorer, Universal, blue	1.00	3.00	2.00
☐ **Patch**, Sea Explorer, Universal, white	1.00	3.00	2.00
☐ **Patch**, Sea Explorer, "bug," blue and white	1.00	2.00	1.50
☐ **Patch**, Sea Explorer, Assistant Crew Leader, blue and white	1.00	3.00	2.00
☐ **Patch**, Sea Explorer, Crew Leader, blue and white	1.00	3.00	2.00
☐ **Patch**, Sea Explorer, Boatswain's Mate, blue and white	1.00	3.00	2.00
☐ **Patch**, Sea Explorer, Boatswain, blue and white	1.00	3.00	2.00
☐ **Patch**, Cabinet Officer, blue and white	1.00	2.00	1.50
☐ **Patch**, Representative, blue and white	1.00	2.00	1.50
☐ **Patch**, Sea Explorer Skipper, blue and white	1.00	5.00	3.00
☐ **Patch**, Sea Explorer Mate, blue and white	1.00	5.00	3.00
☐ **Patch**, Sea Explorer Specialist, blue and white	1.00	4.00	2.00
☐ **Patch**, Sea Explorer Purser, blue and white	1.00	4.00	2.00

	Current Price Range		P/Y Avg.
☐ **Patch,** Sea Explorer Bugler, blue and white	1.00	4.00	2.00
☐ **Patch,** Sea Explorer Scribe, blue and white	1.00	4.00	2.00
☐ **Patch,** Sea Explorer Yoeman, blue and white	1.00	4.00	2.00
☐ **Patch,** Sea Explorer Storekeeper, blue and white.....................	1.00	4.00	2.00
☐ **Patch,** Ship Chairman, blue and white................................	1.00	4.00	2.00
☐ **Patch,** Committeeman, blue and white................................	1.00	4.00	2.00
☐ **Patch,** Local Council Chairman, blue and white.....................	2.00	8.00	5.00
☐ **Patch,** Local Council Committee-man, blue and white...............	2.00	8.00	5.00
☐ **Patch,** National Council Chairman, blue and white.....................	5.00	10.00	7.00
☐ **Patch,** National Council Commit-teeman, blue and white............	5.00	10.00	7.00
☐ **Patch,** Local Council Staff, blue and white	8.00	15.00	10.00
☐ **Patch,** National Professional Staff, blue and white.....................	8.00	15.00	10.00
☐ **Patch,** Cabin Boy	15.00	40.00	20.00
☐ **Patch,** Sea Explorer Apprentice, blue and white.....................	1.00	3.00	2.00
☐ **Patch,** Sea Explorer Ordinary, blue and white	2.00	4.00	3.00
☐ **Patch,** Sea Explorer Able, blue and white................................	2.00	4.00	3.00
☐ **Patch,** Sea Explorer Quartermas-ter, blue and white.................	2.00	4.00	3.00
☐ **Patch,** Long Cruise, blue and white................................	4.00	8.00	6.00
☐ **Patch,** Long Cruise, red arc.......	1.00	2.00	1.50
☐ **Patch,** Long Cruise, white arc	1.00	2.00	1.50

Sea Explorer Universal Badge, *paperweight, bronze, 3", c. 1940s, $10.00–$15.00*

	Current Price Range		P/Y Avg.
NUMERALS			
☐ 1–9, blue felt	1.00	2.00	1.50
☐ 1–9, white felt	1.00	2.00	1.50
☐ 1–9, blue-embroidered	.50	1.00	.75
☐ 1–9, white-embroidered	.50	1.00	.75
SEA SCOUT RATINGS (Titles)			
☐ **Sea Scout Airman,** blue & white ...	20.00	35.00	25.00
☐ **Sea Scout Artist,** blue & white ...	20.00	35.00	25.00
☐ **Sea Scout Seaman,** blue & white ..	20.00	35.00	25.00

	Current Price Range		P/Y Avg.
☐ **Sea Scout Naturalist,** blue & white	20.00	35.00	25.00
☐ **Sea Scout Artisan,** blue & white	20.00	35.00	25.00
☐ **Sea Scout Sportsman,** blue & white	20.00	35.00	25.00
☐ **Sea Scout Gardener,** blue & white	20.00	35.00	25.00
☐ **Sea Scout Journalist,** blue & white	20.00	35.00	25.00
☐ **Sea Scout Radioman,** blue & white	20.00	35.00	25.00
☐ **Sea Scout Citizen,** blue & white	20.00	35.00	25.00
☐ **Sea Scout Craftsman,** blue & white	20.00	35.00	25.00
☐ **Sea Scout Forester,** blue & white	20.00	35.00	25.00
☐ **Sea Scout Livestockman,** blue & white	20.00	35.00	25.00
☐ **Sea Scout Conservationist,** blue & white	20.00	35.00	25.00
☐ **Sea Scout Farm Manager,** blue & white	20.00	35.00	25.00
☐ **Sea Scout Dairyman,** blue & white	20.00	35.00	25.00
☐ **Sea Scout Poultryman,** blue & white	20.00	35.00	25.00

MEDAL

	Current Price Range		P/Y Avg.
☐ **Medal,** Sea Explorer Quartermaster	25.00	75.00	35.00

PIN

	Current Price Range		P/Y Avg.
☐ **Pin,** Sea Explorer Quartermaster, Miniature	15.00	30.00	20.00

KNOT	Current Price Range		P/Y Avg.
☐ **Knot,** Sea Explorer Quartermaster, blue, white, khaki..............	4.00	8.00	6.00

CUB SCOUTS

HISTORY

Rudyard Kipling's famous classic children's novel *The Jungle Book* gave Robert Baden-Powell the solution to the problem of establishing a separate program for boys who were too young to join the Boy Scouts.

After obtaining permission from Kipling, Baden-Powell produced *The Wolf Cubs Handbook* in 1916. The program of "Wolf Cubs" utilized the characters appearing in *The Jungle Book,* and many of the early games and activities were designed around the action in the book.

The Boy Scouts of America studied various ideas for a program that would best serve the interests of American prescout-age boys, and in 1929 the first cub packs were organized to test the ideas. In 1930 the "Cubbing" program became official, and it became available to all scout councils by 1933.

In 1945, the name was changed to "Cub Scouts." The program is divided into age groups known as Wolf, Bear, Lions, and Webelos.

COLLECTIBLES	Current Price Range		P/Y Avg.
☐ **Cubbing, The Boys' Cub Book, Wolf Rank,** first edition, cover had Indian drawing, known cover, 1930	12.00	15.00	12.50
☐ **1931**	10.00	12.00	10.50
☐ **1932–1935**	8.00	10.00	8.50
☐ **1936,** change in cover design.....	7.00	9.00	7.50
☐ **1937–1942**	6.00	8.00	6.50
☐ **1943–1944,** various printings of wartime editions	4.00	6.00	4.50

Cub Scout Knife, Brush and Comb

	Current Price Range		P/Y Avg.
☐ **Wolf Cub Scout Book,** second edition, 1948, first printing........	4.00	6.00	4.50
☐ **1949–1953**	3.00	5.00	3.50
☐ **Wolf Cub Scout Book,** revised edition, 1954–1965	2.00	4.00	2.50
☐ **Wolf Cub Scout Book,** fourth edition, 1967–1978	2.00	4.00	2.50
☐ **Bear Rank,** first edition, green cover with Indian drawing, 1930...	12.50	20.00	16.00
☐ **1931**	9.00	14.00	11.00
☐ **1932–1937**	8.00	10.00	8.50

	Current Price Range		P/Y Avg.
☐ **1938–1942,** gold cover with "Bear" on spine	5.00	7.00	5.50
☐ **1943–1945,** wartime edition	5.00	7.00	5.50
☐ **Bear Cub Scout Book,** 1948–1953	3.00	5.00	4.50
☐ **Bear Cub Scout Book,** revised edition, 1954–1958	2.50	4.00	3.25
☐ **Bear Cub Scout Book,** fourth edition, 1967–1978	2.00	4.00	2.50
☐ **Lion Rank,** first edition, blue cover with Indian drawing, 1930	20.00	25.00	20.50
☐ **1931–1937**	9.00	12.00	9.50
☐ **1938,** reddish color on cover, "Lion" on spine	7.50	12.50	8.50
☐ **1943–1945,** wartime edition	5.00	7.00	5.50
☐ **Lion Cub Scout Book,** 1948–1953	4.00	6.00	4.50
☐ **Lion Webelos Cub Scout Book,** 1954	3.00	5.00	4.00
☐ **1955–1966**	3.00	4.00	3.10
☐ **Webelos Scout Book,** revised program, 1967 to present	1.00	3.00	2.50
☐ **Den Chief's Denbook,** first edition, blue cover with gold printing, 1932	10.00	12.50	11.00
☐ **1934 and 1935**	6.00	8.00	6.50
☐ **1937–1941**	4.00	6.00	4.50
☐ **Den Leader's Book,** Cubmaster's Pack book, first edition, blue cover, revised program, 1932	10.00	15.00	12.00
☐ **1932**	9.00	12.00	9.50
☐ **1933–41**	6.00	7.00	6.25
☐ **1943,** second edition	6.00	7.00	6.25
☐ **1944–1954**	4.00	5.00	4.25
☐ **1954–1966,** dark blue hardcover, entitled *Pack Book*	3.00	4.00	3.10
☐ **1967 to present,** blue card cover	2.00	3.00	2.10

Cub Scout Cap

	Current Price Range		P/Y Avg.
☐ **Den Mother's Denbook,** first edition, blue cover, gold print, 1937 ..	8.00	10.00	8.50
☐ **1938–1941**	5.00	7.00	5.50
☐ **1942–1950,** red covers............	4.00	6.00	4.50
☐ **1951–1964,** multicolored cover ...	2.50	4.00	3.10
☐ **1967–1973,** third edition	2.00	3.00	2.10
☐ **How-to Book of Cubbing,** gold hardcover, 1938	7.00	10.00	7.50
☐ **1939–1942**	6.00	8.00	6.50
☐ **1943–1945,** yellow cover..........	3.00	4.00	3.25
☐ **1946–1949,** brown cover	2.00	4.00	3.10
☐ **1950,** green question mark........	1.50	3.00	2.00

	Current Price Range		P/Y Avg.
☐ **1951–1966**, red question mark....	1.00	3.00	2.00
☐ **Staging Den and Pack Ceremonies**, 1953	4.00	5.00	4.50
☐ **1955–1973**	3.00	4.00	3.10
☐ **Cub Scout Songbooks**, 1947–1976	1.00	4.00	2.50
☐ **Representative Cub Scout Collectibles**, Avon Cub "Knife," brush and comb set	10.00	15.00	10.50
☐ **Cubmaster Collar Pins**, "Cub Scouts"...........................	15.00	18.00	15.50
☐ **Den Mother Award Medal**, gold filled	10.00	12.00	10.50
☐ **"Cub BSA" Plaques**	5.00	7.00	5.50
☐ **"Cub BSA" Ring**	7.00	8.00	7.50

CAMP FIRE, INC.

HISTORY

Founded in 1910, this first national nonsectarian interracial organization for girls in the United States of America has had a rich and innovative history.

"Work, Health, and Love" (Wo-He-Lo) were the objectives set by Luther Halsey Gulick, M.D., and his wife, Charlotte Vetter Gulick, for a gathering of young girls at a campsite on Lake Sebago, near South Casco, Maine. Dr. and Mrs. Gulick, along with William Chauncy Langdon, in Vermont, Mrs. Mary Schenck Woolman, Mrs. Charles H. Farnsworth, Ernest Thompson Seton and Miss Lina Beard were all instrumental in the development of an organization dedicated to the creation of opportunities for girls similar to the opportunities afforded boys and young men through the Boy Scouts program. The efforts of these groups became the core of the Camp Fire Girls program. According to Wo-He-Lo: The Camp Fire History, "All these people were friends as well as professional associates in advanced educational and recreational work with youth, and all were to be involved in forming that new creation unlike anything that had ever existed—Camp Fire Girls."

After early summer camp experimentation, the basic philosophies of the new group were discussed by Dr. Gulick before the development committee, which included James E. West, executive secretary of the Boy Scouts of America. It was determined that a program entirely different from the Boy Scouts would be developed for the girls.

On April 10, 1911, the following news release was made by Boy Scout Headquarters:

NATIONAL SOCIETY
FOR GIRLS LIKE THE BOY SCOUTS

Prominent New York men and women organize "The Camp Fire Girls of America"—success of the Boy Scout movement paves the way for the new organization, but methods will be different.

Plans are now being made for a temporary organization called "The Camp Fire Girls of America," which may develop into a national society in the fall if such a step seems justified. The aim of the organization is to provide outdoor activities for girls corresponding to those furnished boys by the Boy Scout movement. It seeks to encourage a greater interest among girls in exercises in the open with the threefold aim of developing their bodies, minds and characters. It is recognized, however, that the activities provided for the girls must be fundamentally different from those of the boys and that special attention must be paid to the home. . . .

While plans were being made for the Camp Fire Girls, Clara A. Lisetor-Lane of Des Moines, Iowa, had formed a group called Girl Scouts (not to be confused with the Girl Scouts of America founded by Mrs. Juliette Gorden Low in Savannah, Georgia, in 1912) and the Reverend David Ferry of Spokane, Washington, had begun a group called the Girl Guides.

These three groups hastily banned together and adopted the name "Girl Pioneers of America," but the experiment was unsuccessful and disbanded in late 1911.

Undaunted, Dr. and Mrs. Gulick continued to develop the Camp Fire Girls concepts. Mrs. Gulick prepared the first manual and the fledgling group was incorporated March 15, 1912.

Originally there were three ranks; Wood Gatherer, Fire Maker and Torch Bearer. In 1936, when the age was lowered to ten, the rank of Trail Seeker was added. Achievement honors were grouped in seven elective fields: Health Craft, Home Craft, Nature Lore, Camp Craft, Hand Craft, Business and Patriotism.

The Camp Fire Girls were immediately embraced by young girls through-

Camp Fire Balloon Launch—Seventy-fifth Birthday Week

out the country and within a year forty-two states, Hawaii, and Canada had local Camp Fires.

The Camp Fire Outfitting Company of New York arranged for the clothing and equipment supplies with the National Headquarters receiving a two percent royalty on all sales. The uniforms were designed for comfort with innovative pockets and short skirts that were six inches from the floor. The official hat was of blue cloth with a silver W on the dark red Cockade. The W stood for Wo-He-Lo, which represented the basic goals of the girls, i.e., Work, Health, and Love.

By 1912 there were 1,387 Guardians of the Fire appointed as leaders of local groups, and by the end of 1913 the number reached 4,709. With the cooperation and help of the Camp Fire Girls, the Mormon Church established The Bee Hive Girls program in 1912.

In 1913, the Blue Birds group was established by the Camp Fire Girls for the younger girls ages seven, eight, and nine, and their groups were called "Nests." First a girl would be a Nestling, then a Fledgling, and finally a Flier.

The Blue Birds program was built on the ideas of "Sing, Grow, and Help," and included all the things that little girls would enjoy doing and learning. As explained in *Wohelo* magazine, "Dolls could be dressed and cared for; a love of the outdoors developed; little gardens started, perhaps in a box; the old songs, now dying out, learned: 'Ring-Around-the-Rosy,' and 'Here We Go Round the Mulberry Bush.' "

In 1914, the manual was printed in Braille to assist the great number of groups of blind Camp Fire Girls. In 1915 a novel wall calendar was designed by Lydia Bush-Brown and Mrs. Gulick produced three booklets to aid the program: *A Book of Symbolic Names For Camp Fire Girls*, *The Shul-u-tam-na* (ceremonial costumes), and *Air Pictures* (hand signs and signals).

With the outbreak of World War I, Dr. Gulick established a Minute Girl program, endorsed by President Woodrow Wilson, which taught food economy, health, gardening, waste avoidance, cooperation with the American Red Cross, and other matters important to a country at war. Through this program, nearly 100,000 Camp Fire Girls contributed directly to our victory.

Throughout the years, great artists gave their public approval and support to the creative Camp Fire Girls program. Booth Tarkington, Zona Gale and Many Austin were consulting editors to *Wohelo* magazine for years. The name of this outstanding youth magazine was changed to *Every Girl's* in 1920. The Camp Fire Girls, through this magazine, urged action on child labor protective laws, relief for the American Indian, respect and understanding of conservation, migratory birds and many other noble causes. Famous artists, writers, and actresses continued to advocate growing recognition of the worthiness of the Camp Fire Program.

In 1941, The Horizon Club was developed for high school age Camp Fire Girls. The new program emphasized personality development, wholesome relations with others, social activities, vocational exploration, and community service. The "three mountain peaks" insignia of the Horizon Club represent the three character traits developed: fun-loving, purposeful, and idealistic.

In 1953, the Camp Fire Girls acquired the Camp Fire Outfitting Company, and now operate as their supply division. The equipment was redesigned and quality was improved. As a result, national headquarters was now on a solid financial footing for the first time in over forty years.

The National Council then helped strengthen the financial resources of the local councils and proceeded to strengthen their recruiting and organization programs, leadership training, and professional staff training.

The 1960 Golden Jubilee Convention, held in New York, featured a special Camp Fire Girls post office which issued the "First Day Cover" of the four-cent Commemorative Stamp issued in honor of the Camp Fire Girls.

Throughout the 1960s and 1970s the marvelous work of the Camp Fire Girls continued and changed without ever losing sight of the importance it had always placed on the development of the individual girl.

In September 1960, recognizing the earlier maturing of the modern girl, certain age and program changes were introduced. The Blue Bird program was reduced to two years, and a new program level, Junior Hi, was developed to serve girls twelve and thirteen years old. Many innovations were made to help the modern girl reach her full potential. Soon after, third graders were added to the Blue Bird level and the program was re-extended to three years.

From 1971 through 1973, Horizon Club's new books and materials prepared for the entrance of boys into the club. This began a study that culminated in a program for all youth, including boys and girls.

1975. In the 1970s, the world of women changed significantly from what it was in 1910. Following the Equal Opportunity legislation, opportunities for women seemed almost unlimited in the areas of employment and education. It was this promise that inspired the Camp Fire leaders to offer the Camp Fire opportunity to both boys and girls. In November of 1975, the sixty-six-year-old organization adopted a renewal program called A New Day. The Group was expanded to include youth of both sexes from birth to twenty-one years.

1976. An implementation plan for A New Day was launched in January. In the plan, individuals became members of the Council, and not Camp Fire, Inc. A bright future for Camp Fire as an independent, voluntary agency has been charted, a future dedicated to the development of caring, self-directed youth through a myriad of innovative programs, services, and organizational projects. The major beneficiaries of this important struggle will be the neighborhood youth of all ethnic and economic backgrounds.

1977. The national headquarters moved from New York City to Kansas City, Missouri. The first congress was held in Kansas City. A Washington, D.C., office was opened.

1979. The second congress was held in Portland, Oregon, in November, 1979.

1980. A two-year youth employment project funded by the Department of Labor launched in nine councils. A week-long Horizon Conference for over 1,000 young people and adults was held at the United States Air Force Academy in Colorado Springs in July.

1981. Congress was held in Dallas, Texas, at which time Martha F. Allen and Roberta van der Voort presented the first "Pride" award for program excellence to ten Camp Fire councils. A week-long Horizon Conference for over 1,000 young people and adults was held at the United States Air Force Academy in Colorado Springs in July.

1982. The new Horizon and Discovery programs were introduced. Development of the Discovery program was partially funded by Lilly Endowment and Reader's Digest. Funds from Eastman Kodak were received.

1983. A new program level was created for children five years old and under called Aparks. The fourth congress was held in Philadelphia with a focus on advocacy.

Delegates to their biannual congress voted to change the name from Camp Fire Girls to Camp Fire, Inc., to reflect their changed image. During the previous five years, boys had been participating in Camp Fire at all ages and now made up about five percent of the over half million memberships. Beginning in 1975, Camp Fire had become the first agency to develop a "nonsexist" program which will help all youth to reach their full potential rather than be restricted by stereotype programs which tend to limit their full achievements. The new Camp Fire program offers a variety of activities from which youth may choose, and which will help them to discover their own interests and talents.

Camp Fire, Inc. has therefore evolved into an exciting multipurpose and multiprogram for boys and girls of all ages. This program is offered in more than 320 councils in 35,000 communities.

1985. "Celebrate Friendship—Celebrate Camp Fire." The Seventy-fifth Anniversary Congress was held at national headquarters in Kansas City, Missouri. To celebrate its birthday week, Camp Fire, Inc., launched a massive float of red, white, and blue balloons at 3:00 PM, on March 23, 1985. An estimated 300,000 friendship balloons were launched simultaneously across the country. Each balloon carried a friendship message from an individual member. Replies to these messages have been received from hundreds of miles away. During its Seventy-fifth Anniversary Celebration, Camp Fire, Inc., renewed its objective to become the primary coeducational youth agency in the United States.

Camp Fire and its chartered councils actively seek the organization and/

or sponsorship of Camp Fire programs by institutions, religious organizations, agencies, and clubs that subscribe to the purpose and the fundamental principles of Camp Fire. For further details and information, visit your local council or write: Camp Fire, Inc., 4601 Madison Avenue, Kansas City, Missouri 64112.

COLLECTIBLES

A group of historical items, donated to the Seventy-fifth Anniversary Congress by past members and collectors, was exhibited in an auditorium of the national headquarters, in display cubes from each decade, and sold during the congress.

HISTORICAL ITEMS

1910–1919	Price
☐ **Program Books,** tan-colored paperback books used by members	18.00
☐ **Equipment Books,** uniforms and other merchandise for members	6.00
☐ **Song Sheets,** one-page Camp Fire songs, campsite and ceremonial	4.00
☐ **Wo-He-Lo Magazine, 1913–1916,** oversized monthly magazine published by Camp Fire for leaders	8.00
☐ **Wo-He-Lo Magazine, 1917–1919,** oversized monthly magazine published by Camp Fire for leaders	7.00

1920–1929	
☐ **Program Books,** tan-colored paperback books for members	15.00
☐ **Handbook for Leaders**	8.00
☐ **Guardian Magazine,** monthly, for leaders, black and white matte photos, 1920–1929	4.00
☐ **Symbol Book,** orange and tan with symbols common to Indian tribes as guide to members for creating own designs	5.00
☐ **Everygirl Magazine,** glossy with photographs, 1922–1929	8.00
☐ **Annual Reports,** Bylaws, Addresses	3.00

1930–1939	**Price**

☐ **Program Books,** tan-colored paperback books used by members.. 12.00
☐ **Handbook for Leaders** 6.00
☐ **Guardian Magazine,** monthly magazine for leaders, black and white matte photographs, 1930–39.......... 3.00
☐ **Miscellaneous Small Program Books** 3.00
☐ **Annual Reports,** Bylaws, Addresses 2.00
☐ **Library of Seven Crafts** 5.00
☐ **Everygirl Magazines,** glossy with photographs, 1930–1939 .... 6.00

1950–1959

☐ **Program Book,** red and blue pattern, for members 3.50
☐ **Program Book of Camp Fire Girls,** red and blue pattern, for members 3.50
☐ **Program Book, Horizon Club,** royal blue, for high-school age... 2.50
☐ **Handbook for Guardians,** used by leaders:
☐ **Green,** 1950... 1.00
☐ **Brown,** 1952 .... 1.00
☐ **Blue,** 1950 .... 1.00
☐ **Song Sheets,** 1950–1959 .... .75
☐ **Publications/Equipment Catalogs** 1.00
☐ **Annual Reports/Wo-He-Lo Dispatch,** internal information to Board Members................................ .50
☐ **The Camp Fire Girl Magazine,** glossy, monthly from 1950–1959... 1.00

1960–1969

☐ **Program Level Books,** red and blue, for members 2.00
☐ **Handbooks for Leaders** 1.00
☐ **Braille Book,** oversized, white with spiral binding, for members.. 5.00
☐ **The Camp Fire Girl Magazine,** glossy monthly, with photographs, 1960–1969 .... 1.00

1970–1980	Price
☐ **New Day Bricks,** clay 1″ × 2½″, coeducational, 1977	3.00
☐ **Outdoor Book,** paperback, about camping, glossy, brown cover	1.00

OFFICIAL MEMENTOS OF CAMP FIRE'S SEVENTY-FIFTH ANNIVERSARY YEAR

☐ **Seventy-fifth Anniversary Paperweight,** Armetale, pewter-like, Seventy-fifth Anniversary design:	
☐ **In Relief,** limited edition, 8″ × 1⁷⁄₁₆″ × ½″	6.95
☐ **Mounted,** on 3″ × 6″ walnut base	14.95
☐ **Seventy-fifth Anniversary Tankard,** 5⅜″, white tankard with red and blue anniversary design.............	2.50
☐ **Seventy-fifth Anniversary Bumper Sticker,** "Celebrate Camp Fire," 3″ × 11½″	.75
☐ pkg. of 50	10.50
☐ **Celebration Stickers,** sheet in red, white and blue, 26 per sheet, pkg. of 10 sheets (260 stickers).............	5.00
☐ **Special Seventy-fifth Anniversary Emblems:**	
☐ "Friendship Across the Ages"	.35
☐ "Celebrate Camp Fire"	.35
☐ "Save Our Statue"	.35
☐ **Camp Fire Magnet,** "Camp Fire since 1910," red, flexible vinyl	.98
☐ **The Thrill of Bluebirds,** a set of three 14½″ × 19½″ bluebird prints, by wildlife artist Edward J. Bierly, in handsome portfolio:	
☐ **Series A,** limited edition, signed and numbered......	150.00 set
☐ **Series B,** initialed by the artist.......................	75.00 set
☐ **Series C,** small-size youth prints, 8″ × 10″..........	15.00 set

MISCELLANEOUS

☐ **Camp Fire Shoe Pocket,** laces to shoe to keep money, red and blue vinyl with white logo imprint, two inner compartments, includes ID card and instructions.	1.25
☐ **Camp Fire "Showlaces,"** washable polyester, bluebirds; stripes; horizontal woven rainbow	1.75

	Price
☐ **Camp Fire Pocket Flashlight,** compact, in red or blue with gold embossed "Camp Fire" imprint	2.50
☐ **Camp Fire Kite,** 40″ red inflatable, with 9″ white "The Camp Fire Spirit Is Soaring" imprint.	3.25
☐ **Camp Fire Cross Pen,** chrome with Camp Fire logo, lifetime guarantee	14.95
☐ **Camp Fire Mugs,** red and blue with white letters	2.25
☐ **Camp Fire Desk Flag,** 8″ × 10″, official flag screened on Copen nylon background. Comes with black staff, gold spear and black stand.	2.95
☐ **Camp Fire Cookie Cutter,** 3¾″ jumbo size, in official colors, with loop for hanging	1.25
☐ **Camp Fire Napkins,** paper, 12″ square, red, white and blue, pkg. of 100	3.95
☐ **Camp Fire Pillow,** red and blue, white logo on both sides	5.75
☐ **Camp Fire Iron On,** for T-shirts, etc., 7″ × 7″, official logo, pkg. of 25	5.00
☐ **Camp Fire Teddy Bear,** 7″, plush, stuffed	4.50

	Current Price Range		P/Y Avg.
☐ **Bicycle Reflector,** red emblem and words "Camp Fire Girls", c. 1940s	4.00	6.00	4.50
☐ **Bookends,** triangular, solid copper, emblems on sides, c. 1930s	9.00	13.00	9.50
☐ **Bookmark,** Blue Birds emblem, slips over corner of page, leather, c. 1940s	2.00	3.00	2.10
☐ **Bookmark,** Camp Fire emblem, slips over corner of page, leather, c. 1940s	2.00	3.00	2.10
☐ **Bookmark,** Horizon Club emblem, slips over corner of page, leather, c. 1940s	3.00	4.00	3.10
☐ **Bracelet,** Blue Bird, emblem on gold toned metal, spring hinge, two bands, c. 1965	8.00	11.00	8.50

	Current Price Range		P/Y Avg.
☐ **Bracelet,** emblem on gold toned metal, spring hinge, two bands around wrist, c. 1965	8.00	11.00	8.50
☐ **Bracelet,** Firemaker's, adjustable, sterling silver, Wo-He-Lo on front in decorative letters, c. 1911	9.00	11.00	9.50
☐ **Bracelet,** Blue Birds spelled out in charms, gold plated, c. 1954	15.00	17.00	15.50
☐ **Bracelet,** The Seven Crafts Charm, sterling silver, c. 1940s	30.00	40.00	30.00
☐ **Buttons,** Candy for Sale, salesgirl, c. 1972............................	2.00	4.00	2.50
☐ **Buttons,** Wo-He-Lo, glass, blue or white, set of two, c. 1912..........	5.00	7.00	5.50
☐ **Calendar,** monthly symbols, c. 1914	8.00	11.00	8.50
☐ **Calendar,** by Ruth Kemp, pictures four seasons, heavy cardboard with easel on back, c. 1930s	5.00	7.00	5.50
☐ **Calendar,** leather with law of the Camp Fire burned into it, thong and beads at top, 1916................	10.00	15.00	10.50
☐ **Canteen,** aluminum, shoulder straps with insignia, 1950s	6.00	11.00	6.50
☐ **Christmas Cards,** Blue Bird, three different designs, 12 cards, 4″ × 5″, c. 1962..........................	13.00	17.00	13.50
☐ **Christmas Cards,** three different subjects, color, 3¼″ × 6½″, c. 1962	7.00	10.00	7.50
☐ **Cocoa,** Camp Fire Girl Cocoa, one-half pound tins, c. 1914–1915.....	15.00	19.00	15.50
☐ **Comb Set,** topaz color, insignia and crossed logs on handle, comb fits on top of brush, c. 1930s......	6.00	9.00	6.50
☐ **Comb Set,** saddle color leather, comb, mirror, and emery board, emblem on front, c. 1940s.........	8.00	11.00	8.50

	Current Price Range		P/Y Avg.

☐ **Comb Set,** purse set, slim, red leather case, mirror, comb, and emery board, snap front, Camp Fire Girl emblem in gold, 6″, c. 1965 .... 6.00 9.00 6.50

☐ **Comb Set,** purse set, slim, red leather case, mirror, comb, and emery board, snap front, Blue Bird emblem in gold, c. 1965 .... 5.00 8.00 5.50

☐ **Compact,** gold metal, round, Camp Fire Girl insignia, mirror, sifter and puff, c. 1950s 5.00 7.00 5.50

☐ **Compact,** round, lacquer finish, Horizon Club emblem in sterling and enamel, c. 1955 .... 6.00 8.00 6.50

☐ **Compass,** Taylor Inst. Co., lightweight, blue plastic case, emblem on face, c. 1930s 7.00 9.00 7.50

☐ **Compass,** silver, plastic base, aluminum casing, emblem on base, c. 1953–54 .... 6.00 8.00 6.50

☐ **Cushion Cover,** sofa, felt, brown and flame color, lacing thongs, symbol on front, 22″ × 22″, c. 1916 .... 6.00 9.00 6.50

☐ **Decorative Plate,** smoked crystal, Camp Fire Girl emblem embossed in gold, 7″, c. 1962 .... 9.00 13.00 9.50

☐ **Diary,** 128 pp., 100 illustrated, clothbound, 4½″ × 6½″, c. 1925.... 11.00 15.00 11.50

☐ **Diary,** 128 pp., spiral, red cover, blue plastic spine, lettering and campfire imprinted on front, 4″ × 5″, c. 1940s 9.00 13.00 9.50

☐ **Diary,** two color plastic covers, Jr. High or Horizon Club emblems, 4½″ × 6½″, c. 1965 .... 6.00 8.00 6.50

	Current Price Range		P/Y Avg.
☐ **Doll,** Autograph Hound, design changed, upright standing dog with large head, c. 1971	7.00	9.00	7.50
☐ **Doll,** Autograph Hound, toy dog, used to write signatures on, red ribbon collar, blue felt saddle with Camp Fire emblem, c. 1955	6.00	8.00	6.50
☐ **Doll,** large, Blue Bird, vinyl, silk rooted hair, moveable arms, legs, head, uniformed, 11″, c. 1965	20.00	30.00	21.50
☐ **Doll,** small, Blue Bird, same as above, except 8″, c. 1965	12.00	22.00	12.50
☐ **Doll,** Blue Bird, blond, pigtails, 13½″, c. 1950s	12.00	17.00	12.50
☐ **Doll,** paper doll, color, *McCall's* magazine, 1922	9.00	13.00	9.50
☐ **Doll,** large, vinyl, silk rooted hair, moveable arms, legs, head, uniformed, 11″, c. 1965	25.00	35.00	25.50
☐ **Doll,** small, same as above except 8″ tall, c. 1965	12.00	22.00	12.50
☐ **Doll,** Indian, "Emgom," little brave, 13″, c. 1915	30.00	35.00	30.50
☐ **Doll,** Indian, "Harmar," little sister of Lodorbes, 13″, c. 1915	30.00	35.00	30.50
☐ **Doll,** Indian, "Jagom," big brave, 30″, c. 1915	40.00	50.00	41.50
☐ **Doll,** Indian, "Lodorbes," Camp Fire Girls, 30″, c. 1915	40.00	50.00	41.50
☐ **Earrings,** screw back, gold plate and red enamel, Camp Fire design, c. 1950s	7.00	9.00	7.50
☐ **Emblem,** bathing suit, circles with logs in center, white and brown on blue, c. 1911	8.00	10.00	8.50
☐ **Emblem,** Blue Bird, blue on white background, c. 1940s	5.00	7.00	5.50

	Current Price Range		P/Y Avg.
☐ **Emblem,** Blue Bird Fly-Up, symbols of bird and flame on square felt, c. 1967	3.00	4.00	3.10
☐ **Emblem,** Fire Maker's emblem, two crossed logs and flame, brown and orange on blue, c. 1911	8.00	10.00	8.50
☐ **Emblem,** hat, white on blue, shows symbol and Wo-He-Lo, c. 1911....	5.00	7.00	5.50
☐ **Emblem,** health, white on blue, shows symbol and Wo-He-Lo, c. 1911	5.00	7.00	5.50
☐ **Emblem,** Horizon Club-Community Volunteer Service, embroidered felt, 3″ × 2″, c. 1967.......	3.00	5.00	3.50
☐ **Emblem,** National Lifesaving Award, square, embroidered on felt, c. 1967	25.00	35.00	26.00
☐ **Emblem,** Service, red stars on white felt, c. 1940s	6.00	9.00	6.50
☐ **Emblem,** Torch Bearer, two crossed logs, flame and smoke, brown, orange, and white on blue, c. 1911..............................	8.00	10.00	8.50
☐ **Emblem,** Wo-He-Lo medallion, 14K rose gold, solid, Camp Fire on shield, c. 1967	25.00	35.00	25.50
☐ **Emblem,** Wood Gatherer's, two crossed logs, brown and orange on blue, c. 1911.......................	6.00	8.00	6.50
☐ **Firemaking Supplies,** equipment contains: wood, tinder, bow, thong, spindle, baseboard, handle and leather pouch, c. 1916.............	8.00	10.00	8.50
☐ **First Aid Kit,** blue and white metal case, Johnson and Johnson first aid travel kit, Camp Fire Girl emblem on front, c. 1962.............	7.00	11.00	7.50

	Current Price Range		P/Y Avg.
☐ **First Aid Kit,** Johnson and Johnson first aid compact kit, blue and white metal case, c. 1965	8.00	10.00	8.50
☐ **First Aid Kit,** Johnson and Johnson first aid travel kit, blue and white metal case, wording on top of each other and staggered, c. 1965	8.00	10.00	8.50
☐ **First Aid Kit,** leatherette case stamped with Camp Fire insignia, c. 1940s	10.00	14.00	10.50
☐ **Flag,** Blue Bird, cotton with blue emblem, 2' × 3', c. 1940s	9.00	16.00	9.50
☐ **Flag,** cotton, red and brown emblem and letters on white, 2' × 3', c. 1940s	7.00	13.00	7.50
☐ **Flag,** cotton, red and brown emblem and letters on white, 3' × 5', c. 1940s	11.00	17.00	11.50
☐ **Flag,** wool bunting, crossed logs and fire emblem, white, brown and scarlet, 24" × 36", c. 1923	13.00	22.00	13.50
☐ **Flag,** wool bunting, crossed logs and fire emblem, white, brown, and scarlet, 36" × 56", c. 1923	16.00	23.00	16.50
☐ **Flag,** desk set, plastic base, United States flag and Camp Fire Girl flag, 20", c. 1940s	5.00	7.00	5.50
☐ **Flag,** Horizon Club, white cotton, emblem in blue, 2' × 3', c. 1940s	7.00	13.00	7.50
☐ **Flashlight,** Bantamlite, small, pocket model, Camp Fire Girl or Blue Bird emblem on handle, c. 1965	3.00	5.00	3.50
☐ **Flashlight,** metal barrel, red reflector rim, push bottom, emblem on barrel, two batteries, c. 1965...	9.00	11.00	9.50

	Current Price Range		P/Y Avg.

☐ **Flashlight,** Camp Fire emblem, 3″, c. 1930s .... **5.00 7.00** | 5.50

☐ **Flashlight,** mini, striped in red and blue with key chain attached, one battery, c. 1971 .... **3.00 4.00** | 3.10

☐ **Flashlight,** red and black plaid, metal, red reflector, emblem on barrel, two batteries, c. 1960s ..... **4.00 6.00** | 4.50

☐ **Flashlight,** signalling, white, green, and red lights, nickel plated, c. 1914 .... **8.00 11.00** | 8.50

☐ **Flavor Bottles,** almond, cherry, cinnamon, ginger, lemon, orange, peppermint, strawberry, raspberry, vanilla, wintergreen, two ounce, c. 1916, ea............................ **13.00 19.00** | 13.50

☐ **Game,** Game of Honors, card, devised by Mary Black, c. 1923 ...... **9.00 13.00** | 9.50

☐ **Glove Case,** brown leather, two snaps, designs are burnt-in, 4″ × 10″, c. 1916 .... **8.00 11.00** | 8.50

☐ **Graduation Certificate,** Blue Bird to Camp Fire Girl, has girls around border, 6″ × 9″, c. 1954 .... **2.00 3.00** | 2.10

☐ **Handkerchief,** Blue Bird, embroidered emblem, linen, c. 1940s .... **3.00 4.00** | 4.10

☐ **Handkerchief,** Camp Fire Girl, embroidered, linen, c. 1940s ...... **3.00 4.00** | 4.10

☐ **Handkerchief Case,** leather, designs are burned into it, 6″ × 6½″, c. 1916 .... **5.00 7.00** | 5.50

☐ **Honor Beads,** colors represent skills, c. 1911:

☐   **Health Craft,** bright red .... **1.00 2.00** | 1.10

☐   **Home Craft,** orange .... **1.00 2.00** | 1.10

☐   **Nature-lore,** blue .... **1.00 2.00** | 1.10

☐   **Camp Craft,** wood brown .... **1.00 2.00** | 1.10

☐   **Local Honors,** uncolored .... **1.00 2.00** | 1.10

	Current Price Range		P/Y Avg.
☐ **Hand Craft,** green	1.00	2.00	1.10
☐ **Business,** yellow.................	1.00	2.00	1.10
☐ **Patriotism,** red, white, and blue	1.00	2.00	1.10
☐ **Required,** purple.................	1.00	2.00	1.10
☐ **Honor Beads,** shapes and colors became distinctive, set of 4, c. 1912	1.00	2.00	1.10
☐ **Honor Disks,** wood decorations, hole at top for thong, worn on ceremonial gowns, set of ?, c. 1925	1.00	2.00	1.10
☐ **Ink Bottle,** Official Camp Fire Girl ink, brown, new bottle design, pyramid type top, 1 ounce, c. 1917...	12.00	15.00	12.50
☐ **Ink Bottle,** Official Camp Fire Girl ink, brown, round top, 1 ounce, c. 1915	9.00	11.00	9.50
☐ **Jacket,** Camp Fire Girl ceremonial, navy blue, felt, c. 1950s	9.00	13.00	9.50
☐ **Jewelry,** cuff links and tie bar, matching Florentine finish, square, gold finish, Camp Fire Girl emblem, c. 1962	9.00	13.00	9.50
☐ **Jewelry,** men's, tie bar, gold finish, Camp Fire Girl crossed logs and flame in enamel, c. 1962	6.00	9.00	6.50
☐ **Jewelry,** men's, tie tack, 14K gold with emblem in enamel, button and chain attachment, c. 1962.........	7.50	7.00	9.00
☐ **Key Chain,** Camp Fire emblem on round piece, c. 1940s	4.00	5.00	4.10
☐ **Key Chain,** silver metal finish, raised Camp Fire Girl emblem, triangular shield, c. 1971	4.00	5.00	4.10
☐ **Knife,** New York Knife Co. manufactured the first Camp Fire Girl knife in 1910 or 1911 until 1930. The four blades were a large spear blade, awl, can opener, cap lifter,			

	Current Price Range		P/Y Avg.

and nail file. Camp Fire Girls and triangular emblem etched on blade, long shield with Wo-He-Lo, bone stag handle, nickel plated blades **110.00** **160.00** **112.00**

☐ **Knife,** same as above except screwdriver blade replaced awl ... **110.00** **160.00** **112.00**

☐ **Knife,** same as above except a Mother-of-Pearl handle was introduced in 1916, extremely rare..... **185.00** **260.00** **190.00**

☐ **Knife,** same as above except a special wood-carving blade replaced the fingernail file, bone stag handle and new shield **95.00** **130.00** **100.00**

☐ **Knife,** Remington, smaller, bone stag handle, four blades, 3⅜", c. 1930–1937...................... **80.00** **110.00** **85.00**

☐ **Knife,** Utica Kutmaster, black plastic handle, four blades, emblem and name etched on spear blade, 3¾" **40.00** **55.00** **42.00**

☐ **Locket,** gold-toned metal, opens like book, holds two photos, Camp Fire insignia or Blue Bird, fine chain, c. 1965 .... **7.00** **9.00** **7.50**

☐ **Luggage Tags,** triangular, Camp Fire Girl emblem, c. 1925 .... **3.00** **4.00** **3.10**

☐ **Magazine article,** The Camp Fire Girls Lend a Helping Hand, *Red Cross Magazine,* 1917 .... **8.00** **10.00** **8.50**

☐ **Magazine article,** Camp Fire Girl, in *National Geographic Bulletin,* 4pp., 1969 .... **3.00** **4.00** **3.10**

☐ **Magazine article,** Camp Fire Girl Movement and Education, *Journal of Education,* 1912................. **8.00** **10.00** **8.50**

	Current Price Range		P/Y Avg.

☐ **Manicure Kit,** red vinyl case, scissors, file, emery boards, orange stick and comb, Camp Fire insignia, c. 1962 .... 6.00 9.00 6.50

☐ **Match Container,** waterproof, galvanized rubber, screw on top, c. 1916 .... 9.00 11.00 9.50

☐ **Match Container,** waterproof, Marbles Co., of Gladstone, Michigan, lid swings out, c. 1930s 9.00 11.00 9.50

☐ **Match Container,** watertight, metal, 3″ × 1½″, c. 1914 .... 9.00 11.00 9.50

☐ **Mess Kit,** chrome plated utensils, red pigskin case, Geo. Schrade and Co., c. 1940s................ 35.00 45.00 37.00

☐ **Mess Kit,** chrome plated utensils, red plastic case, c. 1953 .... 15.00 17.00 15.50

☐ **Mirror,** suede leather case, stamped with Camp Fire emblem, c. 1930s 6.00 8.00 6.50

☐ **Outfit,** Blue Bird, blue, brown, and gray, cloth, cut into shape of bird and feathers, c. 1911 .... 80.00 110.00 85.00

☐ **Outfit,** Camp Fire Girls ceremonial gown, leather trimmed dress, khaki, includes stockings, moccasins and headband, c. 1925 .... 110.00 135.00 115.00

☐ **Paperweight,** clear plastic, triangle, red, white and blue, Camp Fire Girl emblem embedded, 3″, c. 1962 .... 6.00 8.00 6.50

☐ **Pencil,** Blue Birds printed on side and emblem 3.00 4.00 3.10

☐ **Pencil,** Camp Fire Girls printed on side and emblem 3.00 4.00 3.10

☐ **Pencil Box,** tin, Wallace Pencil Co., Camp Fire Girl scene on cover, c. 1920 .... 25.00 30.00 25.50

	Current Price Range		P/Y Avg.

	Current Price Range		P/Y Avg.
☐ **Pencil Set,** sterling silver, pencil and nickel-silver bookmark paper cutter with emblem	26.00	32.00	27.00
☐ **Pennant,** Blue Bird, copper blue, royal blue screened emblem and border, c. 1954	5.00	6.00	5.25
☐ **Pennant,** Blue Bird, all wool felt, white and blue, c. 1935...........	5.00	6.00	5.10
☐ **Pennant,** triangular, felt, red on navy, 9″ × 27″, c. 1953	6.00	8.00	6.50
☐ **Pennant,** pine tree design on felt, brown or green, c. 1916	8.00	10.00	8.50
☐ **Pin,** adult, gold and enamel finish, Camp Fire design, c. 1940s	5.00	7.00	5.50
☐ **Pin,** large, adult, shield shape, two color, Camp Fire emblem, rhodium finish, 2″ × 1¾″, c. 1953	8.00	10.00	8.50
☐ **Pin,** Blue Bird, blue, white outline, bird shape, c. 1940s..............	4.00	5.00	4.10
☐ **Pin,** Blue Bird, shape of bird, blue, c. 1935.	4.00	5.00	4.10
☐ **Pin,** sterling silver, red enamel, shield and Camp Fire emblem, no lettering, c. 1962...................	5.00	7.00	5.50
☐ **Pin,** guardian, solid Roman gold and black enamel, pictures the sun, c. 1911.............................	20.00	25.00	21.00
☐ **Pin,** hat, head is emblem of Camp Fire girl, silver plate and blue enamel, c. 1911	12.00	16.00	12.50
☐ **Pin,** Horizon Club, sterling silver, blue enamel, Horizon emblem, c. 1962	4.00	6.00	4.50
☐ **Pin,** Junior High, sterling silver, dark blue and red enamel, shield and emblem, "Jr.Hi" underneath, c. 1962.............................	5.00	7.00	5.50

	Current Price Range		P/Y Avg.
☐ **Pin,** Leader's, gold and red enamel, Camp Fire Girl emblem, c. 1940s ...	9.00	11.00	9.50
☐ **Pin,** Leader's, sterling silver, enamel, triangular, Camp Fire Girl emblem and "Leader" on face, ⅝" × ½", c. 1954	7.00	10.00	7.50
☐ **Pin,** membership, sterling silver, Wo-He-Lo design, c. 1923	10.00	13.00	10.50
☐ **Pin,** Torch bearer–Craftman, sterling silver, design of the tendril, c. 1940s	8.00	10.00	8.50
☐ **Pin,** Torch bearer, sterling silver, round and sectioned, c. 1011	11.00	13.00	11.50
☐ **Post Cards,** picture of a Camp Fire Girl on front, set of ten, c. 1940 ...	7.00	10.00	7.50
☐ **Post Cards,** official, set of six, hand painted, color, c. 1911.......	13.00	19.00	13.50
☐ **Poster,** advertising, "Camp Fire Girl" on top, shows three Camp Fire Girls, 15" × 24", c. 1925	8.00	11.00	8.50
☐ **Poster,** Camp Fire Girl health chart, 10" × 14", c. 1929.........	4.00	5.00	4.10
☐ **Poster,** standing Camp Fire Girls, Christy, 14" × 22", c. 1925.......	8.00	11.00	8.50
☐ **Poster,** five designs: Credo; The Law; The Woodgatherer's; The Firemakers; The Torch Bearers, 10" × 14", c. 1925	8.00	10.00	8.50
☐ **Poster,** The Law of the Camp Fire, seven paintings in the set on canvas, art by Helen Fuchs, 16" × 24", c. 1915	85.00	125.00	90.00
☐ **Poster Stamp Album,** black paper, 32pp., My Poster Stamp Collection on cover, 10¾" × 7"	9.00	11.00	9.50
☐ **Poster Stamps,** 72 available, 2" × 2¾", set	55.00	85.00	60.00

	Current Price Range		P/Y Avg.
☐ **Record,** Album of Camp Fire Songs, 78 rpm, 2″ × 10″, c. 1960s	8.00	10.00	8.50
☐ **Record,** One Little Girl, album, presented by Camp Fire Girl, Inc., 33⅓ rpm, 12″, c. 1962	4.00	5.00	4.10
☐ **Record,** Sing Along With Bing, 33⅓ rpm, Camp Fire, Inc., c. 1971	7.00	9.00	7.50
☐ **Record,** Songs for Blue Birds, girls on jacket, 45 rpm, c. 1971	4.00	5.00	4.10
☐ **Record,** Songs for Camp Fire Girls, girls on jacket, 45 rpm, c. 1971	4.00	5.00	4.10
☐ **Ring,** Blue Bird, sterling silver, emblem on face in blue enamel, adjustable, c. 1954	6.00	8.00	6.50
☐ **Ring,** sterling silver, emblem on face in blue enamel, adjustable, c. 1954	7.00	9.00	7.50
☐ **Ring,** Woodgatherer, five vertical fagots, two across the five, sterling silver, c. 1911	13.00	18.00	13.50
☐ **Rubber Mold,** with Camp Fire emblem, c. 1953	4.00	6.00	4.50
☐ **Sewing Kit,** Blue Bird, contains thread, thimble and needles, c. 1940s	8.00	10.00	8.50
☐ **Sheet Music,** Kaninto Kamya, Hughes, processional chant, c. 1925	6.00	8.00	6.50
☐ **Sheet Music,** Zuni Indian songs by Carlos Taylor, seventeen songs available, each	5.00	6.00	5.10
☐ **Slides,** stereopticon, Camp Fire Girl promotional slides to raise money, sixty-slide set, c. 1923	110.00	130.00	115.00
☐ **Songbook,** by Neidlinger, ten songs, c. 1911	16.00	22.00	16.50

	Current Price Range		P/Y Avg.
☐ **Songbook,** Folk Songs, Chanteys and Singing Games, Farnsworth, c. 1916	10.00	14.00	10.50
☐ **Songbook,** Gay Songs for Blue Birds, Kelly, c 1950s	7.00	9.00	7.50
☐ **Songbook,** Hiawatha's Childhood, an operetta by Whiteley, 44pp., c. 1916	11.00	15.00	11.50
☐ **Songbook,** Indian Games, Dances and Songs, Fletcher, 130pp c. 1916	11.00	16.00	11.50
☐ **Songbook,** Indian Tribal Songs, Cadman, c. 1925	9.00	13.00	9.50
☐ **Songbook,** Mystic Fire Songbook, illustrated song showing motions to be used, Bradshaw, c. 1914	16.00	21.00	16.50
☐ **Songbook,** Songs for Community Singing, Birchard and Co., 18 songs, c. 1916	9.00	13.00	9.50
☐ **Stationery,** Happy Blue Bird, box of twenty, decorated with Blue Bird activities, c. 1962	7.00	9.00	7.50
☐ **Stationery,** includes leather case, dark brown sheepskin, burnt design on cover, 9½″ × 7″, c. 1915	21.00	26.00	21.50
☐ **Stationery,** Official Guardian's, engraved in gold with Guardian's emblem, 24 sheets, c. 1940s	16.00	21.00	16.50
☐ **Stationery,** sheet design is crossed logs and flame at top, c. 1914	9.00	13.00	9.50
☐ **Stencils,** stiff paper material, c. 1925	7.00	9.00	7.50
☐ **Suspenders,** Blue Bird, blue on red felt, birds on straps, c. 1940s . . .	5.00	7.00	5.50
☐ **Suspenders,** Blue Bird, red wool felt, lined with white felt, nickel snaps, c. 1954	6.00	8.00	6.50

	Current Price Range		P/Y Avg.
☐ **Tie Slide,** silver finished, enameled disc, Camp Fire girl emblem and colors, c. 1971	3.00	4.00	3.50
☐ **Toilet Kit,** red and blue plastic case, contains washcloth, comb, mirror, soap and toothbrush cases, Camp Fire emblem, c. 1962	6.00	8.00	6.50
☐ **Utility Book,** autograph album, padded maroon leatherette cover, Camp Fire Girl or Blue Bird emblem on front in gold, outlined with gold border, c. 1965	7.00	9.00	7.50
☐ **Utility Book,** autograph album, pastel pages, red leather bound, Camp Fire Girl or Blue Bird emblem in lower right corner, c. 1955	5.00	7.00	5.50
☐ **Utility Book,** address, leatherette bound, stamped with Camp Fire emblem, c. 1940s	6.00	8.00	6.50
☐ **Utility Book,** Camp Fire memo book, leatherette bound, stamped with emblem and "Memorandum," c. 1940s	4.00	6.00	4.50
☐ **Utility Book,** Certificate of Honor in folder cover, c. 1914, each	2.00	3.00	2.10
☐ **Utility Book,** clipboard folder, Camp Fire insignia in gold on front, 2", c. 1971	4.00	6.00	4.50
☐ **Utility Book,** nature notebook, study sheets of birds, trees, etc., Camp Fire Girl and emblem stamped on front, c. 1940s	7.00	9.00	7.50
☐ **Utility Book,** photo folder, leather, Camp Fire emblem, 2¾" × 3¼", c. 1950s	8.00	10.00	8.50

	Current Price Range		P/Y Avg.
☐ **Utility Book,** snapshot album, leather, burnt-in design, bound by thongs, 26pp., 5½″ × 3¾″, c. 1916	11.00	13.00	11.50
☐ **Utility Book,** three ring binder notebook, "Camp Fire Girls" on binder, design on cover, c. 1971	4.00	5.00	4.10
☐ **Vanity Kit,** red leather case with Blue Bird or Camp Fire Girl emblem, comb and clothes brushes, lucite and nylon, c. 1962	9.00	13.00	9.50
☐ **Wallet,** leather, red and blue, gold stamped emblem of Blue Birds, Camp Fire Girls, or Horizon Club, c. 1940s	6.00	8.00	6.50
☐ **Watch,** curved chrome case, black suede band, crossed logs and flame emblem, c. 1965	11.00	13.00	11.50
☐ **Watch,** gold-toned, Timex, shock resistant, gold numerals, Camp Fire Girl emblem on face, black suede band, c. 1962	15.00	19.00	15.50
☐ **Whisk Broom,** broom with case, case is leather with emblem burned into it, 9″, c. 1916	11.00	13.00	11.50
☐ **Whistle,** nickel, Camp Fire Girl design on face plate, c. 1925	7.00	9.00	7.5.00

BOOKS

FICTION

☐ **Armstrong,** Camp Fire Girls on Hurricane Island	3.00	4.00	3.10
☐ **Barnum,** Our Aunt From California, 1925	5.00	6.00	5.10
☐ **Bayliss,** The Camp Fire Girls, play, 1914	6.00	8.00	6.50

	Current Price Range		P/Y Avg.
☐ **Benson,** How Ethel Hollister Became a Campfire Girl	5.00	7.00	5.10
☐ **Benson,** Ethel Hollister's First Summer as a Campfire Girl	4.00	6.00	4.10
☐ **Benson,** Ethel Hollister's Second Summer as a Campfire Girl	5.00	7.00	5.10
☐ **Blanchard,** Fagots and Flames, 1916	11.00	15.00	11.50
☐ **Blanchard,** In Camp with the Moscoday Camp Fire Girls	4.00	5.00	4.10
☐ **Blanchard,** The Camp Fire Girls of Brightwood, 1916	4.00	5.00	4.10
☐ **Brooke,** Peg Lends a Hand, 1925	5.00	6.00	5.10
☐ **Crane,** The Honor of the Class, 1925	4.00	5.00	4.10
☐ **Davidson,** The Camp Fire Girls on the Ice, 1913	7.00	8.00	7.10
☐ **Devries,** The Camp Fire Girls at Holly House	4.00	6.00	4.25
☐ **Devries,** The Camp Fire Girls as Detectives	4.00	6.00	4.25
☐ **Devries,** The Camp Fire Girls Flying Around the Globe	4.00	6.00	4.25
☐ **Devries,** The Camp Fire Girls as Federal Investigators	5.00	7.00	5.25
☐ **Devries,** The Camp Fire Girls on Caliban Island, 1933	4.00	6.00	4.25
☐ **Devries,** The Camp Fire Girls at the White House	5.00	7.00	5.50
☐ **Eastman,** The Eagle and the Star, play	6.00	8.00	6.50
☐ **Fox,** The Returning of Rosalia, play, 1923	6.00	8.00	6.50
☐ **Francis,** Camp Fire Girls in the Country	4.00	6.00	4.25
☐ **Francis,** Camp Fire Girls Trip up the River	5.00	7.00	5.25
☐ **Francis,** Camp Fire Girls Outing	4.00	6.00	4.25

A Campfire Girl's Chum, Jane Stewart, Saalfield Publishing Co., 1915, $3.50–$5.00

	Current Price Range		P/Y Avg.
☐ **Francis,** Camp Fire Girls on a Hike	4.00	6.00	4.25
☐ **Francis,** Camp Fire Girls at Twin Lakes	5.00	7.00	5.25
☐ **Frey,** The Camp Fire Girls in the Maine Woods	4.00	6.00	4.50
☐ **Frey,** The Camp Fire Girls at Onoway House	5.00	7.00	5.50

The Campfire Girls Success, Helen Hart, $2.50–$5.00

	Current Price Range		P/Y Avg.
☐ **Frey,** The Camp Fire Girls Go Motoring	4.00	6.00	4.50
☐ **Frey,** The Camp Fire Girls' Larks and Pranks	4.00	6.00	4.50
☐ **Frey,** The Camp Fire Girls on Ellen's Isle	4.00	6.00	4.50
☐ **Frey,** The Camp Fire Girls on the Open Road	5.00	7.00	5.50
☐ **Frey,** The Camp Fire Girls Do Their Bit	4.00	6.00	4.50

	Current Price Range		P/Y Avg.
☐ **Frey**, The Camp Fire Girls Solve a Mystery	4.00	6.00	4.50
☐ **Frey**, The Camp Fire Girls at Camp Keewaydin	5.00	7.00	5.50
☐ **Frey**, The Camp Fire Girls at School, 1916	4.00	6.00	4.50
☐ **Getchell**, Spruce, Cone & Bunchbarry, play, 1916	0.00	8.00	6.50
☐ **Grove**, The Camp Fire Girls on the Trail, 1931	4.00	5.00	4.10
☐ **Hartman**, The Wheatless Meal, play 1923	6.00	8.00	6.50
☐ **Hary**, The Camp Fire Girls at Work	4.00	5.00	4.10
☐ **Hornibrook**, Girls of the Morning Glory Camp Fire, 1916	7.00	9.00	7.50
☐ **Hyde**, Little Sisters to the Camp Fire Girls, 1918	6.00	8.00	6.50
☐ **Knevels**, Minnetoska's Dream, 1916	6.00	8.00	6.50
☐ **Knevels**, Skyboy, play, 1916	7.00	9.00	7.50
☐ **Lounsbury and Jeffery**, Any Girl, play, 1916	6.00	8.00	6.50
☐ **Partridge**, Joyful Star, 1916	4.00	6.00	4.50
☐ **Penrose**, Camp Fire Girls of Roselawn	4.00	6.00	4.50
☐ **Penrose**, Camp Fire Girls on the Program	5.00	7.00	5.50
☐ **Penrose**, Camp Fire Girls on Station Island	4.00	6.00	4.50
☐ **Rietz**, The Camp Fire Girls Week-End Party	4.00	6.00	4.50
☐ **Reitz**, The Camp Fire Girls and Aunt Madge	5.00	7.00	5.50
☐ **Rogers**, Sebago—Wo-He-Lo Camp Fire Girls, 1915	13.00	19.00	13.50
☐ **Sanderson**, The Camp Fire Girls on a Yacht, 1922	5.00	7.00	5.50

	Current Price Range		P/Y Avg.
☐ **Sanderson,** The Camp Fire Girls in Old Kentucky, 1919	5.00	7.00	5.50
☐ **Sanderson,** The Camp Fire Girls at Driftwood Heights	6.00	9.00	6.50
☐ **Sanderson,** The Camp Fire Girls at Hillside	5.00	7.00	5.50
☐ **Sanderson,** The Camp Fire Girls at Pine-Tree Camp	6.00	9.00	6.50
☐ **Stewart,** A Camp Fire Girl's First Council Fire......................	5.00	7.00	5.50
☐ **Stewart,** A Camp Fire Girl's Chum	5.00	7.00	5.50
☐ **Stewart,** A Camp Fire Girl in Summer Camp	5.00	7.00	5.50
☐ **Stewart,** A Camp Fire Girl's Adventures	5.00	7.00	5.50
☐ **Stewart,** A Camp Fire Girl's Test of Friendship......................	6.00	9.00	6.50
☐ **Stewart,** A Camp Fire Girl's Happiness................................	6.00	9.00	6.50
☐ **Stewart,** The Camp Fire Girls on the Farm...........................	5.00	7.00	5.50
☐ **Stewart,** The Camp Fire Girls at Long Lake	5.00	7.00	5.50
☐ **Stewart,** The Camp Fire Girls in the Mountains	6.00	9.00	6.50
☐ **Stewart,** The Camp Fire Girls on the March...........................	5.00	7.00	5.50
☐ **Vandercook,** The Camp Fire Girls at Half Moon Lake, 1921	6.00	7.00	6.10
☐ **Vandercook,** The Camp Fire Girls at Sunrise Hill	7.00	9.00	7.50
☐ **Vandercook,** The Camp Fire Girls at the End of the Trail	6.00	7.00	6.10
☐ **Vandercook,** The Camp Fire Girls Amid the Snows	7.00	9.00	7.50
☐ **Vandercook,** The Camp Fire Girls by the Blue Lagoon, 1921	7.00	9.00	7.50

	Current Price Range		P/Y Avg.
☐ **Vandercook,** The Camp Fire Girls in the Outside World..............	6.00	7.00	6.10
☐ **Vandercook,** The Camp Fire Girls Across the Sea	6.00	7.00	6.10
☐ **Vandercook,** The Camp Fire Girls' Careers	6.00	7.00	6.10
☐ **Vandercook,** The Camp Fire Girls in After Years......................	6.00	7.00	6.10
☐ **Vandercook,** Tho Camp Fire Girls in Merrie England, 1920	6.00	7.00	6.10
☐ **Vandercook,** The Camp Fire Girls at the Edge of the Desert..........	7.00	9.00	7.50
☐ **Vandercook,** The Camp Fire Girls Behind the Lines	6.00	7.00	6.10
☐ **Vandercook,** The Camp Fire Girls on the Field of Honor..............	6.00	7.00	6.10
☐ **Vandercook,** The Camp Fire Girls in Glorious France.................	6.00	7.00	6.10
☐ **Vanderlaan,** The Magic Flute, a musical, 1923......................	4.00	5.00	4.10
☐ **Widdemer,** Winona of the Camp Fire, 1915...........................	9.00	11.00	9.25
☐ **Williams,** The Healing Spring, play, 1916	8.00	10.00	8.50

NONFICTION

☐ **Beard & Beard,** On the Trail, 1916	16.00	21.00	16.50
☐ **Camp Fire Girls,** The Blue Bird Wish Come True, 1965	5.00	6.00	5.10
☐ **Camp Fire Girls,** Camp Fire Ceremonials, 1950s	7.00	9.00	7.50
☐ **Camp Fire Girls,** Ceremonials for Camp Fire Girls, 1947–68	4.00	6.00	4.50
☐ **Camp Fire Girls,** Child Care Course, 1965	4.00	5.00	4.10
☐ **Camp Fire Girls,** Conservation Book, 1965	4.00	5.00	4.10

	Current Price Range		P/Y Avg.
☐ **Camp Fire Girls,** Discovery Club, 1971	3.00	4.00	3.10
☐ **Camp Fire Girls,** *Everygirl's* magazine, 1920–33	4.00	5.00	4.10
☐ **Camp Fire Girls,** Handbook for Guardians, 1924.....................	10.00	13.00	10.50
☐ **Camp Fire Girls,** Handbook for Guardians, 1925–66	5.00	8.00	5.50
☐ **Camp Fire Girls,** Junior High Supplement	4.00	5.00	4.10
☐ **Camp Fire Girls,** The Library of the Seven Crafts, 1930s:			
☐ **Your Symbol**	8.00	10.00	8.50
☐ **Book of Ceremonials**	8.00	10.00	8.50
☐ **The Outdoor Book**	8.00	10.00	8.50
☐ **Rainbow Book**....................	8.00	10.00	8.50
☐ **Clay Craft**	9.00	11.00	9.50
☐ **Book Craft**	9.00	11.00	9.50
☐ **Block Printing and Stenciling** ...	8.00	10.00	8.50
☐ **Leathercraft and Beading**	7.00	9.00	8.50
☐ **Camp Fire Girls,** The Outdoor Book, 1962	7.00	9.00	7.50
☐ **Camp Fire Girls,** Recipe Books, 1916:			
☐ **The Candy Book**	4.00	6.00	4.50
☐ **The Salad Book**	5.00	7.00	5.50
☐ **The Sandwich Book**	5.00	7.00	5.50
☐ **The Cake Maker**	4.00	5.00	4.50
☐ **Dainty Luncheons**..............	4.00	5.00	4.50
☐ **The Dessert Book**	4.00	6.00	4.50
☐ **Ten-Minute Recipes**...........	4.00	6.00	4.50
☐ **Camp Fire Girls,** Vacation Book of the Camp Fire Girls, 1966	10.00	13.00	10.50
☐ **Camp Fire Girls,** Wo-He-Lo I and II	4.00	5.00	4.10
☐ **Camp Fire Girls,** *Wo-He-Lo* magazine, July 1913	16.00	21.00	16.50
☐ **Additional copies,** 1913–1920 ...	6.00	9.00	6.50

Wo-He-Lo, *Book I, 1910–1960; Book II, 1961–1979,* ***$3.00–$4.00***

	Current Price Range		P/Y Avg.
☐ **Clark,** Camp Fire Girls Pageant, 1923	11.00	15.00	11.50
☐ **Donahue, Camp Fire Girls, 1916** ..	11.00	15.00	11.50

	Current Price Range		P/Y Avg.
☐ **Gulick,** Air Picture Book, 1916	15.00	19.00	15.50
☐ **Gulick,** Book of Indian Names and Meanings, 1916....................	11.00	13.00	11.50
☐ **Gulick,** The Shulutamna, 1916....	13.00	16.00	13.50
☐ **Gulick,** Symbol Book, 1916	13.00	16.00	13.50
☐ **Gulick,** Written Thoughts Series:			
☐ **WAPA I**—Camp Fire Girls and the New Relation of Women to the World..........................	8.00	10.00	8.50
☐ **WAPA II**—The Desires of the American Girls	8.00	10.00	8.50
☐ **WAPA III**—Patriotism and Team-work in Social Life..............	9.00	11.00	9.50
☐ **Hall & Perkins,** Handicraft for Handy Girls, 1923	10.00	13.00	10.50
☐ **Hood,** For Girls and the Mothers of Girls, 1916..........................	9.00	11.00	9.50
☐ **Lowry,** Confidence, 1923	8.00	11.00	9.50
☐ **Lowry,** Herself, 1923..............	8.00	10.00	8.50
☐ **MacMillan,** Camping Out, 1925 ...	11.00	13.00	11.50
☐ **Malone,** Poems by Camp Fire Girls, 1940s	9.00	11.00	9.50
☐ **Thurston,** The Torch Bearer, 1912	13.00	16.00	13.50

MANUALS

	Current Price Range		P/Y Avg.
☐ **Girl Pioneers of America,** Bulletin Manual, June 1911	65.00	95.00	70.00
☐ **Same as above,** late editions...	25.00	35.00	26.00
☐ **Manual,** first edition, March 1912, 100 pages, tan kraft paper cover with ''Camp Fire Girls'' and symbol of crossed logs and flame, printed in dark brown and Chinese red, about half of pages were photographs	110.00	160.00	115.00

Left to Right: **1914 Manual,** *symbol of crossed logs and flame, brown and red paperback, fourth edition,* **$20.00–$30.00;** *1937* **Manual,** *red and blue paperback, first edition,* **$7.00–$10.00**

		Current Price Range		P/Y Avg.
☐	**Second edition,** September 1912, increased by 14 pages of text, two pages of honors, an enlarged bibliography, and additional camp fire ceremonies.....	55.00	80.00	60.00
☐	**Third edition,** August 1913, 130 pages, included advertisements for Baker's Cocoa and Waterman's Ideal Fountain Pen.......	40.00	60.00	41.00
☐	**Fourth edition,** 1914	25.00	35.00	26.00
☐	**Fifth edition,** 1914–15	25.00	35.00	26.00
☐	**Sixth edition,** includes "War Call to the Girls of America," 1917...............................	30.00	40.00	31.00
☐	**Seventh edition,** "Manual of Activities and War Programs for the Girls of America," 1918.....	30.00	40.00	31.00
☐	**Eighth edition,** "Manual of Activities for the Girls of America," 1920............................	19.00	28.00	20.00
☐	**Ninth edition,** 1921	16.00	21.00	16.50
☐	**Tenth edition,** 1922	13.00	98.00	13.50
☐	**Manual,** first printing, revised edition, 1924	13.00	17.00	13.50
☐	**Second printing,** 1925	11.00	16.00	11.50
☐	**Third printing,** 1927	9.00	13.00	9.50
☐	**Fourth printing,** 1929	8.00	11.00	8.50
☐	**Fifth printing,** 1931	9.00	11.00	9.50
☐	**Sixth edition,** revised edition, 1933	8.00	11.00	8.50
☐	**Manual,** first printing, new edition, 1936, cloth-paper cover	8.00	11.00	8.50
☐	**Same as above,** leather cover	11.00	16.00	11.50
☐	**Second printing,** 1938	6.00	9.00	6.50
☐	**Third printing,** 1940	6.00	8.00	6.50
☐	**Fourth printing,** 1942	6.00	8.00	6.50
☐	**Revised edition,** June 1946	5.00	7.00	5.50
☐	**All subsequent editions**	5.00	7.00	5.50

GIRL SCOUTS

HISTORY

The Girl Scouts of America have a history rich in tradition and service to millions of girls, not only in the United States but throughout the world. In 1912, when Juliette Gordon Low organized the first Girl Scout troop in Savannah, Georgia, she initiated an informal education program for girls that would cross all cultural groups within the United States. This tradition has grown and endured for seventy-five years and has influenced the lives of over fifty million girls and adults.

Girl Scouting goes back to the early 1900s, when Juliette Low lived in England. At a Boy Scout rally held in the Crystal Palace in London, the King of England proclaimed Lt. General Robert Baden-Powell "The Hero of Mafeking." At a parade of Scouts in his honor, to the surprise of all, hundreds of girls dressed in khaki shirts, skirts and wide-brimmed hats marched right along with the boys. Sir Robert Baden-Powell discovered that 6,000 girls were enrolled in his Boy Scouts program. He enlisted the aid of his sister, Agnes, and other English women, to create a separate program for the girls with equal challenges devoted to scouting ideals. His Girl Guide Program became extremely successful. As a friend and colleague of Sir Robert Baden-Powell and his sister, Juliette Gordon Low served as a leader of the Girl Guide "companies" in London and Scotland, on a volunteer basis. Through this work, she experienced first-hand the rewards and responsibilities of working with young women, a career she followed all through her life.

In 1912, she returned to her home in Georgia full of enthusiasm and ideas for girls in the United States. On March 12, she called a friend to say, "Come right over. I've got something for the girls of Savannah, and all America, and the world. We're going to start it tonight." Thus was founded the first Girl Guide troop in the United States. In 1913, she changed the name of the group to the Girl Scouts and established a national headquarters in Washington, D.C. That same year the first Girl Scout Handbook, *How Girls Can Help Their Country*, was published. For the rest of her life, Juliette gave unsparingly of herself, often selling her own jewelry to continue the work of the Girl Scouts. At the time of her death in 1927, there were over 150,000 Girl Scouts in the United States.

Through the years, Girl Scouting has maintained its role and tradition in our country, identifying and serving the needs of girls on five different levels. It offers "Discovery" for the six- to eight-year-old Brownie Girl Scouts, who learn to function in a group, and "Adventure" for Junior Girl Scouts, ages

The Girl Scout Family, five age levels, in official uniforms: Daisy Girl Scout, Brownie Girl Scout, Junior Girl Scout, Cadette Girl Scout, Senior Girl Scout

nine to eleven, who learn to organize to get things done. "Action" is the activity for Cadette Girl Scouts, ages twelve through fourteen, who learn to meet the challenges of today's world, and the program of "self-awareness" for Senior Girl Scouts, ages fourteen through seventeen, offers them an opportunity to fulfill a promise to themselves and society. In 1984, the organization recognized the maturity of today's younger girls by creating Daisy Girl Scouts for girls five years old or in kindergarten.

Handbooks and program materials have been updated and changed, always highlighting activities that help girls develop skills and reach their fullest potential. In the late 1970s, career exploration materials were published, offering Cadette and Senior Girl Scouts an opportunity to expand their options even further. In 1986, new handbooks for Brownie and Junior Girl Scouts introduced challenging activities specifically related to the development of young women in today's society.

The progressive organization that Juliette Low started in 1912 continues to serve girls from all segments of the community, and remains a viable and important force in society today. Its plans for tomorrow are embodied in its Seventy-fifth Anniversary theme, . . . Tradition with a Future. For more information about Girl Scouting, contact Media Services, Girl Scouts of the USA, 830 Third Avenue, New York, New York 10022.

SEVENTY-FIFTH ANNIVERSARY

In 1987, nearly three million Girl Scouts will mark the Seventy-fifth Anniversary of the organization with gifts of service to their communities, time-travel activities, and a world-wide event called the Promise Circle. The Promise Circle begins in Washington, D.C., on March 12, when Girl Scouts and friends recite the Girl Scout Promise. In each time zone at 4 P.M., Girl Scouts will repeat the ceremony, creating a continuous chain around the world.

OFFICIAL SEVENTY-FIFTH ANNIVERSARY COMMEMORATIVE ITEMS

The following items can be purchased through Girl Scouts of the USA/National Equipment Service, 830 Third Avenue, New York, N.Y. 10022.

All Seventy-fifth Anniversary items shown are copyrighted by the *Girl Scouts of the USA.* All rights reserved.

Seventy-fifth Anniversary Embroidered Patch, 3'' round symbol has solid-stitched white background, blue/green design and lettering, silvertone metallic stars. Unofficial. May only be worn on back of uniform sash of vest or on a patch jacket. 27–102, **$2.50.** Not shown: **Seventy-fifth Anniversary Photo Art Patch.** Same as above except stars are white. 27-114, **$.75**

Seventy-fifth Anniversary T-Shirt, royal blue poly/cotton with white symbol. Available in adult sizes. 27-100, **$8.50.** Also available in girls' sizes. 27–112, **$7.00**

Seventy-fifth Anniversary Tile, silhouette figures and symbol printed in black on white. 6" x 6" tile/plaque comes with a hanger backing. 27–109, **$4.00**

Seventy-fifth Anniversary Balloon, blue symbol on white balloon. Ideal for all Girl Scout celebrations! Packaged in bags of 100. 27–113–100, **$20.00 bag**

Seventy-fifth Anniversary Collector's Plate, *handsome 6" round spun brass plate has contrasting shiny/matte goldtone symbol. Gift boxed. 27–110,* **$25.00**

Seventy-fifth Anniversary Pencil *has #2 lead and eraser. Available in assorted blue and green with white symbol. 27–106,* **$.30 each**

Seventy-fifth Anniversary Mug, *elegant navy blue vitreous china with goldtone symbol and rim. 12 oz. capacity. Individually boxed.* 27–108, **$11.50**

Seventy-fifth Anniversary Pin, *⁷⁄₈" round. Silvertone metal base with patterned back. Blue/green symbol on white has silvertone stars. Nail/clutch closing.* 27–101, **$2.50**

Seventy-fifth Anniversary Stickers, *pressure-sensitive 1½" round stickers carry the message on stationery, books, etc. Blue/green symbol embossed on white. 100 to a roll. 27–107–100,* **$3.75 roll**

Seventy-fifth Anniversary Plaque, *walnut finish with blue/green symbol on silvertone. 6" x 8", ⅝" thick. Engraving plate. Individually boxed. 27-111.* **$13.25**

1954 Handbook, *blue and green with Girl Scout symbol,* *hardcover, $3.00–$4.00*

HANDBOOKS

GIRL SCOUT HANDBOOKS

Initially the Girl Scouts produced one handbook to cover all age groups, and then developed different handbooks for each separate program.

	Current Price Range		P/Y Avg.
☐ **How Girls Can Help Their Country,** adapted by W.J. Hoxie from the British *Girl Guide Handbook,* 1913	75.00	95.00	80.00
☐ **How Girls Can Help Their Country,** rewritten by Juliette Low, 1916	55.00	65.00	30.00
☐ **Scouting for Girls,** adapted by Juliette Low from British *Handbook of Scouting For Girls* by Sir Robert Baden-Powell, includes introductory section on Brownies, 1918	32.00	42.00	25.00
☐ **Scouting for Girls,** Official Handbook of the Girl Scouts, light brown cover, preface by Sir Robert Baden-Powell, 558 pages; 5¼" × 7½", 1920	5.00	10.00	8.00
☐ **Second Edition,** 1921	5.00	10.00	8.00
☐ **Third Edition,** 1922	5.00	10.00	8.00
☐ **Fourth Edition,** 1923	5.00	10.00	8.00
☐ **Fifth Edition,** 1924	5.00	10.00	8.00
☐ **Sixth Edition,** 1925	5.00	10.00	8.00
☐ **Scouting for Girls,** abridged edition, copyright 1927, brown cover with Girl Scout Trefoil. Preface states in part: "Since much of the material is out of date, this abridged edition, omitting obsolete sections, has been prepared for use until a new handbook can be published." This edition contained 464 pages, 5¼" × 7½", 1927	11.00	15.00	11.50

	Current Price Range		P/Y Avg.

☐ **Girl Scout Handbook,** revised edition, green cover with silhouettes of three Girl Scouts hiking, minor revisions, 464 pages, 5¼″ × 7½″, 1929	11.00	15.00	11.50
☐ **Same as above,** but 1930	9.00	13.00	9.50
☐ **Same as above,** but 1931	9.00	13.00	9.50
☐ **Same as above,** but 1932	9.00	13.00	9.50
☐ **Girl Scout Handbook,** new edition, olive cover with "Girl Scout Handbook" and trefoil at top, 575 pages, 5¼″ × 7¼″, for the Intermediate Program, October 1933	5.00	9.00	7.00
☐ **Second Impression,** June 1934	5.00	9.00	7.00
☐ **Third Impression,** June 1936	5.00	9.00	7.00
☐ **Fourth Impression,** February 1938	5.00	9.00	7.00
☐ **Girl Scout Handbook,** new edition, bright green, lightweight cover with Girl Scout Handbook, trefoil and nine horizontal lines in yellow, 694 pages, 5″ × 7″, for the Intermediate Program, October 1940	9.00	13.00	9.50
☐ **Second Impression,** April 1941	7.00	9.00	7.50
☐ **Third Impression,** January 1942	7.00	9.00	7.50
☐ **Fourth Impression,** July 1942	7.00	9.00	7.50
☐ **Fifth Impression,** March 1943	7.00	9.00	7.50
☐ **Sixth Impression,** July 1944	7.00	9.00	7.50
☐ **Sixth Edition,** November 1944	7.00	9.00	7.50
☐ **Seventh Edition,** 1944	7.00	9.00	7.50
☐ **Eighth Edition,** 1945	7.00	9.00	7.50
☐ **Ninth Edition,** September 1946	7.00	9.00	7.50

	Current Price Range		P/Y Avg.
☐ **Girl Scout Handbook,** new edition, bright green cover with script Girl Scout Handbook and outline of the trefoil in silver on two dark green horizontal bars, 527 pages with additional pages for notes and autographs, 4½″ × 6½″, Intermediate Program, October 1947	9.00	11.00	9.25
☐ **Second Impression,** January 1948	7.00	9.00	7.25
☐ **Third Impression,** August 1948	6.00	9.00	6.25
☐ **Fourth Impression,** March 1949	6.00	9.00	6.25
☐ **Fifth Impression,** July 1949	5.00	7.00	5.25
☐ **Sixth Impression,** January 1950	5.00	7.00	5.25
☐ **Seventh Impression,** June 1950	5.00	7.00	5.25
☐ **Eighth Impression,** October 1950	5.00	7.00	5.25
☐ **Ninth Impression,** May 1951	5.00	7.00	5.25
☐ **Tenth Impression,** September 1951	5.00	7.00	5.25
☐ **Eleventh Impression,** January 1952	5.00	7.00	5.25
☐ **Twelfth Impression,** May 1952	5.00	7.00	5.25
☐ **Girl Scout Handbook,** new edition, cover is dark green on left and light green on right with large trefoil and small printing of Girl Scout Handbook, 511 pages 5¼″ × 8¼″, Intermediate Program, September 1953	5.00	7.00	5.25
☐ **Second Impression,** November 1953	5.00	6.00	5.10
☐ **Third Impression,** January 1954	5.00	6.00	5.10

	Current Price Range		P/Y Avg.
☐ **Fourth Impression,** March 1954	5.00	6.00	5.10
☐ **Fifth Impression,** August 1954 ...	5.00	6.00	5.10
☐ **Sixth Impression,** January 1955	5.00	6.00	5.10
☐ **Seventh Impression,** April 1955	5.00	6.00	5.10
☐ **Eighth Impression,** November 1955	5.00	6.00	5.10
☐ **Ninth Impression,** May 1956 ...	5.00	6.00	5.10
☐ **Tenth Impression,** August 1956	5.00	6.00	5.10
☐ **Eleventh Impression,** November 1956	5.00	6.00	5.10
☐ **Twelfth Impression,** January 1957	5.00	6.00	5.10
☐ **Thirteenth Impression,** April 1957	5.00	6.00	5.10
☐ **Fourteenth Impression,** July 1957	5.00	6.00	5.10
☐ **Fifteenth Impression,** September 1957	5.00	6.00	5.10
☐ **Sixteenth Impression,** six pages of new badges added, December 1957	7.00	9.00	7.10
☐ **1958–1962 Printings**	5.00	6.00	5.10

BROWNIE HANDBOOKS

☐ **Brownie Handbook,** first edition, gray and rose-tan cover, with five Brownie Scouts at play, 95 pages, 6¼″ x 9¼″, December 1951	7.00	9.00	7.50
☐ **Same as above,** twenty-four impressions, January 1952–1962	5.00	6.00	5.10

	Current Price Range		P/Y Avg.

☐ **Brownie Handbook,** new edition, orange soft cover with full color illustrations, 224 pages of new content, 8¼" × 8¾", April 1963 ...... | 3.00 | 4.00 | 3.10
☐ **Same as above,** approximately 20 printings 1963–1976 .... | 3.00 | 4.00 | 3.10
☐ **World To Explore,** combined the Brownie and Junior Handbooks, 1977–present .... | 3.00 | 4.00 | 3.10

JUNIOR HANDBOOKS

☐ **Careers to Explore,** for Brownie and Junior Girl Scouts............ | 3.50 | 4.00 | 3.50
☐ **Leader's Guide** .... | 1.40 | 1.40 | 1.40
☐ **First Separate Junior Handbook,** light blue, soft cover, well illustrated in color, 371 pages, 6½" × 8¾", April 1963.................... | 3.00 | 4.00 | 3.10
☐ **Same as above,** approximately 20 reprints, 1963–1976.......... | 3.00 | 4.00 | 3.10
☐ **Worlds to Explore,** for Brownies and Junior Girl Scouts, replaced the separate Handbooks, 1977.... | 6.00 | 8.00 | 6.50

CADETTE HANDBOOKS

☐ **Cadette Handbook,** first edition, purple soft cover, April 1963 ...... | 5.00 | 7.00 | 5.50
☐ **Same as above,** but new edition, 1950........................ | 5.00 | 7.00 | 5.25
☐ **Same as above,** but revised edition, 1957........................ | 5.00 | 7.00 | 5.25
☐ **Same as above,** additional reprints, 1963–1979 .... | 3.00 | 4.00 | 3.50
☐ **You Make the Difference,** combined handbook, beautiful abstract on cover, 72 pages, 8½" × 11", 1980–present .... | 4.00 | 6.00 | 4.50

SENIOR HANDBOOKS	Current Price Range		P/Y Avg.

☐ **Idea Book for Senior Girl Scouts,** published as first half of original Senior Handbook, 1939	15.00	19.00	15.50
☐ **Planning Book for Senior Girl Scouts,** published as second half of original Senior Handbook, 1940	14.00	16.00	14.50
☐ **Senior Girl Scouting,** first complete Senior Handbook, tan with red lettering and trefoil, 216 pages, 6¼″ × 9¼″, September 1945	11.00	13.00	11.00
☐ **Same as above,** but revised edition, September 1952	7.00	8.00	7.10
☐ **Same as above,** but new soft cover handbook, 1963	5.00	7.00	5.25
☐ **Same as above,** but additional reprints, 1963–1979	3.00	4.00	3.10

OTHER MANUALS

☐ **Mariner Scout Manual,** July 1948	11.00	13.00	11.50
☐ **Mariner Scouting and Wing Scouting,** issued as pamphlet suppliments to Senior Girl Scouting, 1953............................	6.00	9.00	6.50

OLDER GIRL MANUALS

☐ **Let's Make It Happen**	6.00	9.00	6.50
☐ **Dreams to Reality**	6.00	9.00	6.50
☐ **You Make the Difference**	6.00	9.00	6.50

PROGRAM BOOKS FOR LEADERS	Current Price Range		P/Y Avg.
☐ **Brownie Book for Leaders,** Junior Girl Scouts, 1922..............	16.00	19.00	16.50
☐ **Brown Book for Brown Owls,** first official leader's guide to United States Brownie program, 1926	7.00	9.00	8.00
☐ **Leader's Guide to Brownie Scout Program,** October 1939	5.00	7.00	6.00
☐ **Moreabouts,** for Brownie leaders, 1968	4.00	6.00	4.25
☐ **Worlds to Explore,** Brownie and Junior leader's guide, 1977	4.00	6.00	4.25
☐ **Leadership of Girl Scout Troops,** Intermediate program, 1943.......	5.00	7.00	5.25
☐ **Girl Scout Leader's Guide,** 1955...	5.00	7.00	5.25
☐ **Senior Leader's Guide,** published first time as a book, 1956	5.00	6.00	5.10
☐ **Guide for Girl Scout Trainers,** booklet, 1963	3.00	4.00	3.10
☐ **You Make the Difference,** leader's guide for Cadette and Senior Girl Scouts, 1980–present	3.00	5.00	3.25

MISCELLANEOUS GIRL SCOUTS COLLECTIBLES

☐ **Axe,** Girl Scouts hand model, hickory, 1920s	14.00	19.00	14.50
☐ **Axe,** Girl Scouts hand model, handle and head are stained green, 1930s	13.00	16.00	13.50
☐ **Badges,** Assistant Patrol Leader's bar.....................................	9.00	11.00	9.25
☐ **Badges,** Ex-Patrol Leader's Chevron.....................................	11.00	15.00	11.50
☐ **Badges,** First Class, oval, 1930	19.00	23.00	19.50
☐ **Badges,** First Class embroidered on rectangular green backing, round, 1960s.......................	2.00	5.00	3.00
☐ **Badges,** First Class, round, 1940s ..	3.00	6.00	4.00

Girl Scout Canteen and Cloth Case

	Current Price Range		P/Y Avg.
☐ **Badges,** gold wing on green felt Brownie Wings.....................	.65	4.00	1.00
☐ **Badges,** Jack Tar insignia, on white chevron.....................	5.00	7.00	5.50
☐ **Badges,** Mariners, woven rayon ..	6.00	8.00	6.50
☐ **Badges,** Patrol Leader's Chevron ..	9.00	11.00	9.50

	Current Price Range		P/Y Avg.
☐ **Badges,** Second Class, embroidered, curved bar, oval, 1940s	8.00	10.00	8.50
☐ **Badges,** Second Class, square, 1930			
☐ **Badges,** senior service, Scout emblem, 1940s	9.00	11.00	9.50
☐ **Badges,** Wing Scout insignia, embroidered, 1930s...................	13.00	16.00	13.50
☐ **Bookends,** bronze metal, shows Girl Scout feeding rabbit	21.00	26.00	21.50
☐ **Bookends,** Girl Scout trefoils, made of wood, 1940s..............	9.00	16.00	9.50
☐ **Bracelet,** charm, wide price range, 1930	15.00	30.00	10.00
☐ **Bracelet,** silver color, Girl Scout, spring closure, adjustable	7.00	9.00	7.50
☐ **Buttons,** Girl Scout, four, metal...	3.00	4.00	3.10
☐ **Camera,** Jem Jr. 120, box	28.00	38.00	20.00
☐ **Camera,** official Girl Scout Kodak, folds, 1929.........................	12.00	35.00	20.00
☐ **Camera,** official Girl Scout 620, box....................................	17.00	25.00	20.00
☐ **Camera,** Univex Girl Scout model, cast aluminum, black and green, small	40.00	40.00	20.00
☐ **Candles,** Girl Scout, stamped insignia	7.00	9.00	7.50
☐ **Canteen,** Girl Scout insignia, aluminum, green cloth case, 1930s ..	11.00	16.00	11.50
☐ **Coin Purse,** Girl Scout, sheepskin, dark green, snap button	5.00	7.00	5.50
☐ **Collar Monograms,** G-S collar letters, copper.......................	13.00	16.00	8.00
☐ **Comb,** gilt metal case	8.00	11.00	8.50
☐ **Comb Set,** Girl Scout handy comb, black plastic, green leather case ..	5.00	7.00	5.50
☐ **Comb Set,** mirror, comb and file, green leather case................	8.00	10.00	8.50

	Current Price Range		P/Y Avg.
☐ **Compact**, Girl Scouts, gray-green enamel, nickelplated...............	8.00	10.00	8.50
☐ **Compact**, Girl Scout, wood, trefoil in brown plastic, 3″ square........	7.00	9.00	7.50
☐ **Compass**, official Girl Scout, blue bakelite case, 1930s...............	10.00	13.00	10.50
☐ **Compass**, official Girl Scout, green bakelite, 1930s	9.00	13.00	9.50
☐ **Compass**, official Girl Scout, nickel plated brass case..................	11.00	16.00	11.50
☐ **Cup**, aluminum, folding	3.00	4.00	3.10
☐ **Decal**, Girl Scouts Fiftieth Anniversary, 1962	4.00	6.00	4.25
☐ **Diary**, Girl Scouts, 1930s	11.00	15.00	5.00
☐ **Diary**, Girl Scouts, green leather, gold trim, 1930s	8.00	10.00	5.00
☐ **First Aid Kit**, Girl Scout, canvas case, 1920s........................	15.00	21.00	10.00
☐ **First Aid Kit**, Girl Scout, Johnson and Johnson, 1930s...............	10.00	12.00	10.00
☐ **Flashlight**, L-shaped, Girl Scout model, gray-green, 1920s	11.00	15.00	9.00
☐ **Games-Toys**, Girl Scout paper dolls, worldwide uniforms..........	11.00	13.00	11.50
☐ **Hat**, Girl Scout leader, twill, Mariner's patch.......................	4.00	7.00	4.50
☐ **Hat Band**, embroidered felt Girl Scout band	5.00	7.00	5.50
☐ **Knife**, Brownie, one blade, Kutmaster, aluminum liner and bolsters, orange and white handle.....	6.00	9.00	6.50
☐ **Same as above**, but red and white handle....................	6.00	9.00	6.50
☐ **Knife**, current light green plastic handle with new logo, four blade, 3⅝″	8.00	10.00	8.50

	Current Price Range		P/Y Avg.
☐ **Knife,** Remington #4373, bone stag handle, from about late 1920s to late 1930s, four blade, 3⅜″	70.00	90.00	75.00
☐ **Knife,** Remington R251 Sheath Knife, 4″ blade in green sheath, 1930s	45.00	55.00	46.00
☐ **Knife,** Remington R251 Sheath Knife and Remington #4373, four blade, gift set	130.00	180.00	135.00
☐ **Knife,** Girl Scout model 311, Utica Kutmaster, green marbilized handle, four blades, 3¾″, mid-1930s ...	20.00	50.00	20.00
☐ **Knife,** Utica Kutmaster, heavy, brown bone stag handle, no shield, trefoil etched on blade only, four blade, 3¾″	30.00	50.00	30.00
☐ **Knife,** Kutmaster, Utica, New York, green plastic, not celluloid handle, four blades, 3¾″, 1970s	18.00	23.00	13.00
☐ **Knife,** Kutmaster, Utica, New York, large size, green celluloid handle, large gold trefoil, four blade, 3⅜″, this size is comparatively scarce, 1950s	38.00	48.00	38.50
☐ **Same as above,** except for reduced size to 3³/₈″, for more comfortable holding, 1950s and 1960s	11.00	15.00	9.00
☐ **Knife,** Girl Scout Woodman's Sheath, 1930s	21.00	31.00	21.50
☐ **Lunch Pail,** tin, litho scenes on five sides	12.00	32.00	12.00
☐ **Magazine,** article and color cover by Jessie Wilcox Smith, *Good Housekeeping*......................	3.00	5.00	3.25
☐ **Magazine,** Girl Scout history article from *American Heritage*, 1961 ...	3.00	5.00	3.25

	Current Price Range		P/Y Avg.
☐ **Magazine,** Girl Scout Equipment Catalog 1930	10.00	25.00	10.00
☐ **Magazine,** Girl Scout Equipment Catalog 1942	11.00	13.00	11.50
☐ **Magazine,** First National Roundup, 2 pp. in *Life*, 1956	7.00	9.00	7.50
☐ **Magazine,** Regional Encampment, 3 pp, in *life*, 1966	7.00	9.00	7.50
☐ **Magnifying Glass,** green leather case, 1⅝", 1930s	7.00	9.00	7.50
☐ **Medal,** Life-Saving Cross, bronze, red ribbon..........................	15.00	19.00	15.00
☐ **Medal,** Honorable Mention, Life Saving Award, bronze, red ribbon	15.00	19.00	15.50
☐ **Medal,** official Girl Scout, 12 Norman Rockwell silver medals produced in 1977 by Franklin Mint, 2,182 sets produced...............	400.00	450.00	410.00
☐ **Medal,** Special Camp Award, pictures a Girl Scout feeding a rabbit, 1930s	13.00	15.00	13.50
☐ **Medal,** Thank You, 10K gold, blue ribbon...............................	45.00	60.00	46.50
☐ **Membership Card,** Brownie, 1932 ..	5.00	9.00	4.00
☐ **Mess Kit,** green and red plaid cover	6.00	8.00	6.50
☐ **Neckerchief Slide,** green, knot style..................................	5.00	7.00	5.50
☐ **Paperweight,** metal casting of Girl Scout feeding a rabbit, bronze	9.00	10.00	9.10
☐ **Pen and Pencil Set,** mottled green, gold filled trefoil clips, pen point is 14K, 1930s	17.00	23.00	17.50
☐ **Pin,** Brownie metal attendance rosette	3.00	4.00	3.10
☐ **Pin,** curved bar.....................	7.00	11.00	7.50
☐ **Pin,** Fiftieth Anniversary, ¹¹/₁₆"	8.00	10.00	5.00

	Current Price Range		P/Y Avg.
☐ **Pin,** Girl Scout attendance, star...	.35	4.00	1.00
☐ **Pin,** Girl Scout, gold filled.........	7.00	10.00	7.50
☐ **Pin,** Girl Scout in brown uniform, yellow, pinback, ⅞"...............	13.00	16.00	8.00
☐ **Pin,** Girl Scout logo, stickpin, gold	5.00	7.00	5.50
☐ **Pin,** Girl Scout Mariners, gold trefoil on chrome ship's wheel	4.00	6.00	3.00
☐ **Pin,** Girl Scout Senior, gold on green enamel, ½"	3.00	4.00	3.00
☐ **Pin,** Golden Eaglet, 10K, gold.....	15.00	17.00	15.50
☐ **Pin,** Midget Girl Scout, gold filled	5.00	7.00	5.50
☐ **Pin,** Midget Golden Eagle, 10K, gold....................................	11.00	13.00	11.50
☐ **Pin,** red trefoil, gold border........	4.00	6.00	4.50
☐ **Pin,** World friendship...............	3.00	4.00	3.10
☐ **Planter,** bisque porcelain by Relpo Manufacturing Company	13.00	17.00	13.50
☐ **Plaque,** Masonite, standing	13.00	15.00	13.50
☐ **Plate,** china, Girl Scout Senior Roundup, Idaho, 7", 1965..........	15.00	20.00	15.50
☐ **Postcard,** camp, set of eight, 1930s	8.00	24.00	3.00 each
☐ **Postcard,** Our Chalet, set of two, 1930s	9.00	11.00	9.50
☐ **Poster,** Buy for Victory.............	10.00	13.00	10.50
☐ **Poster,** Girl Scout camp	8.00	10.00	8.50
☐ **Poster,** Girl Scout promise, 7½" x 11"......................................	5.00	7.00	5.50
☐ **Poster,** Girl Scouts of Japan, set of three, 24" x 30"	7.00	9.00	7.50
☐ **Poster,** Girl Scouts, Trustees of Tomorrow, 1940s	11.00	13.00	11.50
☐ **Poster,** Picture of standing Girl Scout	9.00	11.00	9.50
☐ **Record,** Girl Scouts Sing Around the World, GSA, 33⅓ rpm, 8"	5.00	7.00	5.50

	Current Price Range		P/Y Avg.

☐ **Record,** Sing Around the World, GSA, 45 rpm, 6″	5.00	7.00	5.50
☐ **Record,** Sing High, Sing Low, Nanette Guilford, 45 rpm, 6″	4.00	6.00	4.50
☐ **Record,** Sounds of Roundup, GSA, Farragut, Idaho Roundup, 33⅓ rpm, 12″, July 1965	6.00	8.00	6.50
☐ **Record,** Where Do We Go from Here, Wake Dafne, 33⅓ rpm, 6″ ..	4.00	6.00	5.50
☐ **Ring,** Brownie, sterling silver.....	9.00	11.00	9.50
☐ **Ring,** Collegiate, gold on green enamel..................................	22.00	25.00	22.50
☐ **Ring,** Girl Scout, adjustable, sterling silver, logo on rectangle	11.00	13.00	10.00
☐ **Ring,** new logo, on green enamel...	6.00	8.00	6.50
☐ **Ring,** silver and gold on blue enamel..................................	18.00	23.00	18.50
☐ **Ring,** spoon, 1970s...............	6.00	8.00	6.50
☐ **Ring,** sterling silver with lattice work on sides.......................	10.00	16.00	10.00
☐ **Ring,** sterling silver with ribbed sides	10.00	12.00	10.00
☐ **Seal Set,** bronze, signet, trefoil, seal, sealing waxes of green, gold and lavendar, 1930s...............	18.00	23.00	18.50
☐ **Sewing Kit,** Brownies, red case, 1940s	10.00	12.00	10.50
☐ **Sewing Kit,** Girl Scout, official, 1930s	11.00	16.00	11.50
☐ **Sheet Music,** America Needs You, copper, 1940s	4.00	6.00	4.50
☐ **Sheet Music,** Blessing the House, ceremony	7.00	9.00	7.50
☐ **Sheet Music,** Girl Scouts Are We, Rivenburg, 1945	3.00	4.00	3.50
☐ **Sheet Music,** Girl Scouts Together, Goff, 1940s................	4.00	6.00	4.50

	Current Price Range		P/Y Avg.
☐ **Sheet Music,** Growing Up Tree, The	3.00	4.00	3.10
☐ **Sheet Music,** No Man Is an Island, 1950	2.00	3.00	2.10
☐ **Sheet Music,** World Song, The, Jean Sibelius	6.00	8.00	6.50
☐ **Stamp,** First-Day Cover, Golden Anniversary	6.00	8.00	6.50
☐ **Tray,** Girl Scout, trefoil, wood, 1940s	13.00	16.00	13.50
☐ **Tray,** small, from Juliette Low House	7.00	8.00	7.50
☐ **Utility Book,** Girl Scout "Don't Forget" book, trefoil on wine red cover, 1930s	9.00	13.00	9.50
☐ **Utility Book,** memory, embossed leather	13.00	16.00	13.50
☐ **Utility Book,** photograph, green and gold, 1940s	9.00	13.00	9.50
☐ **Utility Book,** scrap, green leather and gold trim, full color picture on cover of Girl Scout, 1930s	10.00	13.00	10.50
☐ **Utility Book,** snapshot album, green leather, gold trim, 1930s	10.00	13.00	10.50
☐ **Wallet,** green sheepskin, ostrich grained, stamped insignia	8.00	10.00	8.50
☐ **Watch,** Ingersoll, trefoil on face ...	15.00	20.00	15.00
☐ **Watch,** official Sunwatch, brass, 1920s	15.00	20.00	15.00
☐ **Whistle,** cylindrical with green bakelite finish	5.00	7.00	5.50
☐ **Whistle,** gunmetal finish, insignia ...	10.00	12.00	10.50
☐ **Whistle,** nickel finish, insignia	7.00	10.00	7.50

BOOKS

FICTION

	Current Price Range		P/Y Avg.
☐ Brave Girls, Philmus	6.50	8.50	6.75
☐ Brownie Scouts and Their Tree House, Wirt.......................	4.50	6.50	4 75
☐ Brownie Scouts at Silver Beach, Wirt	3.50	6.50	3.75
☐ Brownie Scouts at Snow Valley, Wirt	4.50	5 50	4.75
☐ Brownie Scouts at the Circus, Wirt	3.50	4.50	3.75
☐ Brownie Scouts at Windmill Farm, Wirt.......................	3.50	4.50	3.75
☐ Brownie Scouts in the Cherry Festival, Wirt	4.50	6.50	4.75
☐ Friend to All, Kohler	7.50	9.50	7.75
☐ Girl in Green, Beatty.............	8.50	10.50	8.75
☐ Girl Scouts at Camp, Lavell	4.50	6.50	4.75
☐ Girl Scouts at Camp Comalong, Garis................................	4.50	5.50	4.75
☐ Girl Scouts at Home, Galt........	3.50	5.50	3.75
☐ Girl Scouts at Mystery Mansion, Wirt	5.50	7.50	5.75
☐ Girl Scouts' Canoe Trip, Lavell ..	4.50	6.50	4.75
☐ Girl Scouts' Director, Lavell......	4.50	6.50	4.75
☐ Girl Scout Good Turn, Lavell.....	4.50	6.50	4.75
☐ Girl Scouts' Rally, Galt...........	3.50	5.50	3.75
☐ Girl Scouts' Triumph, Galt	2.50	4.50	2.75
☐ Mystery of the Water Witch, American Girl Book.................	3.50	5.50	3.75
☐ Mystery of the Old Fisk House, The, Fishler and Fuller	3.50	4.50	3.75
☐ When Girls Meet Boys, American Girl Book........................	3.50	5.50	3.75

	Current Price Range		P/Y Avg.

NONFICTION

☐ **Beginners Cookbook,** Dell Paperback	2.50	3.50	2.70
☐ **Big Test, The,** Christian	5.50	6.50	5.60
☐ **Blue Book of Rules for Girl Scout Captains, The,**	12.50	15.50	13.00
☐ **Camp Memory Book,** no date	2.50	3.50	2.60
☐ **Cooking Out of Doors,** 1960	5.50	7.50	5.75
☐ **Dramatics and Ceremonies,** Girl Scouts	3.50	4.50	3.60
☐ **Education for Parenthood,** 1973	2.50	3.50	2.60
☐ **Exploring the Hand Arts,** Girl Scouts	3.50	4.50	3.60
☐ **Games for Girl Scouts**	4.50	5.50	4.60
☐ **Girl Guides Policy, The,** organization and rules, 1938	4.50	6.50	5.00
☐ **Girl Scout Game Book,** 1930s	9.50	10.50	10.00
☐ **Girl Scout Leaders Nature Guide,** 1930	8.50	12.50	8.75
☐ **Girl Scouts, Inc.,** Nature Notebook, ring binder	10.50	12.50	11.00
☐ **Girl Scout Song Book,** 1925	4.50	5.50	4.75
☐ **Same as above,** but 1929	3.50	5.50	3.75
☐ **Girl Scouting and the Catholic Girl**	1.00	2.00	1.10
☐ **Girl Scouting and the Jewish Girl**	1.00	2.00	1.10
☐ **Girl Scouting and the Lutheran Girl**	1.00	2.00	1.10
☐ **Girl Scouting and the Protestant Girl**	1.00	2.00	1.10
☐ **Guide, The,** English Girl Guide Publication	5.00	20.00	5.50
☐ **Handcraft for Handy Girls**	18.50	22.50	19.00
☐ **Hands Around the World,** 1951	3.50	5.50	3.75
☐ **Happily Appley,** Munz	2.50	3.50	2.75
☐ **Here Come the Girl Guides,** Barne	3.50	4.50	3.75

	Current Price Range		P/Y Avg.
☐ Hiking in Town or Country	1.50	2.50	1.75
☐ If I Were a Girl Scout in 1776 ...	1.00	3.50	1.00
☐ Juliette Low and the Girl Scouts, 1928	7.00	12.50	7.00
☐ Kettles and Camp Fires, pamphlet	7.00	15.00	7.00
☐ Knife and Axe-Campcraft Skills, 1953	2.50	3.50	2.75
☐ Lady from Savannah	6.50	7.50	6.75
☐ Leader's Nature Guide, 1942	3.50	4.50	3.75
☐ Let Us Go Camping Together, 1960	1.00	2.00	1.10
☐ On My Honor, 1951	5.50	7.50	5.75
☐ Patrol and Their Court of Honor ..	1.75	5.50	1.75
☐ Patrol Book for Cadette and Senior Girl Scouts	1.50	2.50	1.75
☐ Pocket Songbook, 1956	.60	3.50	.75
☐ Programs in Girl Scout Camping	2.50	3.50	2.75
☐ Safety-Wise	1.50	2.50	1.75
☐ Senior Planning Boards, booklet...	1.50	2.50	1.75
☐ Sing Together, 1936..............	4.50	5.50	4.75
☐ Sing Together, 1949..............	3.50	4.50	3.75
☐ Sing Together, 1973..............	3.50	4.50	3.75
☐ Summer Activities for Girl Scouts, 1944	2.50	3.50	2.75
☐ Tramping and Trailing with the Girl Scouts	4.50	6.50	5.00
☐ Trefoil Around the World, 1958....	4.50	5.50	4.75
☐ Way of Understanding, The, 1934	10.50	12.50	11.00
☐ Wide World of Girl Guiding and Girl Scouting, The	3.50	4.50	3.75

RECOMMENDED READING

The Official Price Guide to Scouting Collectibles is designed as a basic introductory course for the beginning collector and flea market shopper, as well as a handy, tote-along reference book for the more seasoned hobbyist.

This guide offers the beginner a general over-view of collecting techniques, tips and prices for the collectibles most commonly bought and sold on the market today.

You can slip this price guide into a pocket or a purse and take along your own "official" expert on your next shopping excursion.

As your interest and your collection grow, you may want to start a reference library of your fa-vorite areas. For the collector who needs a more extensive coverage of the collectibles market, The House of Collectibles publishes a complete line of comprehensive companion guides to the pocket-sized books. These larger price guides, which are itemized at the back of this book, con-

$11.95, 8th Edition, 766 pgs. Order #290-6

tain full coverage on buying, selling, and care of valuable articles, plus list-ings with thousands of prices for rare, unusual and common antiques and collectibles.

The House of Collectibles recommends *The Official Price Guide to Col-lector Knives,* eighth edition, as the companion to this pocket book.

- **Over 14,000 current collector values,** including the most comprehen-sive listings of collector pocket and sheath knives in print. A complete price listing for **1,250 U.S. and foreign knife manufacturers.**
- *FEATURING NEW AND EXPANDED PRICING SECTIONS*—Buck, Cat-taraugus, Colt, Fightin' Rooster, Keen Kutter, Kinfolks, Landers-Frary-and-Clark, Maher & Grosh, New York, Parker, Remington, Robeson, Russell, Schatt & Morgan, Schrade, Shapleigh, Winchester and more!!
- *CASE KNIVES*—Every known Case pocket and sheath knife is listed and pictured according to pattern number. Detailed information includes all handle and blade variations.
- *KA-BAR KNIVES*—A complete pictorial price reference in over 100 pages includes a special section on Ka-Bar Dogshead knives.

Available from your local dealer or order direct from:
THE HOUSE OF COLLECTIBLES, see order blank

SCOUT MEMORABILIA

Published during the months of January, March, May, September and November.

SUBSCRIPTION: One Year

☐ USA only $5.00 a year
☐ Canada/Mexico via air $7.00
☐ Foreign via airmail $10.00

SPONSORSHIP: One Year ☐ USA only $10.00
Includes your own subscription and your choice:
3 Ads or 2 Gift Subscriptions

I COLLECT THE FOLLOWING: _____

_____

MY PRESENT SCOUTING POSITION: _____

_____

Ads Single $2.00
Same ads in
2 issues $3.00
(Your camera ready copy
must be in **black** ink.)

Name: _____

Address: _____

City: _____

State: _____ Zip: _____

checks payable to: **HARRY THORSEN**
7305 Bounty Drive
Sarasota, Florida 33581

APPLICATION FOR MEMBERSHIP IN THE FEDERATION OF SCOUT MUSEUMS INTERNATIONAL

Please mail to
Harry D. Thorsen, 7305 Bounty Drive
Sarasota, Florida 33581:

Name of Museum: _____

Address: _____

Owner of Association: _____

_____

Curator: _____

Address: _____

_____

Days or times open: _____

_____

Brochure ? (please enclose)

_____

Displays and features

_____

Will you trade or loan items to other member museums?

_____

Signed: _____

Title: _____

Date: _____

Federation Directors are
Harry D. Thorsen, Max J. Silber, and Ralph E. Zitelman.

Not affiliated with the World Scout Bureau.

☐ *Please send me the following price guides—*
☐ *I would like the most current edition of the books listed below.*

THE OFFICIAL PRICE GUIDES TO:

☐ 199-3	**American Silver & Silver Plate** 5th Ed.	11.95
☐ 513-1	**Antique Clocks** 3rd Ed.	10.95
☐ 283-3	**Antique & Modern Dolls** 3rd Ed.	10.95
☐ 287-6	**Antique & Modern Firearms** 6th Ed.	11.95
☐ 517-4	**Antiques & Collectibles** 7th Ed.	9.95
☐ 289-2	**Antique Jewelry** 5th Ed.	11.95
☐ 270-1	**Beer Cans & Collectibles,** 3rd Ed.	7.95
☐ 262-0	**Bottles Old & New** 9th Ed.	10.95
☐ 255-8	**Carnival Glass** 1st Ed.	10.95
☐ 295-7	**Collectible Cameras** 2nd Ed.	10.95
☐ 277-0	**Collectibles of the Third Reich** 2nd Ed.	10.95
☐ 281-7	**Collectible Toys** 3rd Ed.	10.95
☐ 490-9	**Collector Cars** 6th Ed.	11.95
☐ 267-1	**Collector Handguns** 3rd Ed.	11.95
☐ 290-6	**Collector Knives** 8th Ed.	11.95
☐ 266-3	**Collector Plates** 4th Ed.	11.95
☐ 296-5	**Collector Prints** 7th Ed.	12.95
☐ 489-5	**Comic Books & Collectibles** 8th Ed.	9.95
☐ 433-X	**Depression Glass** 1st Ed.	9.95
☐ 472-0	**Glassware** 2nd Ed.	10.95
☐ 243-4	**Hummel Figurines & Plates** 6th Ed.	10.95
☐ 451-8	**Kitchen Collectibles** 2nd Ed.	10.95
☐ 291-4	**Military Collectibles** 5th Ed.	11.95
☐ 268-X	**Music Collectibles** 5th Ed.	11.95
☐ 313-9	**Old Books & Autographs** 7th Ed.	11.95
☐ 298-1	**Oriental Collectibles** 3rd Ed.	11.95
☐ 297-3	**Paper Collectibles** 5th Ed.	10.95
☐ 276-0	**Pottery & Porcelain** 5th Ed.	11.95
☐ 263-9	**Radio, T.V. & Movie Memorabilia** 2nd Ed.	11.95
☐ 288-4	**Records** 7th Ed.	10.95
☐ 247-7	**Royal Doulton** 5th Ed.	11.95
☐ 280-9	**Science Fiction & Fantasy Collectibles** 2nd Ed.	10.95
☐ 299-X	**Star Trek/Star Wars Collectibles** 1st Ed.	7.95
☐ 248-5	**Wicker** 3rd Ed.	10.95

THE OFFICIAL:

☐ 445-3	**Collector's Journal** 1st Ed.	4.95
☐ 365-1	**Encyclopedia of Antiques** 1st Ed.	9.95
☐ 369-4	**Guide to Buying & Selling Antiques** 1st Ed.	9.95
☐ 414-3	**Identification Guide to Early American Furniture** 1st Ed.	9.95
☐ 413-5	**Identification Guide to Glassware** 1st Ed.	9.95
☐ 448-8	**Identification Guide to Gunmarks** 2nd Ed.	9.95
☐ 412-7	**Identification Guide to Pottery & Porcelain** 1st Ed.	9.95
☐ 415-1	**Identification Guide to Victorian Furniture** 1st Ed.	9.95

THE OFFICIAL (SMALL SIZE) PRICE GUIDES TO:

☐ 473-9	**Antiques & Flea Markets** 3rd Ed.	3.95
☐ 269-8	**Antique Jewelry** 3rd Ed.	4.95
☐ 509-3	**Baseball Cards** 6th Ed.	4.95
☐ 488-7	**Bottles** 2nd Ed.	4.95
☐ 468-2	**Cars & Trucks** 2nd Ed.	4.95
☐ 260-4	**Collectible Americana** 1st Ed.	4.95
☐ 294-9	**Collectible Records** 3rd Ed.	4.95
☐ 469-0	**Collector Guns** 2nd Ed.	4.95
☐ 474-7	**Comic Books** 3rd Ed.	3.95
☐ 486-0	**Dolls** 3rd Ed.	4.95
☐ 292-2	**Football Cards** 5th Ed.	4.95
☐ 258-2	**Glassware** 2nd Ed.	4.95
☐ 487-9	**Hummels** 3rd Ed.	4.95
☐ 279-5	**Military Collectibles** 3rd Ed.	4.95
☐ 480-1	**Paperbacks & Magazines** 3rd Ed.	4.95
☐ 278-7	**Pocket Knives** 3rd Ed.	4.95
☐ 479-8	**Scouting Collectibles** 3rd Ed.	4.95
☐ 439-9	**Sports Collectibles** 2nd Ed.	3.95
☐ 494-1	**Star Trek/Star Wars Collectibles** 3rd Ed.	3.95
☐ 307-4	**Toys** 4th Ed.	4.95

THE OFFICIAL BLACKBOOK PRICE GUIDES OF:

☐ 510-7	**U.S. Coins** 25th Ed.	3.95
☐ 511-5	**U.S. Paper Money** 19th Ed.	3.95
☐ 512-3	**U.S. Postage Stamps** 9th Ed.	3.95

THE OFFICIAL INVESTORS GUIDE TO BUYING & SELLING:

☐ 496-8	**Gold, Silver and Diamonds** 2nd Ed.	9.95
☐ 497-6	**Gold Coins** 2nd Ed.	9.95
☐ 498-4	**Silver Coins** 2nd Ed.	9.95
☐ 499-2	**Silver Dollars** 2nd Ed.	9.95

THE OFFICIAL NUMISMATIC GUIDE SERIES:

☐ 481-X	**Coin Collecting** 3rd Ed.	9.95
☐ 254-X	**The Official Guide to Detecting Counterfeit Money** 2nd Ed.	7.95
☐ 257-4	**The Official Guide to Mint Errors** 4th Ed.	7.95
☐ 162-4	**Variety & Oddity Guide of U.S. Coins** 8th Ed.	4.95

SPECIAL INTEREST SERIES:

☐ 506-9	**From Hearth to Cookstove** 3rd Ed.	17.95
☐ 508-5	**Lucky Number Lottery Guide** 1st Ed.	3.50
☐ 504-2	**On Method Acting** 8th Printing	6.95

TOTAL	

SEE FOLLOWING PAGE FOR ORDERING INSTRUCTIONS

FOR IMMEDIATE DELIVERY

VISA & MASTER CARD CUSTOMERS
ORDER TOLL FREE!
1-800-638-6460

This number is for orders only; it is not tied into the customer service or business office. Customers not using charge cards must use mail for ordering since payment is required with the order — sorry no C.O.D.'s.

OR SEND ORDERS TO

THE HOUSE OF COLLECTIBLES, *201 East 50th Street New York, New York 10022*

——— POSTAGE & HANDLING RATES ———

First Book	$1.00
Each Additional Copy or Title	$0.50

Total from columns   Quantity_____ $ _____

[ ] Check or money order enclosed $_____ (include postage and handling)

[ ] Please charge $_____ to my: [ ] MASTERCARD [ ] VISA

Charge Card Customers Not Using Our Toll Free Number Please Fill Out The Information Below

Account No. (All Digits) _____ Expiration Date _____

Signature_____

NAME (please print) _____ PHONE _____

ADDRESS _____ APT. # _____ **10**

CITY _____ STATE _____ ZIP _____